FROMMER'S

FAMILY TRAVEL GUIDE

SAN FRANCISCO WITH KIDS

W9-CMH-483

by Carey Simon and
Charlene Marmer Solomon

PRENTICE HALL TRAVEL

NEW YORK • LONDON • TORONTO • SYDNEY • TOKYO • SINGAPORE

To Barbara—This one is for you.

—C.M.S.

This book is dedicated to my loving and supportive traveling partners—my husband Danny and my daughter Janey.

—C.S.

FROMMER BOOKS
Published by Prentice Hall General Reference
A division of Simon & Schuster Inc.
15 Columbus Circle
New York, NY 10023

ISBN 0-13-333345-0
ISSN 1058-4951

Design by Robert Bull Design
Maps by Geografix Inc.

Manufactured in the United States of America

FROMMER'S SAN FRANCISCO WITH KIDS '92–'93

Editor-in-Chief: Marilyn Wood
Senior Editors: Judith de Rubini, Amit Shah
Editors: Alice Fellows, Paige Hughes, Theodore Stavrou
Assistant Editors: Suzanne Arkin, Peter Katucki, Lisa Renaud, Ellen Zucker
Managing Editor: Leanne Coupe

CONTENTS

LIST OF MAPS

ACKNOWLEDGMENTS

This book is a natural outgrowth of our *Frommer's California with Kids*. It gave us the marvelous opportunity to focus in on one of our favorite destinations: San Francisco and the Bay Area. Just like our other new city guide book, *Frommer's Los Angeles with Kids,* this book required the assistance and support of many people.

A family travel book relies heavily on family support to be written. Thank you to my extended family—Shirley and Sid, Michele, Melinda and David, for their smiles and love; to Andrew and Elizabeth and my best friend Alan, for making it worth it all. And to my parents, who were always my champions and taught me the joy of traveling with children.—**C.M.S.**

My personal thanks again go to Helen Hawekotte and Joe Stewart, and to Magdalena Diaz Velasquez, without whom I could never finish any writing project. I am also delighted I could once again work with such a talented writing partner.—**C.S.**

OUR THANKS GO TO: Among the many people who sustained our efforts on this book, we would especially like to thank Marilyn Wood and Judith de Rubini at Prentice Hall. Special thanks go also to Margaret Basalone, Jody Welborn, and Pooky Garthoff.

We won't forget the continuing assistance of Fred Sater of the California Office of Tourism, and the support of Helen Chang and Sharon Rooney of the San Francisco Visitors and Convention Bureau and to Lauren Wilkens of the Monterey County Visitors and Convention Bureau.

INVITATION TO THE READERS

In researching this book, we have come across many wonderful establishments, the best of which we have included here. We are sure that many of you will also come across family-friendly hotels, inns, restaurants, guesthouses, shops, and attractions. Please don't keep them to yourself. Share your family's experiences, especially if you want to comment on places that have been included in this edition that have changed for the worse. You can address your letters to:

Carey Simon and Charlene Marmer Solomon
Frommer's San Francisco with Kids
c/o Prentice Hall Travel
15 Columbus Circle
New York, NY 10023

A DISCLAIMER

Readers are advised that prices fluctuate in the course of time and travel information changes under the impact of the varied and volatile factors that affect the travel industry. Neither the authors nor the publisher can be held responsible for the experiences of readers while traveling. Readers are invited to write to the publisher with ideas, comments, and suggestions for future editions.

SAFETY ADVISORY

Whenever you're traveling in an unfamiliar city or country, stay alert. Be aware of your immediate surroundings. Wear a moneybelt and keep a close eye on your possessions. Be particularly careful with cameras, purses, and wallets, all favorite targets of thieves and pickpockets.

CHAPTER 1

PLANNING A FAMILY TRIP TO SAN FRANCISCO

San Francisco has often been voted America's favorite city. It is one of the most breathtakingly beautiful cities in the world—at once both quaint and cosmopolitan. Shiny, stunning steel bridges and pinnacle-like skyscrapers sit within minutes of Victorian dwellings and classic cathedrals. And, of course, there's the weather. The city can be thick with fog or crystalline bright. Or, it can be both—in different parts of town.

Many people think of San Francisco as an adult city, and indeed it is . . . but not exclusively. It is a cosmopolitan city abundant with activities for both parents and children. Children can experience the excitement of an urban community like New York, London, or Tokyo or retreat to the beautiful outdoor areas that offer so much to families.

1. TOURIST INFORMATION

Before you visit, you'll want to contact the **California Office of Tourism,** P.O. Box 9278, Dept. A-1003, Van Nuys, CA 91409 (tel. toll free 800/TOCALIF), and the **San Francisco Convention & Visitors Bureau's Visitor Information Center,** P.O. Box 6977, San Francisco, CA 94101 (tel. 415/391-2000). The bureau will send you a visitor's kit for $1, which contains maps and invaluable information.

WHAT THINGS COST IN SAN FRANCISCO	U.S. $
Taxi from the airport to downtown S.F.	25.00
Shuttle from airport to downtown S.F.	11.00
Bus from airport to downtown S.F.	7.00
Local telephone call	.20
Double room at the Four Seasons Clift (expensive)	250.00
Double room at the Villa Florence (moderate)	119.00
Double room at the Chelsea (inexpensive)	74.00

	U.S. $
Lunch for one adult at the French Room (expensive)	20.00
Lunch for one child at the French Room (expensive)	8.00
Lunch for one adult at Mama's of S.F. (moderate)	8.00
Lunch for one child at Mama's of S.F. (moderate)	4.00
Dinner for one adult at A. Sabella's (expensive)	30.00
Dinner for one child at A. Sabella's (expensive)	7.75
Dinner for one adult at MacArthur Park (moderate)	18.00
Dinner for one child at MacArthur Park (moderate)	6.00
Coca-Cola	.65
Ice-cream cone	1.25
Hot dog	1.00
Roll of ASA 100 Kodacolor film, 36 exposures	5.00
Admission to Marine World Africa USA	
Adult	19.95
Child	14.95
Movie ticket	
Adult	7.00
Child	3.50
Theater ticket at American Conservatory Theater (ACT)	10.00 to 29.00

2. WHEN TO GO

THE CLIMATE San Francisco enjoys mild weather year round, with temperatures seldom rising above 70°F or falling below 40° F. Morning and evening fogs roll in during the summer months. September and October are generally the warmest months in San Francisco; January, with an average high of 56°F, is normally the coldest.

KIDS' FAVORITE EVENTS

JANUARY

✪ *CHINESE NEW YEAR CELEBRATION* This is a favorite of locals as well as visitors. There are all kinds of festivities, culminating with the Golden Dragon Parade.

Where: Chinatown *When:* January or February *How:* For more information and this year's date, call the Chinese Chamber of Commerce, 415/982-3000. Or send a self-addressed stamped envelope to: Chinese New Year Celebration, P.O. Box 6977, San Francisco, CA 94101.

□ **SEA LION SEA-LEBRITIES** Sea lions have taken up permanent residence at Pier 39. In tandem with the Marine Mammal Center, there are guided tours during January weekends from noon to 4pm.

□ **MARTIN LUTHER KING BIRTHDAY CELEBRATION** A parade and other festivities go on throughout the city in celebration on January 21. Call 415/771-6300 for more information.

FEBRUARY

□ **CHILDREN'S KITE FESTIVAL** Celebrate the art and craft of kite-making and kite-flying at the Children's Kite Festival on Pier 39. As part of the Chinese New Year festivities, it features a Chinese kite-decorating contest for children in grades K–5. Chinese cultural entertainment and kite-flying demonstrations. Call 415/981-8030 for details.

MARCH

✪ *CHERRY BLOSSOMS IN BLOOM AT THE JAPANESE TEA GARDEN* You'll think you're in Japan when you see the spectacular beauty of the cherry blossoms in bloom.
Where: Golden Gate Park *When:* Last week in March. *How:* Call 415/387-6787 for information.

□ **AFRICA FOCUS WEEKS** Fairs, exhibits, concerts, and interpretive talks about Africa, its culture and people. March 1–15. Call 415/775-9622.

□ **JUNIOR GRAND NATIONAL RODEO, HORSE AND STOCK SHOW** Participate or watch kids 18 and under demonstrate their horsemanship skills and showcase their animals at the Cow Palace. There is a livestock show the first five days, then a full horse show with both English and Western tradition. The California high school rodeo finals are the finale of this event. Call 415/469-6057 for this year's dates and details.

✪ *ST. PATRICK'S DAY CELEBRATION* A Sunday parade kicks off the event. There are flag-raising ceremonies at the Civic Center and festivities at the United Irish Cultural Center.
Where: Civic Center. *When:* March 17. *How:* For more details, call 415/467-8218.

APRIL

✪ *CHERRY BLOSSOM FESTIVAL* This is a wonderful event for children. It includes Japanese music, dancing, flower arranging, bonsai show, martial arts, calligraphy, origami, tea ceremony, films, food bazaar, and a marvelous parade.

Where: Japantown. *When:* Usually two weekends in late March to mid-April. *How:* For specific details, call 415/992-6776.

❍ *SAN FRANCISCO GIANTS BASEBALL SEASON* Play ball! Everyone's all-time favorite—complete with hot dogs and Cracker Jacks—begins its yearly tradition.
Where: Candlestick Park. *When:* April–September. *How:* Call 415/467-8000 for dates and ticket information.

☐ **SAN FRANCISCO INTERNATIONAL FILM FESTIVAL** This is Northern California's longest-running film festival, lasting from mid-April to early May. Call 415/567-4641 to find out which movies are appropriate for children, as well as ticket information and location of theaters.

MAY

❍ *CINCO DE MAYO PARADE AND CELEBRATION* There are two days of cultural activities and entertainment to celebrate Mexico's Independence Day. A fiesta queen is crowned.
Where: Mission District. *When:* Weekend of May 5. *How:* For further information call 415/826-1401. The local newspapers carry daily listings of events.

❍ *SAN FRANCISCO EXAMINER BAY TO BREAKERS FOOT RACE* This has been called a "moving block party" rather than a race, so don't expect a serious marathon. Parents with children in strollers jog/walk alongside waiters carrying trays. It's a lot of fun, albeit very crowded, with at least 100,000 participants, and maybe twice that number of spectators.
Where: S.F. city streets. *When:* mid-May. *How:* Grab hold of your sense of humor, and start to train. Call 415/777-7770 for specific details.

❍ *CARNIVAL* This street festival is like Mardi Gras elsewhere. It includes a parade, music, dance, and a costume contest.
Where: Mission District. *When:* End of May. *How:* For detailed information call 415/826-1401.

JUNE

❍ *STERN GROVE MIDSUMMER MUSIC FESTIVAL* Free concerts are held every Sunday in Golden Gate Park, with dance, music, theater, and jazz. Youth-oriented music is often featured as well as full-length symphony and operatic performances. Come early to get the best lawn or bench seating. Bring a picnic and a blanket (as well as a ball or Frisbee). About half the concerts are preceded by lectures at Trocadero Clubhouse, the purpose of which is to give young people an understanding of the performance of the day.
Where: Sigmund Stern Grove at 19th Avenue at Sloat Boulevard (see our map of Golden Gate Park, Chapter 4, in "What Kids Like to See &

Do"). ***When:*** *Mid-June through mid-August, 2–4pm.* ***How:*** *Call 415/252-6252 for further information.*

☐ **UNION STREET SPRING FESTIVAL OF ARTS AND CRAFTS** Considered the city's most "elegant street event," the Union Street Spring Festival (between Gough and Steiner streets) features outdoor cafés, continuous musical entertainment, street performers, and fine arts and crafts. The festivities, held the first weekend of June, start with the waiter's race; then there is a fashion show and dancing in the streets. Call 415/346-4561 for specific details.

☐ **INTERNATIONAL STREET PERFORMERS FESTIVAL** A San Francisco tradition during the first week of June that includes jugglers, comedians, musicians, and mimes who perform on Pier 39. Call 415/981-8030 for further details.

☐ **KITEMAKERS ANNUAL FATHER'S DAY KITE FESTIVAL** Join in the festivities on the Marina Green on Father's Day. A treat not to be missed.

☐ **NORTH BEACH FAIR** San Francisco's longest running street fair is held in the city's historic Italian neighborhood (on Grant Avenue between Columbus Avenue and Filbert Street and on Green Street from Columbus Avenue to Grant Avenue) in mid-June. Arts and crafts and music are featured and outdoor cafés serve food and wine. North Beach chefs compete for "the best of North Beach awards." Call 415/346-4561 for specific details.

☐ **FESTIVAL OF THE VIEWING OF THE MOON, TSUKIMI** This three-day event in early June celebrates the moon with traditional Japanese arts and crafts, music, and Japanese and California food. There is a free jazz concert at sunset. Call 415/346-4561 for more information.

JULY

☐ **MIDSUMMER MOZART FESTIVAL** Festivities are held at the Louise M. Davies Symphony Hall (tel. 415/431-5400) and Herbst Theater (tel. 415/552-3656) during July and August. Obtain tickets at major ticket agencies or from the theaters directly.

○ *FOURTH OF JULY CELEBRATION AND FIREWORKS* A truly American treat.
   Where: *Crissy Field.* ***When:*** *July 4.* ***How:*** *Dress warmly and don't forget the picnic blankets and food.*

AUGUST

☐ **SAN FRANCISCO 49ERS FOOTBALL SEASON** Kick-off is at Candlestick Park in early August. For schedule information, call 408/562-4949; for tickets, call 415/468-2249.

☐ **NIHONMACHI STREET FAIR** Like visiting Tokyo, this festival at Japantown and Japan Center during the first weekend in August abounds with the sights and smells of the Far East. Call 415/922-8700 for specific details.

☐ **RENAISSANCE PLEASURE FAIRE** This trip back to merry ole' England in Blackpointe Forest in Novato is a fun day for the entire family. Call 415/892-0937 for further information.

☐ **SAUSALITO ART FESTIVAL.** This is held the last weekend in August. Call 415/332-9378 for exact details.

SEPTEMBER

☐ **ANNUAL L.E.A.P. SANDCASTLE-BUILDING CONTEST FOR ARCHITECTS** See what pros do with the sand, in Aquatic Park. Sponsored by the Learning through Education in the Arts Project. Call 415/775-5327 for further details.

☐ **WEST COAST NATIONAL STUNT KITE CHAMPIONSHIP** This is a parade of colors in the air that you can watch with the kids on the Marina Green. Call 415/652-4003 for more information.

○ *DISPLAY OF BOATS AND ANNUAL RACE TO PRESERVE HISTORIC SHIPS* Cheer on your favorite historic ship or offshore powerboat in this annual race held the first weekend in September at the Pier 39 marina. Call 415/981-8030 for details.

☐ **FESTIVAL DE LAS AMERICAS (LATIN-AMERICAN FOODS AND ARTS FESTIVAL)** Latin beats pulsate in the Mission District streets during this lively fair in mid-September. There are several café areas, with emphasis on different kinds of Latin food, including Caribbean, Puerto Rican, and Latin American. There is a huge arts and crafts section that is arranged in conjunction with the Mexican Museum. Call 415/826-1401 for further information.

○ *BLESSING OF THE FISHING FLEET* This takes place at the Church of Saints Peter and Paul.
Where: Fisherman's Wharf. *When:* The last weekend in September.
How: For further information and this year's date, call 415/434-1492.

OCTOBER

☐ **INTERNATIONAL PUMPKIN ASSOCIATION'S WORLD PUMPKIN WEIGH-OFF** Heavyweight pumpkins from around the world (U.S., Canada, Japan, U.S.S.R., Great Britain) compete. The winner is honored at the Great Halloween & Pumpkin Festival later in the month. This event takes place at City Hall at the beginning of the month. Call 415/346-4561 for this year's dates and further information.

○ *FESTA ITALIANA* This family-oriented event features food, continuous entertainment (including puppets, jugglers, and magic)—things that will make the whole family happy—as well as an art exhibit, opera, and dancing at night.
Where: Fisherman's Wharf. *When:* Weekend before Columbus Day in October. *How:* For further information and this year's date, call 415/434-1417.

○ *COLUMBUS DAY CELEBRATION* See "Queen Isabella's" coronation, a pageant that celebrates the landing of Columbus, civic ceremonies, and a Sunday parade. There is also the blessing of the fishing fleet.
Where: North Beach. *When:* Weekend nearest Columbus Day. *How:* For more information and this year's date, call 415/434-1492.

○ **FLEET WEEK** These festivities are dedicated to the United States Navy. There are aerial performances by the Blue Angels, and a parade of naval vessels around the Golden Gate Bridge. You can tour ships and take boat rides.

    Where: San Francisco's waterfront, Pier 39, Fisherman's Wharf. **When:** mid–October. **How:** Call 415/765-6056 for specific details and dates.

○ **GREAT HALLOWEEN & PUMPKIN FESTIVAL** Celebrate the Great Pumpkin during this event with pumpkin treats, arts and crafts, and musical entertainment. Get ready for Halloween with pumpkin-carving demonstrations and a pumpkin parade. Children can trick-or-treat in neighborhood stores, and adults can join in with the pie-eating contests and hayrides.

    Where: Richmond District (Clement Street between Third and Ninth avenues). **When:** Mid–October. **How:** Call 415/346-4561 for further details.

☐ **HARVEST FESTIVAL** This festival in early November is claimed to be the largest crafts fair in the nation with original American crafts and unusual entertainment, such as vaudeville acts.

NOVEMBER

☐ **GRAND NATIONAL RODEO, HORSE & STOCK SHOW** Ten days of festivities at the Cow Palace include 11 rodeo performances and full-scale horse shows. This is a major rodeo for the cowboys. For specific dates and ticket information, call 415/469-6057.

○ **TRADITIONAL TREE LIGHTING CEREMONY** Thanksgiving Eve is the kick-off for the holiday season with the Tree Lighting at Pier 39. Christmas carolers sing traditional holiday songs around the 65-foot white fir tree. The kids will love the Disney characters who come out in full force along with Santa.

    When: Thanksgiving Eve. **Where:** Pier 39. **How:** Call 415/981-8030 for more information.

DECEMBER

☐ **AMERICAN CONSERVATORY THEATER (ACT)** Begins its performances of *A Christmas Carol.* Call 415/749-2228 for dates and ticket information.
☐ **SAN FRANCISCO BALLET** Begins performances of *The Nutcracker* at the War Memorial Opera House in the Civic Center. Call 415/621-3838 for ticket information and dates.

    For more information about any of these events, write for a copy of *The San Francisco Book.* Send $1 to the San Francisco Information Center, P. O. Box 6977, San Francisco, CA 94101-6977, or call 415/391-2001 for a daily recording of events anytime during your stay.

3. WHAT TO PACK

FOR YOU   The temperature in San Francisco is rarely above 70° F during the day and rarely below 40° F at night. But don't be fooled if you're going during the summer: that's when the fog can be at its thickest in the early morning and evening.

The San Francisco Convention and Visitors Bureau suggests that visitors keep a light jacket or all-weather coat handy. You will rarely need summertime clothes (shorts and sleeveless shirts and dresses) in the city. If you leave the city, however, to such areas as the East Bay and the Napa Valley you'll find them considerably warmer. This is true for parts of Marin County as well. It's best to check ahead with the visitor information centers or your hotel front desk staff.

FOR THE KIDS   Do you ever feel like you have to be a wizard to pack for your family? Yes, it takes some magic, but successful packing can be done! Before we even take down the suitcases, we first decide whether we're going to use coin-operated laundries and hotel cleaning services while we're traveling or whether we're going to bring all the soiled laundry home. We basically try to take as little as we can, and then we review our list to see if we can cut back further. This requires planning—actually laying out clothes a few days or more ahead and making lists for each family member. We start planning about a week in advance and ask the kids to start thinking about what they'll want to take. We encourage them to bring along only what they can carry, so we're not bogged down with backpacks and extra luggage.

Of course, kids get dirty, wet, and messy, and we've learned that we'll need an extra outfit per day for each of our kids over the age of 3 (excluding teens). For tots, we pack at least three outfits, or plan which ones we'll hand-wash.

4. HEALTH & OTHER PRECAUTIONS

HEALTH   Be sure to pack all the **medications** your children may need, and have your doctors' phone numbers. (Even if it's long distance, call your physician if you have a serious problem.) If you're going to be flying, be sure that any signs of congestion or a cold are seen by your doctor before departure. He or she can tell you what to do to prevent inner ear injury. You might also ask about nasal sprays and oral decongestants for your kids for takeoffs and landings.

Be prepared for **motion sickness.** Kids who never get motion sickness in a car can get it on a boat, in a stuffy airplane, or on a train. Those of you who have tried to get a pill down the throat of an uncooperative child will appreciate liquid Dramamine, which you can give to kids over the age of 2 (we mix it with soda before getting on the boat). Dramamine also comes in chewable tablet form. Ask your pediatrician about other remedies.

You'll want a **first-aid kit.** A small, basic kit is available at most pharmacies. For a more comprehensive kit, contact the American Red Cross (tel. 201/568-8787) and ask how to obtain a Top Gun EMS Kit, which is endorsed by the Red Cross. It comes in a compact easy-to-pack size, but is filled with all you'll need in most emergencies.

SAFETY   There are a few general safety precautions that should be discussed ahead of time, and one that especially applies to the San Francisco area.

If You Become Separated When visiting crowded sightseeing attractions, dress your kids in bright-colored clothing so it will be easy for you to keep an eye on them. Also, talk with them about what they should do if you become separated. Theme-park employees are all schooled to handle the problem of lost children, so tell your kids it's safe to walk up to any park employee and report they are lost. At most theme parks, special name tags can be obtained to aid identification should a child become separated from his or her party.

Fire Every time you check into a new hotel room, it's a good idea to consider what you would do if there was a fire. Where are the exits? Which adult is responsible for which children? Be sure you don't try to leave by elevator. Feel the door to the stairwells before pushing it open. If it's hot, don't attempt to open the door—the fire could be traveling through that stairwell.

Earthquakes Earthquakes do occur here. They are usually quite small, and you may never know one even happened. But if a more significant quake should occur, remember the following: If you are inside a building, *don't run outside.* Keep away from windows and other large glass items. Get under a sturdy piece of furniture, such as a desk or dining table, or stand under a doorway. Never use the elevator to get out, only the stairwells, and don't try to get out if the building is still shaking.

Should you be in your car when a quake hits, pull over and stop—but not under power lines or near trees. Don't stop on a bridge or overpass, and don't get out of the car.

If you're out walking, get into the open, but stay clear of trees, power lines, signs, and the sides of buildings.

OTHER PRECAUTIONS On a less threatening note, we always have all **reservation confirmations** sent to us in writing. Whenever possible, it's best to have something written to show in the event of a problem.

If you are planning to register your kids for a **children's program** at a hotel or in the day-care or ski schools we describe, be sure to find out if you need to make your reservations for those programs in advance. You don't want to make big vacation plans that include children's programs only to get there and find out that your kids can't get in.

5. GETTING THE KIDS INTERESTED

Assuming that you've included the children in your decision to vacation in San Francisco, and that you've decided how long you're going to stay, it's time to get the kids involved again.

SPECIAL PROJECTS

Take them with you to get travel brochures and maps. Once you have a map, plot out your route with a yellow marking pen, circling points of interest and milestones. On the trip, when we pass those points (or a few minutes before), we talk about them. This not only gives children the sense of accomplishing the miles, but also tends to make them take a more active interest in the landmarks of the trip. This works best for car trips, of course, but you can also do it on an airplane if you have a cooperative flight attendant who will indicate the points of interest during your journey.

Get empty notebooks so the kids can keep a journal of their trip. Don't overlook those single-use cameras available at drugstores and camera shops. For $12, your child can have his/her own camera without you having to worry about keeping track of it during the trip. A nice treat.

RECOMMENDED BOOKS FOR KIDS

These books might serve to stimulate your children's interest in San Francisco before they travel.

Aylesworth, Thomas and Virginia, *The Pacific* (Chelsea House Publishers, $6.95).

Boyd, Candy Dawson, *Charlie Pippin* (Macmillan Publishing Co., $3.95). A novel for 8- to 12-year-olds.

Caen, Herb, *The Cable Car and the Dragon* (Chronicle Books, $9.95). Fiction.

Delehanty, Randolph, *The Ultimate Guide to San Francisco* (Chronicle Books, $14.95).

Dudman, John, *The San Francisco Earthquake* (Franklin Watts, $10.90).

Haddoc, Patricia, *San Francisco* (Dillon, $12.95).

Horton, Tom, *SupersSpan, The Golden Gate Bridge* (Chronicle Books, $10.95). With photographs by Baron Wolman.

Kingston, Jeremy, *How Bridges are Made* (Facts on File, $12.95).

Levine, Ellen, *If You Lived at the Time of the Great San Francisco Earthquake* (Scholastic, Inc., $2.50).

Martin, Don, and Betty Woo Martin, *The Best of San Francisco* (Chronicle Books, $9.95).

Pelta, Kathy, *Bridging the Golden Gate* (First Avenue Editions, $4.95).

Tokuda, Wendy, and Hall, Richard, *Humphrey the Lost Whale* (Heian International, Inc., $11.95). Fiction.

Wilder, Laura Ingalls, *West From Home: Letters of Laura Ingalls Wilder* (Harper, $3.50). For 9-year-olds and older.

Yep, Laurence, *Child of the Owl* (Harper, $3.95). A novel for 10- to 14-year-olds.

Yep, Laurence, *Dragonwings* (Harper, $3.50). A novel for 10- to 14-year-olds.

Zibart, Rosemary, *Kidding Around San Francisco* (John Muir Publications, $9.95).

6. GETTING THERE

TRANSPORTATION

BY PLANE

AIRPORTS San Francisco International Airport (tel. 415/761-0800), about 13 miles south of San Francisco near San Bruno, is served by all major domestic and foreign passenger carriers.

You might instead choose to fly into Oakland International Airport (tel. 415/577-4000), a smaller airport that is easier to navigate.

AIRLINES Here's a list of toll-free numbers of the major carriers that fly in and out of San Francisco: **Air Canada** (tel. toll free 800/776-3000); **Air France** (tel. toll free 800/237-2623); **Alaska Airlines** (tel. toll free 800/426-0333); **American Airlines** (tel. toll free 800/433-7300); **America West Airlines** (tel. toll free 800/247-5692); **Braniff Airways** (tel. toll free 800/272-6433); **British Airways** (tel. toll free 800/247-9297); **Canadian Airlines International** (tel. toll free 800/426-7000); **Cathay Pacific Airways** (tel. toll free 800/233-2742); **China Airlines** (tel. toll free 800/227-5118); **Continental Airlines** (tel. toll free 800/435-0040); **Delta Air** (tel. toll free 800/221-1212); **Hawaiian Airlines** (tel. toll free 800/367-5320); **Japan Air Lines** (tel. toll free 800/525-3663); **Korean Airlines** (tel. toll free 800/531-2626); **Lufthansa** (tel. toll free 800/645-3880); **Mexicana Airlines** (tel. toll free 800/531-7921); **Northwest Airlines** (tel. toll free 800/225-2525); **Philippine Airlines** (tel. toll free 800/435-9725); **Qantas Airlines** (tel. toll free 800/227-4500); **Scandinavian Airlines System (SAS)** (tel. toll free 800/221-2350); **Singapore Airlines** (tel. toll free 800/742-3333); **Southwest Airlines** (tel. toll free 800/531-5601); **Trans World Airlines (TWA)** (tel. toll free 800/221-2000); **United Airlines and United Express** (tel. toll free 800/241-6522); **USAir** (tel. toll free 800/428-4322); **UTA French Airlines** (tel. toll free 800/237-2623).

Many chartered flights also fly into San Francisco. Check the newspapers for ads or consult a travel agent specialist.

BY CAR

Scenic north-south routes passing directly through San Francisco are U.S. 101 and Calif. 1. They enter the city separately from the south, merge on the San Francisco

 FROMMER'S SMART FAMILY TRAVELER: AIRFARES

VALUE-CONSCIOUS TRAVELERS SHOULD TAKE ADVANTAGE OF THE FOLLOWING:

1. Shop all the airlines that fly to your destination.
2. Always ask for the lowest fare, not just a discount fare. Ask about special family fares.
3. Keep calling the airline of your choice—availability of cheap seats changes daily. Airlines would rather sell a seat at a discount than have it fly empty. As the departure date nears, additional low-cost seats may become available.
4. Ask about frequent-flier programs that give you bonuses and free flights when you use an airline regularly.
5. Ask airlines about their family tour packages. Land arrangements are often cheaper when booked with an air ticket.
6. Be flexible with your times and days of departure—the best prices are often offered midweek.

approach to the Golden Gate Bridge, and continue as one through a few miles of southern Marin County. Because Calif. 1, the coastal route, is subject to dense fog and the likelihood of landslides, the AAA recommends that you check weather and road conditions before driving it.

The fast north-south route, I-5, lies east of San Francisco; connections to the San Francisco-Oakland Bay Bridge are via I-580 and I-80 from the north and I-580 and I-80 from the south. Another route, Calif. 99, closely parallels I-5 and also has connections into the city.

Most traffic from the east approaches via I-80 across the Sierras. Interstate-80 is closely paralleled by U.S. 50 to Sacramento, from where the Interstate heads west, leading into the city over the San Francisco-Oakland Bay Bridge.

BY TRAIN

The train is an exciting way to travel. **Amtrak,** with its San Francisco office in the Trans-Bay Terminal, First and Mission streets (tel. 415/558-6600, or toll free 800/USA-RAIL), is the way to go. Amtrak's *Coast Starlight* runs the length of the California coast and inland up to Portland and Seattle. The train disembarks in Oakland and a shuttle takes you to the Trans-Bay Terminal in San Francisco. The *California Zephyr* comes from parts east, through Chicago and Denver.

Some of the trains have complete dining cars with full-service restaurants; others have snack bars. Some have bedrooms with sleeping berths; others offer family bedrooms—rooms that are the full width of the train, with windows on both sides.

When you consider train travel, ask about family fares and package tours. They make it considerably more affordable.

BY BUS

The major transcontinental bus line that services the Bay area is **Greyhound/ Trailways Bus Lines,** with its main depot at the San Francisco Trans-Bay Terminal at First and Mission streets (tel. 415/558-6789).

KEEPING THE KIDS ENTERTAINED

People have different opinions about the number of toys you should take on a trip. We bring some new toys and some old favorites. The kids each get their own backpack (or small toy box in the backseat of the car) in which they pack the toys and books they especially want. We stash new toys in our suitcases or bags and dole them out when the kids tire of what they've brought. When the trip is a long one, we actually wrap the new toys and distribute them to the kids at key moments—timed to hold their interest. We alternate creative-type toys, such as crayons, with toys and games that require some concentration and thinking. We always include toys that *we* enjoy playing with, too. Most toy stores have a large variety of travel games and toys.

Once your child is old enough to enjoy cassette-tape stories and songs, you've found a real treasure. These kept Andrew occupied for hours at a time, long enough to endure very long car trips.

Be sure to leave the messy, noisy toys and projects at home. Games with little pieces and puzzles can also give you grief. Our least favorite words on a cross-country flight were, "Oh, I dropped some again!" Picture yourself picking up little game pieces

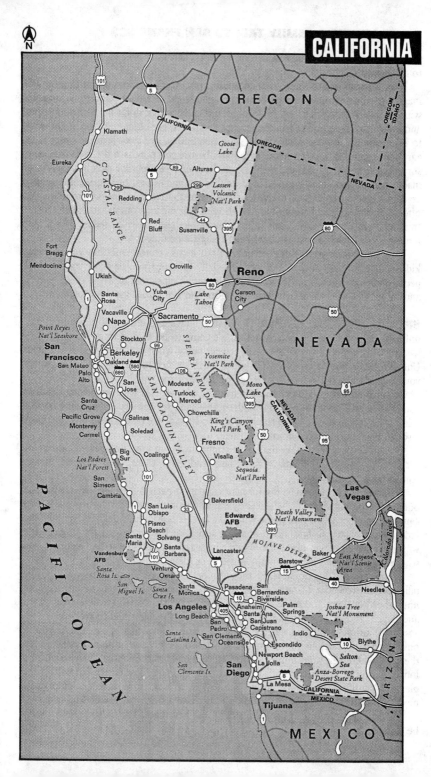

CALIFORNIA

OREGON

CALIFORNIA

OREGON / IDAHO

Klamath

Eureka

COASTAL RANGE

Goose
Lake

OREGON

NEVADA

Alturas

Redding

*Lassen
Volcanic
Nat'l Park*

Red
Bluff

Susanville

Fort
Bragg

Mendocino

Oroville

Ukiah

Reno

Santa
Rosa

Yuba
City

*Lake
Tahoe*

Carson
City

Vacaville

Napa

Sacramento

NEVADA

*Point Reyes
Nat'l Seashore*

Stockton

SIERRA NEVADA

*Yosemite
Nat'l Park*

San
Francisco

Berkeley

Oakland

San Mateo

Palo
Alto

San
Jose

Modesto

Turlock

Merced

*Mono
Lake*

NEVADA
CALIFORNIA

Santa
Cruz

SAN JOAQUIN VALLEY

Chowchilla

Pacific Grove

Salinas

*King's Canyon
Nat'l Park*

Monterey

Carmel

Soledad

Fresno

Big
Sur

Coalinga

Visalia

*Los Padres
Nat'l Forest*

*Sequoia
Nat'l Park*

Las
Vegas

San
Simeon

Cambria

Bakersfield

San Luis
Obispo

*Death Valley
Nat'l Monument*

Pismo
Beach

Edwards
AFB

Santa
Maria

Solvang

Santa
Barbara

Lancaster

MOJAVE DESERT

Baker

*East Mojave
Nat'l Scenic
Area*

Vandenburg
AFB

Ventura

Oxnard

Barstow

*Santa
Rosa Is.*

*San
Miguel Is.*

*Santa
Cruz Is.*

Santa
Monica

Pasadena

San
Bernardino

Needles

Riverside

Los Angeles

Anaheim

Santa Ana

*Joshua Tree
Nat'l Monument*

Long Beach

San
Pedro

San Juan
Capistrano

Palm
Springs

Indio

Blythe

*Santa
Catalina Is.*

San Clemente

Oceanside

Escondido

*Salton
Sea*

Newport Beach

La Jolla

*Anza-Borrego
Desert State Park*

*San
Clemente Is.*

San
Diego

La Mesa

ARIZONA

Colorado River

CALIFORNIA
MEXICO

Tijuana

P A C I F I C   O C E A N

M E X I C O

in a crowded, baggage-filled row of airline seats. There are better toys and better ways to meet your neighbors.

Here are some ideas of things to take along: packages of stickers and sticker books, magnetic drawing and alphabet boards, magnetic games, hand puppets, write-and-wipe boards, Colorforms, coloring books and crayons that don't melt, tracing paper and designs to trace, and self-inking stamps and paper. For older kids, you might want to bring small cars, decks of cards, blank notebooks, and a cassette recorder with earphones. (Check the size of the earphones before you purchase the recorder; after surprising then 4-year-old Jane with one on the plane, we spent the next hour trying to make them fit her small head.) Hand-held video games are, of course, the newest craze, and you probably won't have to remind your child to bring his or hers along. We often make up a crafts box with lots of goodies that the kids can use to create artistic treasures. On car trips, you can bring song books and music cassettes. (If you are renting a car, check ahead as to whether there's a tape deck.)

More and more companies are putting out items created especially for traveling kids: activity books; books of games especially for car, train, or plane travel; travel packs made up of age-appropriate diversions; audio tapes that describe travel games; and more. Check with your favorite toy store and bookstore for the latest items.

SPECIAL TIPS FOR AIRPLANE TRIPS Flying is always an adventure, but unfortunately you can't predict whether it's going to be a good or a bad one.

The kids, especially young ones, get very antsy when confined to a small area. Unlike in a car, you can't stop when you want to let the kids run around. Also, some young children may become frightened on the airplane.

To ward off negative experiences before the trip, we talk with our young children about what will happen. If your children are flying for the first time, some people think it helps if you take them to an airport to look at the planes before your trip. A favorite blanket or stuffed animal will help too.

Once on board, remember that cabin temperature can vary. Bring extra clothes for each child (always a change of clothes) and have them wear layered, loose, comfortable clothing.

Waiting in airports can be the torment of many a parent. Although we try to time our arrival so that we won't be too early but also won't have to run for the plane, you can never predict when that plane will leave late. If our flight is delayed, we take the kids for walks, try to find video arcades, and look for other kids their age in the waiting area for them to play with. When all else fails, we attempt to find a corner area where we can spread out and play on the floor (ugh!).

Whatever you do, don't leave the terminal. We were once assured by airline officials that we had a 3-hour delay, so we took a long walk. When we returned (an hour ahead of time), the plane had departed. The airline officials said they had paged and paged, and all passengers who didn't return to the flight had to rebook.

Many airline personnel suggest bringing your young child's car seat if you've purchased a separate seat for him or her. It helps to protect and, in some cases, to keep the child where you want him or her. Also, your child may be more likely to sit for a longer period of time in a familiar car seat than in a large seat with a lap belt. If the plane isn't full, sometimes the airline staff will try to make sure there's an empty seat next to you for the car seat (if you didn't purchase a ticket for the child).

Always bring a carry-on bag with snacks and beverages. The kids may not always be able to wait for the scheduled airline meals, and you don't even know if they will actually eat the airline food. (Goodness knows, many adults don't!) We pack a full goodie bag, complete with fresh fruit, bread, raisins, crackers and cheese, pretzels, and lots of individual boxes of juice. Kids get very thirsty on flights. We also include several flexible straws, and for little ones, drinking cups with lids.

Finally, airlines allow you to board in advance if you have children. This is wonderful if you're carrying tons of things or have more than one child to settle. If you feel your child needs to expend that last bit of energy before the flight, ask the flight attendant if one adult can board with all the paraphernalia while the other one stays with the child until the last minutes of boarding.

SPECIAL TIPS FOR CAR TRAVEL Traveling in a car with children is unlike any other experience, one you have to undergo to understand. Remember that you'll all be enclosed in a very small space for an extended period of time. Good humor, plenty to do, and food and drink are the order of the day.

The main rule is to stop every few hours to break up the monotony and allow the kids time to get out and move around. Also, instead of stopping at a restaurant to eat, you can stop at a lovely park or where you know there's a special attraction.

Seating arrangements are important. One parent might sit in the backseat with the kids to ward off trouble. It's especially helpful if one child is having a hard time, or if the group of kids tends to bicker or get rowdy when you're on the road. It's better than constantly turning around and leaning over the front seat, and it also protects you from running the risk of being ticketed for not wearing a seatbelt (a California law).

Also, be sure to bring along an adequate supply of pacifiers, bottles, and snacks. Pack enough pillows and blankets for everyone.

To prevent cranky kids, anticipate where the sun will be on their faces. If you can't keep them out of the sun, use a visor. Kids get really uncomfortable with the sun in their eyes, and they can complain unmercifully if they're hot and sweaty. Driving through the California desert can be a grueling experience. Without our knowing it until later, one of our children actually got a sunburn from it. You can get a dark cellophane-like material that sticks to the window and can be moved around depending where the sun is.

To combat motion sickness, experts suggest lemon drops, lemon cookies, peppermint, foods high in carbohydrates, and salt-covered foods such as crackers or pretzels, which cut down the production of what causes nausea. Again, ask your pediatrician for advice. Also remember not to let the kids read while the car is in motion.

The question "When will we get there?" signals the time to take out the prerouted map we suggested you make (see "Special Projects" in Section 5, "Getting the Kids Interested," above). The activity can be as simple as calculating where you'll stop for gas and roadside stretches.

Another game especially well suited for automobile travel (and for kids over 6) is the geography game, in which one player names a place (country, city, region, etc.) and the next player has to come up with a place whose name begins with the last letter of the previous place name.

Other fun ways to pass the time involve using license plates of passing vehicles. Young kids can look for the alphabet in sequence. Older children can try to spell words or find all the states of the United States. Very little children can look for colors of passing cars. And an all-time favorite is to sing songs together.

SPECIAL TIPS FOR TRAIN TRAVEL Although not the luxurious form of transportation it used to be, train travel is still one way to see the scenery without constantly stopping for gas, restaurants, and hotels. Kids can move around, play easier than in a car, and often learn a great deal about this mode of transportation. When you make your reservations, ask about family bedrooms, offered on some Amtrak trains. Short trips in the Bay Area can be fun experiences for children, and the journey itself can be the adventure.

CHAPTER 2

GETTING TO KNOW SAN FRANCISCO

Nearly everyone who comes to San Francisco falls in love with it. A city of sea, hills and parks, cable cars, a bustling waterfront, bridges that span mighty spaces, a warm sun and a romantic fog—San Francisco is alive and lovely.

San Francisco was built on 43 hills and encompasses a total of almost 130 square miles, of which only 46.6 square miles are land. But don't worry: San Francisco is a friendly giant, easy to get to know and easy—at least *possible*—to get around.

1. ORIENTATION

ARRIVING

BY PLANE   Your choice of ground transportation depends on the airport you use and your destination.

From San Francisco International Airport   From San Francisco International Airport, ground transportation is available via shuttle, bus, taxi, limousine, or rental cars. Also, check ahead about courtesy van service available from some hotels.

Door-to-door airport service is available 24 hours a day from **Bay Area Super Shuttle** (tel. 415/558-8500). Once you land at SFO and have gathered your bags, go outside where you'll find the city-bound shuttles. General fare is $10 for adults and children over 5, $5 for children ages 2 to 5; free for children under 2. Make reservations early.

The **SFO Airporter Coaches** (tel. 415/495-8404) provides transfers from the airport to major downtown hotels and hotels in the financial district every 20 to 30 minutes from 5:30am to 10:30pm. Trips take approximately 20 minutes. One-way fare for adults is $6, $3 for children 2 to 12; free for children under 2.

Minivans provide door-to-door service between the airport and hotels. Among the companies offering this service are **Good Neighbors** (tel. 415/777-4899), **Lorries** (tel. 415/334-9000), and **Yellow Airport Service** (tel. 415/282-7433). There are frequent pickups from the red-and-white-striped zones marked at pedestrian islands on the upper level of the airport. One-way fare ranges between $8 and $10 per person, regardless of age.

Associated Limousines of San Francisco (tel. 415/431-7000, or toll free 800/255-2660), offers door-to-door transportation as well. The fare is $8 per person, $4 for children under 5. Two bags per person are permitted, then extra charges apply.

Taxis are plentiful in this city. A trip from the airport to downtown will cost you approximately $25. Taxi fares in San Francisco are approximately $2.90 for the first mile, and $1.50 for each additional mile. You can pick up a cab anywhere, but if you need to call, here are a couple of suggestions: **Luxor Cab** (tel. 415/282-4141) and **Veteran's Taxicab Company** (tel. 415/552-1300).

Rental cars from all the major agencies are available through their airport reservation desks.

From Oakland International Airport   You can easily reach San Francisco and other parts of the Bay area from Oakland International Airport. **AC Transit** (tel. 415/839-2882) will take you to different locations in Oakland. You can then take a bus to the San Francisco Trans-Bay Terminal, where **BART** (Bay Area Rapid Transit; tel. 415/788-BART) will take you directly under the Bay and into the city. **AirBART** (tel. 415/832-1464, or toll free 800/545-2700) is another possibility; the shuttle bus will take you from the airport to the nearest BART station. Buses run about every 15 minutes and stop in front of Terminals 1 and 2 near the GROUND TRANSPORTA-TION signs. AirBART operates Monday through Saturday from 6am to midnight and on Sunday from 9am to midnight. If you prefer a limousine, **569-LIMO, Inc.,** is one choice; dial 415/569-LIMO, of course. **Taxis** from the airport to downtown San Francisco are expensive, costing approximately $55 plus tip. There are car rental agencies as well.

BY TRAIN   All rail service terminates in Oakland at the 16th Street Station and passengers are transported by bus to the Trans-Bay Terminal, First and Mission streets (tel. 415/558-6600).

BY BUS   The **Greyhound/Trailways Bus Lines** has its main terminal at the Trans-Bay Terminal, First and Mission streets (tel. 415/558-6789).

BY CAR   For your information while driving, San Francisco intersections are subject to strict enforcement of the Anti-Gridlock Act, which prohibits pulling into an intersection when traffic makes it questionable that you'll get through before the light turns red. Fines of $50 to $500 are imposed on motorists convicted of violating the act, so drive carefully.

The downtown speed limit is 25 mph unless otherwise posted, 15 mph at blind intersections. Right turns on red are legal unless otherwise posted. Pedestrians using designated crosswalks **always** have the right-of-way.

TOURIST INFORMATION

The **San Francisco Convention and Visitors Bureau Information Center,** 900 Market St. at Powell Street in Hallidie Plaza, lower level, San Francisco, CA 94102 (tel. 415/391-2000), has a multilingual staff to help you. Hours are Monday through

Friday 9am to 5:30pm, Saturday 9am to 3pm, Sundays 10am to 2pm. They are closed New Year's Day, Thanksgiving Day, and Christmas Day.

You can also contact **Traveler's Aid Society** at 415/255-2252. Additional visitor information is available from the **Japan Center,** 1520 Webster St., San Francisco, CA 94115 (tel. 415/922-6776); **North Beach Chamber of Commerce,** 800A Lombard St., San Francisco, CA 94133 (tel. 415/673-2522); and **Union Street Association, Inc.,** 1686 Union St., San Francisco, CA 94123 (tel. 415/441-7055).

When in town, dial 391-2001 any time of day or night for a **recorded message** about current cultural, theater, music, sports, and other special events. This information is also available in German (tel. 391-2004), French (tel. 391-2003), Japanese (tel. 391-2101), and Spanish (tel. 391-2122).

The **Visitors Information Center of the Redwood Empire Association,** 785 Market St., 15th Floor (tel. 415/543-8334), offers informative brochures and a very knowledgeable desk staff who are able to plan tours both in San Francisco and north of the city. Their free annual *Redwood Empire Visitors' Guide* is crammed with detailed information on everything from San Francisco walking tours and museums to visits to Marin County and the timetable of the Super Skunk train through Mendocino County. The office is open Monday through Friday from 9am to 5pm.

CITY LAYOUT

San Francisco may seem confusing at first, but it quickly becomes easy to negotiate. The city's downtown streets are arranged in a simple grid pattern, with the exception of Market Street and Columbus Avenue, which cut across the grid at right angles to each other. Hills appear to distort this pattern, however, and can seem disorienting. But as you learn your way around, these same hills will become your landmarks and reference points.

MAIN ARTERIES & STREETS   Market Street is San Francisco's main thoroughfare. Most of the city's buses ply this strip on their way to the Financial District from the bedroom communities to the west and south. The tall office buildings that create the city's stalactite skyline are clustered at the northeast end of Market; one block beyond lie the Embarcadero and the bay.

The Embarcadero curves north along San Francisco Bay, around the perimeter of the city. It terminates at Fisherman's Wharf, the famous tourist-oriented pier, which is full of restaurants and T-shirt stands. Aquatic Park and the Fort Mason complex are just ahead, occupying the northernmost point of the peninsula.

From here, **Van Ness Avenue** runs due south, back to Market Street. The area just described forms a rough triangle, with Market Street as its eastern, the waterfront as its northern, and Van Ness Avenue as its western boundary. Within this triangle lie most of the city's main tourist sights.

The Golden Gate Bridge   The Golden Gate Bridge is one of the most famous—and beautiful—landmarks in the world. Painted bright red-orange, it stands vibrantly above the white-flecked waters, where the Pacific Ocean meets San Francisco Bay and is framed by dark green rolling hills and crystal waters. Because of the enormous engineering challenges of constructing a bridge spanning over water 318

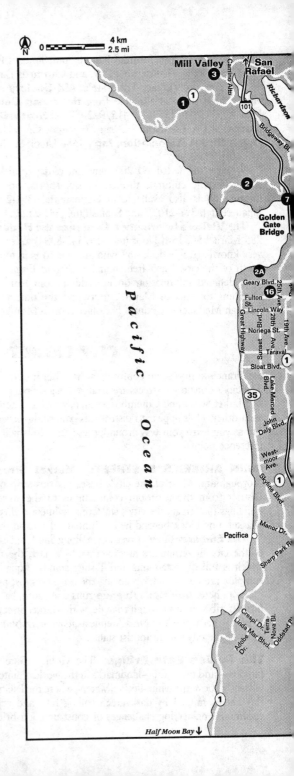

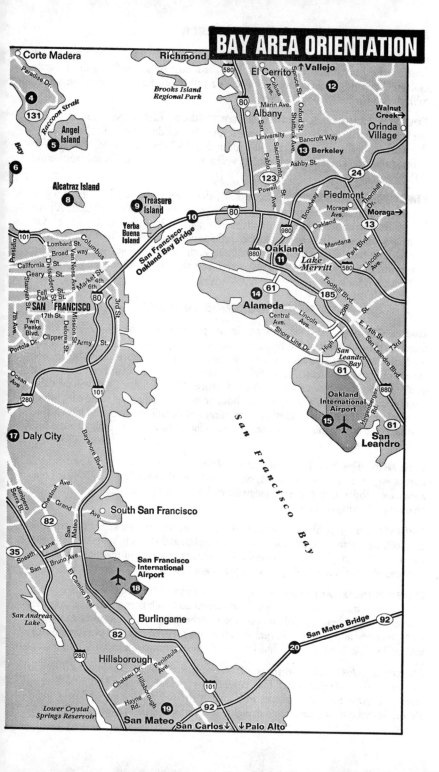

feet deep in some places, the project was originally nicknamed "The Bridge That Couldn't Be Built." But, on May 27, 1937, at a cost of $35 million, the 1.7-mile Golden Gate Bridge was completed. There's a toll booth for southbound traffic ($2 toll); the pedestrian walkway is free.

The San Francisco–Oakland Bay Bridge   Linking San Francisco with the East Bay cities of Oakland and Berkeley, the Bay Bridge is 8½ miles long, one of the world's longest steel bridges. The silver double-decker bridge has five lanes in either direction. There is no pedestrian walkway, and a toll is collected westbound ($1).

FINDING AN ADDRESS   Since most of the city's streets are laid out in a grid pattern, finding an address is easy when you know the nearest cross street. All the listings in this book include cross-street information. In addition, the city of San Francisco encompasses over a dozen distinct neighborhoods. To help you stay oriented, we have listed hotels and restaurants under area headings. When asking for directions, find out the nearest cross street and the neighborhood in which your destination is located.

NEIGHBORHOODS IN BRIEF

Union Square   Although it's not in the geographic center of the city, Union Square is the true heart of San Francisco. Surrounded by both the city's swankiest and seediest shops, the square is also home to large department stores, busy hotels, and tourist-oriented restaurants. It is likely that your hotel will be near here. But even if you're not bedding down within walking distance of Union Square, you will probably pass by on your way to the theater, to shop, or to ride the famous cable cars, which terminate just three blocks south, on the corner of Powell Street and Market Street. During peak hours, this area becomes a bit difficult to navigate, with strollers and children in tow.

Nob Hill   This high hill in the center of the city around California and Mason streets, is quite a swanky spot; it was once called "the hill of palaces" by Robert Louis Stevenson. Today it is home to magnificent hotels, beautiful Grace Cathedral and charming Huntington Park.

Chinatown   Just blocks north of Union Square and the Financial District, this 24-block labyrinth of restaurants, markets, temples, and shops is home to the largest Chinese community in North America. For tourists, it is one of the most marvelous walking, shopping, and eating areas in San Francisco.

North Beach   At Columbus Avenue, Chinatown blends with North Beach, the city's famous Italian quarter. Although you'll find no beach here and no real activities of interest to children, you will discover some of the city's best family restaurants, plus cafés, theaters, and galleries. Telegraph Hill looms over the east side of North Beach, topped by Coit Tower, one of San Francisco's best vantage points.

Financial District   Northeast of Union Square, toward San Francisco Bay, is the city's suit-and-tie district. This conservative quarter, centered around Kearny Street and Sansome Street, swarms with smartly dressed workers on weekdays and is almost deserted on weekends and at night. The Transamerica Pyramid, at Montgomery Street and Clay Street, is one of the district's most conspicuous architectural features. To its east stands the sprawling **Embarcadero Center,** an 8½-acre complex housing offices, shops, and restaurants. Farther east still is the World Trade Center, standing adjacent to the old Ferry Building, the city's prebridge transportation hub. Ferries to Sausalito and Larkspur still leave from this point.

Civic Center   This is an area comprised of government buildings and performing arts centers that are quite lovely. While it doesn't offer much in the way of family sightseeing, a brief walk around the area is a chance to see some wonderful architecture. In fact, San Francisco City Hall is an example of spectacular French Renaissance architecture and has a dome taller than the Capitol building in Washington, D.C.

SoMa   The area south of Market Street, dubbed "SoMa" by young trendies, is in an exciting state of transition. Working warehouses and industrial spaces are rapidly being transformed into nightclubs, galleries, and restaurants. Collectively, they are turning this formerly desolate area into one of the city's most vibrant new neighborhoods, though not really a tourist section for children.

Haight-Ashbury   The Haight, as it is called, was the 1960s stomping ground of America's hippies and the center of the counterculture movement. Today the neighborhood straddling upper Haight Street, on the eastern border of Golden Gate Park, is largely gentrified, but the street life is still colorful, and shops along the strip still include a good number of alternative boutiques.

The Castro   Synonymous with San Francisco's gay community, the Castro is a pretty, residential neighborhood centered around bustling Castro Street. Located at the very end of Market Street, at the corner of 17th Street, Castro Street supports dozens of shops, restaurants, and bars, and has one of the best movie houses in America.

Japantown (or "Nihonmachi")   This is San Francisco's Tokyo-like quarter for things Japanese. Located at Post and Buchanan streets is the five-acre complex known as the Japan Center.

Richmond District & Clement Street   Three and a half miles from downtown is this wonderful international section with shops, restaurants, and cultural buildings. Chinese, Indonesian, Thai, Korean, Vietnamese, Russian, Greek, Italian, and other nationalities are represented here, which makes for a delightful educational stroll.

And now a brief mention of San Francisco's 24 miles of waterfront. The **Embarcadero** starts at the Ferry Building at the foot of Market Street (you'll spot it immediately by its charming clock tower) and continues toward the **Northern Waterfront,** which is roughly the area from **Pier 39** to **Ghirardelli Square** and includes Fisherman's Wharf, the Cannery, and the Hyde Street Pier. Nearby are the Marina District and Union Street. The **Marina District** offers many moderately

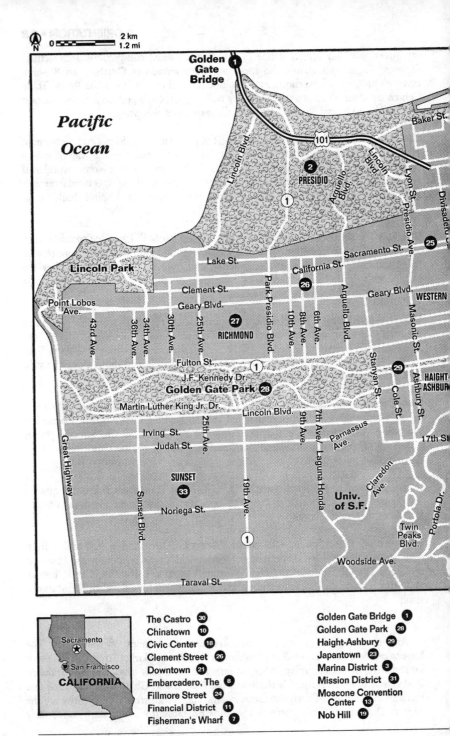

0 ▭▭▭▭ **2 km**
1.2 mi

N

Golden
Gate
Bridge — **1**

Pacific

Ocean

Baker St.

101

Lincoln Blvd.

Lincoln Blvd.

2
PRESIDIO

Arguello Blvd.

Presidio Ave.

Lyon St.

Divisadero

1

25

Lincoln Park

Lake St.

Sacramento St.

California St.

26

Geary Blvd.

WESTERN

Point Lobos Ave.

Clement St.

Geary Blvd.

43rd Ave.

36th Ave.

34th Ave.

30th Ave.

25th Ave.

Park Presidio Blvd.

10th Ave.

8th Ave.

6th Ave.

Arguello Blvd.

Masonic St.

27
RICHMOND

Fulton St.

1

29

HAIGHT ASHBUR

J.F. Kennedy Dr.

Golden Gate Park **28**

Stanyan St.

Cole St.

Ashbury St.

Martin Luther King Jr. Dr.

Lincoln Blvd.

9th Ave.

7th Ave./Laguna Honda

Parnassus Ave.

17th St

Irving St.

Judah St.

25th Ave.

Great Highway

SUNSET
33

Noriega St.

Sunset Blvd.

19th Ave.

**Univ.
of S.F.**

Claredon Ave.

Portola Dr.

Twin
Peaks
Blvd.

1

Woodside Ave.

Taraval St.

Sacramento ★

● San Francisco

CALIFORNIA

The Castro **30**
Chinatown **10**
Civic Center **18**
Clement Street **26**
Downtown **21**
Embarcadero, The **8**
Fillmore Street **24**
Financial District **11**
Fisherman's Wharf **7**

Golden Gate Bridge **1**
Golden Gate Park **28**
Haight-Ashbury **29**
Japantown **23**
Marina District **3**
Mission District **31**
Moscone Convention
  Center **13**
Nob Hill **19**

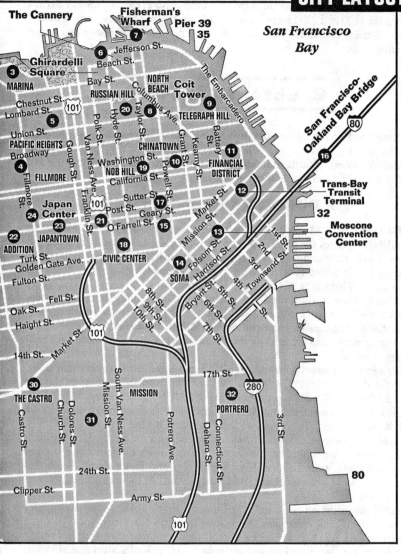

CITY LAYOUT

The Cannery

Fisherman's Wharf

Pier 39
35

San Francisco Bay

Jefferson St.

Beach St.

Ghirardelli Square

MARINA

Bay St.

Chestnut St.

Lombard St.

101

Union St.

PACIFIC HEIGHTS

Broadway

FILLMORE

Fillmore St.

Japan Center

JAPANTOWN

ADDITION

Turk St.

Golden Gate Ave.

Fulton St.

Fell St.

Oak St.

Haight St.

14th St.

Market St.

THE CASTRO

Castro St.

NORTH BEACH

Columbus Ave.

RUSSIAN HILL

Taylor St.

Hyde St.

Polk St.

Van Ness Ave.

Gough St.

Franklin St.

CHINATOWN

Washington St.

NOB HILL

California St.

Sutter St.

Post St.

O'Farrell St.

Geary St.

CIVIC CENTER

8th St.

9th St.

10th St.

Coit Tower

TELEGRAPH HILL

Grant St.

Kearny St.

Battery St.

Powell St.

FINANCIAL DISTRICT

Market St.

Mission St.

Folsom St.

Harrison St.

SOMA

Bryant St.

5th St.

6th St.

7th St.

17th St.

MISSION

Mission St.

South Van Ness Ave.

Dolores St.

Church St.

24th St.

Clipper St.

Army St.

PORTRERO

Potrero Ave.

Connecticut St.

Deharo St.

3rd St.

The Embarcadero

San Francisco Bay

San Francisco-Oakland Bay Bridge

80

Trans-Bay Transit Terminal

Moscone Convention Center

32

1st St.

2nd St.

3rd

4th St.

Townsend St.

I St.

280

80

101

North Beach   8
Northern Waterfront   6
Pacific Heights   4
Potrero   32
Presidio   2
Richmond   27
Russian Hill   20
Sacramento Street   25
San Francisco-Oakland Bay Bridge   16

San Francisco Visitor Information Center   15
South of Market (SoMa)   14
Sunset District   33
Telegraph Hill   9
Trans-Bay Terminal   12
Union Square   17
Union Street   5
Western Addition   22

priced accommodations and some of the best small parks in the city. **Union Street** between the 1600 and 220 blocks is the area known as **Cow Hollow,** now a trendy, upscale shopping and restaurant area with restored Victorian buildings and quaint little courtyards.

2. GETTING AROUND

For starters, pick up a good map of San Francisco. You'll find that walking is the most enjoyable way to go, and you can walk almost anywhere (especially if you've brought comfortable shoes). When you get tired of walking, there's convenient—and affordable—public and private transportation.

BY PUBLIC TRANSPORTATION

The **San Francisco Municipal Railway** better known as **MUNI** (tel. 673-6864 or 673-MUNI), operates the city's 700 miles of cable cars, buses, trolly coaches and metros. Together, these three public-transportation services crisscross the entire city, rendering San Francisco fully accessible to otherwise vehicleless visitors. Buses and metros cost 85¢ for adults, 25¢ for young riders aged 5 to 17, and 15¢ for seniors over 65. Cable cars cost a whopping $2 for adults and $1 for young riders; they remain, however, 15¢ for seniors. Needless to say, they're packed primarily with tourists. **Note: Exact change is required on all MUNI vehicles.** Free transfers are issued upon request and are valid for two vehicle changes, in any direction, within 90 minutes of issuance.

You might want to get a map of the MUNI routes and transit connections called *The Official San Francisco Street and Transit Guide,* available at most bookstores for $1.50. You can also get information by writing MUNI, MUNI Map, 949 Presidio Ave., Room 222, San Francisco, CA 94115. Enclose a check or money order for $2 (includes 50¢ postage, etc.) payable to San Francisco City and County.

There are self-service ticket machines at all major stops and terminals on the cable car lines. (These are located at Powell and Market streets, California and Drumm streets, California Street and Van Ness Avenue, Bay and Taylor streets, Beach and Hyde streets, and California Street and Grant Avenue.) At these machines, you can purchase discount tickets.

MUNI discount passes, called "passports," entitle holders to unlimited rides on buses, trams, and cable cars. A passport costs $6 for 1 day and $10 for 3 consecutive days. As a bonus, your passport also entitles you to admission discounts at 27 of the city's major attractions, including: the M. H. de Young Memorial Museum, the Asian Art Museum, the California Academy of Sciences, and the Japanese Tea Garden (all in Golden Gate Park); the Museum of Modern Art; Coit Tower; the California Palace of the Legion of Honor; the Exploratorium; the Zoo; and the National Maritime Museum and Historic Ships (where you may visit the U.S.S. *Pampanito* and the S.S. *Jeremiah O'Brien*). Among the places where you can purchase a pass, or passport, are the San Francisco Visitor Information Center, the Holiday Inn Civic Center, the San Francisco Ticket Box Office Service (STBS) booth at Union Square, and the Cable Car Museum (at Mason Street and Washington Street).

BY CABLE CAR San Francisco's cable cars may not be the most practical means of transport, but these rolling symbols of the city are the best loved. They are also official historic landmarks, designated as such by the National Parks Service in 1964. There are three lines in all. The most scenic—and exciting—is the **Powell-Hyde line,** which follows a zigzag route from the corner of Powell Street and Market Street, over both Nob Hill and Russian Hill, to a turntable at gaslit Victorian Square in front of Aquatic Park. The **Powell-Mason line** starts at the same intersection and climbs over Nob Hill before descending to Bay Street, just three blocks from Fisherman's Wharf. The **California Street line** begins at the foot of Market Street and runs a straight course through Chinatown and over Nob Hill to Van Ness Avenue. All riders must exit at the last stop and wait in line for the return trip. The cable-car system operates from approximately 6:30am to 12:30am.

BY BUS Buses reach almost every corner of San Francisco, and beyond—they travel over the bridges to Marin County and Oakland. Some buses are powered by overhead electric cables; others use conventional gas engines. All are numbered and display their destinations on the front. Stops are designated by signs, curb markings, and yellow bands on adjacent utility poles. Most buses travel along Market Street or pass near Union Square. They run from about 6am to midnight, after which there is infrequent all-night "Owl" service.

Popular tourist routes are traveled by bus nos. 5, 7, and 71, all of which run to Golden Gate Park; by bus nos. 41 and 45, which ply the length of Union Street; and by bus no. 30, which runs between Union Square and Ghirardelli Square.

AC Transit, Trans-Bay Terminal, First and Mission streets (tel. 415/839-2882), is the way to get to the East Bay by way of the San Francisco–Oakland Bay Bridge.

Golden Gate Transit depot, also located in the Trans-Bay Terminal, First and Mission streets (tel. 415/332-6600), is the system that gets you to Marin and Sonoma counties by way of the Golden Gate Bridge.

SAMTRANS (San Mateo County Transit District) Trans-Bay Terminal, First and Mission streets (tel. 415/761-7000), connects San Francisco to San Mateo County and the San Francisco International Airport.

BY METRO MUNI's five metro lines, designated J, K, L, M, and N, run underground downtown and aboveground in the outer neighborhoods. The sleek rail buses make the same stops as BART (see below) along Market Street, including Embarcadero Station (in the Financial District), Montgomery Street and Powell Street (both near Union Square), and the Civic Center (near City Hall). Past the Civic Center, the routes branch off in different directions: The J line goes to Mission Dolores; the K, L, and M lines go to Castro Street; and the N line ends within one block of Golden Gate Park. Metros run about every 15 minutes—more frequently during rush hours. Service is offered Monday through Friday from 5am to 12:30am, on Saturday from 6am to 12:20am, and on Sunday from 9am to 12:20am.

BY BART BART, an acronym for Bay Area Rapid Transit (tel. 788-BART), is a futuristic-looking, $5-billion high-speed rail network that connects San Francisco with the East Bay—Oakland, Richmond, Concord, and Fremont. Four stations are located along Market Street (see "By Metro," above). Fares range from 85¢ to $4, depending on how far you go. Tickets are dispensed from machines in the stations and are magnetically encoded with a dollar amount. Computerized exits automatically deduct the correct fare. Children 4 and under ride free. Trains run every 15 to 20

FROMMER'S SMART FAMILY TRAVELER—HOW TO KEEP KIDS ENTERTAINED WHILE TRAVELING

SUGGESTIONS FOR COMBATTING BOREDOM ON LONG ROAD TRIPS

How often have you heard the words "I'm bored" or "I am tired of sitting in this car . . . what can I do?" from your children in the back seat. With hours of highway driving still to go, you have to come up with something to keep the kids happily occupied. Our family has favorite car activities, as I am sure yours does also—but we just discovered three new boredom-busters we want to tell you about. All are available from any Club office of the American Automobile Association.

1. The first is a publication called the *AAA Travel Activity Book: The Official AAA Fun Book for Kids*. This 144-page book should provide hours of entertainment, along with light doses of historical, geographical, and general information. For example, youngsters can learn a little about Connecticut's shipbuilding heritage while adding designs to and coloring in a clipper ship. And there are also travel-oriented verbal games the whole family can play, anagrams, crossword puzzles, math problems, and dozens of other activities to amuse and inform car passengers of all ages.

2. The second is a "peel 'n press" game kit called *Road Sign Games*. This sticker set satisfies a child's yen for collecting things while offering activities focusing on geography, traffic safety, and just plain fun. There are 88 full-color pressure-sensitive road sign stickers, an album to keep a permanent record of the signs your family has seen, and a 12-page booklet with game suggestions and information about highway road sign.

3. The final offering is another "peel 'n press" game kit, this one called *License Plate Games*. The kit contains 75 color stickers, an album, maps, and a booklet detailing numerous games that your kids and the whole family can play to while away the hours.

Much to our delight, we discovered that the above items are very inexpensive—the book costs $3 ($4.95 mail order) and the games cost $1.50 each ($3 apiece mail order). Call or visit your local AAA Club office before you leave home.

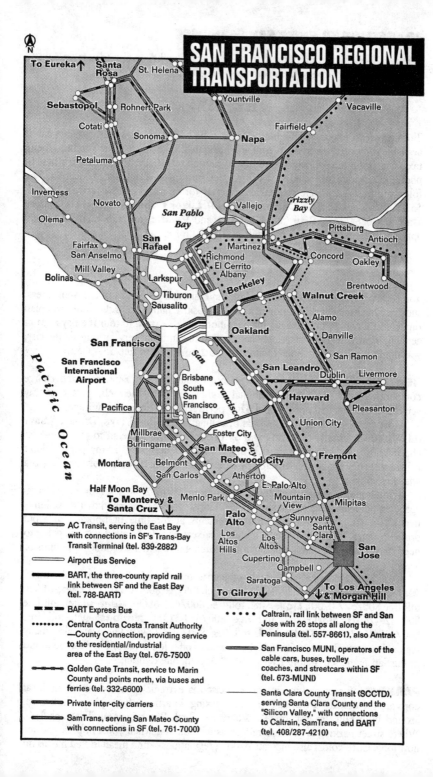

SAN FRANCISCO REGIONAL TRANSPORTATION

AC Transit, serving the East Bay with connections in SF's Trans-Bay Transit Terminal (tel. 839-2882)

Airport Bus Service

BART, the three-county rapid rail link between SF and the East Bay (tel. 788-BART)

BART Express Bus

Central Contra Costa Transit Authority —County Connection, providing service to the residential/industrial area of the East Bay (tel. 676-7500)

Golden Gate Transit, service to Marin County and points north, via buses and ferries (tel. 332-6600)

Private inter-city carriers

SamTrans, serving San Mateo County with connections in SF (tel. 761-7000)

Caltrain, rail link between SF and San Jose with 26 stops all along the Peninsula (tel. 557-8661), also Amtrak

San Francisco MUNI, operators of the cable cars, buses, trolley coaches, and streetcars within SF (tel. 673-MUNI)

Santa Clara County Transit (SCCTD), serving Santa Clara County and the "Silicon Valley," with connections to Caltrain, SamTrans, and BART (tel. 408/287-4210)

minutes, Monday through Friday from 4am to midnight, on Saturday from 6am to midnight, and on Sunday from 8am to midnight.

BY TAXI

Taxis travel on major thoroughfares and can be hailed on the street. When a cab is available for hire, the sign on its roof will be lighted. Like police when you need them, taxis can become suddenly scarce during rain or rush hour. If you can, it's best to phone in advance and request a cab to pick you up at a designated location. The following licensed private companies compete for customers: **Veteran's Cab** (tel. 552-1300), **Desoto Cab Co.** (tel. 673-1414), **Luxor Cabs** (tel. 282-4141), **Yellow Cab** (tel. 626-2345), **City** (tel. 468-7200), and **Pacific** (tel. 986-7220). Rates are approximately $2.90 for the first mile and $1.50 for each additional mile.

BY CAR

You certainly don't need a car to explore San Francisco proper. In fact, in some areas, such as Chinatown and Japantown, a car is a positive handicap. If, however, you plan on extensive exploration of outlying neighborhoods, or want to tour the Bay Area in general, a car will prove extremely handy. Before venturing very far outside the city, you might want to call about California **road conditions** (tel. 557-3755).

RENTALS Scores of car-rental firms are located in San Francisco, and charge competitive rates. The major national companies offer their cheapest economy vehicles for about $30 per day and $100 per week with unlimited mileage.

Most rental firms pad their profits by selling an additional Loss/Damage Waiver (LDW), which usually costs an extra $9 per day. Before agreeing to this, however, check with your insurance carrier and credit-card company. Many people don't realize that they are already covered by either one or both. If you're not, the LDW is a wise investment.

A minimum-age requirement—ranging from 19 to 25—is set by most rental agencies. Some also have a maximum-age limit. If you're concerned that these limits may affect you, ask about rental requirements at the time of booking to avoid problems later. Be sure to reserve a child's carseat ahead of time if you are going to need one. The law requires carseats for children 4 and under weighing 40 pounds or less.

Some of the national car-rental companies operating in San Francisco include: **Alamo** (tel. toll free 800/327-9633), **Avis** (tel. toll free 800/331-1212), **Budget** (tel. toll free 800/527-0700), **Dollar** (tel. toll free 800/421-6868), **General** (tel. toll free 800/327-7607), **Hertz** (tel. toll free 800/654-3131), **National** (tel. toll free 800/328-4567), and **Thrifty** (tel. toll free 800/367-2277). There are also many regional car-rental companies, which sometimes offer lower rates. They can be found in the San Francisco *Yellow Pages* under "Automobile Renting."

PARKING Street parking in San Francisco is extremely limited—and the local cops are the quickest tow I've ever seen. Parking is particularly tough in Chinatown, around Nob Hill, by Fisherman's Wharf, in North Beach, and on Telegraph Hill. Where street parking is not metered, signs will tell you when you can park and for how long. Curb colors also indicate parking regulations—and mean it! *Red* means no

DOWNTOWN SAN FRANCISCO TRANSPORTATION

San Francisco Bay

Aquatic Park
Fort Mason
Ghirardelli Square
Jefferson St.
Beach St.
North Point St.
Bay St.
Chestnut St.
Columbus Ave.
Embarcadero
Lombard St.
Laguna St.
Gough St.
Union St.
Larkin St.
Leavenworth St.
Jones St.
Powell St.
Grant St.
Kearny St.
Montgomery St.
Sansome St.
Battery St.
Jackson St.
Washington St.
Sacramento St.
California St.
Pine St.
Bush St.
Sutter St.
Post St.
Geary St.
Van Ness St.
Polk St.
Hyde St.
Taylor St.
Mason St.
Stockton St.
Drumm St.
Franklin St.
Embarcadero Station
Trans-Bay Terminal
Montg. St. Station
Union Square
O'Farrell St.
Powell St. Station
Market St.
1st St.
McAllister St.
Civic Center Station
Howard St.
Folsom St.
2nd St.
3rd St.
Embarcadero
Grove St.
Hayes St.
6th St.
Harrison St.
4th St.
Van Ness Station
Page St.
Haight St.
Bryant St.
Brannan St.
Market St.
7th St.
8th St.
9th St.
10th St.
11th St.
12th St.
Townsend St.
King St.
Berry St.
14th St.
15th St.
16th St.
16th St./Mission Station
Mission St.
S. Van Ness Ave.
Folsom St.
Bryant St.
Potrero St.
16th St.
17th St.
18th St.

- - - - - AC Transit
••••••• BART
+ + + + + Caltrain/Southern Pacific
———— Golden Gate Transit
———— San Francisco MUNI
- - - - - SamTrans Local Routes
- - - - - SamTrans Local Commute Routes
———— SamTrans Flyer/Express Routes
———— SamTrans Flyer/Express Commute Routes
- - - - MUNI Cable Car
———— MUNI Metro
▭ BART/MUNI Metro Station
▱ MUNI Metro Station

stopping or parking; *blue* is reserved for disabled drivers with a California-issued disabled plate or a placard; *white* means there's a 5-minute limit; *green* indicates a 10-minute limit; and *yellow* and *yellow-black* curbs are for commercial vehicles only. Also, don't park at a bus stop or in front of a fire hydrant; watch out, too, for street-cleaning signs.

When parking on a hill, apply the hand brake, put the car in gear, and *curb your wheels*—toward the curb when facing downhill, away from the curb when facing uphill. Curbing your wheels will not only prevent a possible "runaway" but will also keep you from getting a ticket—an expensive fine that is aggressively enforced.

Parking lots abound, but are usually quite expensive. Parking often costs about $4 to $5 per hour. It's cheaper by the day: from $15 to $20 for 24 hours. In Chinatown the best (and cheapest) place to park is the Portsmouth Square Garage at 733 Kearny Street (enter between Clay Street and Washington Street). Between 10:30am and 2:30pm you may have to wait in line to enter. The price is 75¢ for the first hour, $2 for 2 hours, $4 for 3 hours, $5.75 for 4 hours—up to a maximum of $12.50 for 7 to 24 hours. At the Civic Center, try for the Civic Center Plaza Garage at Taylor Street and O'Farrell Street, where parking is 50¢ per hour, $15 for 24 hours. Downtown, head for the Sutter-Stockton Garage at 330 Sutter Street, where it's 50¢ for the first hour, $1 for the second hour and for each hour thereafter—up to $14 for 24 hours. At Fisherman's Wharf/Ghirardelli Square, try the North Point Shopping Garage at 350 Bay Street, where the tab is $1 per half hour, $8.50 maximum; or the Ghirardelli Square Garage at 900 North Point, which charges $1 per half hour, $6 maximum. There is validated parking in those lots, which make it a lot cheaper. On Nob Hill the least costly we've found is Park & Lock at 877 California Street, where the fee is $1.50 per hour. On Union Street, in the area of high-traffic shopping, try the Cow Hollow Garage at 3060 Fillmore Street for $2 per hour, $7 maximum.

DRIVING RULES   California law requires that both drivers and passengers wear seatbelts. You may turn right at a red light (unless otherwise indicated), after yielding to traffic and pedestrians, *and* after making a complete stop. Cable cars, like sailing ships, always have the right-of-way, as do pedestrians at intersections and crosswalks. Pay attention to signs and arrows on the streets and roadways or you may find yourself suddenly in a lane that requires exiting or turning when you really want to go straight ahead. What's more, San Francisco's profusion of one-way streets can create a few small difficulties, but most road maps of the city indicate which way traffic flows.

BY FERRY

The opening of the Golden Gate Bridge in 1937 signaled the end of the ferry service that plied the bay between downtown San Francisco and the Marin shores. But this ferry tale has a happy ending. In August 1970 service resumed, as a result of growing commuter traffic too great for the bridge to bear alone. The **Golden Gate Ferry Service** (tel. 415/332-6600) fleet dashes back and forth between the San Francisco Ferry Building, at the foot of Market Street, and downtown Sausalito and Larkspur. Family fares are available.

To/From Sausalito   Service to **Sausalito** is frequent, departing at reasonable intervals every day of the year except New Year's Day, Thanksgiving Day, and Christmas Day. Call (tel. 415/332-6600) for exact schedule information. The ride takes a half hour and costs $3.50 for adults and $2.60 for young riders aged 6 to 12. Seniors and physically disabled passengers ride for half price; kids 5 and under ride free. The **Red-and-White Fleet** (tel. 415/546-2628, or toll free 800/445-8880 in California), also operates service to Sausalito (from Pier 43½) and to Tiburon, Angel Island, Alcatraz and Marine World Africa USA.

To/From Larkspur   The **Larkspur** ferry is primarily a commuter service during the week, with frequent departures around the rush hours. Weekend service is offered during the summer only. Boats make the trip in about 50 minutes and cost $2.20 for adults and $1.65 for young riders aged 6 to 12; on weekends, prices rise to $3 for adults and $2.25 for young riders. Seniors and physically disabled passengers ride for half price; kids 5 and under ride free.

ON FOOT

San Francisco is a walking city par excellence. The hills can be challenging, but the best way to explore the city is definitely on foot. Many of the main tourist attractions are within easy strolling distance of one another: The downtown shopping district is adjacent to Chinatown, which runs right into North Beach, which, in turn, buffets Fisherman's Wharf. If at any time you become too tired to hoof it, the city's vast and efficient public transportation system can easily whisk you to your destination.

 SAN FRANCISCO

Airport   See Section 1, "Orientation," above.

American Express   For travel arrangements, traveler's checks, currency exchange, and other member services, American Express has offices at 2500 Mason Street (tel. 788-3025), near Fisherman's Wharf, and at 455 Market Street (tel. 512-8250) in the Financial District.

To report lost or stolen traveler's checks, call toll free 800/221-7282.

Area Code   The area code for San Francisco is **415**. All phone numbers in this book assume this prefix unless otherwise noted. Pacific Bell advises that as of October 7, 1991, Oakland and Berkeley will have the new area code of **510.** The boundary for the new area code is San Francisco Bay. Alameda and Contra Costa counties will also be identified with the new area code. Napa County is area code 707, and Monterey County is area code 408.

Baby-Sitters   Hotels can often recommend a baby-sitter or child-care service. If yours can't, try **Temporary Tot Tending** (tel. 355-7377, or 871-5790 after 6pm), which offers child care by licensed teachers, by the hour or day, for children from 3 weeks to 12 years of age. It's open Monday through Friday from 6am to 7pm (weekend service is available only during convention times).

Bookstores   Chain bookstores can be found in almost every shopping center in the city, including B. Dalton at Embarcadero Center (tel. 982-4278) and Brentano's at Ghirardelli Square (tel. 474-8328) and the San Francisco Shopping Center at Market Street and Fifth Street (tel. 543-0933). See Chapter 5, "Their Shopping List," for a list of the city's excellent specialty booksellers.

Business Hours Banking hours vary, but most **banks** are open Monday through Friday from 9am to 3pm. Several stay open until about 5pm at least one day during the week. Many banks also feature Automated Teller Machines (ATMs) for 24-hour banking (see Section 1, "Information and Money," in Chapter 2).

Most **stores** are open Monday through Saturday from 10am to 6pm; closed Sunday. But there are exceptions: Stores in Chinatown are generally open daily from 10am to 10pm. Ghirardelli Square and Pier 39 shops are open Monday through Saturday from 10am to 9pm (later during the summer). San Francisco Shopping Center shops are open Monday through Saturday from 9:30am to 8pm and on Sunday from 11am to 6pm. Large department stores, including Emporium, Macy's, and Nordstrom, keep late hours and are open Sunday.

Hours in **restaurants** vary, but most serve lunch from about 11:30am to 3pm and dinner from 5:30 to 11pm. You can sometimes get served later on weekends. **Nightclubs and bars** are usually open daily until 2am, when they are legally bound to stop serving alcohol.

As far as **businesses** are concerned, San Francisco is generally a 9am-to-5pm town.

Car Rentals See Section 2, "Getting Around," above.

Climate See Section 2, "When to Go," in Chapter 1.

Currency and Exchange See "Fast Facts: For the Foreign Traveler" in Chapter 3.

Dentist In the event of an emergency, see your hotel concierge or contact the **San Francisco Dental Society** (tel. 421-1435) for referral to a specialist. The **San Francisco Dental Office,** 132 The Embarcadero (tel. 775-5115), between Mission Street and Howard Street, offers 24-hour emergency service and comprehensive dental care by appointment.

Doctor In an emergency, call an **ambulance** by dialing 911 from any phone; no coins are required. **Saint Francis Memorial Hospital,** 900 Hyde Street, on Nob Hill (tel. 775-4321), provides urgent-care service Monday through Friday from 8am to 5pm; no appointment is necessary. The hospital also operates a physician-referral service (tel. 775-4441).

Documents Required See Section 1, "Preparing for Your U. S. Trip," in Chapter 3.

Driving Rules See Section 2, "Getting Around," above.

Drugstores There are **Walgreens Pharmacies** all over town, including one at 135 Powell Street (tel. 391-4433) that's open Monday through Saturday from 8am to midnight and on Sunday from 9am to 8pm. The branch on Divisadero Street at Lombard (tel. 931-6415) is open 24 hours. **Merrill's Drug Center,** 805 Market Street (tel. 781-1669), is open Monday through Friday from 7am to 10pm and on Saturday and Sunday from 7:30am to 8:30pm. Both accept MasterCard and VISA.

Earthquakes There will always be earthquakes in California—most of which you'll never notice. However, in case of a significant shaker, there are a few basic precautionary measures you should know. When you are inside a building, seek cover; *do not run outside.* Move away from windows toward the center of the building. Duck under a large, sturdy piece of furniture or stand against a wall or under a doorway. If you exit the building, use stairwells, not elevators. If you are in your car, pull over to the side of the road and stop—but not until you are away from bridges, overpasses, telephone poles, and power lines. Stay in your car. If you're out walking, stay outside and away from trees, power lines, and the sides of buildings. If you're in an area with tall buildings, find a doorway in which to stand.

Embassies/Consulates See "Fast Facts: For the Foreign Traveler" in Chapter 3.

Emergencies To reach the police, an ambulance, or fire department, dial **911** from any phone; no coins are needed. Emergency hotlines include the Poison Control Center (tel. 476-6600), Suicide Prevention (tel. 221-1423), and Rape Crisis (tel. 647-7273).

Eyeglasses For emergency replacement of lost or broken glasses, **Lens Crafters,** 685 Market Street at Third Street (tel. 896-0680), offers 1-hour service. **Pearle Express,** 720 Market Street (tel. 677-9701), offers similar services, selections, and prices. Both are open daily from 10am to 6pm. For top name-brand frames, visit **Spectacles of Union Square,** 177 Maiden Lane, at Kearny Street (tel. 781-8556). They feature 1-hour service, in-stock contact lenses, and a full-time staff technician. It's open Monday through Saturday from 10am to 6pm.

Hairdressers/Barbers In addition to haircutters in the top hotels, respected salons include the avant-garde **Architects & Heroes,** 207 Powell Street, at O'Farrell Street (tel. 391-8833); the English coiffeur **David Oliver,** 3365 Sacramento Street at Presidio Avenue (tel. 563-2044); and the classic **Vidal Sassoon,** 130 Post Street, at Grant Street (tel. 397-5105).

Hospitals In case of emergency, try the following: **Medical Center at the University of California San Francisco,** 505 Parnassus Avenue, at Third Avenue (tel. 476-1000 or 476-1037); **San Francisco General Hospital Medical Center,** 1001 Potrero Avenue (tel. 821-8200 or 821-8111 for the emergency room); **St. Francis Memorial Hospital,** 900 Hyde Street, on Nob Hill (tel. 775-4321, 775-4441 for physician referral service, 775-4321, ext. 2160, for the emergency room); **Mount Zion Hospital and Medical Center,** 1600 Divisadero Street (tel. 885-7520); and **Pacific Presbyterian Medical Center,** 2300 Sacramento Street, at Buchanan Street (tel. 923-3333). If you need a private ambulance, try **San Francisco Ambulance Service,** 2829 California Street (tel. 931-3900). Remember, for an ambulance in an emergency, dial 911 from any phone.

Laundry/Dry Cleaning Laundries abound; ask at your hotel for the closest one. If you want to have some fun while you wash your clothes, visit **Brain Wash,** 1126 Folsom Street, south of Market (tel. 431-WASH). It features dozens of washers and dryers along with a café and bar, and live music Tuesday through Thursday. It's open daily from 7:30am to 11pm. Dry cleaning is also available.

Libraries The main branch of the San Francisco Public Library (tel. 558-3191) is located in Civic Center Plaza, just north of Market Street, and houses some 1.2 million volumes. It's open on Monday, Wednesday, Thursday, and Saturday from 10am to 6pm, on Tuesday from noon to 9pm, on Friday noon to 6pm, and on Sunday from 1 to 5pm. There is a Chinatown branch at 1135 Powell St. (tel. 989-6770) and a North Beach branch at 2000 Mason St. (tel. 391-9473). Call for the location and hours of other branches. Your kids might love **Dial-A-Story** (tel. 626-6516), where they can call to hear a bedtime story.

Liquor Laws Liquor and grocery stores, as well as some drugstores, can sell packaged alcoholic beverages between 6am and 2am. Most restaurants, nightclubs, and bars are licensed to serve alcoholic beverages during the same hours. The legal age for purchase and consumption is 21; proof of age is required.

Lost Property If you lost any personal property on the street, it's probably gone for good, but call the local police anyway (tel. 553-0123). If you lost it on a MUNI cable car, bus, or train, call the lost-and-found office (tel. 923-6168).

Luggage Repair Ask the concierge in your hotel or check in the *Yellow Pages.*

Mail San Francisco's Main Post Office, Seventh Street and Mission Street, San Francisco, CA 94102 (tel. 621-6838), is located one block south of Market Street, near the Civic Center. Letters addressed to you and marked "General Delivery" can be picked up here. Local branches are located all around town. The closest office to Union Square is inside Macy's department store, 121 Stockton Street (tel. 956-3570). The Airport Mail Facility (tel. 742-1432), on Road 6, at the San Francisco International Airport, is open 24 hours.

Domestic first-class letters cost 29¢ for the first ounce and 23¢ for each additional ounce. Postcards cost 19¢ to any U.S. destination. Letters to Canada cost 40¢ for up to 1 ounce; Mexico-bound letters cost 45¢ for up to 1 ounce. All other international airmail letters cost 50¢ for up to half an ounce and 45¢ for each additional half ounce.

Newspapers/Magazines The city's two main dailies are the *San Francisco Chronicle* and the *San Francisco Examiner;* both are distributed throughout the city. The two papers combine for a massive Sunday edition that includes a pink "Datebook" section—an excellent preview of the week's upcoming events. The free weekly *San Francisco Bay Guardian,* a tabloid of news and listings, is indispensable for nightlife information; it's widely distributed through street-corner dispensers and at city cafés and restaurants.

Of the many free tourist-oriented publications, the most widely read are *Key* and *San Francisco Guide.* Both of these handbook-size weeklies contain maps and information on current events. They can be found in most hotels and in shops and restaurants in the major tourist areas.

Photographic Needs Drugstores and supermarkets are probably the cheapest places to purchase film. You'll pay loads more for the same product at specialized kiosks near major tourist attractions. **Brooks Cameras,** 45 Kearny Street, at Maiden Lane (tel. 392-1900), has a complete inventory of cameras and accessories. It also offers an authorized repair service and 1-hour photo-finishing. It's open Monday through Friday from 9am to 6pm and on Saturday from 9:30am to 5:30pm. Another major location is at 243 Montgomery Street in the Financial District (tel. 392-5815).

Police The **San Francisco Police Department** kobans are kiosks—or mini police stations—to help you. **Hallidie Plaza Koban** is at Market and Powell streets, open Tuesday through Saturday 10am–6pm; **Chinatown Koban** is at Grant Avenue between Washington and Jackson streets, open 1–9pm daily; **Japantown Koban** is at Post and Buchanan streets, open Monday–Friday 11am–7pm; and **Mission District Koban** is at 16th and Mission streets, open 9am–5pm daily. For emergencies, dial 911 from any phone; no coins are needed. For other matters, call 553-0123.

Post Office The main branch was destroyed in the recent earthquake but other convenient branches are at Macy's, 121 Stockton Street; Emporium, 835 Market Street; in Chinatown at 867 Stockton Street; and at City Hall in Civic Center.

Radio About four dozen radio stations can be heard in San Francisco. On the AM dial, 740 (KCBS) and 810 (KGO) are the top picks for news, sports, talk, and information. The best music stations on the FM dial include KQED (88.5) for classical, KSAN (94.9) for country, and KRQR (97.3) and KFOG (104.5) for album-oriented rock; KBLX (102.9) and KUSF (90.3) play dance and alternative rock, respectively.

Religious Services San Francisco has houses of worship for all major faiths, including the following: First Friendship Institutional Baptist Church, 501 Steiner Street (tel. 431-4775); Buddha's Universal Church, 720 Washington Street (tel. 982-6116); Congregation Emanu-El (Jewish), 199 Arguello Boulevard (tel. 751-2535); Mission Dolores Basilica (Roman Catholic), 3321 16th Street (tel. 621-8203); Grace Cathedral (Episcopal), 1051 Taylor Street (tel. 776-6611); St. Paul's Lutheran Church, 944 Eddy Street (tel. 673-0497); and New Liberation Presbyterian Church, 1100 Divisadero Street (tel. 929-8881).

Rest Rooms Stores rarely let customers use the rest rooms, and many restaurants offer their facilities for customers only. But most malls have bathrooms, as do the ubiquitous fast-food restaurants. Many public beaches and large parks provide toilets, though in some places you have to pay or tip an attendant. If you have the time, look for one of the large hotels; most have well-stocked, clean rest rooms in their lobbies.

Safety Innocent tourists are rarely the victims of violent crime. Still, few locals would recommend that you walk alone late at night. The Tenderloin, between Union Square and the Civic Center, is one of San Francisco's most infamous areas. Compared with similar areas in other cities, however, even this section of San Francisco is relatively tranquil. Other areas where you should be particularly alert are the Mission District, around 16th Street and Mission Street; the Fillmore area, around lower Haight Street; and the SoMa area south of Market Street. None of these areas is of particular interest to tourists, except for sociological reasons. See Section 4, "Health & Other Precautions," in Chapter 1 for additional safety tips.

Shoe Repairs There are dozens of shoe- and leather-repair shops around the city. Check the San Francisco *Yellow Pages* for the location nearest you or visit **Jack's Shoe Service,** 53 Sutter Street, between Montgomery Street and Sansome Street (tel. 392-7336). It's open Monday through Friday from 7:30am to 5:30pm.

Taxes A 7¼% sales tax is added at the register for all goods and services purchased in San Francisco. In restaurants, a 7% tax will be tacked onto your bill. The city hotel tax is a whopping 11%. No additional airport tax is charged to international travelers.

Taxis See Section 2, "Getting Around," above.

Television In addition to the cable stations, available in most hotels, all the major networks and several independent stations are represented. They include: Channel 2, KTVU (NBC); Channel 4, KRON (CBS); Channel 5, KPIX (CBS); Channel 7, KGO (ABC); and Channel 9, KQED (PBS).

Time San Francisco, like the entire West Coast, is in the Pacific standard-time zone, which is 8 hours behind Greenwich mean time. To find out what time it is, call 767-8900.

Tipping A 15% tip is standard for waiters and waitresses, bartenders, taxi drivers, and hairdressers. Porters should be tipped 50¢ to $1 per bag, and parking valets should be given $1. It's proper to leave a few dollars on your pillow for the hotel maid; lavatory attendants will appreciate whatever change you have.

Transit Information The San Francisco Municipal Railway, better known as MUNI, operates the city's cable cars, buses, and metros. Information is available 24 hours by calling 673-6864.

Useful Telephone Numbers **Alcoholics Anonymous** (tel. 661-1828), **American Express Global Assist** (for cardholders only) (tel. toll free 800/554-2639), **Amtrak** (tel. toll free 800/USA RAIL), **Better Business Bureau**

of San Francisco (tel. 243-9999), **California road conditions** (tel. 557-3755), **California State Automobile Association (AAA)** (tel. 565-2012), **Directory Assistance** (tel. 411), **emergencies** (tel. 911), **fire** (tel. 861-8020), **highway conditions** (tel. 557-3755), **Poison Control Center** (tel. 476-6600), **recorded listing of special events** (tel. 391-2001), **San Francisco Bar Association Lawyer Referral** (tel. 764-1616), **senior citizens' information** (tel. 626-1033), **time** (tel. 767-8900), **Traveler's Aid Society** (tel. 255-2252).

Weather   Call 936-1212 for the latest information.

CHAPTER 3

FOR FOREIGN VISITORS

1. PREPARING FOR YOUR U.S. TRIP

2. GETTING TO & AROUND THE U.S.

• **FAST FACTS: THE FOREIGN VISITOR**

• **THE AMERICAN SYSTEM OF MEASUREMENTS**

The United States, like any foreign country, can be confusing at times, especially if you aren't totally at ease with the language or familiar with the customs. The purpose of this chapter is to offer practical information to help the foreign visitor have as easy and as pleasant a stay as possible. We've even included information on the American system of measurements. There is also helpful information in "Fast Facts: San Francisco" in Chapter 2.

1. PREPARING FOR YOUR U.S. TRIP

ENTRY REQUIREMENTS

NECESSARY DOCUMENTS Canadian nationals need only proof of Canadian residence to visit the United States. Citizens of the United Kingdom and Japan need only a current passport; a visa is not necessary. Citizens of other countries, including Australia and New Zealand, usually need two documents: a valid passport with an expiration date at least 6 months later than the scheduled end of their U.S. visit, plus a visa available at no charge from a U.S. embassy or consulate.

To get a tourist or business visa to enter the United States, contact the nearest American embassy or consulate in your country. If there is none, you will have to apply in person in a country where there is a U.S. embassy or consulate. Present your passport, a passport-size photo of yourself, and a completed application, which is available through the embassy or consulate.

You may be asked to provide information about how you plan to finance your trip or show a letter of invitation from a friend with whom you plan to stay. Those applying for a business visa may be asked to show evidence that they will not receive a salary in the United States.

Be sure to check the length of time allotted you on the visa; usually it's 6 months. If you want to stay longer, you may file for an extension of the visa with the Immigration and Naturalization Service once you are in the United States. If permission to stay is granted, a new visa is not required unless you leave the country and want to reenter.

MEDICAL REQUIREMENTS You won't need any **inoculations** unless you are arriving from, or have stopped off recently in, a country that is experiencing an outbreak of cholera, yellow fever, or another contagious dangerous disease.

If you have a medical condition requiring you to take **prescription drugs** (or use a syringe), be sure to bring along a valid prescription signed by your doctor.

TRAVEL INSURANCE

Travel insurance and assistance can get you out of a bind or a scrape (literally), but it's not a requirement to visit the United States. Coverage can include loss or stolen baggage, illness or injury, and last-minute or midtrip cancellation due to illness or emergency (a special consideration when traveling with children). Travel insurance and assistance policies are sold through insurance companies, automobile clubs, travel agencies, and at airports.

2. GETTING TO & AROUND THE U.S.

GETTING TO THE U.S. In addition to the domestic American airlines listed in Section 6, "Getting There," in Chapter 1, several international carriers, including Air Canada (tel. toll free 800/776-3000), British Airways (tel. toll free 800/247-9297), Japan Airlines (tel. toll free 800/525-3663), and SAS (tel. toll free 800/221-2350), also serve San Francisco International Airport. For the best rates, compare fares and be flexible with the dates and times of travel.

GETTING AROUND THE U.S. Some large airlines (for example, American Airlines, TWA, Northwest, and Delta) offer travelers on their transatlantic or transpacific flights special discount tickets under the name **Visit USA,** allowing travel between any U.S. destinations at minimum rates. They are not on sale in the United States and must be purchased abroad in conjunction with your international ticket. See your travel agent or airline ticket office for full details, including terms and conditions.

European visitors can also buy a **USA Railpass,** good for unlimited train travel on Amtrak. The pass is available through some airlines and travel agents, including Thomas Cook in Great Britain and Cuoni on the continent. Various itinerary options are available for $299 and up. Amtrak officials suggest that you make route reservations as soon as possible, because many trains are often sold out.

With a foreign passport and airline ticket, you can also buy the passes at Amtrak offices in Seattle, San Francisco, Los Angeles, Chicago, New York, Miami, Boston, and Washington, D.C. For further information, contact the Amtrak Distribution Center, P.O. Box 7700, 1549 West Glen Lake Avenue, Itasca, IL 60143 (tel. toll free 800/USA-RAIL in the U.S.).

FAST FACTS FOR THE FOREIGN TRAVELER

Accommodations Some of the major hotels listed in this book maintain overseas reservation networks and can be booked either directly or through travel agents. Some hotels are also included in tour operators' package tours. Since tour companies buy rooms in bulk, they can often offer them at a discount. Discuss this option with your travel agent and compare tour prices with those in this guide. For accommodations in San Francisco, see Chapter 8.

Auto Organizations If you plan on renting a car in the United States, you will probably not need the services of an additional auto organization. If you are planning to buy or borrow a car, automobile association membership is recommended. The **American Automobile Association (AAA),** 8111 Gatehouse Road, Falls Church, VA 22047 (tel. 703/222-6000), is the country's largest auto club, supplying members with maps, insurance, and, most important, emergency road service. The cost of joining runs $20 to $60, but if you're a member of a foreign auto club with reciprocal arrangements, you can enjoy free AAA service in America. Call the Southern California Automobile Association if you're in San Francisco.

Business Hours In San Francisco, most **banks** are open from 9am to 4pm, with later hours on Friday. A few have Saturday hours. **Bars** can be open all day, but they must stop serving liquor between the hours of 2 and 6am. **Office** hours are generally 9am to 5pm weekdays. **Stores** are open until at least 9pm, and there is usually at least one 24-hour market in a major city. The 7-Eleven stores, a nationwide chain offering limited groceries, sundries, and beverages, are open 24 hours. Downtown **shops** are open Monday through Saturday from 10am to 6pm. Stores in shopping malls tend to have later hours, and are usually open on Sunday. It's safest to call and check.

Climate The California climate varies from north to south and inland. There are hot deserts, cool mountains, and foggy seaside towns. San Francisco rarely gets unbearably hot, but the coastal towns can change from one moment to the next, from sunny and balmy to foggy and misty.

Consulates Consulates in San Francisco area include: **Australian Consulate-General,** 360 Post Street (tel. 415/362-6160); **British Consulate-General,** 1 Sansome Street (tel. 415/981-3030); **Canadian Consulate-General,** 50 Fremont Street (tel. 415/495-7030); **French Consulate-General,** 540 Bush Street (tel. 415/397-4330); **Irish Consulate-General,** 655 Montgomery Street (tel. 415/392-4214); **Japan Consulate-General,** 50 Fremont Street (tel. 415/777-3533); **Mexican Consulate,** 870 Market St. (tel. 415/392-5554).

Currency and Exchange The U.S. monetary system has a decimal base: 1 **dollar** ($1) = 100 **cents** (100¢).

The most common **bills** (all green) are the $1 (colloquially, a "buck"), $5, $10, and $20 denominations. There are also $2 (seldom encountered), $50, and $100 bills (the last two are not welcome when paying for small purchases).

There are six denominations of **coins:** 1¢ (1 cent, or a penny), 5¢ (5 cents, or a nickel), 10¢ (10 cents, or a dime), 25¢ (25 cents, or a quarter), 50¢ (50 cents, or a half dollar), and the rare—prized by collectors—$1 piece (both the older, large silver dollar and the newer, small Susan B. Anthony coin).

Foreign-exchange bureaus are rare in the United States, and most banks are not equipped to handle currency exchange. San Francisco's money-changing offices include: **Bank of America,** 345 Montgomery Street (tel. 415/622-2451), open Monday through Thursday from 9am to 4pm, on Friday from 9am to 6pm, and on Saturday from 9am to 3pm; and **Deak International,** 100 Grant Avenue (tel. 415/362-3452), open Monday through Friday from 9am to 5pm. The **Thomas Cook Currency Exchange,** located at San Francisco International Airport, International Terminal, Departure Level (tel. 415/583-4029), is convenient for in-bound and out-bound travelers. It offers a wide array of foreign-exchange services, including the exchange of over 100 currencies. There is another branch downtown at 100 Grant Avenue (tel. 415/362-3452).

Traveler's checks are widely accepted. Make sure, however, that they are denominated in U.S. dollars, as foreign-currency checks are difficult to exchange.

Customs and Immigration   Every visitor over 21 years of age may bring in, free of duty, the following: (1) 1 liter of wine or hard liquor; (2) 200 cigarettes, 100 cigars (but *not* from Cuba), or 3 pounds of smoking tobacco; and (3) $400 worth of gifts. These exemptions are offered to travelers who spend at least 72 hours in the United States and who have not claimed them within the preceding 6 months. It is altogether forbidden to bring into the country foodstuffs (particularly cheese, fruit, cooked meats, and canned goods) and plants (vegetables, seeds, tropical plants, and the like). Foreign tourists may bring in or take out up to $10,000 in U.S. or foreign currency with no formalities; larger sums must be declared to Customs on entering or leaving.

Drinking Laws   The legal age for purchase and consumption of alcoholic beverages is 21; proof of age is required. In San Francisco, liquor is sold in supermarkets and grocery stores, daily from 6am to 2am. When licensed, restaurants are permitted to sell alcohol during the same hours. Note that many eateries are licensed only for beer and wine.

Electricity   U.S. wall outlets give power at 110–115 volts, 60 cycles, compared with 220 volts, 50 cycles, in most of Europe. In addition to a 110-volt transformer, small foreign appliances, such as hairdryers and shavers, will require a plug adapter with two flat, parallel pins.

Embassies and Consulates   All embassies are located in the national capital, Washington, D.C. In addition, several of the major English-speaking countries also have consulates in San Francisco or in Los Angeles. The embassy of **Australia** is at 1601 Massachusetts Avenue NW, Washington, DC 20036 (tel. 202/797-3000), and there's a consulate at 360 Post Street, San Francisco, CA 94108 (tel. 415/362-6160). The embassy of **Canada** is at 501 Pennsylvania Avenue NW, Washington, DC 20001 (tel. 202/682-1740), and a consulate is at One Maritime Plaza, Golden Gateway Center, San Francisco, CA 94111 (tel. 415/981-8541). The embassy of the **Republic of Ireland** at 2234 Massachusetts Avenue NW, Washington, DC 20008 (tel. 202/462-3939), and there's a consulate at 655 Montgomery Street, Suite 930, San Francisco, CA 94111 (tel. 415/392-4214). The embassy of **New Zealand** is at 37 Observatory Circle NW, Washington, DC 20008 (tel. 202/328-4800); the nearest consulate is in the Tishman Building, 10960 Wilshire Boulevard, Westwood Suite 1530, Los Angeles, CA 90024 (tel. 213/477-8241). The embassy of the **United Kingdom** is at 3100 Massachusetts Avenue NW, Washington, DC 20008 (tel. 202/462-1340); the nearest consulate is at 3701 Wilshire Boulevard, Suite 312, Los Angeles, CA 90010 (tel. 213/385-7381). If you are from **another country,** you can get the telephone number of your embassy by calling "Information" (directory assistance) in Washington, D.C.: 202/555-1212.

Emergencies   You can call the police, an ambulance, or the fire department through the single emergency telephone number **911.** Another useful way of reporting an emergency is to call the telephone company operator by dialing **0** (zero, not the letter "O").

Gasoline   Prices vary, but expect to pay anywhere between $1.15 and $1.45

for 1 U.S. gallon (about 3.75 liters) of "regular" unleaded gasoline (petrol). Higher-octane fuels are also available at most gas stations for slightly higher prices. Taxes are already included in the posted price. Many California gas stations have self-serve islands, in which you pay first and pump your own gas.

Holidays   On the following legal national holidays, banks, government offices, post offices, and many stores, restaurants, and museums are closed: New Year's Day (Jan 1), Martin Luther King, Jr., Day (third Mon in Jan), Presidents' Day (third Mon in Feb), Memorial Day (last Mon in May), Independence Day (July 4), Labor Day (first Mon in Sept), Columbus Day (second Mon in Oct), Veterans' Day (Nov 11), Thanksgiving Day (last Thurs in Nov), and Christmas Day (Dec 25). Election Day, for national elections, falls on the Tuesday following the first Monday in November. It is a legal national holiday during a presidential election, which occurs every fourth year.

Information   See Section 1, "Tourist Information," in Chapter 1.

Legal Aid   Happily, foreign tourists rarely come into contact with the American legal system. If you are stopped for a minor driving infraction (speeding, for example), *never* attempt to pay the fine directly to a police officer; fines should be paid to the Clerk of the Court, and a receipt should be obtained. If you are accused of a more serious offense, it is wise to say and do nothing before consulting a lawyer. Under U.S. law, an arrested person is allowed one telephone call to a party of his or her choice. You may wish to contact your country's embassy or consulate (see above). Should you require legal assistance while visiting, the **Bar Association, Lawyer Referral Service** (tel. 415/764-1616) will refer you to an appropriate attorney based on your need.

Mail   If you want to receive mail, but aren't exactly sure where you'll be, have it sent to you, in your name, **c/o General Delivery** (Poste Restante) at the main post office of the city or region you're visiting. The addressee must pick it up in person and produce proof of identity (driver's license, credit card, passport). Most post offices will hold your mail up to 1 month.

Generally found at street intersections, **mailboxes** are blue and carry the inscription U.S. MAIL. If your mail is addressed to a U.S. destination, don't forget to add the five-figure ZIP Code, after the two-letter abbreviation of the state to which the mail is addressed (CA for California).

For domestic and international postage rates, see "Mail" in "Fast Facts: San Francisco" in Chapter 2.

Medical Emergencies   To call an **ambulance,** dial 911 from any phone. No coins are needed. For a list of hospitals and other emergency information, see "Fast Facts: San Francisco" in Chapter 3.

Newspapers and Magazines   Many of San Francisco's newsstands offer a selection of foreign periodicals and newspapers, such as *The Economist, Le Monde,* and *Der Spiegel.* For information on local literature and specific newsstand locations, see "Fast Facts: San Francisco" in Chapter 3.

Post   See "Mail," above.

Radio and Television   The audiovisual media play a major role in the cultural life of San Francisco, as they do elsewhere in the United States. A variety of radio stations broadcast classical, country, jazz, and pop music, punctuated by regular news reports and advertisements (commercials). Broadcast television offers access to several channels, including those of the three coast-to-coast commercial networks— the American Broadcasting System (ABC), the Columbia Broadcasting System (CBS), and the National Broadcasting Company (NBC)—as well as the noncommercial Public Broadcasting System (PBS) and the emerging commercial Fox network. Also, in most cities local cable franchises offer a number of additional channels delivered by cable to their subscribers, including the Cable News Network (CNN) and Home Box Office (HBO, mostly movies), as well as sports, music, and movies. Most hotels have TVs in their rooms, and many offer both broadcast and some cable channels; some may offer special programs or movies on a pay-per-view basis.

In San Francisco KGO (ABC) is Channel 7, KPIX (CBS) is Channel 5, KRON (NBC) is Channel 4, and KQED (PBS) is Channel 9. If you have cable TV in your hotel room, check for the Disney Channel, Nickelodeon, and USA for children's programming.

Safety   In general, the United States is a pretty safe place, especially for tourists, who are rarely the victims of crime. However, there are "danger zones" in the big cities that should be approached only with extreme caution.

As a general rule, isolated areas, such as parks and parking lots, should be avoided after dark. Elevators and public-transportation systems in off-hours, particularly between 10pm and 6am, are also potential crime scenes. You should drive through decaying neighborhoods with your car doors locked and the windows closed. Never carry valuables like jewelry or large sums of cash; traveler's checks are much safer.

Taxes   In the United States there is no VAT (Value-Added Tax) or other indirect tax at a national level. Every state, as well as every city, is allowed to levy its own local **sales tax** on all purchases, including hotel and restaurant checks and airline tickets. Taxes are already included in the price of certain services, such as public transportation, cab fares, phone calls, and gasoline. The amount of sales tax varies from 4% to 11%, depending on the state and city, so when you are making major purchases, such as photographic equipment, clothing, or high-fidelity components, it can be a significant part of the cost.

In addition, many cities charge a separate "bed" or room tax on accommodations, above and beyond any sales tax.

For information on sales and room taxes in and around San Francisco, see "Fast Facts: San Francisco" in Chapter 2.

Telephone, Telegraph, Telex, and Fax   Pay phones can be found almost everywhere—at street corners, in bars and restaurants, and in hotels. Outside the metropolitan area, however, public telephones are more difficult to find; stores and gas stations are your best bet.

Phones do not accept pennies, and few will take anything larger than a quarter. Some public phones, especially those in airports and large hotels, accept credit cards, such as MasterCard, VISA, and American Express. Credit cards are especially handy for international calls; instructions are printed on the phone.

In San Francisco, **local calls** cost 20¢. For domestic **long-distance calls or international calls,** stock up with a supply of quarters; a recorded voice will instruct you when and in what quantity you should put them into the slot. For direct overseas calls, dial 011 first, then the country code (Australia, 61; Republic of Ireland, 353; New Zealand, 64; United Kingdom, 44) followed by the city code, and then the number you wish to call. To place a call to Canada or the Caribbean, just dial 1, the area code, and the number you wish to call.

Before calling from a hotel room, always ask the hotel phone operator if there are any telephone surcharges. These can sometimes be reduced by calling collect or by using a telephone charge card. Hotel charges, which can be exorbitant, may be avoided altogether by using a public phone.

For **collect (reversed-charge) calls** and for **person-to-person calls,** dial 0 (zero, not the letter "O"), followed by the area code and the number you want; an operator will then come on the line, and you should specify that you are calling collect or person-to-person, or both. If your operator-assisted call is international, ask for the overseas operator.

For local **"information" (directory inquiries),** dial 411; for long-distance information in Canada or the United States, dial 1, then the appropriate area code and 555-1212.

Like the telephone system, **telegraph and telex services** are provided by private corporations, such as ITT, MCI, and, above all, Western Union. You can take your telegram to a Western Union office or dictate it over the phone (tel. toll free 800/325-6000). You can also telegraph money, or have it telegraphed to you, very quickly. In San Francisco, a Western Union office, centrally located in the Financial District, is at Supermail International, 4 Embarcadero Center, lobby level (tel. 415/392-7788). There are several other locations around town, too.

Most copy shops also offer **fax services.**

Time   The United States is divided into six time zones. From east to west, these are eastern standard time (EST), central standard time (CST), mountain standard time (MST), Pacific standard time (PST), Alaska standard time (AST), and Hawaii standard time (HST). San Francisco is on Pacific standard time, which is 8 hours behind Greenwich mean time. Noon in New York City (EST) is 11am in Chicago (CST), 10am in Denver (MST), 9am in San Francisco (PST), 8am in Anchorage (AST), and 7am in Honolulu (HST).

Daylight saving time is in effect from 1am on the first Sunday in April until 2am on the last Sunday in October, except in Arizona, Hawaii, part of Indiana, and Puerto Rico.

Tipping   Service in America is some of the best in the world, and tipping is the reason why. The amount you tip should depend on the service you have received. Good service warrants the following tips: bartenders, 15%; bellhops, $2 to $4; cab drivers, 15%; cafeterias and fast-food restaurants, no tip; chambermaids, $1 per person per day; cinemas, no tip; checkroom attendants, 50¢ to $1 (unless there is a charge, then no tip); gas-station attendants, no tip; hairdressers, 15% to 20%; parking valets, $1; redcaps (in airports and railroad stations), $2 to $4; restaurants and nightclubs, 15%, 20% for excellent service.

Toilets   Public toilets can be hard to find. There are none on the streets, and few small stores will allow you access to their facilities. You can almost always find a toilet in restaurants and bars, but if you are not buying from them, you should ask first. Large hotels and fast-food restaurants are probably the best bet for good, clean facilities. Museums, department stores, shopping malls, and, in a pinch, gas stations all have public toilets.

Yellow Pages   The *Yellow Pages* telephone directory lists all local services, businesses, and industries by category; it also has an index for quick reference. Categories range from automobile repairs (listed by make of car) and drugstores, or pharmacies, to places of worship and restaurants (listed according to cuisine and geographical location). The *Yellow Pages* directory is also a good source for information of particular interest to the traveler; among other things, it has maps of the city, showing sights and transportation routes. Such information can be found in the "Community Interest Pages" of San Francisco's directory, at the beginning of volume 1.

THE AMERICAN SYSTEM OF MEASUREMENTS

LENGTH

1 inch (in.)			=	2.54cm		
1 foot (ft.)	=	12 in.	=	30.48cm	=	.305m
1 yard (yd.)	=	3 ft.			=	.915m
1 mile	=	5,280 ft.			=	1.609km

To convert miles to kilometers, multiply the number of miles by 1.61 (example: 50 mi. × 1.61 = 80.5km). Also use to convert speeds from miles per hour (mph) to kilometers per hour (kmph).

To convert kilometers to miles, multiply the number of kilometers by .62 (example: 25km × .62 = 15.5 mi.). Also use to convert kmph to mph.

CAPACITY

1 fluid ounce (fl. oz.)			=	.03 liters		
1 pint	=	16 fl. oz.	=	.47 liters		
1 quart	=	2 pints	=	.94 liters		
1 gallon (gal.)	=	4 quarts	=	3.79 liters	=	.83 Imperial gal.

To convert U.S. gallons to liters, multiply the number of gallons by 3.79 (example: 12 gal. × 3.79 = 45.48 liters).

To convert liters to U.S. gallons, multiply the number of liters by .26 (example: 50 liters × .26 = 13 U.S. gal.).

To convert U.S. gallons to Imperial gallons, multiply the number of U.S. gallons by .83 (example: 12 U.S. gal. × .83 = 9.95 Imperial gal.).

To convert Imperial gallons to U.S. gallons, multiply the number of Imperial gallons by 1.2 (example: 8 Imperial gal. × 1.2 = 9.6 U.S. gal.).

WEIGHT

1 ounce (oz.)			=	28.35g		
1 pound (lb.)	=	16 oz.	=	453.6g	=	.45kg
1 ton			=	2,000 lb.	=	907kg	=	.91 metric tons

To convert pounds to kilograms, multiply the number of pounds by .45 (example: 90 lb. × .45 = 40.5kg).

To convert kilograms to pounds, multiply the number of kilograms by 2.2 (example: 75kg × 2.2 = 165 lb.).

AREA

1 acre   = .41ha
1 square mile = 640 acres = 259ha= 2.6km^2

To convert acres to hectares, multiply the number of acres by .41 (example: 40 acres × .41 = 16.4ha).

To convert hectares to acres, multiply the number of hectares by 2.47 (example: 20ha × 2.47 = 49.4 acres).

To convert square miles to square kilometers, multiply the number of square miles by 2.6 (example: 80 square miles × 2.6 = 208km^2).

To convert square kilometers to square miles, multiply the number of square kilometers by .39 (example: 150km^2 × .39 = 58.5 square miles).

TEMPERATURE

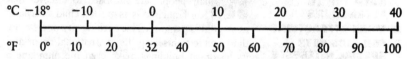

To convert degrees Fahrenheit to degrees Celsius, subtract 32 from °F, multiply by 5, then divide by 9 (example: 85°F – 32 × 5/9 = 29.4°C).

To convert degrees Celsius to degrees Fahrenheit, multiply °C by 9, divide by 5, and add 32 (example: 20°C × 9/5 + 32 = 68°F).

CHAPTER 4

WHAT KIDS LIKE TO SEE & DO

1. KIDS' TOP 10 ATTRACTIONS

2. MORE ATTRACTIONS

3. FOR KIDS WITH SPECIAL INTERESTS

4. LETTING OFF STEAM

5. PERFECT FOR STROLLING

6. ORGANIZED TOURS

Many people are surprised to discover that San Francisco is as much a child's playland as an adult's paradise. This exciting city offers more than simple sightseeing. Its international flavor and its historical buildings make even the mundane a lively—often educational—experience.

SUGGESTED ITINERARIES

Everybody's children are different: Some are early risers and only make it until 3pm, at which point they turn into people you'd rather not know. Other kids can go all day and into the evening—only to fall apart at dinner. Then there are those rare ones you see fast asleep on dad's shoulder, quiet, angelic, sleeping right on until morning, allowing parents to make it back to the hotel with time to read a good book. We don't know your kids or their ages. So the itineraries that follow can be customized to fit your children's ages and needs.

IF YOU HAVE 2 DAYS

Day 1: Take the cable car to Fisherman's Wharf. Visit Pier 39, Fisherman's Wharf, U.S.S. *Pampanito*, the Hyde Street Pier, and Ghirardelli Square. Have lunch on the Wharf or at Ghirardelli, then take a Bay cruise. Have dinner in Chinatown.

Day 2: If you have a car, take part of the 49-mile drive to acquaint yourself with the city. Visit the Exploratorium, then have lunch or grab a picnic basket. Spend the rest of the day at Golden Gate Park. (Don't miss the California Academy of Sciences, the Japanese Tea Garden, and Stow Lake.) Have dinner in North Beach.

IF YOU HAVE 3 DAYS

Days 1–2: Spend days 1–2 as outlined above.

Day 3: Spend a day in Marin County. Drive across the Golden Gate Bridge, and go to the Bay Area Discovery Museum. Then, stroll around and have lunch in Sausalito or Tiburon. Consider going to Muir Woods or Angel Island for the rest of the day.

IF YOU HAVE 4 DAYS OR MORE

Days 1–3: Spend days 1–3 as outlined above.

Day 4: Visit Berkeley or spend more time at Golden Gate Park (roller skating, bike riding, going to the other museums, or riding the carousel) and go to the San Francisco Zoo.

Days 5–6: If you have 5 days or more, you might consider going to Monterey or Carmel on Days 5 and 6. If you want to stay a day longer, you can then visit Big Sur. After that, if you're looking for another excursion, Napa would be a good choice.

1. KIDS' TOP 10 ATTRACTIONS

CABLE CARS. Tel. 673-6864.

Just getting from one place to another can be exhilarating in this city. In fact, cable cars—that rare form of transportation—is very high on our kids' list of things to see and do. Designated official historic landmarks by the National Parks Service in 1964, these delightful, clattering, open-air cars go up and down the steep San Francisco terrain at speeds of up to 9½ miles per hour, creating rollercoaster fun while simply getting from one point to another. At one time, there were over 600 cars on 100 miles of track; today, fewer than 40 cars ride the 12 miles of track, offering passengers grand vistas of the city and the bay.

The **Powell-Hyde cable car line** offers what some people think is the most thrilling ride. This car goes down the steepest grade of all, presenting spectacular views of Alcatraz, Angel Island, and Marin County. It runs from Powell and Market streets through Union Square to Victorian Park near Ghirardelli Square. During the course of its ride to the Wharf, it passes Lombard Street (the crookedest street in the world), from which you can see the skyscrapers of downtown.

The **Powell-Mason line** also starts at Powell and Market streets, but it goes to

---

RAINY-DAY SUGGESTIONS

Our number one rainy-day choice is the **Exploratorium.** Next on our list are the **California Academy of Sciences,** the **Bay Area Discovery Museum,** and the **Lawrence Hall of Science** (in Berkeley). There's also the **M.H. De Young** and **Asian Art museums,** the **San Francisco Museum of Modern Art,** and the **California Palace of the Legion of Honor.** Find out about activities at **Fort Mason Center** and the **Mexican Museum.** (If there is an indoor event at Fort Mason Center, you can also go to the Mexican Museum and make it a good part of the day.) Also, check out the public libraries, the movie theaters in **Japantown** (AMC Kabuki 8 Theaters, tel. 931-9800), and the **Japantown Bowl** (tel. 921-6200).

If you're going to be in Monterey, the **Monterey Aquarium** is a perfect choice. In San Jose there is the **Winchester Mystery House** and the **Children's Discovery Museum of San Jose.**

the other end of the Wharf, near Pier 39. On its run, you'll see part of North Beach, Coit Tower, and glimpses of the bay.

The **California Street line** starts at Market and Drumm streets near the Hyatt Regency San Francisco and ends at Van Ness Avenue, taking you through the towering canyons of the financial district, and passing through Chinatown and Nob Hill, where you see the Mark Hopkins and Fairmont hotels and beautiful Grace Cathedral.

Here are some tips for riding cable cars with kids: Cable cars can be crowded, so travel as light as you can. Remember to hang on to the kids around those curves, and be sure they don't lean out while standing on the running boards.

For more information, call 673-MUNI. You can purchase an all-day MUNI pass (See Chapter 2 under "Getting Around, By Public Transportation," for details).

Admission: Rides cost $2 adults, $1 children 5–17, and 15¢ seniors.

Open: Cable cars run from 6am–1am.

PIER 39, on the waterfront at Embarcadero and Beach Street. Tel. 981-PIER.

⭐ This festive $54-million two-tiered marketplace of more than 100 specialty shops, video arcades, and restaurants is a special treat for kids. Chosen as their favorite place in San Francisco in a survey of 45,000 San Francisco schoolchildren, Pier 39 offers a little bit of all San Francisco in one spot. Located at the northernmost point of the San Francisco peninsula, you can see all the major landmarks from here: the two bridges, Alcatraz, Angel Island, Coit Tower, the Transamerica Pyramid, the skyline, and the exquisite panoramic views of the East Bay and Marin County.

One of the major attractions here is the **San Francisco Experience** (tel. 982-7394, or 982-7550 for recorded information), a 30-minute multimedia show that covers the history of San Francisco. Learn about the city's Barbary Coast origins and how the cable cars came into existence. Experience the 1906 and 1989 earthquakes. Learn about the 1960s—the Summer of Love and the Flower Children. Although children over 5 shouldn't have any problems with the show, there are a few things you should tell your younger kids about the three-dimensional effects: During the Chinese New Year scenes, a dragon pops out of one of the walls; during the Barbary Coast scenes, two bodies drop out of the ceiling; and during the earthquake, the seats rumble. (On your way out of the theater, look at the fascinating earthquake exhibit. The display of the 1906 and 1989 earthquakes combines stunning photographs, instructive material about the quakes, and safety information.) Tickets cost $6 adults, $5 seniors over 55, $3 children 6–16, under-6s free. Show times are daily every half hour—10am–8:30pm Jan–Mar, 10am–9:30pm the rest of the year.

Another spectacular attraction at Pier 39 is **Underwater World,** opened in fall 1991. Designed to be a "dry journey through the sea," it transports visitors on a moving footpath through a clear, acrylic 400-foot-long underwater tunnel. The experience is one of feeling surrounded by the sea and the species of aquatic life indigenous to Northern California including sharks and sea turtles. There are also interactive displays and exhibits. Admission is $7.50 adults, $3.75 children and seniors. The attraction is open daily 10am–10pm.

For older kids and teens, head for **Music Tracks,** where the kids can sing and record their favorite hit songs. And, there is always **Atari Expo,** a large, clean video arcade with wide aisles and plenty of room between games so that children don't

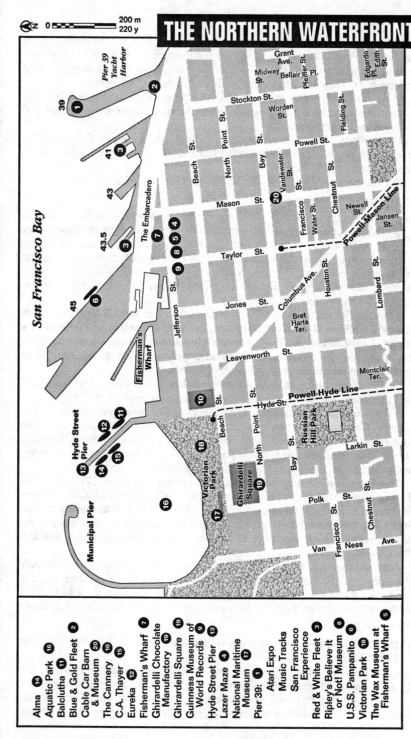

THE NORTHERN WATERFRONT

0   200 m
      220 y

San Francisco Bay

Pier 39 Yacht Harbor

Grant Ave.
Midway St.
Bellair Pl.
Pfeiffer St.
Edgardo Pl.
Edith St.

Stockton St.
Worden St.
Fielding St.

Point St.
Bay St.
Powell St.

Beach St.
North St.
Vandewater St.

Mason St.
Francisco St.
Water St.
Chestnut St.
Newell St.
Jansen St.

The Embarcadero

Taylor St.
Columbus Ave.
Houston St.
Lombard St.

Jones St.

Jefferson St.

Bret Harte Ter.

Leavenworth St.

Montclair Ter.

Powell-Mason Line

Fisherman's Wharf

Hyde St.
Powell-Hyde Line

Beach St.
North Point St.
Russian Hill Park

Hyde Street Pier

Larkin St.

Victorian Park

Bay St.

Ghirardelli Square

Municipal Pier

Polk St.

Francisco St.
Ness
Chestnut St.

Van Ness Ave.

Cable Car – – – –

Legend

- Alma **14**
- Aquatic Park **16**
- Balclutha **11**
- Blue & Gold Fleet **2**
- Cable Car Barn & Museum **20**
- The Cannery **10**
- C.A. Thayer **15**
- Eureka **12**
- Fisherman's Wharf **7**
- Ghirardelli Chocolate Manufactory **19**
- Ghirardelli Square **19**
- Guinness Museum of World Records **9**
- Hyde Street Pier **13**
- Lazer Maze **4**
- National Maritime Museum **17**
- Pier 39: **1**
  - Atari Expo
  - Music Tracks
- San Francisco Experience **3**
- Red & White Fleet **8**
- Ripley's Believe It or Not! Museum **6**
- U.S.S. Pampanito **18**
- Victorian Park **18**
- The Wax Museum at Fisherman's Wharf **5**

elbow each other as they're playing. For Younger Kids, head for the double-decker **carousel,** where the music isn't too loud and the carousel isn't too big. They will also enjoy the street performers—mimes, dancers, musicians, and jugglers—who perform daily. There are also innovative shops that parents will love.

Most shops are open daily 10:30am–8:30pm—longer during holidays and summer. Restaurants are open 11am–11:30pm. American Express, MasterCard, and VISA are usually accepted.

To get there, take the Powell-Mason cable car, which ends at Taylor and Bay streets. Walk two blocks north to Beach Street and go east until you see the colorful flags beckoning you to Pier 39.

You can also take the 15, 19, 30, 32, 39, 42, 47, or the 49 bus.

FISHERMAN'S WHARF

World-famous Fisherman's Wharf is a panorama of sights, smells, and sounds, with souvenir vendors selling T-shirts, cable-car renditions, posters, and books, and sidewalk seafood stands with their bubbling cauldrons of crab and inviting sourdough bread. Fishermen work on their vessels alongside mimes, jugglers, and street performers plying their trades. We love the general hubbub, although during the weekends and busy summer days it's too difficult to navigate a stroller through the crowds. (We recommend a baby carrier.)

There are also several fun attractions in the area, such as the **U.S.S. *Pampanito*, Ripley's Believe It or Not! Museum,** the **Wax Museum at Fisherman's Wharf, Lazer Maze,** and the **Guinness Museum of World Records.** This is also where you can take a cruise to **Alcatraz** or other destinations. (See "More Attractions" in this chapter for details on all these attractions.)

On Pier 39, you can cruise with the **Blue-and-Gold Fleet** and on Piers 41 and 43½ you can sail with the **Red & White Fleet**—more about this later on.

If you would like to stay on dry land, take a horse-drawn carriage ride around the area, offered by **Carriage Charter,** located at Pier 41 (tel. 398-0857). Our kids also enjoy the **Dog House Video Arcade,** 2693 Taylor St., between Beach and North Point (tel. 928-3083), so named because it sells hot dogs and different snacks. It is one of the few arcades in the area. Open daily 10am–midnight; Fri–Sat 10am–2am.

The Cannery is also in the vicinity at 2801 Leavenworth St. (tel. 771-3112). It is a shopping area (see Chapter 5, "Their Shopping List," for details) and it has many delight-ful places to sit and enjoy the sights. It houses the hands-on **San Francisco International Toy Museum** (tel. 441-TOYS). Unfortunately, at the time of publication, the museum was temporarily closed, but it's worth calling to see if it has reopened. Kids ages 10 and under will enjoy it.

Admission: Free. **Open:** The Wharf, daily 24 hours; most area shops, daily 11am–8pm; most restaurants, Sun–Thurs 10am–midnight, Fri–Sat 10am–2am. To get to Fisherman's Wharf, take the Powell-Mason cable car to its terminus at the Wharf; walk 3 blocks north to Jefferson Street. You can also take the 15, 19, 30, 32, 39, 42, 47, or the 49 bus.

HYDE STREET PIER (across from Ghirardelli Square). Tel. 929-0202 or 556-6435.

Shaped like an art deco ship and located near Fisherman's Wharf, the **National Maritime Museum** is a treasure trove of sailing, whaling, and fishing lore. Remarkably good exhibits include intricate model craft, scrim-shaw, and a terrific collection of shipwreck photographs and historic marine scenes, including an 1851 snapshot of hundreds of abandoned ships, deserted en masse by crews rushing off to participate in the latest gold strike. The museum's walls are lined with beautifully carved, high-busted, brightly painted wooden figureheads from old windjammers.

Two blocks east, on Aquatic Park's Hyde Street Pier, are several museum-operated historic ships, now moored and open to the public.

The **S/V Balclutha** (tel. 929-0202), one of the last surviving square-riggers and the handsomest vessel in San Francisco Bay, was built in Glasgow, Scotland, in 1886 and used to carry grain from California at a near-record speed of 300 miles a day. The *Balclutha* was one of the legendary "Cape Horners" of the windjammer age; it rounded the treacherous cape 17 times in its career. It survived a near wreck off the coast of Alaska and was refitted in 1906. The ship is now completely restored. Visitors are invited to spin the wheel, squint at the compass, and imagine they're weathering a mighty blow. Kids can climb into the bunking quarters, visit the "slop chest" (galley to you, matey), and read the sea chanties (clean ones only) that decorate the walls.

The 1890 **Eureka** still carries a cargo of nostalgia for San Franciscans. It was the last of 50 paddle-wheeled ferries that regularly plied the bay; it made its final trip in 1957. Restored to its original splendor at the height of the ferryboat era, the side-wheeler is loaded with deck cargo, including antique cars and trucks. Kids can go into the wheel house and pretend they're captains. There are tours of the engine room daily at 3pm, but check ahead because times vary.

The "steam schooner" **Wapama,** built in 1915, is a good example of shipping in the Industrial Revolution. Originally built as a sailing ship, it was later fitted with a steam engine, after the technology became available.

The black-hulled, three-masted **C. A. Thayer,** built in 1895, was crafted for the lumber trade and carried logs felled in the Pacific Northwest to the carpentry shops of California.

Other historic ships docked here include the tiny two-masted **Alma,** one of the last scow schooners to bring hay to the horses of San Francisco; the **Hercules,** a huge 1907 oceangoing steam tug; and the **Eppleton Hall,** a side-wheeled tugboat built in England in 1914 to operate on London's River Thames.

At the pier's small-boat shop, visitors can follow the restoration progress of historic boats from the museum's collection. It's located behind the Maritime Book Store on your right as you approach the ships.

Stop in at the Maritime Book Store (tel. 775-2665) devoted to books, maps, posters, cards, and gifts on sailing and marine life. This is a place that local kids enjoy after school. There's also a small boat shop on the pier that gives boatbuilding classes.

Admission: Museum, free; ships, $3 adults, free for children under 16 and seniors over 62.

Open: June–Aug, daily 10am–6pm; the rest of the year, daily 10am–5pm. **Closed:** Thanksgiving Day, Christmas Day, and New Year's Day. Take the Powell-Hyde cable car to Victorian Park. You can also get there on bus 19, 30, 32, 39, 42, 47, or 49. If you choose to drive to the area, there are several all-day parking lots.

GHIRARDELLI SQUARE, 900 North Point St. (bordered by Beach, Larkin, Polk, and North Point streets). Tel. 775-5500.

 That famous red-brick chocolate factory with the 15-foot-high illuminated sign has greeted millions of tourists and delighted the kid in all of us. In fact, we never miss a trip to Ghirardelli Square when we're in San Francisco, sometimes making a quick stop for an Emperor Norton at the **Ghirardelli Chocolate Manufactory** (see Chapter 7, "Where Kids Like to Eat," for details). This is a great place to have dinner after a walk on the Wharf. In the evening, you can watch the sun set over the Golden Gate Bridge. By day, you can see Alcatraz Island, Sausalito, and the East Bay. In addition, there are numerous clothing and accessory stores, craft and art galleries, gift stores, and import shops. (See Chapter 5, "Their Shopping List," for more details.)

Warning: This delightfully constructed set of buildings is tricky to navigate with a stroller unless you know where you're going. If you have stroller, don't attempt the stairs from Beach Street. Enter at Larkin Street or North Point Street and ask at the Information Desk (fountain level) for directions to ramps and elevator access.

Admission: Free.

Open: Shops, Memorial Day–Labor Day, Mon–Sat 10am–9pm, Sun 11am–6pm; the rest of the year, Mon–Thurs 10:30am–6:30pm, Fri–Sat 10:30am–9pm, Sun 11am–6pm. Restaurants, times vary; see the individual listings in Chapter 7, "Where Kids Like to Eat," for complete information. Take the Powell-Hyde cable car to Victorian Park. You can also get to Ghirardelli Square on bus 19, 30, 32, 39, 42, 47, or 49. If you choose to drive to the area, there are several all-day reasonably priced parking lots, some with validations.

THE EXPLORATORIUM, in the Palace of Fine Arts, 3601 Lyon St. Tel. 563-7337, or 561-0368 for recorded information.

Don't miss this 86,000-square-foot children's delight. The Exploratorium is like nothing else you've ever seen. Also called the "Playful Museum," this innovative, hands-on science fair is a participatory venture, where you use all your senses and stretch them to new dimensions. There are over 700 exhibits for children to explore and learn about light, color, sound, motion, language, touch, and electricity. Throughout the museum, exhibit "explainers" work with children to encourage their explorations.

Younger kids especially enjoy the Balancing Ball (a traffic cone standing up with a column of air blowing through, and a beach ball that levitates from the air, which kids chase after); the Shadow Box (a walk-in box where a strobe light casts kids' shadows on a phosphorescent wall); the Distorted Room (with a slanted floor that has no right angles; when someone outside looks into the room, people inside look like dwarves or giants); and Duck Into Kaleidoscope (where children duck under partitions and then see infinite number of reflections in the three mirrors set up).

Older kids enjoy Light Strokes (a converted Macintosh Computer that offers a sensitive, sophisticated finger-painting experience) and Everyone Is You and Me (a two-way mirror that both reflects and can be seen through, so that by adjusting knobs, two kids can superimpose their images one on the other).

The Tactile Dome is another exhibit—adults and kids crawl through this darkened area using their sense of touch to experience another dimension. You must make a reservation several days in advance (tel. 415/561-0362 between 2 and 4pm) and pay an extra fee to enjoy this experience, which is recommended for children over 7.

Yes, we have our favorite exhibits. Andrew couldn't get enough of the Momentum Machine, on which he and five other school-agers pushed off on a scooter-like structure that kept them spinning as long as they balanced evenly. Then, we discovered "Viewing the Golden Gate," an interactive video disk where, by moving a rotary control ball, you "fly" over the Golden Gate Bridge. While moving the steering wheel you see the blips on the radar screen, and if you look over that small air-traffic-controller-like screen, you can see a larger screen of the scenery you'd be flying over. This is such a big hit that it was difficult to get kids to take turns. Once on, they wanted to stay.

If you know ahead when you'll be at the Exploratorium, call for information on special events, workshops, and field trips. The museum is completely stroller-accessible.

The museum is located on one of the prettiest parcels in the city, in the only building left standing from the Panama-Pacific Exposition of 1915, which celebrated the opening of the Panama Canal. The adjoining lagoon is home to ducks, swans, and seagulls.

Admission: $6 adults, $3 senior citizens, $1.50 children 6–17, free for children under 6; free for everyone Wed after 6pm.

Open: Wed 10am–9:30pm, Thurs–Sun 10am–5pm. **Closed:** Mon–Tues (except when they're holidays), Thanksgiving Day, and Christmas Day. You can take bus 30 from Stockton Street to the Marina stop. Buses 28, 41, 43, and 45 also stop within walking distance. If driving, from U.S. 101 north, take the last exit before the bridge.

GOLDEN GATE PARK (Park Headquarters are at McLaren Lodge). Tel. 666-7106 or 666-7200.

This is one of the places that make San Francisco special and is a *must-see* for anyone visiting the city. There are so many faces to the park, so many things to see and do—fabulous museums, a planetarium and an aquarium, a buffalo grazing paddock, a lake with boats, an antique carousel, great playground equipment, and of course the famous, authentic Japanese Tea Garden. So plan to spend lots of time here, at least a half day each time you go—a few hours for the planetarium or aquarium, some time to meander, and some time at the playground or Stow Lake. If you want to hike, rollerskate, or bike ride, you can do that, too.

Stretching from the ocean (be sure to drive there just to see the Dutch Windmill welcoming visitors to San Francisco) to 3 miles inland and 1½ miles wide, Golden Gate Park is a recreation area par excellence for families.

For an overall look at the park, you can drive west on John F. Kennedy Drive toward the ocean. At the Great Highway, take a left, and another left onto Martin Luther King, Jr., Drive, which will bring you back into the park heading east. The Music Concourse is considered the heart of the park. On Sundays, weather permitting, you can hear everything from opera to Irish folk bands.

The area that most families consider the hub is near the de Young Compound (also called the Music Concourse). There are many picnic areas here, and museums, too. This is where you'll find roller skaters and bicyclists.

Admission: Park, free. Most museums charge fees (see individual writeups).

Open: Daily. Parking is a problem. Park authorities suggest that the best place to park for the Academy of Sciences, the children's playground, the Music Concourse, and Japanese Tea Garden is outside the park on Fulton Street between 7th and 11th avenues. Then walk into the park following the directions to the Music Concourse. On Sundays, John F. Kennedy Drive is closed as far as Crossover Drive, about a mile.

You can take a bus. From Market Street take the No. 5 ("Fulton"), or the No. 21 ("Hayes"), which runs along the north side of the park; the No. 71 ("Noriega") runs along the south side of the park on Lincoln Avenue; the No. 7 ("Haight") goes to the east end of the park, from which you'll have to walk a block or two. The only bus that stops in the park itself is the No. 44 ("O'Shaughnessy"), which stops in the Music Concourse area. We always call MUNI (tel. 673-MUNI) for specific bus information before we go.

The **California Academy of Sciences,** on the Music Concourse (tel. 221-5100, or 750-7145 for recorded information), is one of the finest natural science museums in the country. Natural science exhibits include **Life Through Time,** a 3.5 billion-year journey through life on Earth. Ten-year-old Andrew was able to appreciate evolution in a new way, while 4-year-old Elizabeth squealed when she saw the life-size dinosaurs. It's a good exhibit for all ages. **Wild California** is an exhibit hall devoted to the vastness and diversity of this amazing region. **African Safari** has a lifelike African watering hole exhibit that has realistic sound and lighting effects. If you have a budding gemologist as we do—and I don't know many kids who don't "ooh" and "ah" over stones that glimmer—take at least a brief look-see at the **Gem and Mineral Hall.** Imagine a child's delight at the 1,350-pound quartz crystal! It is a treat. The **SafeQuake Ride** is part of a large exhibit on earthquakes. Here, you stand on a platform and watch a video about earthquakes. At the same time, the platform is programmed to simulate the vibrations of different strengths. This is a great favorite of the 8- through 11-year-old set. You'll also want to see **The Discovery Room,** a small, quiet area (designed for family interaction) with lots to see and touch. "Please Touch!" are the words you'll hear. Children are invited to handle such things as shark jaws, dinosaur bones, and birds' nests. Even though your toddler won't be able to participate fully, this is a good place to calm him or her down if overstimulated. (The Discovery Room is open Tues–Fri 1–4pm, Sat–Sun 11am–3:30pm; summer hours from July 1 through Labor Day are Tue–Sun 11am–3:30pm. The room is staffed by volunteers, so call ahead for exact hours.)

The **Steinhart Aquarium** houses one of the largest and most diverse collections of aquatic life in the nation. Some 14,000 specimens call Steinhart home, including amphibians, reptiles, marine mammals, and penguins. The aquarium contains a California tidepool and a "hands-on" area where children can touch starfish and sea urchins. Their living coral reef is the largest display of its kind in the country and the only one in the West. In the Fish Roundabout—a unique, 100,000-gallon tank—visitors are surrounded by fast-swimming schools of open-ocean fish. Seals and dolphins are fed every 2 hours, beginning at 10:30am; the penguins are fed at 11:30am and 4pm.

The **Morrison Planetarium** is northern California's largest indoor theater of the outdoors. Its awesome sky shows are projected onto a 65-foot domed ceiling. School-age children and those older love to spend the hour gazing up at the "night sky," learning about the celestial bodies. Our only qualifier (which applies to all planetarium shows) is that children under 6 find the shows very long, and the darkness seems to scare many of them. The planetarium staff agrees. Approximately four major exhibits, with titles such as *Star Death: The Birth of Black Holes* and *The Universe Unveiled,* are presented each year. Related cosmos exhibits are located in the adjacent Earth and Space Hall. Call for show schedules and information.

In the **Wattis Hall of Human Cultures,** life-size tableaux depict life in various parts of the world. Step into the icy environs of the Arctic Eskimo during a midwinter seal hunt, then warm yourself in the parched desert campsite of Australian aborigines.

GOLDEN GATE PARK

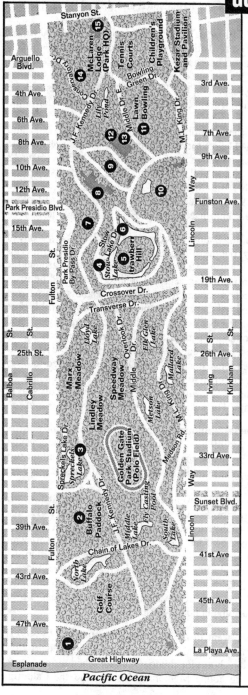

0   500 m
     550 y

Stanyon St.

Arguello
Blvd.

Lily
Pond

McLaren
Lodge
(Park HQ)

Tennis
Courts

Bowling
Green Dr.

Children's
Playground

Kezar Stadium
and Pavilion

Bowling
Lawn

Stow
Lake

Strawberry
Hill

Park Presidio
By-Pass Dr.

Crossover Dr.

Transverse Dr.

Lloyd
Lake

Overlook Dr.

Elk Glen
Lake

Marx
Meadow

Speedway
Meadow

Lindley
Meadow

Metson
Lake

Mallard
Lake

Golden Gate
Park Stadium
(Polo Field)

Spreckels
Lake

Fly Casting
Pool

Medson Rd.

Buffalo
Paddock

Middle
Lake

South
Lake

Chain of Lakes Dr.

North
Lake

Golf
Course

Esplanade

Great Highway

La Playa Ave.

Pacific Ocean

Arguello Blvd. · 4th Ave. · 6th Ave. · 8th Ave. · 10th Ave. · 12th Ave. · Park Presidio Blvd. · 15th Ave.

3rd Ave. · 7th Ave. · 9th Ave. · Funston Ave. · 19th Ave. · 26th Ave. · 33rd Ave. · Sunset Blvd. · 39th Ave. · 41st Ave. · 43rd Ave. · 45th Ave. · 47th Ave.

Balboa · Cabrillo · 25th St.

Irving St. · Kirkham St.

Fulton St. · J.F. Kennedy Dr. · Conservatory Dr. · Middle Dr. E. · M.L. King Dr.

Spreckels Lake Dr. · Stow Lake Dr.

Spreckels Lake 3
Steinhart Aquarium 13
Stow Lake 4
Strybing Arboretum 10

Japanese Tea Garden 6
McLaren Lodge (Park Headquarters) 15
M.H. de Young Memorial Museum 8
Morrison Planetarium 12
Music Concourse 9

Asian Art Museum 7
Buffalo Paddock 2
California Academy of Sciences 11
Chinese Pavilion 5
Conservatory of Flowers 14
Dutch Windmill 1

Golden Gate Park

SAN FRANCISCO

A dozen such exhibits show how humanity has adapted and thrived in our planet's most adverse climates.

In **Meyer Hall,** the "Wild California" exhibition includes a 14,000-gallon aquarium and seabird rookery, life-size battling elephant seals, and two larger-than-life views of microscopic life forms. There's also a poisonous twin-headed snake.

In **McBean-Peterson Hall,** visitors are encouraged to "walk through time" as they are presented with evidence supporting the Theory of Evolution. This massive exhibit walks you through 3.5 billion years of history, from the Garden of Eden to the present day.

Admission: Aquarium and science exhibits, $6 adults, $3 students 12–17 and seniors 65 and over, $1 children 6–11, free for children under 6; free for everyone the first Wed of every month. Planetarium shows, $2.50 adults, $1.25 children under 18 and seniors 65 and over. Show a valid MUNI transfer for $2 off the admission price.

Open: Labor Day–July 4, daily 10am–5pm; July 4–Labor Day, daily 10am–7pm; first Wed of every month 10am–9pm. **MUNI Metro:** N line ("Judah") to Golden Gate Park. **Bus:** 5 ("Fulton"), 71 ("Haight-Noriega"), or 44 ("O'Shaughnessy").

The **Japanese Tea Garden,** the Band Concourse area (tel. 752-1171), is one of the most popular, and possibly the most unique attraction of the park. This handsome, delicate Asian garden is a delightful step into a world halfway around the globe. Pathways meander through Japanese greenery, koi-filled ponds, and bonsai.

Kids particularly love the arched moon bridge and the elaborate five-tiered dark-red pagoda. The hand-carved red gateway entrance and the wonderful bronze Buddha intrigue them. If you're in the city during March and early April, you'll find the Japanese cherry trees blossoming. There is a lovely little teahouse in which kimono-clad women serve Japanese tea and cookies. Stroller-access is to the left of the main gate entrance on Tea Garden Drive (marked "Exit"), but be prepared to carry little children, as certain areas are not open to strollers. Admission is $2 for adults, $1 for children 6–12 and seniors. There is free admission for all on the first Wednesday of each month and on major holidays. The tea garden is open daily 9am–5:30pm.

The **M. H. de Young Memorial Museum,** near 10th Avenue and Fulton Street (tel. 750-3600, or 863-3330 for recorded information), is the most comprehensive museum in the city, with artwork from ancient Egypt, Greece, and Rome, all the way to 20th century America. It also features sculpture, decorative arts, tapestries, and oils from the old European Masters.

This is where you can take the kids to introduce them to Rembrandt, Reubens, El Greco, and Goya. There are also Saturday workshops for children ages 7–13. The children visit a different museum gallery each week, and then participate in an artistic experience in which they create their own art. These occur every Saturday at 10:30am and are available to the first 25 children on a drop-in basis. (For more information, call 750-3658.) Admission (including the Asian Art Museum and the California Palace of the Legion of Honor) is $4 adults; $2 children 12–17 and seniors; children under 12, free; free for everyone first Wed and first Sat of each month. The museum is open Wed–Sun 10am–5pm; also open some holidays—call.

The **Asian Art Museum,** adjacent to the de Young Museum (tel. 668-8921), houses an internationally acclaimed collection of almost 12,000 objets d'art from Asia. There are films and story-telling hours for children. Call for schedules and times. Admission (including the M.H. de Young Memorial Museum and the California

Palace of the Legion of Honor) is $4 adults, $2 children 12–17 and seniors, children under 12, free (fees may be higher for some special exhibitions); free for everyone first Wed and first Sat of each month. The museum is open Wed–Sun 10am–5pm, till 8:45pm first Wed of the month.

Stow Lake, is a delightful little retreat—a place where you can rent boats or hike. The lake comes complete with an island. You can see the **Chinese Pavilion,** and visitors are allowed inside. Wander to the top of the hill to the reservoir that feeds **Huntington Falls,** a lovely artificial waterfall with hand-sculpted rocks. There is stroller-access all around the lake (although it can get muddy) and to the top of the falls.

Plan to spend about an hour if you're going to walk around the lake and walk up to the top. You can picnic anywhere around this area or on the top of the hill but carry out what you bring in. Electric motorboats can be rented by the hour, as can rowboats and pedal boats. A deposit is required for all rentals.

Nearby **Spreckels Lake** is a delight of hobbyists, who bring out their remote-controlled model sailboats and powerboats on the weekends. When Elizabeth was two years old, she squealed when she saw the buffalo feeding nearby at the **Buffalo Paddock.** The boathouse is open Tue–Sun 9am–4pm.

Golden Gate Park's magnificent **carousel** has a wonderful menagerie of animals. Recently restored at a cost of $800,000, it is one of the last complete Hershell-Spillman carousels still operating. Rides cost $1 adults, 25¢ children over 3 feet tall; under 3 feet, free. The carousel operates daily June–Sept 10am–5pm, Oct–May Wed–Sun 10am–4pm.

The nearby **Children's Playground** can rightfully be called a young one's exercise complex. Several huge slides, tires for swinging, and huge wooden climbing structures beckon kids from all over the city . . . and all over the world. Outside the playground are meadows for picnicking. And for the babies, there is a tiny elephant slide and low swings. This is where the **Petting Zoo** is located.

SAN FRANCISCO ZOOLOGICAL GARDENS AND CHILDREN'S ZOO, Sloat Boulevard and 45th Avenue Tel. 753-7061, or 753-7083 for recorded information.

Located between the Pacific Ocean and Lake Merced, in the southwest corner of the city, the San Francisco Zoo is among America's highest-rated animal parks. Begun in 1889 with a grizzly bear named Monarch donated by the *San Francisco Examiner,* the zoo now sprawls over 65 acres and is growing. It attracts over a million visitors each year.

A large bank of children's swings greets you as you enter the 45th Avenue entrance. Our children took off to play on the equipment and were so content to amuse themselves that animal viewing took a backseat.

The zoo boasts over 1,000 animals and birds, and is considered a special treat for resident and visiting children. One innovation is the Zoo Key. You purchase a key for $1.50. At exhibits throughout the zoo, there are boxes with locks. The key unlocks an audio explanation of the animals. Children are delighted with this key, and scramble to be the one to "unlock" the information.

Most of the 1,000-plus inhabitants are contained in realistically landscaped enclosures guarded by cunningly concealed moats. The innovative Primate Discovery Center is particularly noteworthy, known for its many rare and endangered species. Soaring outdoor atriums, sprawling meadows, and a midnight world for exotic nocturnal primates house a speedy Patas monkey that can run up to 35 miles per hour and the Senegal bush baby, a pint-size primate that can jump up 4 feet.

Other highlights of interest to families include Koala Crossing, patterned after an Australian outback station; Gorilla World, one of the world's largest exhibits of these gentle giants; and Wolf Woods, exhibiting the remarkably sophisticated social behavior of the North American timber wolf. Musk Ox Meadow is a 2½-acre habitat for a herd of rare white-fronted musk oxen brought from Alaska. And the Lion House is home to four species of cats, including Prince Charles, a rare white tiger (you can watch them being fed at 2pm daily except Monday).

The **Children's Zoo,** a four-acre park adjacent to the main park, allows both kids and adults to get close to animals, including zoo babies being tended in the nursery. The Barnyard is alive with strokable, cuddly baby animals. And then there's our kids' personal favorite, the fascinating Insect Zoo—the only one in the western United States and one of only three such exhibits in the country. Over 6,000 specimens include a colony of velvet ants, honey bees, scorpions, and several hissing cockroaches. On weekends at 2:30pm you can see the popular show *Amazing Insects in Action,* which gives an intimate look at live insects through a "macro" video system. Our kids talk about it for days afterward.

A free, informal walking tour of the zoo leaves from Koala Crossing at 12:30 and 2:30pm on weekends. The *Zebra Zephyr* train tour takes visitors on a 20-minute "safari" daily (in winter, only on weekends). The tour is $2 for adults, $1 for children 15 and under.

Admission: Main zoo, $6 adults, $3 seniors and children 12–15, free for children 11 and under if accompanied by an adult; children's zoo, $1.50, free for children under 2.

Open: Main zoo, daily 10am–5pm; children's zoo, daily 11am–4pm. You can get to the zoo by MUNI Metro—take the line from downtown Market Street to the end of the line.

GOLDEN GATE NATIONAL RECREATION AREA (GGNRA), Fort Mason. Tel. 556-0560.

Not to be confused with Golden Gate Park, GGNRA is an enormous urban coastal preserve—a U.S. National Park—of over 114 square miles that stretches from San Mateo County (in the south) through parts of the city's waterfront (including the San Francisco Maritime National Historical Park) to the Cliff House and Fort Point, to Alcatraz, and then across Golden Gate Bridge north to parts of Marin County. This most popular of the U.S. National Parks attracts upward of 20 million visitors a year (more than twice the combined total of the Grand Canyon, Yosemite, and Cape Cod). Within its boundaries are abundant adventures for families. It offers miles of trails, ranger-conducted walks, and historical tours, all within minutes of downtown San Francisco. (Some of the park's attractions are covered later in this chapter under "More Attractions" and "Letting Off Steam.")

Be sure to pick up a copy of the invaluable book *Golden Gate National Recreation Area Park Guide,* published by the Golden Gate National Park Association.

Fort Mason, Bay and Franklin streets (tel. 441-5705 or 556-0560), is where the GGNRA park headquarters are located (the Fort Mason Center). You can pick up maps and other information about GGNRA here. The center is a complex of buildings housing theaters, art galleries, museums, and various arts programs. More than 1,000 activities are held here monthly, including concerts and fairs on the adjacent piers.

Anchored at Pier 3 in Fort Mason is the last unchanged ship of the fleet of 2,751 Liberty ships built for World War II. The *Jeremiah O'Brien* (Tel. 441-3101) is open daily 9am–6pm. Admission is $2 adults, $1 children and seniors.

Fort Mason also offers beautiful picnic facilities and is a favored spot by hikers, joggers, and bicyclists. You'll find Green's Restaurant here (see Chapter 7, "Where Kids Like to Eat," for details).

Golden Gate Promenade (tel. 556-0560) is a spectacular 4-mile walk on a footpath along the shoreline from Aquatic Park to Fort Point at the foot of the Golden Gate Bridge. The Promenade passes Marina Green (great for kite flying), the yacht harbor, and Fort Mason, offering lovely views through the trees. There is parking at Fort Point, and the walk toward the city provides very dramatic views.

Fort Point (tel. 556-1693) is a brick fort that was built during the Civil War. It now houses a museum (open daily 10am–5pm, free admission), an old jail cell, and the old army barracks. The best thing about Fort Point are the views of Golden Gate Bridge and San Francisco. Be sure to go all the way out to the Fort itself for the fantastic views of the city and Bay Bridge crossing over to the East Bay.

Cliff House and Seal Rocks, 1090 Point Lobos (tel. 556-8642), is located above Ocean Beach and has some of the best views of The Golden Gate National Recreation Area. The original Cliff House burned to the ground. One-time San Francisco mayor Adolph Sutro built the second Cliff House in 1895, the year before he built the nearby Sutro Baths. The baths (which burned down in 1966), a swimming/bathing complex that could accommodate 24,000 people in either salt-water or fresh-water pools, resembled the baths of Imperial Rome. Today the remains look like classical ruins.

The second Cliff House burned down in 1896 and the present building opened in 1909, the fifth on the spot. Cliff House is the place to view **Seal Rocks,** a group of rocks 400 feet offshore that is home to sea lions and various sea birds. It's a great place to bring binoculars and watch the scenery.

BAY AREA DISCOVERY MUSEUM, 557 East Fort Baker. Tel. 332-9646.

This wonderful museum on the north side of the Golden Gate Bridge is targeted for children from 2 to 12. It is an imaginative, creative space for children to learn. Fort Baker was restored to house the exhibitions, which are a *must-see.* With its myriad exhibits, all of which offer exciting ways to stretch your child's mind, the museum is designed so that every child, no matter what his or her learning style is, no matter what age, will be enticed into learning—and, of course, into having fun.

Exhibits include "Transportation" (where kids play "the gridlock game" as they hear traffic reports and try to remedy the difficult Bay Area transportation situation); "Building the City" (an architecture exhibit that allows children to build and experiment); "San Francisco Bay" (which focuses on the interaction between people and the natural environment, including sea life, commerce, and industry connected to the sea, such as fishing and navigation, and the city high-rises that ring the bay). There is even a "Children's Bank" exhibit, where an ATM teaches the concept of value.

Admission: $5 adults, $4 seniors, $3 children.

Open: Wed–Sun 10am–5pm; summers Tues–Sun 10am–5pm. To get to East Fort Baker from San Francisco, take U.S. 101 north across the Golden Gate Bridge to the Alexander Avenue exit. Turn off and follow the signs to East Fort Baker.

2. MORE ATTRACTIONS

ALCATRAZ ISLAND, San Francisco Bay. Tel. 546-BOAT.

Spanish explorer Juan Manuel de Ayala sighted this oblong chunk of rock in 1775 and christened it "Isla de los Alcatraces," or Island of the Pelicans, after the thousands of birds that made their home here. American settlers drove the birds off and successively transformed the island into a fortress, an army prison, and finally a maximum-security prison. The last incarnation occurred in 1934, at the peak of America's gangster scare, when tough guys like John Dillinger and "Pretty Boy" Floyd seemed to bust out of ordinary jails with toothpicks. An alarmed public demanded n escape-proof "tiger cage"—and the federal government fingered Alcatraz for the part.

The choice seemed ideal. The Rock, as it became known, is ringed by strongly swirling, bone-chilling water, enough to defeat even the strongest swimmer. At great cost, the old army cages were made into tiers of tiny, toolproof one-man cells, guarded by machine-gun turrets, high walls, steel panels, and electronic metal detectors called "snitch boxes." Even more forbidding than the walls were the prison rules: No talking, no newspapers, no canteen, no playing cards, and no inducement to good behavior—merely punishment for bad.

The Rock resembled a gigantic, absolutely spotless tomb with the hush of death upon it. Into that living cemetary went most of the criminal big shots who let themselves be taken alive—Al Capone, "Machine Gun" Kelly, "Doc" Barker, "Creepy" Karpis, and a dozen more. All were broken by Alcatraz . . . except those who died while trying to escape from it.

While, in some respects, Alcatraz seemed a macabre success, it was a huge white elephant from the start. Its cells were designed to hold 300 convicts, but there simply weren't that many top torpedoes in captivity. Consequently, more and more small fry were added just to maintain the population, which eventually included ordinary car thieves, forgers, and burglars—crooks who could just as well have been jailed elsewhere. Yet the cost of maintaining the prison was colossal (drinking water, for instance, had to be ferried across in tank boats), and by the 1950s the money required to keep a single inmate on the Rock could have housed him in a luxury hotel suite. When three men seemed to have staged a successful escape from Alcatraz in June 1962, the federal government took the opportunity to order the prison "phased out"—closed. (It's far from certain whether the trio actually got away.)

In the decade that followed, Alcatraz was abandoned, a rock without a purpose. The only tenants were a caretaker, his wife, and an assistant. In 1969 a group of protesters occupied the island with the intention of establishing a Native American cultural center; they left in 1971.

Today great numbers of visitors explore the island's grim cells and fortifications on tours conducted by the U.S. National Parks Service—fascinating accounts by park rangers on the island's history, an award-winning audio tour in the prison cell house, and a slide show.

A trip to Alcatraz is a popular excursion, and space is limited. Try to make reservations as far in advance as possible. Tours and tickets are available through **Red and White Fleet** (tel. 415/546-BOAT, or toll free 800/229-2784 in California) and can be charged to your American Express, MasterCard, or VISA card. You can also purchase tickets on the day of sailing from the Red and White Fleet ticket office on Pier 41.

Be sure to wear comfortable shoes and take a heavy sweater or windbreaker. Even if the sun is shining when you embark, the bay can turn bitterly cold in minutes. You should know that hiking around the island is not easy; there's a steep rise, and you have to climb several flights of stairs. The National Parks Service advises those with heart or respiratory conditions to reconsider taking the tour if climbing stairs leaves them short of breath.

For those who want to get a closer look at Alcatraz without all the hiking, two boat-tour operators offer short circumnavigations of the island. (See Section 4, "Letting Off Steam" below, for complete information.)

Admission: Tours, $7.50 adults, $7 seniors 55 and older, $4 children 5–11.

Open: Winter, daily 9:45am–2:45pm; summer, daily 9:15am–4:15pm. Ferries depart from Pier 41 by Fisherman's Wharf every half hour, at 15 and 45 minutes after the hour. Arrive at least 20 minutes prior to sailing time.

CHINATOWN, Gateway on Grant Avenue at Bush Street

San Francisco boasts the largest Chinese community outside of Asia, and once you see Chinatown you will believe it. It's a neighborhood where you'll see pagoda-style roofs, Chinese-style filigreed balconies, and lots of bright red paint. The gateway to Chinatown is a two-level structure with dragons and guard dogs. This bustling section of town is one of the most popular tourist attractions in all San Francisco. And no wonder . . . it's like stepping into another world of sights, sounds, and smells. Exotic shops, grocery stores, herb stands, souvenir vendors, tearooms, and plenty of people, all make you feel as if you're part of a parade. Kids love it.

Chinese New Year (which occurs every year between mid-January and late February) is a week in which Chinatown comes alive with folk dancing, pageants, and the Miss Chinatown USA Beauty Contest. There are Chinatown festival walks, exhibits, and displays, all culminating in a spectacular finale called the Golden Dragon Parade. Usually 450,000 spectators line the parade route. The Chinese Culture Center also offers special activities. For information about tickets to the pageant—and the exact dates—call 415/982-3000.

The **Chinese Culture Center,** 750 Kearny St., on the third floor of the Holiday Inn (tel. 986-1822), offers educational and cultural programs, including lectures, art exhibits, films and festivals. Changing exhibits are presented year round, but you should call for schedules. Some of the performing arts include such children's favorites as the Shanghai Puppeteers and the Shanghai Children's Music and Dance Corps. Admission is free and it is open Tues–Sat 10am–4pm.

You might also want to stop at the **Chinese Historical Society,** 17 Adler Place, near Grant Avenue and Broadway (tel. 391-1188), where you'll see the important role Chinese immigrants played in the Gold Rush and railroad eras. Admission is free and the office is open Tues–Sat 1–5pm.

Directions: You can get to Chinatown by the California Street cable car or by bus 1, 15, 30, 41, and 83, or check with MUNI (tel. 673-MUNI).

JAPAN CENTER, Post and Buchanan Streets. Tel. 922-6776.

The immense yet graceful Japan Center is an Asian-oriented shopping mall located in San Francisco's revitalized Japantown, about a mile west of Union Square. At its center is a serenely noble five-tiered Peace Pagoda, designed by world-famous Japanese architect Yoshiro Taniguchi "to convey the friendship and goodwill of the Japanese to the people of the United States." Surrounding the pagoda, in a network of arcades, squares, and bridges, are dozens of shops and showrooms featuring everything from cameras and transistor radios to pearls, bonsai (dwarf trees), and kimonos. When it opened, with fanfare, in 1968, the complex seemed as modern as a jumbo jet. Today the aging concrete structure seems less impressive, but it still holds some interesting surprises. The renowned **Kabuki Hot Spring,** 1750 Geary Boulevard (tel. 922-6000), is the center's most famous tenant. The Kabuki is an authentic traditional Japanese bathhouse with deep ceramic communal tubs, as well as private baths. In addition to steaming water and restful tatami rooms, the Kabuki features Japanese-style shiatsu finger-pressure massages. Facilities include a *furo* (hot bath) and *mizoburo* (cold bath), dry-heat saunas, a steam room, steam cabinets, and Japanese-style sit-down showers. Appointments are required. The Japan Center also houses several restaurants (including sushi bars) and teahouses, the AMC Kabuki 8 cinema, and the luxurious 14-story Miyako Hotel.

There is often live entertainment on summer weekends, including Japanese music and dance performances, tea ceremonies, flower-arranging demonstrations, martial-arts presentations, and other cultural events. Japanese festivals are celebrated here thrice yearly: a **Cherry Blossom festival** (Sakura Matsuri) in April, the **Buddhist Bon festival** in July, and an **Autumn Harvest festival** (Aki Matsuri) in September. Each is a colorful occasion, complete with beautiful costumes and traditional Japanese music and dance.

Japantown, or Nihonmachi, San Francisco's Japanese quarter, occupies four square blocks directly north of the Japan Center. Though less exotic and colorful than Chinatown, this area is notable for some interesting gift stores, a movie theater showing Japanese films, and several good Japanese restaurants. In the Buchanan Street Mall, between Post Street and Sutter Street, is a cobblestone walkway designed to resemble a meandering stream. It is lined on either side with flowering cherry and plum trees, and contains two origami-inspired fountains by Ruth Asawa.

Admission: Free.

Open: Mon–Fri 10am–10pm, Sat–Sun 9am–10pm. By bus, take either 22 or 38 (exit on the northeast corner of Geary Boulevard and Fillmore Street).

LOMBARD STREET, between Hyde and Leavenworth Streets.

Known as the "crookedest street in the world," the whimsically winding block of Lombard Street, between Hyde Street and Leavenworth Street, puts smiles on the faces of thousands of visitors each year, and we couldn't let you or the kids miss it. The elevation is so dramatic that the road has to snake back and forth to make a descent possible. The street zigzags around bright flower gardens that explode with

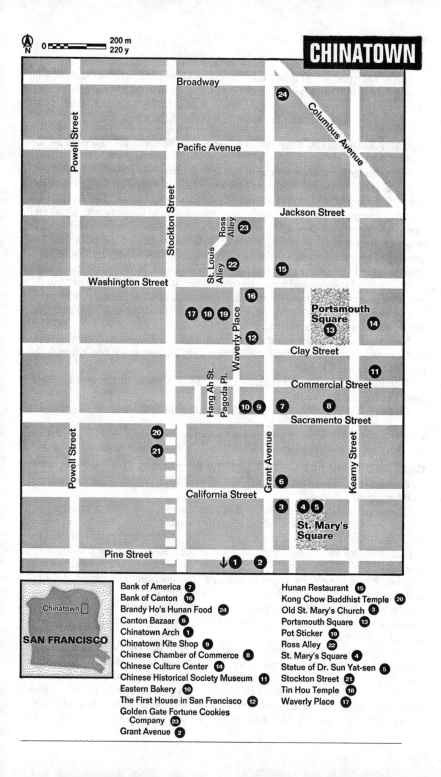

CHINATOWN

0 — 200 m
  — 220 y

Broadway

24

Pacific Avenue

Columbus Avenue

Powell Street

Stockton Street

Jackson Street

Ross Alley 23

St. Louis Alley 22

15

Washington Street

16

17 18 19

Portsmouth Square 13

14

Waverly Place

12

Clay Street

11

Hang Ah St.
Pagoda Pl.

Commercial Street

10 9 7

8

Sacramento Street

20

21

Grant Avenue

Kearny Street

Powell Street

6

California Street

3

4 5

St. Mary's Square

Pine Street

↓ 1 2

SAN FRANCISCO

Chinatown

Bank of America 7
Bank of Canton 16
Brandy Ho's Hunan Food 24
Canton Bazaar 6
Chinatown Arch 1
Chinatown Kite Shop 9
Chinese Chamber of Commerce 8
Chinese Culture Center 14
Chinese Historical Society Museum 11
Eastern Bakery 10
The First House in San Francisco 12
Golden Gate Fortune Cookies
  Company 23
Grant Avenue 2

Hunan Restaurant 15
Kong Chow Buddhist Temple 20
Old St. Mary's Church 3
Portsmouth Square 13
Pot Sticker 19
Ross Alley 22
St. Mary's Square 4
Statue of Dr. Sun Yat-sen 5
Stockton Street 21
Tin Hou Temple 18
Waverly Place 17

color during warmer months. This short stretch of Lombard Street is one way, downhill, and great fun to drive. Take the curves slowly and in low gear. Save your photographing for the bottom, where you can find a parking space and gaze to your heart's content. You can also walk the block, if your family is up to it, either up or down, via staircases (without curves) on either side of the street.

U.S.S. *PAMPANITO*, Pier 45, Fisherman's Wharf. Tel. 929-0202 or 441-5819

This popular battle-scarred World War II fleet submarine is part of the Historic Ships Collection of the San Francisco Maritime National Historical Park. It has been completely restored, and visitors are free to meander around inside. This is especially great for children who are interested in ships, torpedoes, and maritime war. Eight- and nine-year-old boys are particularly enchanted with the idea of living underwater in those tiny quarters for a period of time. Walk the deck and go below on this submarine, taking a step back in time to World War II. This is delightful for children because everything is on a small scale and tidily arranged, as you might expect.

Be careful of toddlers and babies too old to carry in a Snuggly. The steps from the deck that go into the main part of the sub are steep ladders, and the doors from room to room are like windows forcing you to bend down while lifting each leg. There is no way to take a stroller, and it's tough to carry a baby.

Not only is the submarine fun, but on clear days, this location affords great views of Alcatraz Island, Sausalito, and the East Bay. Try looking at Alcatraz through the powerful telescopes at the foot of the pier.

Admission: $4 adults, $3 students 12–17, $2 children 6–12 and seniors 65 and over, free for children under 6.

Open: May–Oct, daily 9am–9pm; Nov–Apr, daily 9am–6pm.

MUSEUMS

CALIFORNIA PALACE OF THE LEGION OF HONOR, Lincoln Park, 34th Avenue and Clement Street. Tel. 750-3600, or 863-3330 for recorded information.

The white architectural sculpture that rises unexpectedly from a green hilltop above the bay is San Francisco's most beautiful museum. Designed as a memorial to California's World War I casualties, the neoclassical structure is an exact replica of the Legion of Honor Palace in Paris, right down to the inscription HONNEUR ET PATRIE above the portal. Visitors enter through rows of Ionic columns and a starkly massive archway. Appropriately, the museum houses a fine collection of European painting, sculpture, and graphic art. Several masters are represented, including El Greco, Rembrandt, Rubens, Manet, Renoir, and Degas. The museum also contains a comprehensive collection of sculptures by Rodin, including a cast of **The Thinker,** located in the inner courtyard.

A well-planned variety of rotating exhibits is drawn from the museum's extensive collection of prints and drawings—the largest graphics collection in the western United States. Visiting exhibitions run the gamut from paintings and posters to jewelry and ornamental objects. The museum also arranges a series of auxiliary attractions, including classical music concerts on weekend afternoons. The museum's well-stocked gift shop and the Café Chanticleer are open during museum hours. The

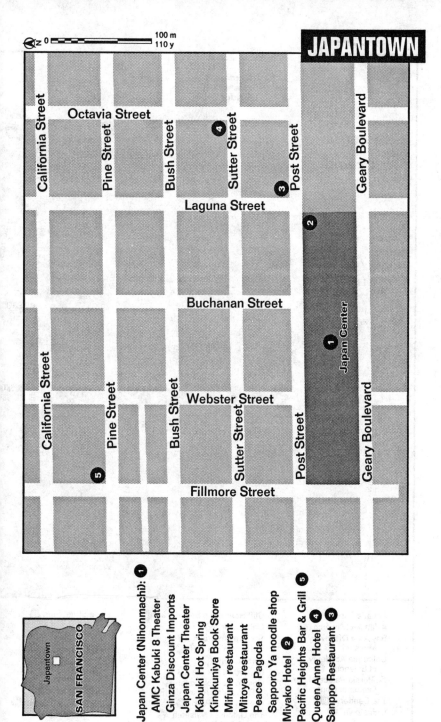

JAPANTOWN

Octavia Street
California Street
Pine Street
Bush Street
Sutter Street
Post Street
Geary Boulevard
Laguna Street
Buchanan Street
Japan Center
Webster Street
Sutter Street
Bush Street
Pine Street
California Street
Post Street
Geary Boulevard
Fillmore Street

100 m
110 y

Japantown
SAN FRANCISCO

Japan Center (Nihonmachi): ❶
  AMC Kabuki 8 Theater
  Ginza Discount Imports
  Japan Center Theater
  Kabuki Hot Spring
  Kinokuniya Book Store
  Mifune restaurant
  Mitoya restaurant
  Peace Pagoda
  Sapporo Ya noodle shop
Miyako Hotel ❷
Pacific Heights Bar & Grill ❺
Queen Anne Hotel ❹
Sanppo Restaurant ❸

N

0 | 2 km
| 1.2 mi

Pacific
Ocean

Golden
Gate
Bridge

9A

101

10

Baker St.

11

12

Lincoln Blvd

Lyon St.

Presidio Ave.

Divisadero St.

PRESIDIO

Arguello Blvd

1

Lincoln Blvd.

Lake St.

Sacramento St.

California St.

9

Lincoln Park

WESTERN

Point Lobos
Ave.

Clement St.

Geary Blvd.

Geary Blvd.

1

Masonic St.

Arguello Blvd.

43rd Ave.

36th Ave.

34th Ave.

30th Ave.

25th Ave.

Park Presidio Blvd.

10th Ave.

8th Ave.

6th Ave.

RICHMOND

HAIGHT-
ASHBURY

Fulton St.

1

Ashbury St.

J.F. Kennedy Dr.

2

Golden Gate Park

3

5

6

4

7

8

Stanyan St.

Cole St.

Martin Luther King Jr. Dr.

Lincoln Blvd.

9th Ave.

7th Ave.

Laguna Honda

Parnassus
Ave.

17th St.

Irving St.

Judah St.

25th Ave.

SUNSET

19th Ave.

Univ.
of S.F.

Claredon Ave.

Portola Ave.

Sunset Blvd.

Noriega St.

1

Twin
Peaks
Blvd.

Woodside Ave.

Great Highway

28

Taraval St.

Aquatic Park 15
Asian Art Museum 3
Bay Area Discovery
    Museum 9A
California Academy
    of Sciences 6
California Palace of the
    Legion of Honor 9
The Cannery 19
Chinatown 23

Cliff House and Seal Rocks 1
Coit Tower 22
The Exploratorium 12
Fisherman's Wharf 20
Fort Mason 13
Ghirardelli Square 17
Golden Gate National 10
    Recreation Area (GGNRA)
Golden Gate Park 2
The Guinness Museum 2
    of World Records

Hyde Street Pier: 18
    Alma
    C.A. Thayer
    Eppleton Hall
    Eureka
    Hercules
    S/V Balclutha
    Wapama
Japan Center 24
Japanese Tea Garden 4
Lazer Maze 20

SAN FRANCISCO ATTRACTIONS

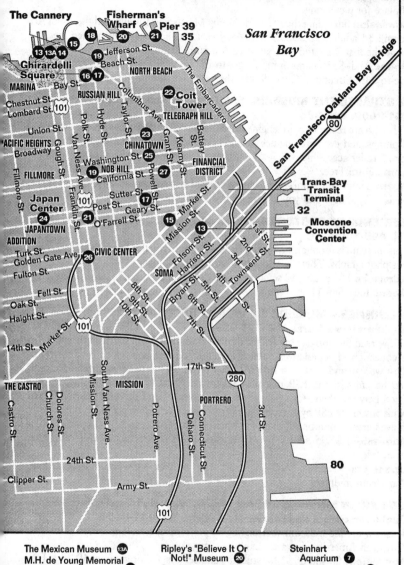

The Cannery

Fisherman's Wharf

Pier 39 35

18 20 21

15

San Francisco Bay

13 13A 14

19 Jefferson St.
Beach St.

Ghirardelli Square

16 17

MARINA Bay St.

NORTH BEACH

Chestnut St.
Lombard St. 101

RUSSIAN HILL

Columbus Ave.

The Embarcadero

22 Coit Tower

TELEGRAPH HILL

Union St.

PACIFIC HEIGHTS
Broadway

23 CHINATOWN

25

FINANCIAL DISTRICT

San Francisco-Oakland Bay Bridge

80

FILLMORE

Washington St.

19 NOB HILL
California St.

27

Trans-Bay Transit Terminal

Japan Center

24

Sutter St.
Post St.

17

Geary St.

15

Market St.

32

JAPANTOWN

21

O'Farrell St.

Mission St.

13

Moscone Convention Center

ADDITION

Turk St.
Golden Gate Ave.

26 CIVIC CENTER

Folsom St.

1st St.

Fulton St.

SOMA

Harrison St.

2nd

Fell St.

8th St.

Bryant St.

3rd

Oak St.

9th St.

5th St.

Townsend St.

Haight St.

10th St.

6th St.

14th St.

Market St.

7th St.

101

17th St.

South Van Ness Ave.
Mission St.

280

THE CASTRO

MISSION

PORTRERO

3rd St.

Castro St.

Dolores St.
Church St.

Potrero Ave.

Connecticut St.
Deharo St.

24th St.

80

Clipper St.

Army St.

101

Attractions List

The Mexican Museum 13A
M.H. de Young Memorial Morrison Planetarium 8
National Maritime Museum 15
Palace of Fine Arts 11
Pier 39: 21
  Atari Expo
  Music Tracks
  S.F. Experience
  Underwater World

Ripley's "Believe It Or Not!" Museum 20
San Francisco Cable-Car Barn Museum 25
San Francisco Craft and Folk Art Museum 14
San Francisco Museum of Modern Art 26
San Francisco Zoological Gardens & Children's Zoo 28

Steinhart Aquarium 7
U.S.S. Pampanito 20
Wax Museum 20
Wells Fargo History Museum 27

surrounding grounds sport a magnificent view of the Golden Gate Bridge and are a good place for picnicking.

Admission (including the M. H. de Young Memorial Museum and the Asian Art Museum): $4 adults, $2 seniors over 65, free for children 18 and under; free for everyone the first Wed and first Sat of each month 10am–noon.

Open: Wed–Sun 10am–5pm. To get to the museum, take bus 38 from Union Square to 33rd Street and Geary Street; then transfer to bus 18 into Lincoln Park.

FIRE DEPARTMENT MUSEUM, 655 Presidio Ave. at Bush Street. Tel. 861-8000, ext. 365.

Kids who are really into fire engines love this museum. They can see old uniforms, hand pumps, and even fire engines (the firehouse is next door). Good for children 6 and up. Stroller accessible.

Admission: Free.

Open: Thurs–Sun 1pm–4pm, but call ahead because hours vary. To get there, take bus 1, 2, 3, or 4 and you'll have a one-block walk.

THE FRIENDS OF PHOTOGRAPHY, Ansel Adams Center, 250 Fourth St. Tel. 495-7000.

This museum is for photography lovers. One of the five galleries is devoted to Ansel Adams photographs. There is also a bookstore and a library.

Admission: $3 adults, $2 seniors and children 12–17; children under 12 are free.

Open: Tues–Sun 11am–6pm.

THE GUINNESS MUSEUM OF WORLD RECORDS, 235 Jefferson St. (Fisherman's Wharf). Tel. 771-9890.

You've read the books, now see the displays! Kids over 9 will particularly enjoy this large collection of superlatives opened in 1980. See the shoes worn by the world's smallest woman and the tallest man. Although Andrew (when he was age 7) was a bit young, he enjoyed the ESP machine, where two people face each other with a partition between them. One person chooses a symbol and the other person has to show his powers of ESP by guessing the correct one. As children get older, they marvel at an even greater number of exhibits. There is stroller-access.

Admission: $5.95 adults, $4.75 students, $4.95 seniors, $2.75 children 5–12; under 5, free.

Open: Daily summer 9am–midnight; rest of year Sun–Thurs 10am–10pm; Fri–Sat 10am–midnight.

THE MEXICAN MUSEUM OF SAN FRANCISCO, Building D, Fort Mason, Buchanan Street and Marina Boulevard. Tel. 441-0404.

This is a unique museum that highlights pre-Hispanic, colonial, folk, Mexican, and Mexican-American fine arts. Exhibits change often.

Admission: $2 adults, $1 for students and seniors, children under 10, free. Free admission for all first Wed of month.

Open: Wed–Sun noon–5pm; first Wed of month noon–8pm.

THE OLD MINT, 88 5th St. at Mission Street. Tel. 744-6830.

This is a great little museum to learn about the turn of the century, the Gold Rush, and the San Francisco earthquake. This building was built in 1870 and survived the Earthquake and fire. There is a dramatic documentary film of the building and why this building survived. You'll find restored rooms, including a miner's cabin, and exciting displays of gold bullion and gold coins. The vaults are used as exhibit space, one of which has a stack of $5 million in gold bars.

Admission: Free.

Open: Mon–Fri 10am–4pm; closed holidays. The mint is near the Powell Street BART Station, so you can take any cable car.

RANDALL (CHILDREN'S) MUSEUM, 199 Museum Way, near Buena Vista Park. Tel. 554-9600.

This museum has ravens, hawks, raccoons, opossum, lizards, and snakes that the kids can interact with and a mineral exhibit that the children can handle. There is also a working seismograph. During the summer there are nature movies and Walt Disney films for a small additional charge. The museum also offers special workshops on weekends and during summer. Call ahead for information about workshop times and fees.

Admission: Free.

Open: Mon–Fri 10am–5pm during summer; Tues–Sat 10am–5pm during the school year. To get here, take bus 37 ("Corbett") that runs on Roosevelt Way.

RIPLEY'S "BELIEVE IT OR NOT!" MUSEUM, 175 Jefferson St., Fisherman's Wharf. Tel. 771-6188.

Not only did the kids like it, but because they couldn't believe many of the 2,000-plus exhibits, they begged us to return. Not surprisingly, when Andrew was seven, he was entranced by the child who grew a beard at the age of four and died of "old age" when he was seven! (That was food for thought for many hours.) The two-headed animals were also of interest.

Admission: $6.95 adults, $5.25 teens 13–17 and seniors over 60; $3.75 children 5–12, free for children under 5.

Open: Sun–Thurs 10am–10pm and Fri–Sat 10am–midnight.

SAN FRANCISCO CABLE-CAR BARN MUSEUM, Washington and Mason Streets. Tel. 474-1887.

Of course your children wonder how the cable cars work; everyone does, and this museum explains it all to you. Yes, this is a museum, but the Cable-Car Barn is no stuffed shirt. It's the living powerhouse, repair shop, and storage place of the cable-car system and is in full workaday operation. Built for the Ferries & Cliff House Railway in 1887, the building underwent an $18-million reconstruction to restore its original gaslight look, install a spectator's gallery, and add a museum of San Francisco transit history. The exposed machinery, which pulls the cables under San Francisco's streets, will fascinate the kids.

You can stand in the mezzanine gallery and watch the massive groaning and vibrating winders as they thread the cable that hauls the cars through a huge figure-8 and back into the system via slack-absorbing tension wheels. Don't miss taking the kids through the room where you can see the cables operating underground.

On display here is one of the first grip cars developed by Andrew S. Hallidie and operated for the first time on Clay Street on August 2, 1873. Other displays include an antique grip car and trailer that operated on Pacific Avenue until 1929 and dozens of exact-scale models of cars used on the various city lines. There's also a shop where you can buy a variety of cable-car gifts.

Admission: Free.

Open: Apr–Oct, daily 10am–6pm; Nov–Mar, daily 10am–5pm. Closed Christmas, New Year's, and Thanksgiving Day. Take any of the cable cars, all of which pass within three blocks. Powell-Mason and Powell-Hyde cable cars stop within one block, California Street cable cars are within three blocks. Or take bus 1, 30, or 83; all pass within two blocks.

SAN FRANCISCO CRAFT AND FOLK ART MUSEUM, Landmark Building A, Fort Mason. Tel. 775-0990.

Contemporary and traditional crafts and American folk art are displayed here in this museum at Fort Mason.

Admission: $1.

Open: Tues–Fri and Sun 11am–5pm, Sat 10am–5pm; closed Mon.

SAN FRANCISCO MARITIME NATIONAL HISTORICAL PARK, NATIONAL MARITIME MUSEUM, Aquatic Park at the foot of Polk Street, Fisherman's Wharf. Tel. 556-3002.

This is an extremely fine museum treat for nautical enthusiasts. It features a changing collection of ships models, all kinds of seafaring memorabilia, and special children's programs.

Admission: Free.

Open: Daily 10am–5pm. To get there, take the Powell-Hyde cable car to Victorian Park or take bus 19, 30, 32, 39, 42, 47, or 49.

SAN FRANCISCO MUSEUM OF MODERN ART, 401 Van Ness Ave., at McAllister Street (Civic Center). Tel. 863-8800.

Opened in 1935, the Museum of Modern Art was the first on the West Coast to be devoted solely to 20th-century art. International in scope, the permanent collection consists of more than 4,000 paintings, sculptures, and works on paper, as well as a selection of objects relating to architecture, design, and the media arts. The museum is strong on American abstract expressionism and other major schools, rotating displays of works by Clyfford Still, Jackson Pollock, Mark Rothko, and Willem de Kooning, among others. It also has a strong representation of German expressionism, fauvism, Mexican painting, and local art. It stands out as one of the first major galleries to recognize photography as a serious art form. The collection of approximately 8,000 photographs includes works by Alfred Stieglitz, Ansel Adams, and Edward Weston, as well as good examples of 1920s German avant-garde and 1930s European surrealist photographers. We often see many teens enjoying the exhibits.

Docent tours are offered daily at 1:15pm and on Thursday at 7:15 and 7:45pm. In addition, the museum regularly organizes special artistic events, lectures, concerts, dance performances, poetry readings, conceptual-art events, and special activities for children. Phone for current details.

Admission: $4 adults, $2 students 13–18 and seniors, free for children 12 and under; half price for everyone Thurs 5–9pm, and free for everyone the first Tues of each month.

Open: Tues–Wed and Fri 10am–5pm, Thurs 10am–9pm, Sat–Sun 11am–5pm. **Closed:** Hols. Bus 5, 47, or 49 will get you there. **MUNI Metro** lines stop at Van Ness Avenue, a five-block walk.

WAX MUSEUM, 145 Jefferson St., Fisherman's Wharf. Tel. 885-4975.

Conceived and executed in the Madame Tussaud mold, San Francisco's wax museum features over 250 eerily lifelike figures of the rich and famous. The "museum" donates the lion's share of its space to images of modern superstars like singer Michael Jackson and political figures like President George Bush. Tableaux include "Royalty," "Great Humanitarians," "Wickedest Ladies," "World Religions," and "Feared Leaders," the last including Fidel Castro, Nikita Khrushchev, Benito Mussolini, and Adolf Hitler. The Chamber of Horrors—which features Dracula, Frankenstein, and a werewolf, along with bloody victims hanging from meathooks—is the stuff tourist traps are made of. It may also scare sensitive younger children—we bypass the Chamber of Horrors and head left to the Gallery of Stars.

Admission: $8.50 adults, $6.50 seniors over 60, $3.95 children 6–12, free for children under 6.

Open: Summer, Sun–Thurs 9am–11pm, Fri–Sat 9am–midnight; winter, Sun–Thurs 9am–10pm, Fri–Sat 9am–11pm.

THE HAUNTED GOLD MINE, 113 Jefferson St. (Fisherman's Wharf). Tel. 885-4975.

Under the same ownership as the Wax Museum, the Haunted Gold Mine is a fun house complete with mazes, a hall of mirrors, spatial-disorientation tricks, wind tunnels, and animated ghouls. Even very young children will probably not find it too scary, but it's fun.

Admission: $4.95 adults, $3.45 seniors, $2.25 children 6–12, free for children under 6.

Open: Summer, Sun–Thurs 9am–11pm, Fri–Sat 9am–midnight; winter, Sun–Thurs 9am–10pm, Fri–Sat 9am–11pm.

LAZER MAZE, 107 Jefferson St. (Fisherman's Wharf). Tel. 885-4836.

Also under the same ownership as the Wax Museum, the Lazer Maze is a walk-in video game that consists of four chambers. In each chamber, there are robots that light up. With the purchase of a ticket, the customer gets a lazer gun and wanders through the maze, trying to zap the robots between the eyes. There is no minimum age here, but your kids have to be able to handle the gun and know what's going on. (The operators say they get children as young as 6; we suggest 10 or 11 years old.) Each game is about three to four minutes long.

Admission: $3 each play.

Open: Summer, daily 9am–midnight; winter, Sun–Thurs 10am–11pm, Fri–Sat 10am–midnight.

WELLS FARGO HISTORY MUSEUM, 420 Montgomery St., at California Street. Tel. 396-2619.

Wells Fargo, one of California's largest banks, got its start in the Wild West. Its history museum, at the bank's head office, houses hundreds of genuine relics—pistols, photographs, early banking articles, posters, and mining equipment—from the company's whip and six-shooter days.

In the center of the main room stands a genuine Concord stagecoach, probably the most celebrated vehicle in American history. This was the 2,500-pound buggy that opened the West as surely as the Winchester and the iron horse. It's hard to believe that it could hold nine passengers "passing comfortably"—with six more perched on the roof. That's not counting the "knight of the whip," who drove the six-horse team, and the essential "shotgun rider" beside him. Kids love to climb on the authentic Wells Fargo Overland Stage Coach and pretend they're back in the Old West.

Elizabeth learned how to work the telegraph and pretend she knew how to drive a team of horses. Both you and the kids will love this fun exhibit.

Admission: Free.

Open: Mon–Fri 9am–5pm. **Closed:** Bank hols. To get there, take the MUNI metro to Montgomery Street or any bus that goes to Market Street.

3. FOR KIDS WITH SPECIAL INTERESTS

For details about the following special-interest sightseeing, see sections "Kids' Top 10 Attractions" and "More Attractions" in this chapter. You may also find details in Chapter 9, "Easy Excursions."

Art & Architecture
Asian Art Museum
Bay Area Discovery Museum
California Palace of the Legion of Honor
M.H. de Young Memorial Museum
San Francisco Museum of Modern Art

Boats & Ships
Hyde Street Pier
Allen Knight Maritime Museum (Monterey)
San Francisco National Maritime Museum
U.S.S. *Pampanito*

History & Culture
Alcatraz
Carmel Mission (Carmel)
Chinese Culture Center
Chinese Historical Society
Fire Department Museum
Mexican Museum of San Francisco
Monterey State Historic Park (Monterey)
The Old Mint
Roaring Camp & Big Trees Narrow-Gauge Railroad (Santa Cruz)
Rosicrucian Egyptian Museum and Planetarium (San Jose)
San Francisco Cable Car Museum
Wells Fargo History Museum

Photography
Bay Area Discovery Museum
The Friends of Photography

Science & Technology
Bay Area Discovery Museum
California Academy of Sciences

California Marine Mammal Center (Marin Headlands—see below, "Letting off Steam")
Children's Discovery Museum of San Jose (San Jose)
The Exploratorium
Lawrence Hall of Science (Berkeley)
Monterey Bay Aquarium (Monterey Bay)
National Audubon Society's Richardson Bay Audubon Center (Tiburon)
Point Lobos State Reserve (Carmel)
Randall Children's Museum
San Jose Historical Museum (San Jose)
Santa Cruz City Museum of Natural History (Santa Cruz)

4. LETTING OFF STEAM

Museums and theme parks can be a lot of fun, but after a while your kids will probably feel confined and get antsy. With its warm climate and loads of sunshine, San Francisco offers many opportunities to take them outdoors to romp around and generally let off steam. Since you're near the Pacific, we'll begin this section with activities on or near the ocean ("The Beaches," "Whale Watching" and "Boat Cruises" and then move on to inland possibilities ("Bicycling," "Parks," and "Camping & Hiking").

THE BEACHES

Although the area is surrounded by an enticing seashore, San Francisco has only two swimming beaches that we recommend. **Aquatic Park** offers lagoon swimming and fishing. There are rest rooms and showers, and lifeguards from mid-April to mid-October. **China Beach** is a small sandy area that has lifeguards during the summer. There are showers and rest rooms available here. The beach is open 7am to dusk.

Ocean Beach, near the Cliff House and Seal Rocks, is a three-mile shoreline where you'll get lots of wind and perhaps fog. Although it's lovely to look at, the water is dangerous. **Baker Beach** is another pretty little beach just west of the Presidio—pretty to look at, but not to swim at.

BOAT CRUISES

One of the best ways to look at San Francisco is from a boat bobbing on the bay. There are several cruises to choose from, many of which start from Fisherman's Wharf. Two companies are:

RED AND WHITE FLEET, Pier 41, Fisherman's Wharf. Tel. 546-BOAT, or toll free 800/229-2784 in California.

The city's largest boat-tour operator offers more than half a dozen itineraries on the bay. The fleet's primary ships are two-toned double- and triple-deckers, capable of holding 150 to 500 passengers. You can't miss the observation-tower ticket booth, located next to the Franciscan Restaurant and Pier 41.

The **San Francisco Bay Cruise** is a 45-minute historical cruise by the Golden

Gate Bridge, Sausalito, and Alcatraz Island. Tours cost $14 for adults, $10 for juniors 12 to 18 and seniors 55 and older, $7 for children 5 to 11. They depart from Pier 41 and Pier 43½ daily, every 15 minutes from 10:45am to 3:45pm.

Alcatraz II, 'Round the Rock, is narrated by Frank Heaney, a former Alcatraz prison guard, who recounts anecdotes about Al Capone, "Machine Gun" Kelly, and the Birdman of Alcatraz. From Memorial Day through Labor Day there are five departures Wednesday through Sunday between 11:15am and 3:45pm; the rest of the year there are only a few tours per week. Call for schedule information. Tickets cost $9 for adults, $8.50 for seniors, $6.50 for kids 5 to 11.

The summer **Champagne Cruise** is a 1-hour sail past the city's most famous sights. The romantic atmosphere is complimented by light hors d'oeuvres, soft music, and a glass of champagne. Boats depart Thursday through Monday at 5:30pm. Adult tickets cost $19.

BLUE AND GOLD FLEET, Pier 39, Fisherman's Wharf. Tel. 781-7890

Blue and Gold's **Bay Cruise** tours the bay year round in a sleek 400-passenger sightseeing boat, complete with food-and-beverage facilities. The fully narrated 1¼-hour cruise passes beneath the Golden Gate Bridge and the Bay Bridge, and comes within yards of Alcatraz Island. Frequent daily departures from Pier 39's West Marina begin at 10am during summer and 11am in winter. Tickets cost $14 for adults, $7 for juniors 5 to 18 and seniors over 55; children under 5 sail free.

WHALE WATCHING

There are whale-watching excursions (seasonal) offered by the following groups: **Oceanic Society Expedition** at Fort Mason Center (tel. 415/441-1106); **San Francisco Zoological Society,** Sloat Boulevard and the Great Highway (tel. 415/753-7080); and **Princess Monterey Cruises,** in Monterey (tel. 408/372-2628).

BICYCLING

Two city-designated bike routes are maintained by the Recreation and Parks Department. One tours 7½ miles through Golden Gate Park to Lake Merced, perfect for trips with kids; the other traverses the city, starting in the south, and follows a route over the Golden Gate Bridge. These routes are not dedicated to bicyclists, and care must be taken to avoid cars. Helmets are recommended. A bike map is available from the San Francisco Visitor Information Center, at Powell Street and Mason Street, and from bicycle shops all around town.

PARK CYCLERY, 1865 Haight St. Tel. 221-3777.

This is just one of many shops in the Haight Street/Stanyan Street area that rent bikes to day trippers. Located next to Golden Gate Park, the Cyclery rents both mountain bikes and 10-speeds, along with helmets, locks, and accessories. The charge is $4 per hour, and it's open daily from 9:30am to 5:30pm.

LINCOLN CYCLERY, 772 Stanyan St. Tel. 221-2415.

This shop rents three-speed bikes at $2 per hour, 10-speed bikes $3. They also have bicycles for children at $2 per hour. They'll rent you a bike with a toddler carrier only if you have your own helmet. They're open Mon and Wed–Sat 9am–5pm, Sun 11:30am–5pm; closed Tues.

CAMPING & HIKING

CAMPING

There is wonderful camping in the **Golden Gate National Recreation Area.** For information on camping in the **Marin Headlands,** in the **Muir Woods/Mt. Tamalpais** area, and points farther north, contact the Park Office (tel. 331-1540) or ask for a copy of the **Golden Gate National Recreation Area Park Guide.** The Sierra Club (tel. 923-5660) is another good source of information for both hiking and camping. You can also try **Samuel Taylor State Park** (tel. 488-9897), **Mt. Tamalpais State Park** (tel. 398-2078), **China Camp State Park** (tel. 456-0766), or **Half Moon Bay State Park** (tel. 726-6238).

HIKING

For great hiking, you might want to start in the cliffs just west of Sausalito in the **Marin Headlands.** Some of the cliffs are sandstone, and create a dramatic setting with the ocean below. The Marin Headlands Visitor Center (tel. 331-1540) is located in Fort Cronkhite and is open 8:30am to 4:30pm daily. A fine one-mile trail called **Lagoon Loop** is located behind the Visitor Center.

The Visitor Center offers guided family walks in which children learn about the wildlife and habitat of the region. Special art programs for children are also offered at times. Call for information.

Although not really hiking, but located in the same area is the **California Marine Mammal Center** (tel. 331-7325) in the Marin Headlands. It is dedicated to rescuing and treating orphaned and injured sea mammals. When they have recovered, the animals are released in the wild. Children enjoy a visit to the center, where they can see recovering seals, sea lions, and otters and talk with animal caretakers who gladly share their expertise and love of the animals with the kids.

Educational materials instruct children about all the kinds of sea mammals on the West Coast. During the weekends, there are tours of the area. For special educational programs, call 331-0161. There is no charge for admission and the center is open daily 10am–4pm.

In the center of this area is **Rodeo Valley,** a beautiful place that opens into the beach and a lagoon. There is good hiking and a picnic area near the lagoon. To reach Rodeo Valley, heading north on U.S. 101, cross the Golden Gate Bridge and take the first exit after the bridge (Alexander Avenue). As you exit, stay to your left and go back under U.S. 101. Just before getting back on U.S. 101 southbound, there is a road to your right (uphill) with signs announcing the entrance to the GGNRA. Take this road (Conzelman Road) uphill until it forks. At the fork stay to your right (McCullough Road). Go down McCullough all the way to the bottom, then take a left on Bunker Road and follow it toward Rodeo Lagoon and Rodeo Beach (about two miles.)

PARKS

In addition to Golden Gate Park, San Francisco boasts more than 2,000 additional acres of city park, most of which are perfect for family outings and picnicking. For general information about parks, call San Francisco Recreation and Parks at 666-7200.

Alta Plaza, at Clay and Scott Streets, is a gorgeous, quiet little park. You get fabulous views of the bay and Marin County. A nice little park to walk through.

Aquatic Park, near Fisherman's Wharf, across from the Hyde Street Pier, is where our kids love to romp on the grass, an area we also love because of the bayside scenery. The lagoon offers a sand beach and swimming too. (Rest rooms are located in the park.)

Huntington Park is a few blocks from Union Square on top of Nob Hill. There is children's play equipment here, and it is a spectacularly beautiful area.

Marina Green, along the Marina, of course, has acres for running, Frisbee throwing, and kite flying. It is flat and beautiful, but can get very windy and cold. (This is part of the Golden Gate Promenade.)

Don't forget **Charles Lee Tilden Regional Park** in Berkeley (tel. 510/843-2137). It has wonderful programs.

Marin Headlands, across the Golden Gate Bridge, is administered by the Golden Gate National Recreation Area. The headland's 70,000 acres encompass ocean beaches, wildlife sanctuaries, and more than 100 miles of trails. Protected by a 1972 act of Congress, the rolling hills of this expansive park start just across the Golden Gate Bridge, where an excellent view can be had of the entire city.

Justin Herman Plaza, at the foot of Market Street, is more of a landscaped concrete plaza than a park. This square in the Financial District is popular with office workers at lunchtime. At its center is Vaillancourt Fountain, a free-form water sculpture that was designed to be walked through and is fun for kids. The surrounding sidewalks are dotted with cafés and stalls selling leather goods, jewelry, pottery, paintings, and sculpture. The plaza is particularly packed on sunny weekday afternoons.

Lincoln Park, Clement Street and 34th Avenue, is a favorite of many. It is a 270-acre green on the northeastern side of the city, home to the California Palace of the Legion of Honor as well as a scenic 18-hole municipal golf course. But the best thing about this park are the 200-foot cliffs that overlook the Golden Gate Bridge and San Francisco Bay.

The Presidio of San Francisco, Lombard and Lyon Streets, is headquarters for the U.S. Sixth Army. It is one of the biggest boons to locals and visitors, for both biking and hiking. Much of the 15,000-acre park is extremely hilly and heavily wooded.

And, of course, there's always **Golden Gate Park** (for a full description, see "Kids' Top 10 Attractions" above). Jogging trails and nature trails are located throughout the park.

5. PERFECT FOR STROLLING

If your young children are like ours, they aren't really up to a formal "walking tour"—they have either too much energy (and want to run loose) or too little (and have to be pushed in a stroller or carried), or they lose interest too rapidly to enjoy the tour. Thus the following are set up as strolls, sort of "guided walks," around some of San Francisco's more interesting neighborhoods. If you're in one of these areas, these strolls will cover the highlights at a gentle pace. You can pick one (or more) that suit your family's itinerary and interests.

GOLDEN GATE BRIDGE

The year 1992 marks the 55th birthday of what is possibly the most beautiful—certainly the most photographed—bridge in the world. Often half-veiled by the city's trademark rolling fog, San Francisco's Golden Gate spans tidal currents, ocean waves, and battering winds to connect the "City by the Bay" with the "Redwood Empire" to the north.

A walk across **Golden Gate Bridge** is an outing you'll never forget. On the 1.7-mile bridge, you'll be able to see the area around Fisherman's Wharf and the skyline, as well as Angel Island and Alcatraz. Looking north, you can see Marin County and much of the Golden Gate National Recreation Area. Looking back to the city, you'll see incredibly beautiful vistas at the north edge of the bridge.

Be sure to bundle up because it's always windy and often very cold on the bridge. Be sure to bring layers of clothing—the best way to keep warm. We love to take this walk on overcast, drizzly days because it seems more scenic. This is a good time to bring your slickers, if you have them, because the rain and wind make an umbrella useless.

CHINATOWN

This is another perfect place for a family stroll. In fact, the best way to see this city within a city is to take some time to walk it. (*Leave your car at the hotel* and take public transportation or taxis to this area because the two parking lots are likely to be filled.)

Walk down Grant Street or Stockton Street and plan to take some time just getting from one corner to another. Sample the authentic Chinese markets. Look into some of the herb shops. Be sure your walk includes the **Bank of Canton** at the corner of Grant Avenue and Washington Street. Designed like a pagoda, it is a cultural treat for kids—even if it's not the real thing. Take your time here. Explore the area and stop for a dim sum breakfast or Chinese lunch.

Walking tours of the area are very popular. For more information, see the "Organized Tours" section, which follows.

FISHERMAN'S WHARF

This is a perfect place to spend at least a half or a full day. Start at Pier 39 and work your way toward Ghirardelli Square. Be sure to allow lots of time. (For more information, see Section 1 in this chapter.)

RICHMOND DISTRICT/CLEMENT STREET

Another of our favorite places to walk is **Clement Street** in the **Richmond District.** Clement Street is known for the many shops, restaurants, and diverse cultural influences that characterize it. From Arguello Boulevard (the north or lower end of Clement Street) all the way to 15th Avenue, you will find some of the best toy stores, new and used bookstores, antiques shops, produce markets, and restaurants anywhere in San Francisco. In just the first 10 blocks (Arguello to 10th Avenue) on

Clement, there are Chinese, Indonesian, Vietnamese, Thai, Persian, Italian, and French restaurants. The neighborhood is very family-oriented—children are everywhere on the streets, in the stores, and in most restaurants throughout early evening. The parking situation is atrocious, but traffic is not as heavy and fast as downtown.

GOLDEN GATE PARK

Golden Gate Park is an easy six blocks east of Clement Street. Anyone who is hungry or still restless after a day there should come for a stroll here. Beware of the daytime weather, though. Even when it's warm and sunny elsewhere, it can be cooler and foggy in the park. (At night, everywhere in San Francisco is chilly.) For more about the park, see "Kids' Top 10 Attractions," above.

6. ORGANIZED TOURS

Organized tours are always "iffy" with children, so here are some of the ones we think you'll like the best.

WOK WIZ CHINATOWN WALKING TOURS, P.O. Box 1583, Pacifica, CA 94044. Tel. 415/355-9657.

San Francisco's Chinatown is always fascinating, but for many tourists with limited time it's hard to know where to search out the "nontouristy" shops, restaurants, and historical spots in this magnificent microcosm of Chinese culture. Founded by author, TV personality, cooking instructor, and restaurant critic Shirley Fong-Torres, Wok Wiz tours take you and older children into nooks and crannies not usually seen by tourists. Each of her guides is Chinese, speaks fluent Cantonese or Mandarin, and is intimately acquainted with all of Chinatown's backways, alleys, and small enterprises, which are generally known only to those who live here. You'll learn about dim sum (a "delight of the heart") and the Chinese tea ceremony; meet a Chinese herbalist; stop at a pastry shop to watch rice noodles being made (noodles and other pasta forms originated in China, not Italy); watch the famous Chinese artist Y. K. Lau do his delicate brush painting; learn about jook, a traditional Chinese breakfast; stop in at a fortune-cookie factory; and visit a Chinese produce market and learn about the very unusual vegetables you may never identify at lunch or dinner.

All in all, you'll learn more about Chinatown than you'll ever remember. And you'll also learn enough to return on your own because you'll know that there's more to Chinatown than just the Grant Avenue gift shops.

Wok Wiz Chinatown Walking Tours are conducted daily from 10am to 1:30pm. The tour begins in the lobby of the Chinatown Holiday Inn at 750 Kearny Street (between Washington Street and Clay Street). It's an easy walk, fun and fascinating, and you and your older kids are bound to make new friends. Groups are generally held to a maximum of 12, and reservations are essential. The cost is $33 per person and includes a complete lunch. Reservations are essential.

GREY LINE, Trans-Bay Terminal, First and Mission streets. Tel. 558-7300, or toll free 800/826-0202.

San Francisco's largest bus-tour operator offers several itineraries on a daily basis, suitable for families with kids ages 5 and up. There is a free pickup and return service between centrally located hotels and departure locations. Call for reservations.

The 1-hour **Motorized Cable Car Tour** continuously loops around the city's downtown, passing Union Square, Nob Hill, Chinatown, North Beach, and Fisherman's Wharf. Passengers ride aboard an authentic cable car–cum–bus. You can get off the bus at either Union Square or the Cannery and board again later. Tickets cost $8 for adults, $4 for children 5 to 11. Buses depart from Union Square, at the corner of Powell Street and Geary Street; or from the Cannery, by Fisherman's Wharf, at Jefferson Street and Leavenworth Street.

The company's 3½-hour **Deluxe City Tour** is a panoramic ride past the city's major sights. You pass by the Opera House, visit Golden Gate Park, and cross the Golden Gate Bridge for the magnificent view from Vista Point (see Section 1, "Kids' Top 10 Attractions," above). Stops include Mission Dolores, the Japanese Tea Garden, and Cliff House. Most—but not all—tours are led by a guide. During winter, some tours are made with taped commentary. Tours cost $23.50 for adults, $11.75 for children 5 to 11. Buses depart from the Trans-Bay Terminal, at First Street and Mission Street, daily at 9, 10, and 11am and 1:30 and 2:30pm.

OTHER TOUR SUGGESTIONS

The **Friends of Recreation and Parks,** Golden Gate Park (tel. 221-1311), lead free guided walking tours of the park on Saturdays and Sundays at 11am, 2pm, and 3pm, from May to October. These walks include the "Strawberry Hill Tour" (Huntington Falls, Stow Lake, the Chinese Pavilion, and a walk up to the top of Strawberry Hill); the "East End Tour" (Conservatory Valley, Children's Playground, Hippie Hill, the Rhododendron Garden, and the Music Concourse); the "Japanese Tea Garden Tour" (inside the main Japanese Tea Garden gate, it covers the history and design of the Japanese Tea Garden); and "Special-Interest Tours" (such as bicycle tours or statue tours). Call for complete details.

City Guides (tel. 557-4266) offers a wide variety of guided walking tours. Tours include the Gold Rush City Tour, City Hall, Fire Department Museum, North Beach, Japantown, Presidio, Coit Tower, and various mansions and Victorian homes in the city.

CHAPTER 5

THEIR SHOPPING LIST

We know some children who love San Francisco because of the shopping! Our own kids prefer the sightseeing, the restaurants, and the activities, but the shopping is superb also, and if you have little shoppers, they'll get their fill.

Although this family guide focuses on stores that in one way or another relate to your children's interests or needs, you can spend days in San Francisco doing little more than shopping.

GREAT SHOPPING AREAS   San Francisco has many shopping areas that appeal to kids—and parents as well—but the following are among the best:

Union Square   Union Square is the real heartbeat of the city's downtown shopping district. Bordered by Geary Street, Powell Street, Post Street, and Stockton Street (with surrounding blocks that offer good shopping as well), Union Square has been compared to New York's Fifth Avenue. You'll find it all here—from fashionable department stores to specialty shops with kid appeal to some of the most respected names in international retailing.

Chinatown   In many ways, Chinatown is the antithesis of Union Square, selling an exceptional variety of cheap goods, T-shirts, knockoffs, and innumerable tourist-oriented trinkets. The best shops in this crowded area are the colorful bazaars, crammed with an eclectic assortment of unrelated objects, from postcards and water pipes to Chinese tableware and plastic toys. Grant Avenue is the area's main thoroughfare, and side streets between Bush Street and Columbus Avenue are full of restaurants, markets, and interesting shops. Walking is best, since traffic through this area is slow and parking is next to impossible. A short sightseeing-cum-shopping stroll should appeal to most kids. Most of the stores in Chinatown are open daily from 10am to 10pm.

Union Street   Real San Franciscans are those who know the difference between Union *Square* and Union *Street*. Although they are similarly named, these two shopping areas are located far away from one another. The Cow Hollow section of this trendy street, between Van Ness Avenue and Steiner Street, is an "in" stretch for antiques, handcrafts, hip fashions, and deluxe glassware. A stroll along Union Street, poking through the many boutiques and highly original stores, makes for a very pleasant afternoon for teenagers and parents. The area is serviced by bus lines 41 and 45.

Haight Street   The neighborhood known as Haight-Ashbury is most famous as a spawning ground for hippies in the 1960s. Although there are no longer so many Flower Children here, the Haight still has an active street scene and is home to a good number of writers and musicians as well as younger, upwardly mobile types. The six blocks of upper Haight Street, between Central Avenue and Stanyan Street, is a good place in the city to shop for trendy street styles for preteens and teens (and adults) from Europe and America. Along this thoroughfare is a healthy mix of boutiques, secondhand shops, and inexpensive restaurants. Bus lines 7, 66, 71, and 73 run the length of Haight Street. MUNI metro line N stops at Waller Street and Cole Street.

Fisherman's Wharf and Environs   The nonstop strip of waterfront malls that runs along Jefferson Street includes hundreds of shops, restaurants, and attractions. Ghirardelli Square, Pier 39, the Cannery, and the Anchorage are all outlined under "Shopping Centers & Complexes," below.

HOURS, TAXES & SHIPPING   Store **hours** are generally Monday through Saturday from 10am to 6pm and on Sunday from noon to 5pm. Most department stores stay open later, as do shops around Fisherman's Wharf—the most heavily touristed area.

   Sales tax in San Francisco is 7¼% added on at the register for all goods and services purchased.

   Shipping: Most of the city's shops can wrap your purchase and ship it anywhere in the world via United Parcel Service (UPS). If they can't, you can send it yourself, either through UPS (tel. 952-5200) or through the U.S. mail. If you don't feel like finding a box and waiting in line, visit **Boxworks,** 2106 Chestnut St. (tel. 921-1964). This full-service packing, wrapping, and shipping store will do all the work for you.

BOOKS

A CLEAN, WELL-LIGHTED PLACE FOR BOOKS, 601 Van Ness Ave., at Turk and Golden Gate (Civic Center). Tel. 441-6670.

   There are over 60,000 titles crammed into this store, where children routinely plop themselves down at a table in the kid's section to read while grownups browse among the adult sections of books, magazines, and newspapers. Tables are set up all over the store and people are encouraged to browse or to stay and read. The staff is helpful and pleasant to children. Book signings and readings are held for adults, and on occasion for children. Open Monday through Thursday from 10am to 11pm and on Friday and Saturday until midnight.

   There's another branch at 2417 Larkspur Landing Circle in Larkspur in Marin County (tel. 461-0171). This branch features regular story hours for children on Sunday. Call for details.

B. DALTON BOOKSELLER, 200 Kearny St. at Sutter Street, Tel. 956-2850.

   This chain stocks over 25,000 titles, including computer and travel books, and they have a fine children's section. Open Monday through Friday from 9am to 6pm and on Saturday from 10am to 5pm.

   There's another location at 2 Embarcadero Center, street level (tel. 982-4278).

BRENTANO'S, Ghirardelli Square, first floor of the Mustard Building, Tel. 474-8328.

   A large line of travel books (domestic and international) and a very large selection of books on San Francisco are featured, as are some children's books. Open Monday through Saturday from 10am to 9:30pm and on Sunday from 10am to 6pm.

   Another branch is located downtown at the San Francisco Shopping Centre at 5th and Market streets (tel. 543-0933).

CHARLOTTE'S WEB CHILDREN'S BOOKSTORE, 1207-F Bridgeway, Sausalito. Tel. 332-2244.

Set in the theme of *Charlotte's Web,* the inside of this shop looks like the inside of a barn. Wilbur the pig is here, and a goose and sheep, too. This children's bookstore has a huge selection of picture books (including hard-to-find ones), as well as children's videos and cassettes. There is a tremendous selection of folk and fairy tales and some foreign-language books as well. The owner is a teacher who did his postgraduate work in education and creative writing and consequently takes a shining to education books.

Regularly scheduled story hours take place on Saturday at 10:30am.

CITY LIGHTS BOOK STORE AND PUBLISHERS, 261 Columbus Ave. at Broadway. Tel. 362-8193.

You can't get much more famous than this publisher/bookstore. Founded in 1953 by beat-generation poet Lawrence Ferlinghetti, the trivia experts tell us that City Lights was the first paperback bookstore in the country. The avant-garde bookstore is noted for its having published poet Allen Ginsburg's *Howl* in the late 1950s. This two-level bookshop prides itself on a comprehensive collection of art, poetry, and political paperbacks, as well as more mainstream books, including many hard-to-find titles. There's a selection of children's books as well. Open daily from 10am to midnight.

CODY'S BOOKS, 2454 Telegraph Ave., Berkeley. Tel. 510/845-7852.

When you're in the neighborhood, don't miss this place. Cody's has over 100,000 titles in stock, including a huge selection of children's books. Open Sunday through Thursday from 9:15am to 9:45pm and on Friday and Saturday from 9:15am to 10:45pm.

DOUBLEDAY BOOK SHOP, 265 Sutter St., near Kearny Street and Grant Street. Tel. 989-3420.

This bookstore is spread over three floors and has an inviting children's section with plenty of room so that the kids can sit and look through books. Open Monday through Saturday from 9:30am to 6:30pm and on Sunday from noon to 5pm.

FANTASY ETC., 808 Larkin St., between Geary Street and O'Farrell Street. Tel. 441-7617.

This fun store is for detective- and adventure-book aficionados. You'll find graphics and pulp magazines also. Teenagers like this emporium. Open Monday through Saturday from 10am to 6:30pm and on Sunday from noon to 5pm.

GREEN APPLE BOOKSTORE, 506 Clement St., at Sixth Avenue. Tel. 387-2272.

This is one of our family's favorite bookstores. Be sure to save some time to browse here if you're near Clement Street. They claim 60,000 new titles and twice that in used books. In addition, they have books on tape, New Age music, and a large mask collection on display. There's also a large children's section. Open Sunday through Thursday from 10am to 10pm and on Friday and Saturday from 10am to midnight.

THE MARITIME STORE, 2905 Hyde Street Pier. Tel. 775-BOOK.

In addition to its maps, posters, cards, and gifts relating to sailing and marine life, this store (part of the San Francisco Historic Park and Museum) is thought to have the world's largest collection of books on maritime history. There is an extensive kids' section devoted to books about boating, nature, whaling, and the like. And, you'll find a good selection of literature that deals with the sea, by such authors as Joseph Conrad, Herman Melville, and Jack London. Open daily from 9:30am to 5pm.

MARKUS BOOKS, 1721 Fillmore St. Tel. 751-9211.

Markus has the Bay Area's best selection of books relating to African American and African culture. In addition to a good collection of children's books, there are titles on fiction, history, politics, art, and biography. Open Monday through Saturday from 10am to 7pm.

MOE'S BOOKS, 2476 Telegraph Ave. Berkeley. Tel. 510/849-2087.

This is one of the best bookstores we've ever been in. There is an unbelievable selection of adult books (four floors' worth) both new and used, and a good children's book section. Don't miss it when you're in Berkeley. It's worth the side trip itself from San Francisco to Berkeley to spend time in Moe's and Cody's (see the writeup above). Open Sunday through Thursday from 10am to 11pm and on Friday and Saturday from 10am to midnight.

MR. MOPPS' CHILDREN'S BOOKS AND TOYS, 1405 Martin Luther King, Jr., Way, Berkeley. Tel. 510/525-9633.

See the "Toys" section below for a complete writeup.

QUINBY'S, 3411 California St. in the Laurel Village Shopping Center, Tel. 751-7727.

Quinby's features one of the largest selections of children's books and educational materials in the Bay Area. Calling itself a place for the "curious child," Quinby's specializes in books and products designed to make family travel easier—items like magnetic toys and cassette tapes for the plane, train, or car journey—as well as other products for newborns to children aged 14. Kids are encouraged to spend time trying out some of the toys and books while parents mosey through the store. There are story hours on Wednesdays, with performances usually twice a month. Open Monday through Saturday from 9:30am to 6pm and on Sunday from 11am to 5pm.

RAND-McNALLY MAP AND TRAVEL, 595 Market St. Tel. 777-3131.

Hands down, the best travel-book store in the city, this corner shop features maps, atlases, and travel guides to all destinations. Our kids like to browse and research future trips. Open Monday through Friday from 9:30am to 6pm and on Saturday from 10am to 4pm.

SIERRA CLUB BOOKSTORE, 730 Polk St., Civic Center. Tel. 923-5600.

Here's a bookstore that offers the best for anyone interested in partaking of the outdoors—maps, books, and trail guides to California and the West. Open Monday through Friday from 10am to 5:30pm and on Saturday from 10am to 5pm.

STACEY'S BOOKSTORE, 581 Market St., near Second Street. Tel. 421-4687.

This bookstore has a nice selection of children's books. It also has a very large collection of technical, medical, and general-interest books. Open Monday through Wednesday and Friday from 8:30am to 6:30pm, on Thursday from 8:30am to 7pm, and on Saturday from 9am to 5:30pm. Closed Sunday.

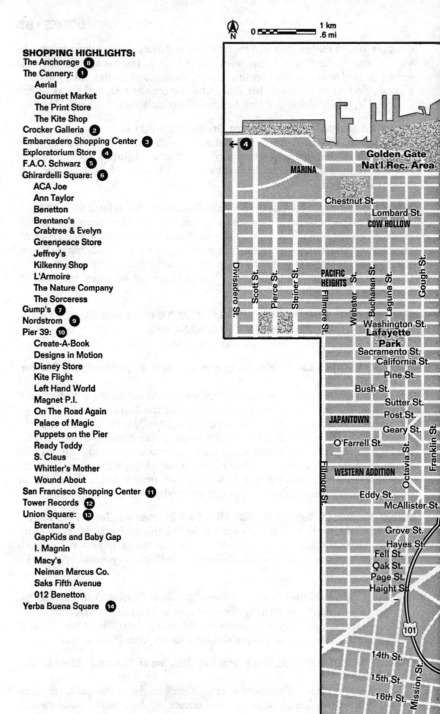

SHOPPING HIGHLIGHTS:
The Anchorage: **8**
The Cannery: **1**
  Aerial
  Gourmet Market
  The Print Store
  The Kite Shop
Crocker Galleria **2**
Embarcadero Shopping Center **3**
Exploratorium Store **4**
F.A.O. Schwarz **5**
Ghirardelli Square: **6**
  ACA Joe
  Ann Taylor
  Benetton
  Brentano's
  Crabtree & Evelyn
  Greenpeace Store
  Jeffrey's
  Kilkenny Shop
  L'Armoire
  The Nature Company
  The Sorceress
Gump's **7**
Nordstrom **9**
Pier 39: **10**
  Create-A-Book
  Designs in Motion
  Disney Store
  Kite Flight
  Left Hand World
  Magnet P.I.
  On The Road Again
  Palace of Magic
  Puppets on the Pier
  Ready Teddy
  S. Claus
  Whittler's Mother
  Wound About
San Francisco Shopping Center **11**
Tower Records **12**
Union Square: **13**
  Brentano's
  GapKids and Baby Gap
  I. Magnin
  Macy's
  Neiman Marcus Co.
  Saks Fifth Avenue
  012 Benetton
Yerba Buena Square **14**

0   1 km
    .6 mi
N

Golden Gate Nat'l. Rec. Area

MARINA

Chestnut St.
Lombard St.
COW HOLLOW

Divisadero St.
Scott St.
Pierce St.
Steiner St.
Fillmore St.
PACIFIC HEIGHTS
Webster St.
Buchanan St.
Laguna St.
Gough St.

Washington St.
Lafayette Park
Sacramento St.
California St.
Pine St.
Bush St.
Sutter St.
JAPANTOWN
Post St.
Geary St.
O'Farrell St.
Octavia St.
Franklin St.

WESTERN ADDITION
Eddy St.
McAllister St.
Grove St.
Hayes St.
Fell St.
Oak St.
Page St.
Haight St.

Fillmore St.

101

14th St.
15th St.
16th St.
Mission St.

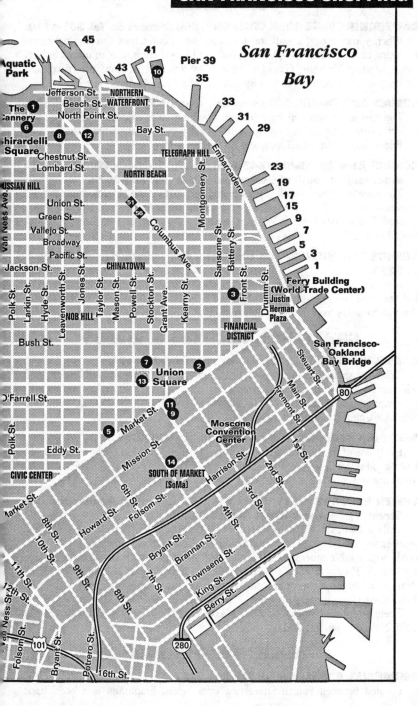

San Francisco
Bay

Aquatic
Park

45

41

Pier 39

43

35

10

Jefferson St.
Beach St.
North Point St.

NORTHERN
WATERFRONT

33

31

The
Cannery

1

6

Bay St.

29

Ghirardelli
Square

8

12

Chestnut St.
Lombard St.

TELEGRAPH HILL

23

19

NORTH BEACH

17

15

RUSSIAN HILL

Union St.
Green St.
Vallejo St.
Broadway
Pacific St.

51

56

9

7

5

Jackson St.

CHINATOWN

3

1

Polk St.
Larkin St.
Hyde St.
Leavenworth St.
Jones St.
Taylor St.
Mason St.
Powell St.
Stockton St.
Grant Ave.
Kearny St.
Sansome St.
Battery St.
Front St.
Drumm St.

Ferry Building
(World Trade Center)
Justin
Herman
Plaza

NOB HILL

Bush St.

3

FINANCIAL
DISTRICT

San Francisco-
Oakland
Bay Bridge

7

2

Union
Square

13

Steuart St.
Main St.
Fremont St.
1st St.

O'Farrell St.

80

11

9

Moscone
Convention
Center

2nd St.

Polk St.

5

Market St.

Eddy St.

Mission St.

14

CIVIC CENTER

SOUTH OF MARKET
(SoMa)

Harrison St.

3rd St.

Market St.

6th St.
Folsom St.

Howard St.

8th St.

4th St.

10th St.

9th St.

Bryant St.

Brannan St.

11th St.

8th St.

7th St.

Townsend St.

12th St.

King St.

Van Ness Ave.

Folsom St.

101

Bryant St.

Berry St.

Potrero St.

280

16th St.

COMIC BOOKS

CALIFORNIA COMIC BOOK COMPANY, 606 Clement St. Tel. 387-4118.

When you're taking a walk on Clement Street, don't miss this unusual store. Featuring comic books, role-playing games, and sports cards, it is an unusual place. Open Monday through Thursday from 11am through 6:30pm; on Friday and Saturday from 11am to 7pm; and on Sunday from 11am to 6pm.

COMICS AND COMIX, 650 Irving St., near 8th Avenue. Tel. 665-5888.

The specialties featured here include innovative independent comic lines and collector comics. Open Monday through Thursday and Saturday from 10am to 7pm; on Friday from 10am to 7:30pm; and on Sunday from 10am to 6pm.

COMICS AND DA-KIND, 1643 Noriega St., between 23rd and 24th avenues, just south of Golden Gate Park. Tel. 753-9678.

There are many new comic books, as well as a large stock of back issues and old comics—many sold at cover price. Sports cards are available, too. Open Monday through Friday from 11am to 7:30pm; Saturday from 11am to 5pm; and on Sunday from 11am to 5pm.

COMICS EXPERIENCE, 305 Divisidero, St., at Page Street. Tel. 863-9258.

Although catering largely to adults, the children's section here does feature some kid favorites: Disney, Ninja Turtles, Archie Classics, and Nintendo. Open Monday through Saturday from 11am to 7pm and on Sunday from noon to 5pm.

CDS, TAPES, RECORDS & VIDEOS

RAINBOW RECORDS, 2222 Fillmore St. Tel. 922-4474.

This store specializes in cassettes, CDs, and videos. It rents and sells videos, and will special-order both CDs and videos.

There are other branches at 838 Market St. (tel. 392-5211), 25 Stanyan St. (tel. 386-6436), and 217 Sutter St. (tel. 956-1072).

RECYCLED RECORDS, 1377 Haight St. Tel. 626-4075.

Easily one of the best used-record stores in the city, this loud shop in the Haight has a good selection of promotional cassettes, and cases of used "classic" rock LPs. Teens are very visible here. Open daily from 10am to 8pm.

TOWER RECORDS, 2525 Jones St., near Columbus Avenue and Bay Street, Fisherman's Wharf. Tel. 885-0500.

Truly a giant, this 10,000-square-foot store is packed with rock, jazz, classical, show tunes, folk, country, and international music—virtually anything you or yours could hope for. No other store in the city carries so large a stock, or can order so large a selection. They also stock a large selection of videos. Open 365 days a year from 9am to midnight. (They have closed only one day, and that was during the Earthquake.)

There are other branches at 2280 Market St. (CDs only) (tel. 621-0588) and at 3205 20th Ave. (tel. 681-2001).

DEPARTMENT STORES

EMPORIUM, 835 Market St. Tel. 764-2222.

Located between Fourth Street and Fifth Street, Emporium is a good basic full-line department store, including gourmet foods, home furnishings, fashions, kitchenware, beauty salon, shoe repair, and post office. In December, there is a popular rooftop Christmas carnival with rides. Open Monday through Friday from 9:30am to 8pm; on Saturday from 9:30am to 8pm; and on Sunday from noon to 6pm.

GUMP'S, 250 Post St. Tel. 982-1616.

No clothing is sold at Gump's, but there is a wonderful place for indoor window shopping of gorgeous, unique items in crystal, silver, and china. Have your littlest ones keep their hands behind their backs. Open Monday through Saturday from 9:30am to 5:30pm.

I. MAGNIN, Geary Street and Stockton Street, Union Square. Tel. 362-2100.

Founded in 1876, this is the flagship I. Magnin store. Ten upscale floors feature clothing for men, women, and children. The merchandise is of high quality and expensive. Sizes are available for newborns to 14. Open Monday, Thursday, and Friday from 9:30am to 8pm; on Tuesday, Wednesday, and Saturday from 9:30am to 6pm; and on Sunday from noon to 6pm.

MACY'S, Stockton Street and O'Farrell Street, Union Square. Tel. 397-3333.

Macy's is a shopper's heaven—divided into two distinct parts. Macy's East has five floors of men's and children's fashions. The clothing departments for girls and boys are very good; it is one of the few places in the city to get children's shoes. The department has sizes for pre-walkers to boys' and girls' sizes 6 and 7, respectively. The seven-story Macy's West features contemporary fashions for women and juniors, including jewelry, fragrances, cosmetics, and accessories. The top floors contain home furnishings, while the Cellar sells upscale housewares and gourmet foods. There is a post office, beauty salon, and personal shopping service here as well. Open Monday through Friday from 9:30am to 9pm; Saturday from 9:30am to 6pm, and on Sunday from 11am to 6pm.

NEIMAN MARCUS CO., 150 Stockton St., Union Square. Tel. 362-3900.

This legendary store offers chic, expensive clothes for men, women, and children (infant to toddler sizes for boys; to size 14 for girls). Also precious gems, cosmetics, and gourmet foods. Open Monday, Thursday, and Friday from 10am to 8pm; Tuesday, Wednesday, and Saturday from 10am to 6pm; and on Sunday from noon to 6pm.

NORDSTROM, 865 Market St., San Francisco Shopping Center. Tel. 243-8500, or toll free 800/289-9190.

Known for its personalized service, Nordstrom is a leading fashion retailer and a wonderful place to shop. Try it once, and you'll see what customer service can be all about. There are excellent children's clothes, especially nice holiday clothes, and a shoe department that features shoe sizes from 0 to girls' size 4 and to boys size 7. Expensive upscale fashion brands include Absorba, Esprit, Adrienne Vittadini, Guess, and Generra. The teenage department is the Brass Plum. The Nordstrom Café, on the top floor, has a terrific view and is a great place for an inexpensive lunch or light snack. Open Monday through Friday from 9:30am to 8pm, Saturday from 9:30am to 7pm, and on Sunday from 11am to 6pm.

SAKS FIFTH AVENUE, 384 Post St., Union Square. Tel. 986-4300.

Saks has an excellent infant department, and a very good children's department with cute accessories for girls. Some items are very expensive. The service is excellent, and mailing and gift-wrapping are available. Open Monday, Thursday, and Friday from 10am to 8pm; Tuesday, Wednesday, and Saturday from 10am to 6pm; and on Sunday from noon to 6pm.

DISCOUNT FACTORY OUTLETS

BABY BOOM, 1601 Irving St. at 17th Avenue. Tel. 564-2666.

Discounts between 25% and 75% are offered on new, used, and sample baby furniture, clothes, and toys. Open Monday through Saturday from 10am to 6pm; and on Sunday from noon to 5pm.

Another branch, Baby Boom Maternity, is located at 1315 17th Ave. (tel. 564-2666).

BURLINGTON COAT FACTORY, 899 Howard St., Yerba Buena Square, (South of Market). Tel. 495-7234.

Coats and clothing for the entire family are offered, including a children's shoe department. Sizes start at kids size 2, and you'll find a full line up from there. Open Monday through Saturday from 9:30am to 8pm and on Sunday from 11am to 6pm.

CHRISTINE FOLEY KNITWEAR WAREHOUSE BOUTIQUE, 430 Ninth St., between Bryant Street and Harrison Street. Tel. 621-8126.

The boutique sells handmade sweaters and has a large selection of 100% cotton outfits that are discontinued. Open Monday through Saturday from 10am to 4pm. Closed Sunday.

ESPRIT OUTLET STORE, 499 Illinois St. Tel. 957-2550.

What a find! People come from all over to shop at this store. Featured is an enormous variety of Esprit clothing from jeans and active sportswear to shoes at 30% or more off regular price. Sizes range from 2 months to adult. Open Monday through Friday from 10am to 8pm; Saturday from 10am to 7pm; and on Sunday from 10am to 5pm. Call for recorded information about available stock.

GUNNE SAX FACTORY OUTLET, 35 Stanford St., between Second Street and Third Street. Tel. 495-3326.

This factory outlet has children's, juniors, and women's clothing. The selection varies daily. Open Monday through Friday from 10am to 5pm; on Saturday from 9am to 5pm; and on Sunday from 11am to 5pm.

MOUSEFEATHERS FACTORY OUTLET STORE, 1001 Camellia St., Berkeley. Tel. 501/526-0261.

Many of the dresses, jumpsuits, and separates for children are discounted up to 50%. Open Monday from noon to 5pm; on Tuesday through Saturday from 10am through 5pm. Call for latest recorded information about what's in stock.

PEEK-A-BOUTIQUE, 1306 Castro St. at 24th Street. Tel. 641-6192.

There is a good selection of quality used clothing and some furniture at this discount outlet. Sizes available are children's 0 to 6X. Open Monday through Saturday from 10:30am through 6pm and on Sunday from noon to 5pm.

SIX SIXTY CENTER, 660 Third St. at Townsend Street, south of Market Street. Tel. 495-6768.

There are 20 factory-outlet stores here, offering children's, women's and men's clothing, shoes, and accessories. Open Monday through Saturday from 10am through 5:30pm.

SWEET POTATOES, 1716 Fourth St., Berkeley. Tel. 510/527-5852.

This factory outlet stocks boys sizes from 12 months to size 7; girls from 12 months to preteen. They sell fabrics and trims also. Open Monday through Saturday from 10am to 5pm and on Sunday from noon to 5pm. A must stop if you're sightseeing in Berkeley.

TOY LIQUIDATORS, Yerba Buena Square, 899 Howard St. at Fifth Street, South of Market. Tel. 974-5136.

This discount store sells overstock. Don't expect the up-to-the-minute hottest toys, but you'll find good value on many name-brand items. For the doll set, there are accessories and clothes for Ken and Barbie and their crowd. Open Monday through Saturday from 9:30am to 7pm and on Sunday from 11am to 5pm.

YERBA BUENA SQUARE, 899 Howard St. at Fifth Street, near the Moscone Center. Tel. 974-5136.

The three floors of retailers at this discount center include a children's store, which you might find of interest. Open Monday through Saturday from 9:30am to 8pm and on Sunday from 11am to 6pm.

ELECTRONICS

MACY'S, Stockton Street and O'Farrell Street, Union Square. Tel. 397-3333.

This department store has an excellent electronics section, with many items of interest to older kids and teens.

RADIO SHACK, 1841 Polk St., near Jackson Street. Tel. 673-9414.

This national chain branch member is open Monday through Saturday from 10am to 7pm and on Sunday to 6pm. There are other branches at 701 Clement St. (tel. 752-5099) and 650 Market St., near Third Street (tel. 986-1004).

WHOLE EARTH ACCESS, 401 Bayshore Blvd., near Army Street. Tel. 285-5244.

This store carries a wide selection of electronics, tools, housewares, cookwares, clothing, and shoes (active wear to dress shoes), even books (nonfiction, reference, cookbooks). You and your older children might find items of interest here. Open Saturday through Wednesday from 10am to 6pm, and on Thursday and Friday from 10am to 8pm.

Other branches are in Berkeley at 2990 Seventh St. (tel. 510/845-3000).

FASHIONS

BANANA REPUBLIC, 256 Grant Ave., downtown. Tel. 788-3087.

If you or your teenager are looking for safari or travel clothes, this is the place to go. Open Monday, Tuesday, Wednesday, and Saturday from 9:30am to 7pm; on Thursday and Friday from 9:30am to 8pm; and on Sunday from noon to 6pm.

There is another branch at 2253 Polk St. (tel. 474-9711).

BEACH BUMS, Pier 39. Tel. 981-7437.

Our teens love this store for its swimwear and beach accessories. Open daily from 10:30am to 8:30pm.

012 BENETTON, 450 Powell St., Union Square. Tel. 391-4146.

This Italian clothing manufacturer has hit it big with our family. At this Benetton branch, you can get kids' imported sweaters, dresses, baby clothes, sweats, and jeans from size 0 to 12—hence the store name. You'll find accessories, sometimes even shoes. Open Monday through Saturday from 10am to 6:30pm, and on Sunday from 10am to 6pm. The Adult Benetton branch is located across the street at 457 Powell St. (tel. 398-4494).

There is also another branch location (adult and 012) at the San Francisco Shopping Center, 865 Market St. (tel. 979-0533).

BELLINI, 418 Sutter St., near Stockton Street. Tel. 391-5417.

Designer clothing sizes 0 to 4T is available here, as well as designer furniture and unique gifts for infants and children. Open Monday, Thursday, and Friday from 9:30am to 8pm; on Tuesday, Wednesday, and Saturday to 6pm; and on Sunday from noon to 4pm.

A CHILD'S PLACE, 1857 Solano Ave., Berkeley. Tel. 510/524-3651.

A multitude of accessories can be found here, along with clothing for babies and children to size 7 and toys. Don't miss stopping by if you visit Berkeley. Open Monday through Saturday from 10:30am to 5:30pm.

CITIKIDS BABY NEWS, 1160 Post St. at Van Ness Avenue. Tel. 673-5437.

This children's department store offers everything you need for infants and toddlers, with sizes up to 6X. You'll also find diapers, furniture, and accessories. Prices are competitive because of the huge volume. Open Monday through Saturday from 10am to 6pm and on Sunday from 11am to 5pm.

COTTON AND COMPANY, 3961A 24th St. Tel. 550-1668.

Adorable all-cotton separates in original designs can be found here along with leggings, turtlenecks, and sweatpants. Open Monday through Saturday from 10:30am to 6:30pm and on Sunday from 11am to 5pm.

There is another branch in Oakland at 5858 College Ave. (tel. 510/653-8058).

DANCE OF LIFE, 1753 Solano Ave., Berkeley. Tel. 510/526-6000.

You'll find a large selection of dance, aerobic, and active wear for children and grownups here. There are also ballet slippers for children and a large selection of Indonesian clothing and handcrafts. Open Monday through Saturday from 10:30am to 5:30pm.

GAP KIDS AND BABY GAP, 100 Post St., Union Square. Tel. 421-4906.

This store features very casual, sporty clothes. Baby Gap has sizes for newborn to

24 months; Gap Kids has clothes for kids ages 2 to 14. The store carries an abundance of jeans and T-shirts, and your teens will love this place if they don't already own Gap clothes—or want more of them. Open Monday through Saturday from 10am to 7pm; and on Sunday from 11am to 6pm.

There are other branches at Laurel Village (offering Gap Kids) (tel. 386-7517); Embarcadero Center, street level, Embarcadero Three (tel. 391-8826); at 2299 Taylor St. at Columbus Avenue, Fisherman's Wharf area (tel. 776-2227); and downtown at 934–936 Market St., at Fifth Street (tel. 397-2266).

THE LIMITED, TOO, 55 Stockton St., across from F.A.O. Schwarz near Union Square. Tel. 391-4439.

You might have to look for this gem because it's hidden. But, it's worth the search because it is one of only a few Limiteds for children, offering stylish European kids' clothes for ages 2 to 14 at reasonable prices. Open Monday through Friday from 10am to 9pm; on Saturday to 7pm; and on Sunday 11am to 6pm.

THE LIMITED EXPRESS, 55 Stockton St. (in the same complex as The Limited, Too). Tel. 433-3320.

Our teens love the selection of trendy clothes and accessories here. Open Monday through Friday from 10am to 9pm and on Saturday to 7pm; Sunday from 11am to 6pm.

MUDPIE, 1699 Union St., near Gough Street. Tel. 771-9262.

Sizes run from infant to size 6 for boys, to size 10 for girls. Underwear, coats, and toys are stocked, and the shoe department has imported and domestic shoes from new-walkers to size 5 for boys and girls. Open Monday through Saturday from 10:30am to 6pm and on Sunday noon to 5pm.

RAGAMUFFIN, 3048 Fillmore St., near Union Street. Tel. 563-7140.

At Ragamuffin sizes range from newborn to 10 years for Italian, French, and English clothing, much of which is 100% cotton. There is also a good selection of sweaters available here. Open Monday through Saturday from 10:30am to 5:30pm; and on Sunday noon to 5pm.

There's another branch at 110 Caledonia St. in Sausalito (tel. 332-1340).

SMALLFRYS, 4066 24th St. Tel. 648-3954.

Get your "California-look" for tots here. Smallfrys stocks all-cotton clothes from size 0 to 7 for boys and up to size 14 for girls. Open Tuesday through Friday from 10am to 6pm; Saturday from 10am to 5:30pm; and on Sunday from 11am to 5pm.

STREET FASHIONS, Anchorage Shopping Center, 333 Jefferson St., Fisherman's Wharf. Tel. 885-3054.

A large selection of Levis at reasonable prices is available in sizes 9 months to adult. Monday through Friday from 10am to 7pm; and on Saturday and Sunday from 10am to 8pm; later hours during summer.

SUCH A BUSINESS—THE KIDS' GENERAL STORE, 1 Rhode Island St. Tel. 431-1703.

This huge place stocks almost anything you can imagine: clothes for infants to sizes for children age 10 as well as shoes, books, tapes, toys, and even furniture. You'll find everything for the layette, including cloth diapers. They even rent strollers, highchairs, and other equipment. There's art supplies, toys and games, costume jewelry—everything, as we said. Open Monday through Saturday from 10am to 6pm (Thursday till 7pm) and on Sunday from noon to 5pm.

There's another branch in Oakland at 5533 College Ave. (tel. 510/655-6641).

FOOD

BEPPLES PIE SHOP AND RESTAURANT, 1934 Union St. Tel. 931-6225.

One of the most celebrated shops on Union Street is this mouth-watering noshery selling soups, muffins, breads, and pies. Kids love to visit here. Open Monday through Thursday from 7am to 11:30pm, on Friday from 7am to 1am, on Saturday from 9am to 1:30am, and on Sunday from 9am to 10:30pm.

THE GOLDEN GATE FORTUNE COOKIES CO., 56 Ross Alley. Tel. 781-3956.

This tiny, touristy factory sells fortune cookies hot off the press. You can purchase them in small bags or in bulk, and if your order is large enough, you may even be able to negotiate your own message. Even if you're not buying, stop in with the kids to see how these sugary treats are made. Open Monday through Friday from 10am to noon.

FURNITURE

BELLINI: see the writeup under "Fashion" above.

CITIKIDS BABY NEWS: see the writeup under "Fashion" above.

JONATHAN-KAY, 3548 Sacramento St., near Laurel Street and Locust Street. Tel. 563-0773.

A wide selection of baby and children's furniture is available here, plus a large selection of educational toys. Open Monday through Friday from 10am to 6pm, Saturday to 5:30pm, and on Sunday from noon to 5pm.

GIFTS & MISCELLANEOUS

AERIAL, 2801 Leavenworth St., at The Cannery. Tel. 474-1566.

This eclectic, artsy, sporty store is one we always like to visit. The kids—especially teenagers—enjoy its odd assortment of items from roller blades to imported toys and graphics books. Open daily from 10am to 7pm.

AUD'S, 1980 Union St. Tel. 931-7765.

Located inside one of the street's most beautiful Victorians, the shop sells one-of-a-kind "fun things," including toys and wearable art. The jewelry is priced from $10 to $60; the shop's proceeds benefit Bay Area artists. Open Monday through Saturday from 10am to 5pm.

COST PLUS IMPORTS, 2552 Taylor St., Fisherman's Wharf. Tel. 928-6200.

This is a must-see if you like imported—but reasonably priced—items. Over 20,000 articles from more than 40 countries are offered, including a large selection of wines. The store is a lot of fun to wander through. Open Monday through Saturday from 9am to 9:30pm and on Sunday from 10am to 8pm.

CREATE-A-BOOK, ETC., Pier 39. Tel. 677-9886.

Create a unique book for your child in this store tucked in at the back of Pier 39. Open daily from 10:30am to 8:30pm.

EXPLORATORIUM STORE, in the Palace of Fine Arts, 3601 Lyon St. Tel. 561-0390.

The best museum gift shop in the city is this fanciful store inside a terrific hands-on science museum (see "What Kids Like to See & Do"). Gifts include the Astronomical Shower Curtain, printed with an accurate map of the stars; Space Super Balls, high-bouncing rubber balls that never seem to slow down; holographic earrings and magnets; and other gizmos and gadgets. Open on Wednesday from 10am to 9:30pm and Thursday through Sunday from 10am to 5pm.

FORMA, 1715 Haight St. Tel. 751-0545.

Perhaps the most unusual store in San Francisco is this celebration of urban kitsch between Cole Street and Shrader Street. In addition to colorful handmade dioramas and rice-paper lamps, you'll find voodoo dolls, ant farms, sea monkeys, Rocky and Bullwinkle toys, Gumby and Pokey dolls, and games like Lite-Brite and Twister. Open Monday through Saturday from noon to 7pm and on Sunday from noon to 6pm.

GINZA DISCOUNT IMPORTS, 44 Peace Plaza, Japantown at the Japanese Cultural & Trade Center. Tel. 922-2475.

We consider this store a "find." It is a huge, traditional Japanese gift store with trinkets, kites, toys, art supplies, and gadgets. We buy the kids inexpensive novelties here such as a little feathered bird, a small abacus, and traditional Japanese dolls. Open daily from 9:30am to 9:30pm.

H. P. CORWITH LTD., 1833 Union St. Tel. 567-7252.

One of the most unusual stores for collectibles is this strange Union Street shop selling bronze puffins and wild boars, teeny Victorian houses, sterling chains and bracelets, lifelike cat and dog sculptures, glass candies, vinyl chocolates, masks, and nested dolls from Russia and China. Get the picture? Your kids will enjoy browsing here—and so will you. Open Monday through Saturday from 10am to 5pm.

LAWRENCE HALL OF SCIENCE MUSEUM SHOP, University of California, at Berkeley. Tel. 510/642-5133.

This is another unique shopping experience in the East Bay area. The museum is known for its wonderful dinosaur exhibits, and you'll find smaller versions of them in the gift shop. Open daily from 10am to 4:30pm.

THE NATURE COMPANY, 900 North Point, Ghirardelli Square. Tel. 776-0724.

You'll find an excellent selection of small toys here, such as tops and YoYos, as well as a good choice of nature-related books. Friendly, relaxed salespeople make shopping here extremely pleasant. Open daily from 10am to 9pm.

ROBISON'S—EXCLUSIVELY FOR PETS, 135 Maiden Lane. Tel. 421-0310.

This little store is perhaps the oldest pet store in the United States, founded in

1849. It carries difficult-to-find products from around the world, as well as a full line of pet supplies and animals for sale. It's a treat to browse through with the kids. Open Monday through Friday from 10am to 5:30pm, and on Saturday till 5pm.

SHOES

KINDER SCHUHE, Shattuck Commons, 1400 Shattuck Ave., Berkeley. Tel. 510/540-8186.

Fine European children's shoes are offered from child's size 0 to adult size 9. Open Monday through Friday from 10:30am to 6pm, Saturday from 10am to 7pm, and on Sunday from noon to 5pm.

MACY'S, Stockton Street and O'Farrell Street, Union Square. Tel. 397-3333.

This department store has a great children's shoe department with sizes for pre-walkers to boys' size 6 and girls' size 7. Open Monday through Friday from 9:30am to 9pm, Saturday from 9:30am to 6pm, and on Sunday from 11am to 6pm.

MUDPIE, 1699 Union St. near Gough Street. Tel. 771-9262.

Mudpie's shoe department features imported and domestic shoes for children in sizes from new-walkers to size 5 for boys and girls. Open Monday through Saturday from 10:30am to 6pm and on Sunday from noon to 5pm.

NORDSTROM, 865 Market St., San Francisco Shopping Center. Tel. 243-8500.

This department store has an excellent children's shoe department, stocking shoe sizes from 0 to girls' size 4 and 0 to boys' size 7. Open Monday through Friday from 9:30am to 8pm, Saturday from 9:30am to 7pm, and on Sunday from 11am to 6pm.

SUCH A BUSINESS—THE KIDS' GENERAL STORE, 1 Rhode Island St. Tel. 431-1703.

This general store has a fine selection of children's shoes in a wide range of sizes. Open Monday through Saturday from 10am to 6pm (Thursday till 7pm) and on Sunday from noon to 5pm.

SHOPPING CENTERS & COMPLEXES

Like any city, San Francisco's malls are filled with carbon-copy chain stores, but they are also dotted with a good selection of local specialty shops, and a taste of the avant garde. Most have stores that will appeal to your kids. We mention some of our favorites below.

THE ANCHORAGE, 2800 Leavenworth St., at Beach Street and Jefferson Street, Fisherman's Wharf. Tel. 775-6000.

The newest of the waterfront complexes, the Anchorage offers shopping and dining near Fisherman's Wharf. The mall is fronted by an impressive two-story anchor sculpture, and continues the nautical theme throughout its outdoor promenades and decks. Close to 50 units offer everything from music boxes to home furnishings. **The Incredible Christmas Store** (tel. 928-5700) sells holiday items year round. There is also a fair assortment of restaurants and specialty food shops. In the courtyard, musicians, mimes, jugglers, and other street performers entertain, a treat for the kids.

Open in summer daily from 10am to 9pm; the rest of the year, daily from 10am to 6pm.

THE CANNERY, 2801 Leavenworth St., at Jefferson Street. Tel. 346-5887.

Once a Del Monte fruit-canning plant, this complex is now occupied by a score or two of shops, restaurants, and nightspots. Top shops include **Aerial,** (tel. 474-1566) for esoteric gifts, architectural books and prints, sports accessories, and art supplies; the **Gourmet Market** (tel. 673-0400), selling international foods, coffees, teas, and a full range of delectables for a fabulous picnic lunch; and **The Print Store** (tel. 252-1314), offering a well-chosen selection of fine art prints and local original art.

Cobb's Comedy Club is also here, along with several restaurants in all cuisines and price ranges.

The Cannery is open Monday through Saturday from 10am to 6pm and on Sunday from 11am to 6pm; extended hours during summer and on holidays.

CROCKER GALLERIA, 50 Post St. Tel. 392-0100.

Modeled after Milan's Galleria Vitorio Emmanuelle, this glass-domed, three-level pavilion, about three blocks east of Union Square, features about 50 high-end shops that will appeal to you and your teenagers. Fashions include Marimekko Finnish designs, Mondi, and Polo. Restaurants, gift, and specialty shops round out the offerings. Open Monday through Friday from 9:30am to 6pm and on Saturday from 10am to 5pm.

EMBARCADERO CENTER, Battery, Sacramento, Drumm, and Clay streets. Tel. 772-0500.

If you've been in San Francisco for more than a few hours, you've probably already seen the buildings of this enormous seven-block complex. Its four tall towers sit next to the Hyatt Regency Hotel. There are 140 shops and restaurants here, many that will appeal to your kids. Validated parking is available—it's free on Sunday. Open daily from 10am to 6pm, later during holidays; restaurants remain open later.

GHIRARDELLI SQUARE, 900 North Point. Tel. 775-5500.

This former chocolate factory is one of the city's largest malls and most popular landmarks. Many chain stores are located here, including the women's clothier **AnnTaylor, ACA Joe** for casual wear, **Benetton** for Italian knitwear, **Crabtree & Evelyn** for English soaps and scents, **The Nature Company** for earth-related gifts, and **The Sharper Image** for unique, upscale electronics and designs. We've poked into every store here and our favorites include: **L'Armoire** (tel. 771-2488) for exquisite lingerie and dainty underthings that are hard to find in major department stores (adult fare, of course); **Jeffrey's** (tel. 776-6780), which is stocked with a good selection of toys, games, and hobby supplies (our kids love to browse here); and the **Kilkenny Shop** (tel. 771-8984) which smells like sheep and specializes in wool suits and blankets, Aran knit sweaters, and other exclusive Irish imports, including Galway crystal. Other stores with kid appeal include **Brentano's** (children's books), **The Sorceress** (fossils, minerals, and jewelry), and a **Greenpeace Store.**

Many good restaurants are located here, too. The complex is open daily from 10am to 6pm. Main plaza shops are open Sunday through Thursday from 10am to 6pm and on Friday and Saturday from 10am to 9pm; extended hours during summer. Restaurant hours vary. Validated parking is offered.

PIER 39. Tel. 981-8030.

This abandoned cargo pier is now one of the most popular tourist destinations in San Francisco. Occupying two levels adjacent to Fisherman's Wharf, this waterfront complex offers almost as many shops as Ghirardelli and the Cannery combined.

Some of the most interesting stores include **Designs in Motion** (tel. 397-5050), which claims the largest collection of kinetic sculpture in the city produced by local artists; **Puppets on the Pier** (tel. 781-4435), selling all kinds of manipulable puppets; and **Ready Teddy** (tel. 781-1255), for bears, bears, and more bears. You can watch wood carvers at work at **Whittler's Mother** (tel. 433-3010); and at **Kite Flight** (tel. 956-3181) you can buy a fanciful creation to fly in the breezes off the bay. At **Left Hand World** (tel. 433-3547), southpaws can stock up on scissors, potholders, watches, and corkscrews, all made for "lefties"; and at the **Palace of Magic** (tel. 346-2218), tricksters can find rubber chickens, fake blood and scars, and unusual masks. Other stores with kid appeal include **Magnet P.I., Create-A-Book,** the **Disney Store, Wound About,** and **S. Claus** (a wonderful Christmas store).

Several Pier restaurants offer great views of the bay.

Pier 39 is open Sunday through Thursday from 10am to 6pm, and on Friday and Saturday from 10am to 9pm. Extended hours are offered during summer. Restaurant hours vary.

SAN FRANCISCO SHOPPING CENTER, 865 Market St. Tel. 495-5656.

Opened in 1988, this $140-million complex is one of the few vertical malls in the United States. Its most stunning feature is the four-story spiral escalator that circles its way up to Nordstrom, the center's primary anchor and the largest unit in the Portland-based fashion specialty chain (see "Department Stores," above). More than 90 specialty shops and restaurants include designer clothiers Adrienne Vittadini, AnnTaylor, Bebe, and Mondi. Lower-fashion outlets include Benetton, Foot Locker, J. Crew, and Victoria's Secret. The mall's nine-story atrium is covered by a retractable skylight. Open Monday through Saturday from 9:30am to 8pm and on Sunday from 11am to 6pm; holiday hours may vary.

SPORTING GOODS

BIG 5 SPORTING GOODS, 2159 Chestnut St. at Steiner Street. Tel. 474-8670.

This chain carries the items for most of your sporting needs. Children's sizes are available. Open Monday through Saturday from 10am to 9pm and on Sunday to 6pm.

COPELAND'S SPORTS, 901 Market St. Tel. 495-0928.

Known as one of the most complete sporting goods stores in the Bay area, this store has ski rentals and backpacking equipment, as well as the more ordinary sporting goods you might want. Children's sizes are available. Open Monday through Saturday from 10am to 8pm and on Sunday to 6pm.

There are two other branch stores in Berkeley—one at 1607 Shattuck Ave. (tel. 510/848-0732) and a second at 1615 University Ave. (tel. 510/843-6505).

FIRST STEP, 216 Powell St. at O'Farrell Street. Tel. 989-9989.

First Step offers a complete line of name-brand athletic shoes for all kinds of sports—basketball, aerobics, walking, tennis, hiking—as well as sports apparel and accessories. Children's sizes are available. Open Monday through Saturday from 9am to 7:30pm.

FTC SKI AND SPORTS, 1586 Bush St., at Franklin Street. Tel. 673-8363.

Our son loves this store, and no wonder. Skateboards, rollerskates and rollerblades, snowboards, and a full line of skiing equipment are the order of the day. Their specialty is skateboards for children and young adults (they have helmets). This full-service ski and rental shop will fit ski boots for adults and children (as young as 5 years old). Open Monday through Friday from 10am to 7pm, on Saturday from 10am to 5pm, and on Sunday from noon to 5pm.

KINDERSPORT, 3566 Sacramento St., at Laurel Street and Locust Street. Tel. 563-7778.

This store offers junior ski and sports outfitting. Open Monday through Saturday from 11am to 6pm.

SPORTS FANTASY, Ghirardelli Square, 2nd floor of Clock Tower Building. Tel. 441-0502.

Licensed sports products such as those endorsed by professional teams of the NBA, NFL, and Major League Baseball teams as well as college teams are offered here. Some children's sizes are available. Open Monday through Thursday from 10am to 7pm, on Friday and Saturday to 9pm, on Sunday to 6pm. Open later in summer. There is another branch at 774 Market St. (tel. 391-9842).

TOYS

THE ARK, 2986 Washington St., at Broderick Street. Tel. 673-2529.

This unusual toy store features many unique handmade toys of natural fibers and materials. There is a fine selection of children's books, many of which are imported. Older children can choose from classics, mythology, and beautiful hardbound books. Craft activities, storytelling, and puppet shows are offered. Call for class reservations and information. Open Monday through Friday from 10am to 6pm, and on Saturday to 5pm. Open later during holidays and summer.

BASIC BROWN BEAR FACTORY & STORE, 444 DeHaro St., between 17th Street and Mariposa Street. Tel. 626-0781.

Get your teddy bears, bunnies, chicks, and stuffed animals of all kinds here. You can also book a tour (for 4 people or more), or drop in on Saturday at 11am or 2pm to see how the bears are made. Open daily from 10am to 5pm.

THE CHINATOWN KITE SHOP, 717 Grant Ave. Tel. 989-5182.

This shop's astonishing assortment of flying objects includes attractive fish kites, windsock kites in nylon or cotton, hand-painted Chinese paper kites, wood-and-paper biplanes, and pentagonal kites—all of which make great souvenirs or decorations. Computer-designed stunt kites have two control lines to manipulate loops and dives. Open daily from 10am to 10pm.

THE DISNEY STORE, Pier 39. Tel. 981-7437.

This shop carries Disney merchandise exclusively. Open daily from 10:30am to 8:30pm.

EXPLORATORIUM STORE, in the Palace of Fine Arts, 3601 Lyon St. Tel. 561-0390.

In this truly unique store, you'll find magical gifts and educational toys for everyone. There are Chinese puzzles, hand-crafted hardwood pieces that form architectural wonders, science packets, and many other treasures. You may also purchase items via mail order (tel. 561-0393). Open on Wednesday from 10am to 9:30pm and on Thursday through Sunday from 10am to 5pm.

F.A.O. SCHWARZ, 48 Stockton St. Tel. 394-8700.

The world's greatest toy store for both children and adults is filled with every imaginable plaything, from hand-carved, custom-painted carousel rocking horses, dolls, and stuffed animals, to gas-powered cars, train sets, and hobby supplies. At the entrance is a singing 22-foot clock tower with 1,000 different moving parts. If you don't want to buy a $5,000 toy car, tell your kids F.A.O. Schwarz is a museum. Open on Monday, Thursday, and Friday from 10am to 8pm; on Tuesday, Wednesday, and Saturday from 10am to 6pm; and on Sunday from 11am to 6pm.

GAMES PEOPLE PLAY, 695 Bridgeway, Sausalito. Tel. 332-4151.

Stuffed animals, kites, a large assortment of travel games, children's books and stocking-stuffer-type items can be found here. Open Monday through Friday from 9:30am to 6pm and on Saturday and Sunday to 6:30pm. Open later in summer.

HEARTH SONG, 1805 Fourth St., Berkeley. Tel. 510/849-3956.

This store offers traditional toys, games, art materials, handmade dolls, and books for children and parents. Hearth Song also holds special holiday events. Open daily from 10am to 6pm, but call ahead because they close a little earlier during the winter weekdays and stay open later during holidays and summer.

HEFFALUMP, 1694 Union St., at Gough Street. Tel. 928-4300.

This chic toy boutique claims to have the best rocking horses in the West. It also stocks an impressive array of European dolls, wooden puzzles and games, and lovely children's books. Validated parking is offered—a real plus in this neighborhood. Open Monday through Saturday from 10am to 6pm and on Sunday from 11am to 5pm.

HOUSE OF MAGIC, 2025 Chestnut St. Tel. 346-2218.

For all those kids who love to play tricks on each other, or learn magic, this store caters to beginners as well as professionals. Open Monday through Saturday from 10am to 7pm and on Sunday from 11am to 4pm.

IMAGINARIUM, 3535 California St. Tel. 387-9885.

This toy chain stocks educational toys that you'll feel good about buying. The staff is trained to help you select age-appropriate toys, and the kids love the hands-on environment where they're encouraged to try out toys. Open Monday through Saturday from 9:30am to 6pm and on Sunday from noon to 5pm.

Another branch is located at 3251 20th Ave. (tel. 566-4111).

JEFFREY'S TOYS, Ghirardelli Square. Tel. 776-6780.

Jeffrey's is a good, solid toy store where you'll find the trinkets and name-brand toys that you want. Open Monday through Thursday from 10am to 6pm, on Friday and Saturday from 10am to 9pm, and on Sunday to 8pm.

There's another Jeffrey's store at 3 Embarcadero Center (tel. 397-8838).

KINDERZIMMER, 556 Sutter St., near Mason Street. Tel. 986-4594.

You can almost imagine Geppetto working in this European-style workshop and toy store. There are many imported handmade wooden toys, dollhouses and accessories, tin toys, and an extensive array of puppets and fine stuffed animals here. Open Monday through Saturday from 10am to 6pm, and on Sunday from noon to 5pm.

THE KITE SHOP, Ghirardelli Square, entrance on Beach Street. Tel. 673-4559 and 673-4557.

This wonderful store has kites from all over the world. Open Monday through Friday from 10am to 6pm, on Saturday and Sunday from 10am to 9pm, and during summer, open daily from 10am to 9pm.

MARINA TOY CHEST, 3259 Pierce St., at Chestnut Street. Tel. 931-5684.

This store stocks games as well as toys. Open Monday through Saturday from 10am to 6pm.

MR. MOPPS' CHILDREN'S BOOKS AND TOYS, 1405 Martin Luther King, Jr., Way., Berkeley. Tel. 510/525-9633.

This beautiful little toy store has a huge bookstore attached, with books for infants to twelfth-graders. It's the place to go if you want to inspire your children to read. Open Monday through Saturday from 9:30am to 5:30pm. Closed Sunday.

PACIFIC HEIGHTS KITES & TOYS, 2801 Leavenworth St., second level of the Cannery. Tel. 775-5483.

This is a wonderful little store with kites galore, little knickknacks, and travel toys. Don't miss it if you're visiting the Cannery. Open Monday through Saturday from 10am to 6pm and on Sunday from 11am to 6pm.

PLAY WITH IT, LTD., 1682 Haight St. Tel. 621-8787.

This store offers a full line of toys, games, and educational toys. Open Monday through Friday from 10am to 7pm, on Saturday to 6pm, and on Sunday from noon to 5pm.

S. F. SCIENCE FICTION TOYS AND HOBBIES, 616 Clement St., between 7th Avenue and 8th Avenue. Tel. 751-7380.

This shop sells mostly science-fiction models such as alien fighters and Japanese animation, and is a good stop for teens. Open Monday through Thursday from 10am to 6pm, on Friday and Saturday to 7pm, and on Sunday to 5pm.

SANRIO, INC., 216 Stockton St., Union Square. Tel. 981-5568.

Don't be misled by the big Hallmark card sign. Downstairs is an enormous "Hello Kitty" store with every accessory girls dream of, but there's much more—little pencil boxes, purses, toothbrush and cup holders, and Hello Kitty makeup. Plan to let them stay for a long time, and be sure to bring the checkbook because there's a lot to buy. Open Monday through Friday from 9:30am to 8pm, on Saturday from 10am to 8pm, and on Sunday from 10am to 6:30pm.

TOY LIQUIDATORS, Yerba Buena Square, 899 Howard St., at Fifth Street. Tel. 974-5136.

This discount store sells overstock toys—not the "hot" items of the moment, but name-brand items at good prices. Ken and Barbie star here. Open Monday through Saturday from 9:30am through 7pm and on Sunday from 11am to 5pm.

TRAVEL GOODS

ON THE ROAD AGAIN, Pier 39. Tel. 434-0106.

In addition to lightweight luggage, this smart shop sells toiletry kits, travel bottles, travel-size items, and a good selection of other related goods. Kids love looking at all the "miniature" items. Open daily from 10am to 8:30pm.

CHAPTER 6

THEIR KIND OF ENTERTAINMENT

1. THEATER & DANCE
2. FILMS
3. CONCERT VENUES
4. CLUBS
5. SPECTATOR SPORTS
6. STORY HOURS

No one can dispute San Francisco's place as a cultural capital. Indeed, it fairly overflows with musical and theatrical events. For a city with fewer than a million inhabitants, San Francisco's overall artistic enterprise is nothing short of phenomenal. You are sure to find much of interest to all family members. You'll also find that spectator sports are very popular here as well.

For up-to-date entertainment information, turn to the *San Francisco Weekly* and the *San Francisco Bay Guardian,* both excellent guides to current activities around the city, with comprehensive listings. They are available free at bars and restaurants, and from street-corner boxes all around the city. *Key,* a free touristy monthly, also has information on programs and performance times; it's available in hotels and around the major tourist sights. The local daily newspapers also have good previews of upcoming events. The Sunday edition of the *San Francisco Examiner and Chronicle,* for example, features a **"Datebook"** section, printed on pink paper, with information and listings on the week's upcoming events.

For the lowdown on daily special events, call 24 hours a day 391-2001. This service, which also offers information in French (tel. 391-2003), Spanish (tel. 391-2122), Japanese (tel. 391-2101), and German (391-2004), gives a summary of daily events, including sports, theater, and museum activities.

And, finally, be sure to get the *San Francisco Book* from the **San Francisco Visitor and Convention Bureau Visitor Information Center** at Hallidie Plaza, 900 Market Street at Powell Street, open weekdays from 9am to 5pm, Saturdays until 3pm, and on Sunday from 10am to 2pm (tel. 391-2000).

TICKETS

You may buy tickets for cultural events at the following agencies: **BASS** ticket center (call information for outlets) or charge tickets by phone (tel. 762-2277); **Ticketron** ticket centers (call information for outlets) or charge by phone (tel. 392-SHOW). The **San Francisco Ticket Box Office Service, STBS** (tel. 433-STBS), sells half-price tickets to theater, dance, and music performances on the day of the show only; tickets for Sunday and Monday events, if available, are sold on Saturday. They also sell advance, full-price tickets through BASS (see above) for most performance halls, sporting events, concerts, and clubs. A service charge, ranging from $1 to $3, is levied on each ticket. Only cash or traveler's checks are accepted for half-price tickets; VISA and MasterCard are accepted for full-price tickets. There are two STBS locations: on Stockton Street, on the east side of Union Square (opposite Maiden Lane); and inside the Embarcadero One office building, at Front Street and

Sacramento Street, in the heart of the Financial District. The Union Square office is open Tuesday through Saturday from noon to 7:30pm; The Embarcadero office is open Monday through Friday from 10am to 6pm.

Tickets to most theater and dance events can also be obtained through **City Box Office,** Sherman Clay & Co., 141 Kearny St. (tel. 392-4400).

BOX OFFICES

The following box offices sell tickets to most major attractions in San Francisco including theater and sporting events. **City Box Office,** 141 Kearny St. (tel. 392-4400), open Monday through Friday from 10am to 5pm. **St. Francis Theater and Sports Tickets,** in the Westin St. Francis Hotel at Union Square (tel. 362-3500), open Monday through Saturday from 9am to 6pm. There is also the **Symphony Box Office** at the Davies Symphony Hall, Van Ness Avenue and Grove Street (tel. 431-5400), and the **Opera Box Office** at the Opera House, Van Ness Avenue and Grove Street (tel. 864-3330).

1. THEATER & DANCE

Most of San Francisco's stages are clustered together, on the blocks just east of Union Square. This semi-official "theater district" is the closest thing San Francisco has to a Broadway or West End. The city's theater offerings—known for solid staging and acting—are among the best in the West. The high quality of performances matches the unusual quantity of productions, a result of the large number of artists who have made the Bay Area their home. And all around town you'll find theater offerings for kids.

FOR KIDS

CALIFORNIA ACADEMY OF SCIENCES, Morrison Auditorium, Golden Gate Park. Tel. 863-1719.
The California Academy of Sciences offers a tremendous variety of children's programs. Call for information and prices.

CHILDREN'S FAIRYLAND, Lake Merritt, Oakland. Tel. 510/452-2259.
This fairy-tale kiddieland frequently has puppet shows for little ones. Call for current information.

KIDSHOWS PERFORMING ARTS SERIES FOR CHILDREN 3 TO 8 YEARS OLD. Berkeley. Tel. 510/527-4977.
Kidshows is a performing arts series for young children. It includes music, puppets, magic, ballet, and folk dance. The season runs from October through April. Performances in Berkeley and San Francisco are offered as well as San Rafael and Walnut Creek.
Prices: $5–$6.

NEW CONSERVATORY CHILDREN'S THEATRE COMPANY, Zephyr Theater Complex, 25 Van Ness Ave., at Market Street. Tel. 861-4915 (for tickets and show information).

Saturday Matinee Club is a program that focuses on kids 4 to 10 with popular stories in dramatized form, for example *Matilda* by Roald Dahl and *Really Rosie* by Maurice Sendak.

The weekend performance program for kids 11 and older focuses on issue-oriented topics. Recent performances were *Broadway Memories, Kegger* (about drinking and driving) and *Earthmatters* (families and the environment).

Prices: $4 up.

YOUNG PERFORMERS' THEATER, Fort Mason Center. Tel. 346-5550.

Presents six to eight stage shows per year on Saturday and Sunday at 1pm and 3:30pm. Performances are approximately 45 minutes long. The troupe performs such classics as *Winnie the Pooh, Hansel and Gretel, Charlotte's Web*, and *Peter and the Wolf*. Good for children 2 to 12. Catered birthday parties. Call for ticket reservations.

Prices: $6 adults, $4 children.

FOR THE WHOLE FAMILY

AMERICAN CONSERVATORY THEATRE (ACT), Stage Door Theatre, 440 Mason St. Tel. 749-2228.

 The American Conservatory Theatre (ACT) made its debut in 1967 and quickly established itself as the city's premier resident theater group. The troupe is so venerated that ACT has been compared to the superb British National Theatre, the Berliner Ensemble, and the Comédie Française. ACT offers solid, well-staged, and brilliantly acted theater, and performs both classical drama and new and experimental works. It won a Tony Award for excellence in repertory theater and actor training in 1979. Whatever's on, the repertoire is always exciting and upbeat. The ACT season runs from October through May. Performances are held at various venues around the city, including the Stage Door Theatre, Theater on the Square, and the Orpheum Theater. Specific locations and transit information can be obtained from the box office.

Prices: $10 to $32.

CURRAN THEATER, 445 Geary St. Tel. 474-3800. THE GOLDEN GATE THEATER, 25 Taylor St. Tel. 474-3800. And THE ORPHEUM THEATER, 1192 Market St. Tel. 474-3800.

These three theaters present big-name Broadway musicals and comedies, such as *Cats* and *H.M.S. Pinafore,* and individual musical talents such as Linda Ronstadt. Matinees on Wednesday, Saturday, and Sunday.

Prices: $14 to $22.

FORT MASON CENTER, Building D, Buchanan Street at Marina Boulevard. Tel. 441-5705.

There are several theaters in Fort Mason, including the highly acclaimed Magic Theatre (tel. 441-8822). Call for specific information about all.

MAKE-A-CIRCUS, Fort Mason, Bldg. C. Tel. 776-8470 for information.

Based in San Francisco 18 years, it is a combination professional one-ring circus (without animals) and audience participation. They teach circus skills such as juggling, stilt walking, tumbling, clowning, and pyramid balancing to anyone in the audience who wants to learn. Call for performance dates.

Price: Free.

PICKLE FAMILY CIRCUS, Palace of Fine Arts Theatre, at Lyon Street and Bay Street. Tel. 826-5678.

This San Francisco–based troupe creates much more than a circus. It takes circus to an art form by combining drama, comedy, dance, and music in a one-ring theatrical ensemble. The current show is an all-clown story. This touring company travels throughout California and the rest of the United States in the spring, summer, and fall.

Performances are generally in December; and on Memorial Day Weekend. Call for exact performance schedule.

Prices: Adults $8–$25; children $8–$15.

SAN FRANCISCO BALLET, War Memorial Opera House, Van Ness Avenue and Grove Street. Tel. 621-3838.

The San Francisco Ballet is known as one of the country's finest ballet companies, and performs some of the classics such as *Sleeping Beauty* and *Swan Lake*. Its regular season runs from January to May (with performances almost nightly except Monday), and there are special holiday performances, such as *The Nutcracker*. There are matinees on Saturday and Sunday at 2pm.

Prices: $10–$70.

2. FILMS

The **San Francisco International Film Festival**, held in March of each year, is one of America's oldest film festivals. Tickets are relatively inexpensive, and screenings are very accessible to the general public. Entries include new films by beginning and established directors. For a schedule or information, call 415/931-FILM. Tickets can be charged by phone through BASS (tel. 835-3849).

Even if you're not here in time for the festival, don't despair. The classic, independent, and mainstream cinemas in San Francisco are every bit as good as the city's other cultural offerings. And children's offerings are fine as well.

FORT POINT NATIONAL HISTORIC SITE THEATER. Tel. 556-1693.

Documentaries, slides, films, and videos are available. Call for information.

LAWRENCE HALL OF SCIENCE, University of California, Berkeley. Tel. 510/642-5133.

A variety of films are shown here, from ones that are good for very little kids to feature films more appropriate for older kids. Call for schedule.

Holiday feature films are shown weekday holidays at 11am and 2:30pm. Films such as *The Little Mermaid* or *The Absent-Minded Professor* are featured.

Prices: $3.50 adults; $2.50 ages 7–18, students and senior citizens; $1 ages 3–6; under 3, free. No additional charge for films.

PACIFIC FILM ARCHIVE, 2625 Durant Ave., Berkeley. Tel. 510/642-1412.

Occasional Saturday and Sunday children matinees are shown at 3:30pm. The films typically feature animation or such films as *The Red Balloon*. There is a yearly Teddy Bear festival. Call for information.

Prices: $5 general admission, including seniors and students; children 12 and under, $3.50.

TIBURON PLAYHOUSE, 40 Main St., Tiburon. Tel. 925-7416.
The playhouse sometimes has a children's film festival. Call for details and prices.

3. CONCERT VENUES

San Francisco is a year-round music festival, with offerings that run the gamut from classical to jazz as well as pop and other styles. There's an abundance of programs for children. One of the best, and longest-running, summer programs is the free **Stern Grove Midsummer Music Festival** (tel. 398-6551), held every Sunday at 2pm in Golden Gate Park. The first concert is traditionally offered by the San Francisco Symphony Orchestra; other performances include ballet, jazz, and theater. For more than 50 years the festival has run from mid-June through August. Stern Grove is located near 19th Avenue and Sloat Boulevard; arrive early for a good view, and bring a picnic.

Other favorites include the following:

CONCERTS FOR KIDS, Davies Symphony Hall, Van Ness Avenue at Grove Street. Tel. 431-5400.
The San Francisco Symphony presents several performances for children. Individual tickets can be purchased if they haven't all been snatched up by school groups. Call for schedule and prices.

SAN FRANCISCO CONSERVATORY OF MUSIC, Hellman Hall, 19th Avenue and Ortega Street (Sunset District), and Agnes Albert Hall, second floor of the Conservatory. Tel. 665-0874.
Every Saturday at 11:30am and 2:30pm, students from the Preparatory Division of the Conservatory (ages 4 to 18) put on recitals. Call for information 665-3818.
Price: Free.

SAN FRANCISCO GIRLS CHORUS, First Unitarian Center, 1187 Franklin St. Tel. 673-1511.
The group is 13 years old, and has a fine reputation regionally and nationally for professional-level concerts. There are Christmas and springtime concerts. Another could be straight classical music (either new or combined with older music), or a children's program (all children's music), or a combination of all the touring programs. There is an annual Christmas singalong concert.
Price: Free.

SAN FRANCISCO SYMPHONY, Davies Symphony Hall, Van Ness Avenue at Grove Street. Tel. 431-5400.
The San Francisco Symphony season runs from September to June. There is a Summer Pops series and a Beethoven Festival in the summer. A Mozart Festival usually takes place in the late spring, early summer. Matinees are offered on Thursday at 2pm and on Sunday at 3pm.

Occasional open rehearsals (probably best for older children) take place on weekdays at 10am, and are very popular. At the open rehearsal, visitors are welcome as early as 8:30am for coffee and donuts; at 9:15 there is a discussion with open seating.

Prices: Concert tickets $10–$70.

SAN FRANCISCO SYMPHONY YOUTH ORCHESTRA, Davies Symphony Hall, Van Ness Avenue at Grove Street. Tel. 552-8000.

This youth orchestra is made up of 110 students up to age 20. Regular performances during the season from January through May (with special concerts during the Christmas season) are held at Davies Symphony Hall. All performances are matinees. Purchase tickets well in advance.

Prices: $6.50 (certain holiday performances are higher).

4. CLUBS

Always a pioneer in arts and entertainment, San Francisco is well known for its liberal policies and alternative culture. And the adult club scene reflects this. But you're visiting with your children, so here's a short list of our family comedy favorites.

BEACH BLANKET BABYLON, at Club Fugazi, 678 Green St., North Beach. Tel. 421-4222.

Now a San Francisco tradition, Beach Blanket Babylon evolved from Steve Silver's Rent-a-Freak service—a group of party-givers extraordinaire who hired themselves out as a "cast of characters" to entertain, complete with fabulous costumes and sets, props, and gags. After their act caught on, it was moved into the Savoy-Tivoli, a North Beach bar. By 1974 the audience grew too large for the facility and Beach Blanket has been at the 400-seat Club Fugazi ever since.

Tiny, candle-topped tables now face the medium-size stage, where one of the most delightful, funny, and original productions is staged nightly. Beach Blanket is a comedic musical send-up that is best known for its outrageous costumes and oversize headdresses. It's been almost 20 years now and almost every performance still sells out. The show is updated with enough regularity that it still draws a fair number of locals along with the hordes of tourists. Minors are welcome at Sunday matinees at 3pm when no alcohol is served; photo ID is required for evening performances. It's wise to write for tickets at least 3 weeks in advance, or obtain them through STBS (see above). *Note:* When you purchase tickets, they will be within a specific section depending upon price; however, seating is still first-come/first-seated within that section. Performances are given on Wednesday and Thursday at 8pm, on Friday and Saturday at 8 and 10:30pm, and on Sunday at 3 and 7:30pm.

Admission: Tickets, $16–$27.

COBB'S COMEDY CLUB, 2801 Leavenworth St. Tel. 928-4320.

Located in the Cannery at Fisherman's Wharf, Cobbs attracts an upscale audience with national headliners such as Emo Philips, Paula Poundstone, and Jim Carrey. There is comedy every night, including a 13-comedian All-Pro Monday showcase (a 3-hour marathon). We love to come here with our teens—Cobb's is open to those 18 and over, as well as kids aged 16 and 17 if they are accompanied by a parent or legal guardian. Shows are on Monday at 8pm, Tuesday through Thursday at 9pm, and on Friday and Saturday at 9 and 11pm.

Admission: Mon $5, Tues–Sun $7–$12, plus a two-drink minimum nightly.

5. SPECTATOR SPORTS

The Bay Area's good sports scene includes several major professional franchises, including football, baseball, and basketball. Check the local newspapers' sports sections for daily listings of local events.

BASEBALL

OAKLAND ATHLETICS, Oakland Coliseum Complex, at the Hegenberger Road exit from I-880, in Oakland. Tel. 510/638-0500 or 638-6300.
The 1989 world-champion As play across the bay in the Oakland Coliseum Stadium. Part of the Oakland Coliseum Complex, the stadium holds close to 55,000 spectators and is serviced by BART's Coliseum station. Tickets are available from the Coliseum Box Office or by phone through Ticketron (tel. 392-7469).

SAN FRANCISCO GIANTS, Candlestick Park, Giants Drive and Gilman Avenue, 8 miles south of SF via the Bayshore Freeway (U.S. 101). Tel. 467-8000.
From April through October the National League Giants play their home games at Candlestick Park, off U.S. 101 about 8 miles south of downtown. Tickets are usually available up until game time (weekend afternoon games—1:05pm; weekday afternoon games—12:35pm; night games—7:35pm), but they can be dreadfully far from the action, so it's best to pick them up as early in your stay as possible. Tickets may be obtained at Candlestick Park, from Giants Dugout, 170 Grant Ave. (tel. 982-9400); or by phone through Ticketron (tel. 392-7469). Special $4 express bus service is available from Market Street on game days; call MUNI (tel. 673-MUNI) for pickup points and schedule information. Bring a coat, as this 60,000-seat stadium is known for chilly winds.

BASKETBALL

GOLDEN STATE WARRIORS, Oakland Coliseum Complex, at the Hegenberger Road exit from I-880, in Oakland. Tel. 510/638-6000.
The NBA Warriors play basketball in the 14,000-seat Oakland Coliseum Arena. The season runs from November through April, and most games are played at 7:30pm. Tickets are available at the arena, and by phone through BASS Ticketmaster (tel. 762-BASS).

FOOTBALL

SAN FRANCISCO 49ERS, Candlestick Park, Giants Drive and Gilman Avenue. Tel. 468-2249.
The football 49ers call Candlestick Park home. The stadium is off U.S. 101 about 8 miles south of downtown. Games are played on Sunday from August through December; kickoff is usually at 1pm. Tickets sell out early in the season, but are available at higher prices through ticket agents beforehand and from scalpers at the gate. Ask your hotel concierge or visit City Box Office, 141 Kearny Street (tel.

392-4400). Special $4 express bus service is available from Market Street on game days; call MUNI (tel. 673-MUNI) for pickup points and schedule information.

UNIVERSITY OF CALIFORNIA GOLDEN BEARS, 61 Harmon Gym, University of California, Berkeley. Tel. 510/642-5150, or toll free 800/GO-BEARS.

The Cal Bears play their home games in Memorial Stadium, on the university campus across the bay. Tickets are usually available at game time. Phone for schedules and information.

HORSE RACING

BAY MEADOWS, 2600 S. Delaware St, off U.S. 101, in San Mateo. Tel. 574-7223.

The nearest autumn racing is at this Thoroughbred and quarter horse track on the peninsula. Located about 20 miles south of downtown San Francisco, the course hosts races 4 or 5 days each week from September through January. Call for admission and post times.

GOLDEN GATE FIELDS, Gilman Street, off I-80, in Albany. Tel. 510/526-3020.

Scenic Thoroughbred races are held here from January to June. The park is located on the seashore, 10 miles northeast of San Francisco. Call for admission prices and post times.

6. STORY HOURS

The following libraries and bookstores offer story hours on a regular basis. Some offer other programs such as films for preschoolers, video programs, and arts-and-crafts activities. Call for times.

LIBRARIES

CHINATOWN BRANCH, 1135 Powell St. (tel. 274-0275); **MARINA BRANCH,** 1890 Chestnut St. (tel. 292-2150); **NOE VALLEY BRANCH,** 451 Jersey St. (tel. 695-5095); **NORTH BEACH BRANCH,** 2000 Mason St. (tel. 274-0270); **RICHMOND BRANCH,** 351 Ninth Ave. (tel. 666-7165).

DIAL-A-STORY, for a bedtime tale (tel. 626-6516).

BOOKSTORES

A CLEAN, WELL-LIGHTED PLACE FOR BOOKS, 2417 Larkspur Landing Circle in Larkspur (in Marin County). Tel. 461-0171.

This location has regular story hours for children on Sunday. Call for times and other special activities.

CHARLOTTE'S WEB CHILDREN'S BOOKSTORE, 1207-F Bridgeway, Sausalito. Tel. 332-2244.

This store has a huge selection of picture books, folk and fairy tales, foreign-language books, and educational books.

Regularly scheduled story hours: Saturday at 10:30am.

CODY'S BOOKS, 2454 Telegraph Ave. Berkeley. Tel. 510/845-7852.

Cody's has over 100,000 titles, and a huge selection of children's books. Open Sunday through Thursday from 9:15am to 9:45pm, on Friday and Saturday from 9:15am to 10:45pm. Call for story hours.

QUINBY'S, 3411 California St. in the Laurel Village Shopping Center. Tel. 751-7727.

Quinby's features one of the largest selections of children's books and educational materials in the Bay Area. Story hours are on Wednesdays, with performances usually twice a month; call for details.

The bookstore is open Monday through Saturday from 9:30am to 6pm and on Sunday from 11am to 5pm.

CHAPTER 7

WHERE KIDS LIKE TO EAT

1. ON THE RUN
2. CANDIES, COOKIES & ICE CREAM
3. KID-RATED RESTAURANTS

San Francisco has so many restaurants that you never need eat in the same place twice when you come for a visit. Of course, we find favorites and love to visit them again and again. Here are just some of the ones we like.

1. ON THE RUN

Much of the eating we do while sightseeing is on the run, so we've come up with some fast—and cute—San Francisco places for you and the kids. Since these are typical fast-food-type eateries, we don't list amenities such as highchairs, and we don't worry about reservations.

APPLE ANNIE'S, Pier 39. Tel. 397-0473.
   Cuisine: AMERICAN.
$ **Prices:** Average $1–$3. No credit cards.
   Open: Daily 10:30am–8:30pm.
Fruit juice, pizza, and sandwiches is the fare here. Apple Annie's is on Pier 39 at Fisherman's Wharf.

AUNT FANNY'S HOT PRETZELS, Pier 39. Tel. 986-0706.
   Cuisine: AMERICAN.
$ **Prices:** Average $1–$2. No credit cards.
   Open: Daily 9:30am–8:30pm.
Feed on hot pretzels, hot dogs, and nachos here. You'll find Aunt Fanny's on Pier 39 at Fisherman's Wharf.

BLONDIE'S PIZZA, 63 Powell St., between Market and Ellis streets. Tel. 982-6168.
   Cuisine: PIZZA.
$ **Prices:** $1 per slice. No credit cards.
   Open: Daily 10:30am–9pm.

⭐ Lines of people standing for delicious pizza-by-the-slice or whole pizzas. There's always a special available—it could be ground beef with mushroom and onion or California with pepperoni and mushroom. No tables. Blondie's is located across from Woolworth's at the cable-car turnaround.

There's another branch in Berkeley at 2340 Telegraph Ave. (tel. 510/548-1129).

BOUDIN SOURDOUGH BAKERY AND CAFE, 156 Jefferson St., Fisherman's Wharf. Tel. 928-1849.
   Cuisine: AMERICAN.
$ **Prices:** $1–$5. MC, V.
   Open: Mon–Thurs 7am–7:30pm, Fri–Sun 7am–8pm; longer hours during summer.

The ultimate in sourdough bread and sandwiches. You can sit and eat or just buy several baguettes and stroll. Boudin's is located on Fisherman's Wharf.

BOUDIN SOURDOUGH BAKERY AND CAFE, Ghirardelli Square. Tel. 928-7404.
   Cuisine: AMERICAN.
$ **Prices:** $1–$5. MC, V.
   Open: Mon–Thurs 8am–8pm, Fri–Sat 8am–9pm, Sun 8am–7pm; longer hours during summer.

San Francisco sourdough bread and sandwiches are the fare here. The Fisherman's Wharf special (hollowed-out bread with clam chowder) is delectable. You'll find this branch at Ghirardelli Square.

BOUDIN SOURDOUGH BAKERY AND CAFE, Pier 39. Tel. 421-0185.
   Cuisine: AMERICAN.
$ **Prices:** $1–$5. MC, V.
   Open: Daily 7am–8:30pm; longer hours during summer.

Get your breads, sandwiches, pizza, and salads here on Pier 39 at Fisherman's Wharf.

There are other branches at 43 Drumm St., downtown (tel. 362-3330) and at Macy's Union Square, 170 O'Farrell St. (tel. 296-4511).

THE BURGER CAFE, Pier 39. Tel. 986-5966.
   Cuisine: AMERICAN.
$ **Prices:** $1.50–$5. No credit cards.
   Open: Daily 8:30am–10pm.

They serve burgers, hot dogs, and salad-bar items here at Pier 39.

CARL'S JR. RESTAURANTS, Hallidie Plaza, 5th and Eddy streets. Tel. 391-5799.
   Cuisine: AMERICAN.
$ **Prices:** $2–$6 average. No credit cards.
   Open: Daily 24 hours.

Fast-food items are served here in the downtown area. There are other branches at 270 Columbus Ave. (tel. 362-0945); 4 Embarcadero Center, street level (tel. 391-7780); and 722 Market St. at Third Street (tel. 398-5495).

CHOWDERS, Pier 39. Tel. 391-4737.
   Cuisine: CHOWDER.
$ **Prices:** $3–$7. No credit cards.

Open: Daily 10:30am–8:30pm.

⭐ For a wonderful lunch or snack of chowder, seafood, and sandwiches, try Chowders. A real treat is the scooped-out sourdough bread served with clam chowder.

DINO'S PIZZA, 2101 Fillmore St. at California Street. Tel. 922-4700.
Cuisine: PIZZA.
$ Prices: $1.50 up. No credit cards.
Open: Mon–Sat 11am–11pm, Sun noon–10pm.

Both thin- and thick-crust pizza are served here. You can sit down and enjoy your snack before continuing on your way. Located in the Marina District.

DOUBLE RAINBOW ICE CREAM AND DESSERT CAFE, 519 Powell St. Tel. 982-3097.
Cuisine: AMERICAN.
$ Prices: $1–$6. No credit cards.
Open: Mon–Fri 8am–11pm, Sat 10am–midnight, Sun 11am–11pm.

⭐ If you're an ice cream lover, this is like finding a pot of gold. An award-winning company known for simply sinful desserts and rich American-style ice cream, Double Rainbow also serves sandwiches and espresso/cappuccino. You'll find it at Union Square.

Other branches are located in the Marina District at 2133 Chestnut St. near Steiner (tel. 922-3920); in Chinatown at 316 Columbus Ave. near Broadway (tel. 956-4095); and near Golden Gate Park at 1724 Haight St. near Stanyan Street (tel. 668-6690).

FRIES INTERNATIONAL, Pier 39. Tel. 986-5111.
Cuisine: AMERICAN.
$ Prices: $1 or so. No credit cards.
Open: Daily 10:30am–8:30pm.

All the fries you could possibly want. Fisherman's Wharf area (Pier 39).

GHIRARDELLI CHOCOLATE MANUFACTORY, plaza level of Clock Tower Building, Ghirardelli Square. Tel. 474-3938.
Cuisine: AMERICAN.
$ Prices: $2 and up. MC, V (candy only).
Open: Daily 10am–10pm.

The ultimate ice-cream shop where you can get sodas, ice-cream sundaes, and Ghirardelli chocolate of all kinds. They even serve one-scoop sundaes for children. If you are going to be in San Francisco for a birthday, call ahead and ask the manager about their special party program. If you stop here for a treat, be prepared to wait in line at peak times in the busy season. You have to fill out your order and present it to the cashier before you enter the restaurant. When it's ready, your number will be called. Our kids love to watch the goings-on at the small chocolate manufactory at the back of the store with all the chocolate-making equipment in motion. Adults will enjoy browsing in the gift shop. There is a candymaker hard at work during the day creating dessert sauces and chocolate candies. The manufactory is in Ghirardelli Square. Where else?

GORDO'S MEXICAN FOOD, 1233 9th Ave., near Lincoln Avenue. Tel. 566-6011.
Cuisine: MEXICAN.
$ Prices: $1–$4. No credit cards.

Open: Daily 10am–10pm.
Stand in line for wonderful burritos, tacos, and quesadillas. They'll wrap it to go. Gordo's is ½ block from Golden Gate Park. There's another branch at 2252 Clement St. near 24th Avenue (tel. 387-4484).

LE CARROUSEL, Pier 39. Tel. 433-4160.
Cuisine: PATISSERIE.
$ Prices: $1–$5. No credit cards.
Open: Daily 8:30am–8:30pm.
You can get croissants, pastries, and deli here in the middle of Pier 39.

LA NOUVELLE PATISSERIE, Ghirardelli Square, Wooden Mill Building, 2nd floor. Tel. 776-5533.
Cuisine: PATISSERIE.
$ Prices: $2–$10. MC, V.
Open: Daily 8am–8:30pm.
Enjoy buttery pastries, gourmet burgers, and garden salads, plus Bay views from the terrace. A Ghirardelli Square favorite. There's another branch at 2184 Union St. (Tel. 931-7655).

McDONALD'S RESTAURANTS, 2 Embarcadero Center. Tel. 397-6333.
Cuisine: AMERICAN.
$ Prices: $1–$4. No credit cards.
Open: Mon–Fri 6:30am–7pm, Sat 8am–5pm, closed Sun.
Andrew and Elizabeth suffer from "withdrawal" if they don't go to McDonald's for a very long stretch of time. If your kids are the same, here's where you come for the fix. In addition to this branch at the Embarcadero Center, there are two other McDonald's near sightseeing venues: near Golden Gate Park at 730 Stanyan St. near Haight Street (tel. 668-4445), open Sun–Thurs 7am–11pm, Fri–Sat 7am–midnight; near Fisherman's Wharf at 2739 Taylor St. (tel. 776-1562), open Sun–Thurs 7am–10pm, Fri–Sat 7am–11pm.

POMPEI'S GROTTO, 340 Jefferson St., Fisherman's Wharf. Tel. 776-9265.
Cuisine: SEAFOOD.
$ Prices: $2–$10. AE, CB, DC, MC, V.
Open: Daily 9am–10pm.
In the San Francisco tradition, this is one of the best stands to buy a crab or shrimp walkaway cocktail as you're making your way down the Wharf. Pompei's Grotto also serves chowder, whole or half crab, oysters, espresso, cappuccino, and cold drinks.

SABELLA AND LA TORRE, 340 Jefferson St., Stall #3, at Fisherman's Wharf. Tel. 673-2824.
Cuisine: SEAFOOD.
$ Prices: $4–$10. AE, DC, MC, V.
Open: Daily 10am–11pm.
Owned by a branch of the Sabella family (see one of our favorite restaurants, A. Sabella's, under "Kid-Rated Restaurants"), this little place is frequented by fishermen. There's a very informal area where you can sit down inside, or you can take your seafood cocktails, crab, prawns, oysters and clams on the half-shell and eat outside. Another Fisherman's Wharf winner.

SAL'S PIZZERIA, Pier 39. Tel. 981-8030.

Cuisine: PIZZA.
$ Prices: $1.50 up. No credit cards.
Open: Daily 11am–9pm.

Pizza, pizza, pizza at Pier 39.

SALMAGUNDI, 422 Geary St. Tel. 441-0894.

Cuisine: AMERICAN/SOUPS & SALADS. **Reservations:** None accepted.
$ Prices: $2.95–$5.50. AE, MC, V.
Open: Mon–Sat 8am–11pm, Sun 11am–9pm.

For a fast, delicious breakfast, lunch, or dinner, the Salmagundi restaurants fit the bill. (For more detail, see the writeup in "Kid-Rated Restaurants" below.) In addition to this Union Square location, there are two other Salmagundi branches: one at 2 Embarcadero Center (tel. 982-5603) and another at the Civic Center, 39 Grove St. (tel. 431-7337).

SIZZLER RESTAURANT, 398 Eddy St. at Leavenworth Street. Tel. 775-1393.

Cuisine: AMERICAN/SALAD BAR.
$ Prices: $2.95–$8.95. MC, V.
Open: Daily 11am–10pm.

This is as quick as you can get without being fast food. One reason we love Sizzler is because everyone in the family gets what they want. Fisherman's Wharf area.

VICOLO PIZZERIA, 900 North Point St. Tel. 776-1331.

Cuisine: ITALIAN.
$ Prices: $1.25 up. No credit cards.
Open: Sun–Thurs 11am–9pm, Fri–Sat 11am–11pm.

Good for deep-dish pizza as well as thin crust. Ghirardelli Square location.

VLAHOS FRUIT ORCHARD, Pier 39. Tel. 981-8030.

Cuisine: FRUIT.
$ Prices: By piece or by pound. No credit cards.
Open: May–Dec daily 10:30am–8:30pm.

Wonderful displays of fruit. This is the ultimate California fruit experience—but only from May through September. Let the kids choose some fruit, wash it off, and eat it as you stroll. A Pier 39 treat.

2. CANDIES, COOKIES & ICE CREAM

CANDIES

THE CANDY STORE, Pier 39. Tel. 981-2649.

Here you can buy wonderful candy—by the pound.

CHOCOLATE HEAVEN, Pier 39. Tel. 421-1789.
Goodies from around the world.

CONFETTI LE CHOCOLATIER, 2801 Leavenworth St., in The Cannery. Tel. 474-7377.
You'll find hand-dipped milk chocolate candied fruit, handmade Swiss chocolates and chocolate truffles, among other goodies. There's another branch at 4 Embarcadero Center (tel. 362-1706).

FINDLEY'S FABULOUS FUDGE, 397 Geary St. at Mason Street in Union Square. Tel. 434-2131.
This place is to die for. Old-fashioned fudge like you wish your Grandma used to make. You'll find a huge variety of choices here.

GHIRARDELLI CHOCOLATE, 44 Stockton St., Union Square. Tel. 397-3615.
Yummy chocolates and gift assortments. (You'll want to take the kids here after a look-around at F.A.O. Schwarz, which is next door.)

GHIRARDELLI CHOCOLATE MANUFACTORY, plaza level of Clock Tower Building, Ghirardelli Square. Tel. 474-3938.
Chocolates, chocolates, and more chocolates.

GHIRARDELLI'S PREMIUM CHOCOLATES, west side, plaza level of Clock Tower Building, Ghirardelli Square, Tel. 474-1414.
Serving up chocolates, espresso, and yogurt. Buy gifts here, too.

STEVE'S SWEETIES, 2nd floor of Wooden Mill, Ghirardelli Square. Tel. 474-3346.
Chocolate candy and brownies are Steve's "Sweeties."

COOKIES & ICE CREAM

BLUE CHIP COOKIES, Pier 39. Tel. 989-9411.
Get your chocolate-chip cookies (15 varieties), brownies, and muffins here.

CONCEPT, Pier 39. Tel. 956-9312.
Delicious ice cream and frozen yogurt are the treats at Concept.

DOUBLE RAINBOW, 519 Powell St., Union Square. Tel. 982-3097.
Dubbed the "Best in the U.S.," the premium ice cream sold here has won numerous prizes. Chocolate Peanut Butter Swirl—yummy! Open Mon–Fri 8am–11pm, Sat 10am–midnight, Sun 11am–11pm. Other branches around town; see the writeup above in "On the Run."

FANTASIA, 3465 California St., between Spruce and Laurel streets. Tel. 752-0825.
With chocolate as their specialty, it's no wonder that most of the cakes are yummy chocolate. They make European-style cakes, milk-chocolate cable cars, plus

cappuccino and other drinks to quench your thirst. There are specials at holiday times. Ask about the cookie-decorating parties that are held four times a year.

GELATO CLASSICO ITALIAN ICE CREAM, 448 Post St. near Powell Street, Union Square. Tel. 989-5884.

The original Italian ice cream. There's another branch in North Beach at 576 Union Street, near Stockton Street (tel. 391-6667).

GHIRARDELLI'S GELATERIA, North Point, Ghirardelli Square. Tel. 474-1115.

This location has gelato and espresso.

GINO GELATERIA, 701 Columbus Ave., North Beach. Tel. 981-4664.

Pastries, espresso, sandwiches, juices, and fresh fruit are the fare here.

GOLDEN GATE FORTUNE COOKIES CO., 56 Ross Alley near Washington Street. Tel. 781-3956.

Tucked away in a little alley, you might find the search for this cookie company almost as much fun as eating the cookies.

JUST DESSERTS, lobby level, 3 Embarcadero Center. Tel. 421-1609.

Old-fashioned baked goods—all manner of cakes and cookies—are made fresh daily. There are other branches at 248 Church St. (tel. 626-5774), 3735 Buchanan St. (tel. 922-8675), and in Berkeley at 1823 Solano St. (tel. 510/527-7344).

LAPPERT'S ICE CREAM, 689 Bridgeway, Sausalito, Tel. 510/332-2019.

Lots of great non-fat flavors as well as your all-time favorites.

LE SCOOP ESPRESSO & FROZEN YOGURT BAR, 2 Embarcadero Center. Tel. 397-4478.

The frozen yogurt served here comes in flavors such as peanut butter and strawberry-banana as well as the usual flavors. Ice cream and espresso are available too.

MARA'S BAKERY, 503 Columbus Ave., North Beach. Tel. 397-9435.

Come to Mara's for Italian pastries, cookies, espresso, tea, and coffee.

MEE MEE BAKERY, 1328 Stockton St., between Broadway and Vallejo Street. Tel. 362-3204.

Fortune cookies, almond cookies, Chinese pastries and cakes are all stars here.

OLD UNCLE GAYLOR'S OLD-FASHIONED ICE CREAM PARLOURS, 221 Irving St., Sunset District. Tel. 759-1614.

Old-fashioned but yummy ice cream is served at Old Uncle Gaylor's. For the locations of other branches, check the telephone directory.

RORY'S TWISTED SCOOP ICE CREAM, 2015 Fillmore St., Western Addition. Tel. 346-3692.

Great ice cream that the locals love. There's another branch of Rory's at 24th Street and Castro Street, Castro District. Tel. 648-2837.

SWENSEN'S ICE CREAM, 1999 Hyde St., corner of Union Street. Tel. 775-6818.

This is America's original Swensen's ice cream parlour—it opened in 1948. They have sundaes, milkshakes, cones, plus ice cream in pints, quarts, and half gallons. Some yogurt as well.

TOY BOAT, 401 Clement St. at Fifth Avenue, Richmond District. Tel. 751-7505.

⭐ A really fun place for desserts. Toys decorate the entire place. There are robots, pandas, dinosaurs, and dolls. Toy Boat serves great floats, smoothies, and sundaes, natural ice creams, cakes, and espressos. In the morning, you and yours can grab a scone or muffin.

3. KID-RATED RESTAURANTS

It's been said that San Francisco has so many restaurants that if you ate in a different one for every meal, it would take you four years to try them all. And new ones open all the time!

San Francisco is an epicurean's dream—even if that food lover has kids and wants to dine with them. Hundreds of restaurants welcome families. We've chosen many of them, listed them by neighborhood first and price second. And we've limited cuisine to the types that children are most likely to eat. Enjoy.

CHINATOWN

There are so many restaurants in Chinatown catering to the family trade that you really could try almost any place that catches your fancy. But here are the ones that we like the best.

Tip: Don't take your car to Chinatown—it's almost impossible to find parking.

MODERATE

THE CANTON TEA HOUSE AND RESTAURANT, 1108 Stockton St. Tel. 982-1032.
Cuisine: CHINESE. **Reservations:** Accepted.
$ Prices: Lunch main courses $4–$7 (dim sum, less), dinner main courses $7.15–$9.55. MC, V.
Open: Daily 7am–4pm and 5pm–10pm.
Children's Services: Highchairs, boosters.
This is a wonderful place to go for breakfast (dim sum), lunch, or dinner. Delectable, reasonably priced food is served by people who are attentive and helpful.

More than 20 kinds of dim sum are made, ranging from barbecued pork buns to sweet lotus buns. This is a fun place for afternoon tea and dim sum, rice, or noodles. But don't limit your eating to lunch or breakfast. The restaurant also serves dinner, and the entrées are delicious. If your kids like soup, the chicken wonton is the one to choose, and the cashew chicken is wonderful. Canton House is a great place to go either before or after wandering around Chinatown.

GOLDEN PHOENIX, 728 Washington St. Tel. 989-4400.
Cuisine: CHINESE. **Reservations:** Accepted.
$ Prices: Main courses $6–$9. AE, CB, DC, MC, V.
Open: Mon–Fri 11:30am–10:30pm, Sat–Sun 2:30–10:30pm.
Children's Services: Highchairs, boosters.

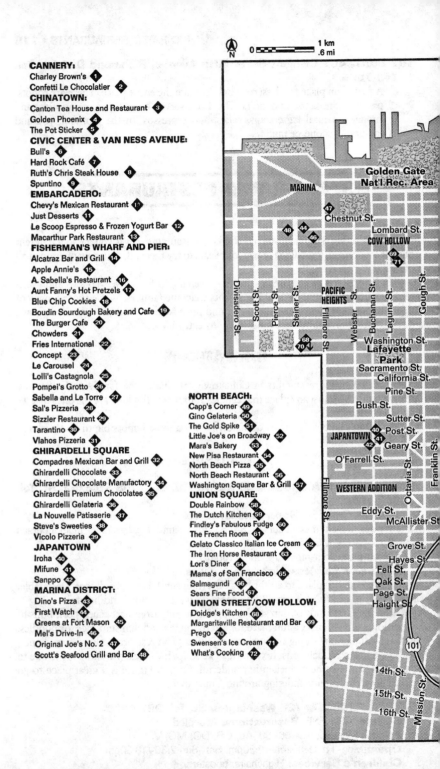

CANNERY:
Charley Brown's 1
Confetti Le Chocolatier 2
CHINATOWN:
Canton Tea House and Restaurant 3
Golden Phoenix 4
The Pot Sticker 5
CIVIC CENTER & VAN NESS AVENUE:
Bull's 6
Hard Rock Café 7
Ruth's Chris Steak House 8
Spuntino 9
EMBARCADERO:
Chevy's Mexican Restaurant 10
Just Desserts 11
Le Scoop Espresso & Frozen Yogurt Bar 12
Macarthur Park Restaurant 13
FISHERMAN'S WHARF AND PIER:
Alcatraz Bar and Grill 14
Apple Annie's 15
A. Sabella's Restaurant 16
Aunt Fanny's Hot Pretzels 17
Blue Chip Cookies 18
Boudin Sourdough Bakery and Cafe 19
The Burger Cafe 20
Chowders 21
Fries International 22
Concept 23
Le Carousel 24
Lolli's Castagnola 25
Pompei's Grotto 26
Sabella and Le Torre 27
Sal's Pizzeria 28
Sizzler Restaurant 29
Tarantino 30
Vlahos Pizzeria 31
GHIRARDELLI SQUARE
Compadres Mexican Bar and Grill 32
Ghirardelli Chocolate 33
Ghirardelli Chocolate Manufactory 34
Ghirardelli Premium Chocolates 35
Ghirardelli Gelateria 36
La Nouvelle Patisserie 37
Steve's Sweeties 38
Vicolo Pizzeria 39
JAPANTOWN
Iroha 40
Mifune 41
Sanppo 42
MARINA DISTRICT:
Dino's Pizza 43
First Watch 44
Greens at Fort Mason 45
Mel's Drive-In 46
Original Joe's No. 2 47
Scott's Seafood Grill and Bar 48

NORTH BEACH:
Capp's Corner 49
Gino Gelateria 50
The Gold Spike 51
Little Joe's on Broadway 52
Mara's Bakery 53
New Pisa Restaurant 54
North Beach Pizza 55
North Beach Restaurant 56
Washington Square Bar & Grill 57
UNION SQUARE:
Double Rainbow 58
The Dutch Kitchen 59
Findley's Fabulous Fudge 60
The French Room 61
Gelato Classico Italian Ice Cream 62
The Iron Horse Restaurant 63
Lori's Diner 64
Mama's of San Francisco 65
Salmagundi 66
Sears Fine Food 67
UNION STREET/COW HOLLOW:
Doidge's Kitchen 68
Margaritaville Restaurant and Bar 69
Prego 70
Swensen's Ice Cream 71
What's Cooking 72

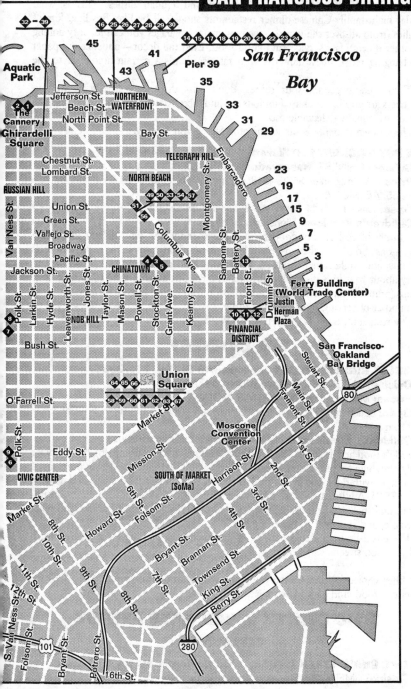

SAN FRANCISCO DINING

San Francisco Bay

Pier 39

Aquatic Park

The Cannery

Ghirardelli Square

NORTHERN WATERFRONT

Jefferson St.
Beach St.
North Point St.
Bay St.

Chestnut St.
Lombard St.

RUSSIAN HILL

TELEGRAPH HILL

NORTH BEACH

Union St.
Green St.
Vallejo St.
Broadway
Pacific St.
Jackson St.

Van Ness St.

Polk St.
Larkin St.
Hyde St.
Leavenworth St.
Jones St.
Taylor St.
Mason St.
Powell St.
Stockton St.
Grant Ave.
Kearny St.

Columbus Ave.

Montgomery St.

Sansome St.

Battery St.

Front St.

Drumm St.

Embarcadero

CHINATOWN

NOB HILL

Bush St.

Ferry Building
(World Trade Center)
Justin Herman Plaza

FINANCIAL DISTRICT

San Francisco-Oakland Bay Bridge

Union Square

O'Farrell St.

Market St.

Steuart St.

Main St.

Fremont St.

1st St.

80

Moscone Convention Center

Harrison St.

2nd St.

3rd St.

Eddy St.

CIVIC CENTER

Polk St.

Market St.

Mission St.

SOUTH OF MARKET (SoMa)

Howard St.
Folsom St.

8th St.
6th St.

7th St.

Bryant St.
Brannan St.
Townsend St.
King St.
Berry St.

4th St.

10th St.
11th St.
12th St.

9th St.

8th St.

S. Van Ness St.
Folsom St.
Bryant St.
Potrero St.

101

280

16th St.

This restaurant offers Cantonese, Szechuan, and Hunan dishes. This is what Sunday-night-family-Chinese-dinner restaurants should all be like. Bustling, lots of families (from all over the world—see how many languages you can identify among the other diners), fast service, and good food. Even the decor—phoenix wallpaper and hanging red Chinese lanterns with tassels—lends a certain ambience to the place.

If you like sweet-and-sour dishes, don't miss them here (the fried wonton appetizers are good). Soups are fabulous too and there's a wide variety of choices. The entrées are equally delectable too.

The Golden Phoenix is on Washington Street near Kearny.

THE POT STICKER, 150 Waverly Place. Tel. 397-9985.
Cuisine: CHINESE. **Reservations:** Accepted.
$ Prices: Main courses $5.25–$18; set meals, lunch $3.50–$4.65, dinner $7.15–$9.55. AE, MC, V.
Open: Daily, lunch 11:30am–4pm; dinner 4:30–9:45pm.
Children's Services: Highchairs, boosters.

This lovely place has very good food and a friendly staff who delight in making suggestions about what the kids might like to eat. Although small, the restaurant feels spacious, and while rather subdued, it's not the kind of quiet in which you have to worry about your kids disturbing anyone. The Pot Sticker is so used to serving large groups (primarily families) that the appetizers and soups are listed with an estimate of the number of servings you'll get per order.

The restaurant is on Waverly Place at Washington Street.

THE CANNERY

CHARLEY BROWN'S, 2801 Leavenworth St. Tel. 776-3838.
Cuisine: AMERICAN. **Reservations:** Advised.
$ Prices: Main courses $13–$25. AE, MC, V.
Open: Lunch daily 11:30am–3pm; dinner Sun–Thurs 3:30–10pm, Fri–Sat 3:30–11pm.
Children's Services: Boosters, highchairs; children's menu.

The adult food here is good (Charley Brown's is known for its prime rib), but the place really rates high for its children's plates, which include extremely generous portions of hamburger with thick-cut fries, sliced tomatoes, soup or salad, beverage, and dessert, all for $5.95. Adults can choose from several fish entrées (all fresh), prime ribs, steaks, pastas, and shellfish. Entrées include soup or salad, freshly baked sourdough bread, vegetable, and rice pilaf or baked potato.

There is 2-hour validated parking at the Anchorage parking lot at Leavenworth and Jefferson streets.

Other choices at the Cannery include the **Chart House** (tel. 474-3476) for American food, and **Las Margaritas** (tel. 776-6996) for Mexican food.

CIVIC CENTER & VAN NESS AVENUE
EXPENSIVE

RUTH'S CHRIS STEAK HOUSE, 1700 California St. Tel. 673-0557.
Cuisine: AMERICAN. **Reservations:** Recommended.

$ Prices: Main courses $19.50–$25. AE, DC, MC, V.
Open: Dinner only, daily 5–10:30pm.
Children's Services: Highchairs, boosters.

Opened 25 years ago in New Orleans by Ruth Fertel, the restaurant is known for juicy steaks and chops. The atmosphere is intimate and cozy, yet tables are widely separated and there are several booths. White tablecloths, mirrored walls, fresh flowers, and dim lighting make this a lovely place to enjoy steak and seafood.

You'll find the entrance to Ruth's Chris Steak House on Van Ness Avenue. The restaurant offers complimentary valet parking.

MODERATE

BULL'S, 25 Van Ness Ave. Tel. 864-4288.

Cuisine: AMERICAN. **Reservations:** For 6 or more only.
$ Prices: Main courses $5–$14. D, MC, V.
Open: Mon–Thurs 11:30am–10pm, Fri–Sat 11:30am–11pm, Sun 12–9pm.
Children's Services: Sassy seats, boosters.

Big and bright, this place is permeated with rustic Texas atmosphere, and kids can move around and make noise while parents can still feel comfortable. Choose from such favorites as deluxe nachos (chips with pit-smoked brisket of beef, black beans, and jalapeños, baked with cheddar and Monterey Jack cheese).

Bull's is on Van Ness Avenue at Market Street, two blocks from City Hall. On-street parking.

HARD ROCK CAFE, 1699 Van Ness Ave. Tel. 885-1699.

Cuisine: AMERICAN. **Reservations:** For 9 or more only.
$ Prices: Main courses $5–$12. AE, MC, V.
Open: Mon–Thurs 11:30am–11pm, Fri–Sun 11:30am–12pm.
Children's Services: Boosters.

For dinner and peak times on weekends you can expect to wait at least a half hour. This Hard Rock (like its sibling restaurants worldwide) is a loud, hard-driving restaurant that serves up rock music (continuous tapes of blues, surf music, golden oldies, and rock 'n roll). Don't expect to carry on a conversation once you're inside, but sit back and enjoy watching your teens do the "people-watch." Don't forget— you're really coming here for the atmosphere (yes, there really is a Cadillac suspended from the wall) and to satisfy your kids' curiosity.

You'll find the Hard Rock Café on Van Ness Avenue at Sacramento Street. On-street parking.

SPUNTINO, 524 Van Ness Ave. Tel. 861-7772.

Cuisine: ITALIAN. **Reservations:** None.
$ Prices: Breakfast $3.50–$7.25, lunch and dinner $3.50–$9.75. AE, MC, V.
Open: Open Mon 7am–10pm, Tues–Thurs 7am–11pm, Fri–Sat 10am–midnight, Sun 10am–9pm.
Children's Services: Boosters.

This casual Italian café has simply delicious food and is a good choice whenever you're in the vicinity of the Civic Center or the Museum of Modern Art, or in need of a late-night after-opera stop. The menu is varied, offering French toast and omelets for breakfast and salads, pastas, pizzettes (small individual pizzas), and Italian sandwiches at other times. It's an upbeat eatery that our kids enjoy—as much for the people-watching as for the good food.

Spuntino is on Van Ness Avenue near McAllister.

EMBARCADERO

MODERATE

CHEVY'S MEXICAN RESTAURANT, 2 Embarcadero—podium level. Tel. 391-2323.

Cuisine: MEXICAN. **Reservations:** Recommended.

$ Prices: Lunch or dinner $10. AE, MC, V.

Open: Sun–Thurs 11am–10pm, Fri–Sat 11am–10pm.

Children's Services: Highchairs, boosters; children's menu.

Part of a Northern California chain, Chevy's is a lively, colorful place. Try the chips and guacamole.

Chevy's is in the Embarcadero Center on the Podium level.

MACARTHUR PARK RESTAURANT, 607 Front St. Tel. 398-5700.

Cuisine: AMERICAN. **Reservations:** Recommended.

$ Prices: Main courses $6.50–$18.75. AE, DC, MC, V.

Open: Breakfast Mon–Fri 7–10am; lunch Mon–Fri 11:30am–2:30pm; dinner Mon–Wed 5–10:30pm, Fri–Sat till 11pm, Sun 4:30pm–10pm. **Closed:** Thanksgiving, Christmas Day.

Children's Services: Highchairs, boosters.

Located across the street from little Jackson Park in a beautiful brick building that recalls the late 1800s and the sensational Barbary Coast days, MacArthur Park has fabulous food and friendly servers. This place is slightly off the beaten path and is a good one to choose for lunch and a park outing either before or after your meal.

Specialties are baby-back ribs, mesquite-grilled fresh fish and steaks, and excellent salads. The desserts here are a real treat. (And most foods can be boxed "to go.")

MacArthur Park is located at Front Street at Jackson Street. Valet parking.

FISHERMAN'S WHARF AND PIER 39

EXPENSIVE

A. SABELLA'S RESTAURANT, 2766 Taylor St., 3rd floor. Tel. 771-6776 and -6775.

Cuisine: ITALIAN. **Reservations:** Advised, but not required (the restaurant is large).

$ Prices: Lunch $6–$12, dinner $12–$35; children's menu $3.25–$7.75. AE, CB, DC, MC, V.

Open: Sun–Thurs 10:30am–10:30pm, Fri–Sat 10:30am–11pm. **Closed:** Christmas Day.

Children's Services: Boosters, highchairs; children's menu.

A. Sabella's has good food, excellent service, and a wonderful view. Large arched windows face across Jefferson Street (the main walkway of the Wharf) onto the Bay so you and the kids can watch as tankers and ferries come and go, and tourists bustle on the street below. Don't let the white linen tablecloths worry you. The restaurant is very spacious and open, so your children are unlikely to disturb other diners (if they're fairly well behaved; although, you should be advised, that the restaurant takes on a decidedly more sophisticated ambience when it's dark outside and the tables are graced with candlelight).

The servers are attentive. Ours was so friendly that he insisted on helping Andrew with his lobster—a good thing since this was Andrew's first encounter with a crustacean and we ourselves needed help negotiating the nutcracker and pick to get the best meat out of the claws. The adult luncheon and dinner menus are tempting, with seafood, pasta, chops, cioppino, and a few unusual items. Crab is the house specialty and is served in a variety of ways, from cold to sautéed with black bean sauce.

You'll find the restaurant on Taylor Street facing the Wharf. They offer validated parking at 350 Beach St.

LOLLI'S CASTAGNOLA, 286 Jefferson St. Tel. 776-5015 or 775-2446.
Cuisine: ITALIAN. **Reservations:** Advised.
$ Prices: Breakfast $4–$9.75, lunch specials (11am–6pm), dinner $7–$27 (lobster). AE, DC, MC, V.
Open: Daily 9am–11pm. **Closed:** Christmas Day.
Children's Services: Boosters, highchairs; children's menu.

⭐ Lolli's Castagnola has been a landmark on Fisherman's Wharf since 1916. We like the very homey atmosphere, even though it's large and located in the midst of the city's tourist mecca. During most of the fall, winter, and spring, kids can watch the sea lions—sometimes there are ten or more—that have come to feed on the bay. During the day (11am to 4pm) you can often watch the fishermen docking their boats and unloading their catch.

Simple decor and white tablecloths are the setting at Lolli's. The floor-to-ceiling windows make you feel like you're sitting on the water. Things are generally fast-paced here, with tables turning over as many as three times during dinner. You set your own pace, though—your server will accommodate your need to get in and out or to dine at a more leisurely pace.

The enormous seafood menu is great and the variety of shellfish and calamari specials is delightful. Kids can choose from the old stand-bys—grilled cheese and tuna sandwiches—or order spaghetti or filet of sole. Many of these selections are served with fries and range in price from $3 to $6.

Lolli's Castagnola Upper Deck (located upstairs) is a moderately priced self-service light-lunch alternative that features soups, seafood salads, sandwiches, fish-and-chips, and beverage service. The huge room with big windows is bright and overlooks the water, while the patio overlooks the Wharf. The Upper Deck is open from 11am to 5pm daily.

TARANTINO'S, 206 Jefferson St. Tel. 775-5600.
Cuisine: SEAFOOD, ITALIAN. **Reservations:** Suggested.
$ Prices: Dinner, main courses $9–$16; lunch $6–$11. AE, CB, DC, MC, V.
Open: Daily 11am–11pm. **Closed:** Thanksgiving, December 24 and 25. Two-hour free validated parking at the lot on Jefferson and Taylor streets.
Children's Services: Boosters, highchairs; children's menu.
Tarantino's has been a Fisherman's Wharf landmark for 43 years, and has served thousands and thousands of families since the Wharf is a family destination. From your table, you'll be able to see the harbor lights at night, the Golden Gate Bridge, and, in the distance, Sausalito. While Mom and Dad are enjoying the splendid view,

servers take care of the children with little oyster crackers and sourdough French bread. As further proof of their friendly attitude, the restaurant provides child-size portions as well as an interesting children's menu.

For lunch and dinner tots can choose from fish-and-chips, seafood plate, linguine, and tortellini, as well as hamburgers. The adult daytime menu (11am–3pm) consists of pasta such as seafood fettuccine Tarantino (scallops, shrimp, and baby clams in a sauce of garlic, herbs, cream, and parmesan cheese), seafood (including calamari, baby salmon, and oysters), soups, salads, and sandwiches. Lunch is semi à la carte and includes clam chowder and bread and butter with every main course. For dinner, you might try a swordfish steak or New York steak with potato and vegetables.

Tarantino's is right on Fisherman's Wharf. Two-hour validated parking is offered.

MODERATE

ALCATRAZ BAR AND GRILL, Pier 39. Tel. 434-1818.

Cuisine: AMERICAN. **Reservations:** Accepted—a good idea.

$ Prices: $5.95–$16.95. AE, DC, MC, V.

Open: Mon–Thurs & Sun 11:30am–9:30pm, Fri–Sat 11:30am–10pm.

Children's Services: Boosters, highchairs; children's menu.

What a fun place to visit! Straightforward American cuisine like barbecued ribs and chicken, burgers and sandwiches (turkey, chicken, sausage, and barbecued beef) are sure bets with any child. And the kid's plate is terrific for those who want grilled cheese, a hot dog, or a small burger.

What makes this place fun? For starters, the back room offers wonderful views of the Golden Gate Bridge, Marin, and the Bay, and on a clear day you can almost touch Alcatraz Island. Everything in the place is a reminder the U.S. Penitentiary in the middle of the Bay. Placemats are black-and-white photographs detailing the prison or pictures of infamous inmates (such as Al Capone and the Birdman of Alcatraz). There's a "rogues' gallery" and an intricate model of Alcatraz. After spending many minutes marveling at the model, Elizabeth and Andrew joined other fascinated children in the authentically styled and sized prison cell. Watch those little fingers as they close the cell door! Our kids had more fun inside that tiny space than we could ever have imagined.

The restaurant is at the end of Pier 39.

Fisherman's Wharf and Pier 39 are simply loaded with eateries. In addition to the ones we've detailed, you'll find pleasant seaside dining at **Alioto's—#8**, 8 Fisherman's Wharf (tel. 673-0183), for seafood; **Pompeii's Grotto**, 340 Jefferson St. (tel. 776-9265), for seafood; and **Scoma's**, Pier 47 (tel. 771-4383), for Italian-style seafood, has valet parking. At Pier 39, you'll find **Swiss Louis** (tel. 421-2913), serving Italian food; the **Eagle Café** (tel. 433-3689), featuring American food; and **Neptune's Palace** (tel. 434-2260), specializing in seafood. Also located here is a branch of **Yet Wah's** (tel. 434-4430), with more than 200 items on the menu.

GHIRARDELLI SQUARE

COMPADRES MEXICAN BAR AND GRILL, 900 North Point St. Tel. 885-2266.

Cuisine: MEXICAN. **Reservations:** Yes, recommended.

$ Prices: Main courses $5.50–$18.95 (Gulf shrimp). AE, DC, MC, V.
Open: Mon–Thurs 11am–10pm, Fri 11am–11pm, Sat–Sun 10am (for brunch)–11pm.
Children's Services: Boosters, highchairs.

This is a lively place with good food, a beautiful view, and very friendly, accommodating service. The boisterous cantina atmosphere inside (we dined on the enclosed patio) was perfect—the adults didn't have to worry about the noise the children created. Watching passers-by was a treat, and when all the kids got restless (although the service was fast), we simply picked them up and went for a walk on the terrace.

Compadres has one fabulous attraction for kids: Two live macaws (parrots) sit at the entrance of the restaurant and charm all who pass by. Also a treat for youngsters are the Chiclets gum offered after dinner and the balloons given out on weekends.

Compadres is located on the second floor of the Mustard Building in Ghirardelli Square. There is validated parking in the underground lot.

Ghirardelli Square has other fine restaurants; among them: **The Mandarin,** 900 North Point St. (tel. 673-8812), for Chinese cuisine, and **Paprika's Fono,** 900 North Point St. (tel. 441-1223), for Hungarian cuisine. You might want to get a baby-sitter so you can enjoy a night out on the town here.

JAPANTOWN

MODERATE

IROHA, 1728 Buchanan St. Tel. 922-0321.
Cuisine: JAPANESE. **Reservations:** For 6 or more only.
$ Prices: Lunch main courses $3.50–$6.50. dinner main courses $8.75–$12.50. AE, DC, MC, V.
Open: Daily 11:30am–9pm.
Children's Services: Highchairs, boosters; children's plate

This part of Buchanan Street is a continuation of the Japan Center shopping area. The plaza area is closed to cars, and the cobblestone walkways are filled with Japanese shops and restaurants. You'll see two huge windows displaying the food specialties in the usual plastic renditions. Enter a tiny courtyard that has a hint of a Japanese garden, complete with bamboo, and walk up a flight of wooden stairs. Walk through the little slats of cloth that greet visitors and you'll be in the mood for a Japanese lunch or dinner. Lots of little booths give the suggestion of privacy, and a painting of Mount Fuji and hanging paper lanterns complete the atmosphere.

For a treat that the kids as well as you will love, try the gyoza (little dough pockets filled with minced pork or beef and shredded vegetables). Other specialties include hot noodles, ramen, and yakitori (chicken, pork, or beef chunks basted and grilled on little skewers).

Iroha is across the street from Japan Center.

MIFUNE, 1737 Post St. Tel. 922-0337.
Cuisine: JAPANESE. **Reservations:** None.
$ Prices: $3–$8.50 main courses (noodles and rice dishes) $8–$13 for others. AE, DC, MC, V.

Children's Services: Boosters, highchairs; children's plate
Open: Daily 11am–9:30pm. **Closed:** Jan 1–3, Thanksgiving, Christmas Day.

Be sure to spend time looking at the plastic models of food in the window before you enter the restaurant. The display is fun to look at, and great for kids who get a kick out of seeing the realistic-looking samples on display. Mama-san and Papa-san dolls are in the display case, beckoning you inside.

All manner of noodles can be sampled. Hot noodles (served in a seasoned broth) are accompanied by chicken, tempura items, shrimp, and even fishcakes. Cold noodles are served with different garnishes ranging from Japanese potato to shrimp-and-vegetable tempura. For those who prefer something other than noodles, there are hearty rice dishes, and after 4pm a choice of tempura or sashimi.

Mifune is in the Kintetsu Building on Post Street. Validated parking in Japan Center lot is offered.

INEXPENSIVE

SANPPO, 1702 Post St. Tel. 346-3486.
  Cuisine: JAPANESE. **Reservations:** None.
  $ Prices: $5.25–$7.75. No credit cards.
  Open: Tues–Sat 11:45am–10pm, Sun 3–10pm.
  Children's Services: Highchairs, boosters.

This is a small, simple Japanese restaurant that has good standard fare at reasonable prices. We love the different donburi (rice with a sweetened sauce and different toppings—egg and vegetables, beef and vegetables, chicken, pork cutlet, even lobster tempura). The kids love the tempura and the ramen (Japanese-style noodles in broth).

Sanppo in on Post Street across from Peace Place. Validated parking in Japan Center lot is offered.

MARINA DISTRICT

EXPENSIVE

GREENS AT FORT MASON, Building A, Fort Mason. Tel. 771-6222.
  Cuisine: VEGETARIAN. **Reservations:** Strongly recommended.
  $ Prices: Main courses $6.50–$10.50 and up; Fri–Sat. $32 prix-fixe. MC, V.
  Open: Lunch Tues–Sat 11:30am–2:15pm; dinner Tues–Thurs 6–9:30pm, Sun brunch 10am–2pm. **Closed:** Mon., Thanksgiving, Christmas Day.
  Children's Services: Boosters, highchairs, toys, crayons, coloring books.

This may be one of the busiest restaurants in town. The food is so good and the place so well known that it operates at capacity almost every night (and they're wonderful with kids, although most children may have difficulty finding something tantalizing on the menu). Owned by the San Francisco Zen Center, Greens may change your opinion about vegetarian dining. (The San Francisco Zen Center also owns the famous Tassajara Zen Center in Carmel, which is known for its food and Tassajara cookbooks.)

Not only is the food good (much of which is organically grown at Greens Gulch), but the view is spectacular. The restaurant is housed in an old World War II army barracks. There is a full wall of windows that overlooks the marina filled with sailboats, and the Golden Gate Bridge in the distance.

The gourmet vegetarian cuisine is quite varied. You can get pizza with sautéed spinach and feta cheese or eggplant and provolone, or fettuccine and vegetables. There are brochettes (tofu takes the place of meat) with marinated vegetables and a wide array of delicious salads. One favorite is the Gujrati dahl (mushrooms, carrots, zucchini, and other vegetables stewed with tomatoes, ginger, chilies, and curry served on rice).

Greens is located in Building A of Fort Mason.

SCOTT'S SEAFOOD GRILL AND BAR, 2400 Lombard St. Tel. 563-8988.

Cuisine: SEAFOOD. **Reservations:** Accepted for early hours—with kids it's best to go before 6:30pm.

$ **Prices:** Entrées $6.50–$19. AE, MC, V.

Open: Sun–Thurs 11:30am–10:30pm, Fri–Sat 11:30am–11pm. **Closed:** Thanksgiving, Christmas.

Children's Services: None.

This may not be the best place for young kids, but it's a winner with older children or those with sophisticated enough palates that they can choose from the almost strictly seafood menu. The line out the door will tell you that there's great fresh seafood here. Scott's Caesar salad is good for starters, and our resident expert on fresh oysters-on-the-half-shell swears to their appeal. The cioppino with fresh local crab is excellent, as is the fettuccine with shucked Willapa Bay oysters in a spicy Cajun beer-butter sauce. For less adventurous appetites, the Hawaiian albacore tuna or local snapper or petrale sole doré might be best. When we go, someone always orders (and shares) the seafood sauté. New York strip steak and filet mignon are available, as are hamburgers and cheeseburgers.

There is another branch of **Scott's** at 3 Embarcadero Center (tel. 981-0622).

INEXPENSIVE

FIRST WATCH, 2150 Lombard St. Tel. 775-9673.

Cuisine: AMERICAN. **Reservations:** For more than 6 only.

$ **Prices:** Main courses $4–$8. MC, V.

Open: Daily 7am–2:30pm.

Children's Services: Boosters, highchairs; children's portions.

This restaurant is clean, has no frills, and serves lots of good food. For breakfast there are all kinds of egg specialties—omelets, frittatas, eggs Benedict (also egg substitutes). Then there's French toast, gourmet pancakes (such as raisin-walnut and wheatberry), and an array of fruit, cereal, and the like. For lunch, they have the expected salads and sandwiches, but even these are a little different. There's the "Chicken Little" sandwich—chicken salad with water chestnuts, raisins, and celery on an English muffin, or the "BLTE"—bacon, lettuce, tomato, and fried egg with melted cheese. And, how about a "Caesar sandwich"? Not what you'd expect. And they make everything "to go" as well, so you can pack yourselves a whopping good picnic.

First Watch is on Lombard Street in the Cow Hollow Motor Inn.

MEL'S DRIVE-IN, 2165 Lombard St. Tel. 921-3039.

Cuisine: AMERICAN. **Reservations:** None.

$ **Prices:** $4.50–$11.95 No credit cards.

Open: Sun–Thurs 6am–1am, Fri–Sat 6am–3am.

Children's Services: Boosters; children's menu.

This place is jumping, and has simply terrific burgers! It isn't a trendy re-creation of a 1950s drive-in—this is an original. Waiters and waitresses wear white shirts and black bowties and soda-jerk-style hats. The kids love it. You might prepare them for a wait if you go at peak times because Mel's can get very crowded.

There are one-third-pound burgers, chili, salads, and specials. The hot dogs are terrific and even 5-year-old Elizabeth wanted seconds of "Samantha's Lunch" (a child's hot dog for $2.75). Don't miss the fountain items—milkshakes, malts, sundaes, and flavored Cokes.

Mel's can be found on Lombard Street at Fillmore Street.

ORIGINAL JOE'S No. 2, 2001 Chestnut St. Tel. 346-3233.

Cuisine: ITALIAN/AMERICAN. **Reservations:** For 4 or more only.

$ Prices: Lunch $3.25–$8.75, dinner $7–$16. MC, V.

Open: Daily 11:30am–1am.

Children's Services: Boosters.

Original Joe's is not much to look at and you could entirely pass it by from the street if you didn't look for the little flashing neon sign (in handwriting/script). Opened in 1938, this Italian restaurant has been serving lunch and dinner to the locals since that time.

The servers bring fresh French bread and butter to the table as soon as you sit down. The lunch menu is so extensive that it runs the gamut from special omelets to sandwiches and burgers. The dinner menu includes pasta and other specialties such as veal, sweetbreads, prime rib, meatloaf, corned beef, roast lamb, pork chops, and New York steak.

You can find Original Joe's No. 2 on Chestnut Street at Fillmore Street.

NORTH BEACH

EXPENSIVE

CAPP'S CORNER, 1600 Powell St. Tel. 989-2589.

Cuisine: ITALIAN/AMERICAN. **Reservations:** None.

$ Prices: Lunch $5.50–$9.50, dinner $9.50–$13.50; children portions: lunch all $5.50, dinner $7.50. D, MC, V.

Children's Services: Highchairs, boosters; children's portions.

Open: Lunch Mon–Fri 11:30am–2:30pm, dinner Sun–Thurs 4:30–10pm, Fri–Sat 4:30–11pm.

This restaurant is one of our favorite places. Homey and warm, tables are set for traditional family-style dining. Entrees range from roast beef and leg of lamb to veal in marsala sauce and eggplant parmigiana. They also serve clams, mussels, and homemade sausage. All entrees come with soup, salad, pasta, dessert, and coffee.

You'll find Capp's Corner on Powell Street at Green Street.

THE GOLD SPIKE, 527 Columbus Ave. Tel. 986-9747.

Cuisine: ITALIAN. **Reservations:** None.

$ Prices: Dinner main courses $12. CB, D, DC, MC, V.

Open: Dinner only, Mon–Tues & Thurs 5–10pm, Fri–Sat 5–10:30pm.

Children's Services: Boosters; special children's prices.

They have been serving huge six-course family-style meals here since 1920. Although the place is small, the walls are filled with business cards, postcards, pictures, signs—it's almost like being in a fantastic old junk store. Kids love to inspect the old treasures everywhere. Dinners include antipasto, minestrone soup, salad, pasta, and dessert. A la carte and side orders are also available. Children can choose from many of the same items as adults at a lower price.

You'll find The Gold Spike on Columbus Avenue between Union Street and Green Street. On-street parking.

LITTLE JOE'S ON BROADWAY, 523 Broadway. Tel. 433-4343.

Cuisine: ITALIAN. **Reservations:** None.
$ Prices: Main courses $6.95–$11.95. No credit cards.
Open: Daily 11am–10:30pm.
Children's Services: Boosters.

The food at Little Joe's is so good, their motto is: "Rain or shine, there's always a line." Call ahead to find out the best time to come—there's usually no wait between 2 and 5pm; between 5:30 and 6pm there may be a short line, but then the crowds arrive; people have been known to stand in line as long as 2 hours. Mounds of cooked spaghetti are in a tray waiting to be smothered with the sauce and used for hungry diners. Fresh French bread is served as soon as you sit down. Daily specials include beef stew, caciucco (fish stew), calamari, and come with a choice of vegetables plus spaghetti or rigatoni or beans. The diverse menu includes sandwiches, omelets, pasta, and entrees such as New York steak, pot roast, lamb chops, and all manner of veal. Although there's no children's menu, a side order of Joe's spaghetti marinara is so large that it's a meal in itself, and certainly enough for a child. Or your server will be happy to bring you an extra plate so that junior can have samples from all the adults. Kids roll up their sleeves for Joe's ravioli, minestrone soup, and spaghetti and meatballs.

Little Joe's is on Broadway at Columbus Avenue. Parking lot across the street on Broadway.

NEW PISA RESTAURANT, 550 Green St. Tel. 362-4726 or 362-5188.

Cuisine: AMERICAN/ITALIAN. **Reservations:** Large parties only.
$ Prices: Lunch $8, dinner $12; children's meals half-price. No credit cards.
Open: Daily except Wed 11:30am–11pm.
Children's Services: Highchairs, boosters; half-price meals.

The choice of entrees here is straightforward—roast beef, roast veal, roast pork, breast of lamb, veal sauté, chicken cacciatore. All meals include soup, salad, pasta, dessert, and coffee.

New Pisa is on Green Street near Powell Street.

NORTH BEACH PIZZA, 1499 Grant Ave. Tel. 433-2444.

Cuisine: ITALIAN. **Reservations:** None.
$ Prices: Dinner $7–$11; pizza by slice or pie. AE, CB, D, DC, MC, V.
Open: Sun–Thurs 10am–1am, Fri–Sat 10am–3am.
Children's Services: Highchairs, boosters.

This is a warm, family place where servers laugh and joke with kid-customers. Small and cozy with traditional red-checked cloths, candles in wine bottles, and garlic ropes hanging along the walls, this restaurant serves up over 20 kinds of pizza—from tame to the exotic.

North Beach Pizza is on Grant Avenue at Union Street.

A second branch, called **North Beach Pizza, Too,** is at 1310 Grant Ave. at Vallejo Street (tel. 433-2444), and is open Mon–Thurs 5pm–1am, Fri–Sat 10am–11pm.

NORTH BEACH RESTAURANT, 1512 Stockton St. Tel. 392-1700.
   Cuisine: ITALIAN. **Reservations:** Recommended.
   $ Prices: Lunch $8.95–$27.95, dinner $17.95–$39.95. AE, CB, DC, MC, V.
   Open: Daily 11:30am–11:45pm. **Closed:** Major holidays.
   Children's Services: Highchairs, boosters.

This restaurant has mouth-watering food. They make their own pasta daily, hang and cure their own prosciutto hams, cut and prepare the veal in their own kitchen, and vow to serve the finest food they can. Choose from among almost 30 different fish entrees, 20 different veal entrees, as well as pasta, lamb, chicken, and steak. Full dinners come with antipasto, salad or soup, pasta, and fresh vegetable.

You'll find the North Beach Restaurant at the intersection of Green, Columbus, and Stockton streets. Valet parking $3.

WASHINGTON SQUARE BAR & GRILL, 1707 Powell St. Tel. 982-8123.
   Cuisine: ITALIAN. **Reservations:** Accepted.
   $ Prices: $7–$16. AE, MC.
   Open: Mon–Sat lunch 11:30am–3pm, dinner 5:30–10:30pm.
   Children's Services: None.

This bustling, comfortable place makes you feel like a local yourself. Opened in 1973, it was the first bar and grill in the Bay Area. The food is good, and while there aren't any special services for children, the staff will use telephone books and cushions to make booster seats. They'll gladly split adult portions in the kitchen for children, serve quarter-size pasta dishes, and warm baby bottles or baby food.

There is jazz at night, during which time the place acquires a more romantic tone. The Italian cuisine ranges from pasta, veal, and chicken to a good selection of seafood. There are hamburgers and daily specials as well.

OCEAN BEACH

CLIFF HOUSE SEAFOOD AND BEVERAGE COMPANY, 1090 Point Lobos. Tel. 386-3330.
   Cuisine: SEAFOOD. **Reservations:** None.
   $ Prices: Main courses $3–$14.75. MC, V.
   Open: Mon–Thurs 11am–10:30pm, Fri 11am–11pm, Sat 10am–11pm; Sun brunch 9am–2pm, dinner 2 to 10:30pm.
   Children's Services: Boosters.

Located at street level, this restaurant at the Cliff House is a large area, dimly lit with nice atmosphere, where you can sit with your food and drinks and watch the waves and seals. While the menu is very limited, it is fast-food style and consequently service is very quick. Kids can munch on sourdough rolls and fruit if they don't like any of the seafood offerings. Adults will enjoy Manhattan clam chowder, the chef and Cobb salads, or steaks, veal scaloppine, and the like.

There is on-street parking available.

UPSTAIRS AT THE CLIFF HOUSE, 1090 Point Lobos. Tel. 387-5847.
   Cuisine: SEAFOOD. **Reservations:** Accepted.

$ Prices: Lunch $5.50–$12, dinner main courses $10–$16.50. MC, V.
Open: Mon–Thurs 9am–4pm and 5–10:30pm, Fri–Sat 9am–4pm, 5–11pm, Sun 8:30am–4pm and 5–10:30pm.
Children's Services: Boosters.

Sitting off by itself, perched on the cliff overlooking Seal Rock, Cliff House is the only San Francisco restaurant overlooking the ocean. This tourist attraction is also popular among the locals, since the view is amazing on clear days—you can see the Golden Gate Bridge. There is also a gift shop, a hot dog stand, and an arcade, called the "Musée Méchanique," which has amusements from the turn of the century as well as modern video games. Kids and adults love the place.

Upstairs at the Cliff House is a lovely restaurant with huge picture windows so guests can enjoy the view. Although it's somewhat pricey, you'll see dozens of families here at any given time—little ones watching for seals, older ones looking at the waves breaking on the rocks. Expect leisurely dining and a long wait for tables on weekends (up to 45 minutes). The varied menu offers such luncheon fare as soup, chili, and hot and cold sandwiches. There is an astonishing array of omelets, 30 in all, as well as daily specials. Dinner entrées include chicken, veal, steaks, fresh pastas, and seafood.

On-street parking is available.

THE RICHMOND DISTRICT [CLEMENT STREET]

Clement Street, part of the Richmond District, is a great place to spend part of the day. You can spend hours window-shopping (or shopping) and then have a good meal, all the while experiencing one of the "neighborhoods" that is not quite as crowded as some of the others in the city. There is a public parking lot on Clement Street at Eighth Avenue and metered street parking everywhere.

MODERATE

YET WAH, 2140 Clement St. Tel. 387-8056.

Cuisine: MANDARIN CHINESE. **Reservations:** Accepted on weekends only for 5 or more.
$ Prices: Main courses $3.50–$10+. AE, MC, V.
Open: Daily 10am–10pm.
Children's Services: Boosters, highchairs.

Choose from such standards as chicken in plum sauce, egg foo yung, and such specialties as Mongolian lamb, almond pressed duck, and a wide variety of fish and shellfish (prawns cooked 17 different ways). Children—and parents as well—enjoy the many kinds of chow mein and noodles.

Yet Wah is on Clement Street near 23rd Avenue.

There's another branch on Pier 39 on the waterfront near Fisherman's Wharf (tel. 434-4430).

INEXPENSIVE

BILL'S PLACE, 2315 Clement St. Tel. 221-5262.

Cuisine: AMERICAN. **Reservations:** None.
$ Prices: Main courses $2.40–$5.15. No credit cards.
Open: Sun–Thurs 11am–10pm, Fri–Sat 11am–11pm.

Children's Services: Boosters, highchairs.

Bill's Place has fabulous hamburgers (a third of a pound of freshly ground choice chuck) and thick milkshakes—so good that many San Franciscans believe that this is the best hamburger place in town. (The owners like to remind you that they're geared for families and that they've been owned by the same family for 30 years.) Unpretentious, with an open grill at which two cooks race to make sure those burgers keep pace with the customers, this place is a treat and is very popular, so expect a brief wait if you come during peak hours. While you're waiting—or while you're eating—be sure not to miss the collection of presidential china that lines the wall. The service is fast, very casual, and friendly. Kids are everywhere.

For hearty souls who like to eat outdoors, even in the Richmond District—which is cooler and foggier than other parts of the city—there is a lovely garden patio.

GIORGIO'S PIZZERIA, 151 Clement St. Tel. 668-1266.
   Cuisine: ITALIAN. **Reservations:** None.
$ **Prices:** Pasta $6.50, extra-large pizzas $11.50–$15.50. No credit cards.
   Open: Mon–Thurs 11:30am–11:30pm, Fri–Sat 11:30am–12:30am, Sun 11:30am–11pm.
   Children's Services: Boosters, highchairs.

Some locals claim that you'll see only families here—possibly because the staff is very experienced with kids and the pizza is terrific. Giorgio's features 18 scrumptious different pizzas. If your kids don't eat pizza (is there a child who doesn't?), the staff will split adult pasta portions and of course bring extra plates. Half orders are available for children under 12.

As Giorgio's is very popular, you should expect a 20-minute wait between 6 and 8pm on weekends. The pizzeria is on Clement Street at 23rd Avenue.

MAI'S VIETNAMESE RESTAURANT, 316 Clement St. Tel. 221-3046.
   Cuisine: VIETNAMESE. **Reservations:** Yes, especially weekends.
$ **Prices:** Main courses approximately $5. AE, MC, V.
   Open: Sun–Thurs 11am–10pm, Fri–Sat 11am–11pm.
   Children's Services: Boosters, highchairs.

You'll see large families digging into soft-shell crab, Imperial rolls (similar to eggrolls), and coconut chicken. This little storefront isn't much to look at, but it has wonderful food. The kids love the Vietnamese rolls, which are similar to Imperial rolls but aren't deep-fried. Hanoi soup is a tempting mixture of sliced beef and noodles in a broth flavored with cilantro and lemon. Ask your server to suggest the least spicy dishes.

Mai's is on Clement Street between Fourth and Fifth avenues. On-street parking. There's another branch in Cow Hollow at 1838 Union St. (tel. 921-2861).

UNION SQUARE

One of the great things about the Union Square area is that it's packed with restaurants, many of them in hotels. You can walk down almost any block and find at least three restaurants. These are the ones we liked best.

EXPENSIVE

THE FRENCH ROOM, in the Four Seasons Clift Hotel, 495 Geary St. Tel. 775-4700.

Cuisine: CONTINENTAL. **Reservations:** Recommended.

$ **Prices:** Breakfast averages $15, lunch $20, dinner $50; Sunday brunch $25 for adults, $17.50 for children. AE, CB, D, DC, MC, V.

Open: Breakfast Mon–Sat 6:30–11am; lunch Mon–Sat noon–2pm; dinner nightly 6:30–10:30pm; brunch Sunday 11am–2pm.

Children's Services: Highchairs, boosters, children's menu.

★ The elegance of the decor is set off by tall tapestry-framed windows and exquisite crystal chandeliers. But this award-winning French-continental restaurant features more than just beautiful surroundings. And to our delight, it welcomes children!

The restaurant is famous for its evening meals and its collection of over 20,000 bottles of fine French and California wines. Prime rib, fresh lamb sausage with wild mushrooms, medallions of veal, and fresh seafood are just a few of the dinner specialties. There is also an alternative menu that offers entrees low in calories, sodium, and cholesterol. Samples from this menu include linguine with clams in chablis sauce, grilled fish (with garlic and roasted peppers), and such delicacies as breast of partridge or warm eggplant salad. The children's menu features macaroni-and-cheese, junior beef or cheeseburgers, chicken fingers, and jumbo hot dogs, with prices ranging from $2.50 to $6. The restaurant is also willing to serve children smaller portions of most items on the regular menu. The staff greets children with a smile and a small trinket—a coloring book, a comic book, or baseball trading cards.

The French Room is in the Four Seasons Clift Hotel on Union Square between Taylor Street and Jones Street. Valet parking is available.

THE IRON HORSE RESTAURANT, 19 Maiden Lane. Tel. 362-8133.

Cuisine: ITALIAN. **Reservations:** Accepted.

$ **Prices:** Lunch $3–$16, dinner $9–$21. AE, CB, D, DC, MC.

Open: Lunch Mon–Sat 11:30am–4pm; dinner nightly 4–10:30pm; Sun dinner–10:30pm only. **Closed:** Thanksgiving, Christmas Day.

Children's Services: Highchairs, boosters.

The restaurant has a British air about it—it's dimly lit and has sconces on the wall and white linen cloths on the tables. It's a lovely place to enjoy an out-of-the-ordinary Italian dinner. We'd suggest this restaurant for well-behaved youngsters or older kids. Go early to avoid the romantic diners and businesspeople. No children's menu here, but the staff is extremely helpful in suggesting items kids might enjoy and is willing to prepare half-orders whenever possible (for half price).

The food is good and the menu is printed daily to feature all the specials. The lunch menu is extensive, offering the likes of 15 different salads, sandwiches, omelets, pasta, seafood, and hot entrees. For dinner, we loved the marinated rack of lamb and the cannelloni della casa. We found the artichoke-and-seafood salad a special treat.

The Iron Horse is tucked behind the chic shops of Union Square, between Post and Geary streets. On-street parking.

MODERATE

THE DUTCH KITCHEN, in the Western St. Francis Hotel, 355 Powell St. Tel. 397-7000.

Cuisine: AMERICAN. **Reservations:** For 6 or more only.

$ **Prices:** Breakfast $4.50–$11.75, lunch and dinner $5.25–$14.50; children's meals $3.75–$6. AE, CB, D, DC, MC, V.

Open: Breakfast daily 6–11:30am, buffet to 11am; lunch and dinner daily 11:30am–11:30pm.

Children's Services: Highchairs, boosters; children's menu.

Crayons and the "Kids' Kruise" menu (which doubles as a coloring page) are handed to each child as quickly as steaming coffee is brought to the table for the grown-ups. Breakfast can be fresh berries, melon, and croissants at the Continental Breakfast Buffet (the children delight in French toast with fruit and pancakes with sausage or bacon) or buttermilk pancakes and full egg breakfasts.

Lunch and dinner run the gamut from salads, sandwiches, and pastas to more elaborate entrées such as salmon and prime rib. There are full early-bird dinners (Monday through Saturday from 5 to 7pm) featuring London broil, chicken, or linguine with clam-and-herb sauce. Kids can have grilled-cheese sandwiches, chicken, or cheeseburgers, with fries, beverage, and dessert.

The Dutch Kitchen is in the Western St. Francis Hotel opposite Union Square. Garage; valet parking available ($20).

LORI'S DINER, 336 Mason St. Tel. 392-8646.

Cuisine: AMERICAN. **Reservations:** None.

$ Prices: Breakfast $3.95–$9, lunch $5–$6, dinner to $11.95. No credit cards.

Open: Daily 24 hours.

Children's Services: Boosters

A fun, trendy eatery with great food. The staff is friendly, and the food is good American fare—a palate pleaser for youngsters of all ages. While there's no children's menu, two children (or an adult and one child) can split one of the enormous burgers, which the cook will cut in half in the kitchen. Great hot dogs and terrific french fries as well. Lori's is on Mason Street at Union Square. Street parking.

MAMA'S OF SAN FRANCISCO, 398 Geary St. Tel. 788-1004.

Cuisine: AMERICAN/ITALIAN. **Reservations:** Accepted

$ Prices: Breakfast $5–$7, lunch averages $6.75, dinner $8.75–$22. AE, CB, D, DC, MC, V.

Open: Sun–Thurs 7am–midnight, Fri–Sat till 1am; lunch served 11am–5pm, breakfast all day.

Children's Services: Highchairs, boosters; children's menu.

An excellent alternative to pricey hotel coffeeshops, Mama's serves tasty American fare for breakfast and lunch, and Italian food for dinner. The restaurant has a reputation among locals for originality and quality food.

For breakfast, munch on fresh-baked muffins, sweet rolls, or croissants while you wait for a truly original omelet or Swedish cinnamon French toast. One great egg dish is the "Eggs Union Square" (scrambled with tomato, green onion, and ham). If you're in the mood for something different, try the three-berry omelet (strawberry, raspberry, and blueberry plus yogurt and sour cream) or the apple pan doré (thin slices of French toast topped with Granny Smith and Red Delicious apples, butter, and cinnamon). Lunch consists of an array of salads ("Nob Hill Salad" is composed of chicken, avocado, and fresh fruit with mixed greens) and Mama's original sandwiches ("Slim Joe" features ground chuck with grilled onion and jack cheese on a French-bread baguette).

The dinner menu is quite extensive. Good sandwiches and hamburgers are available, as are prime rib, veal, and pasta dinners. All dinners include fresh vegetable and pasta or potatoes.

The children's menu features pasta, chicken, and sandwiches. For breakfast, the kids may have smaller portions, or an adult order may be split in the kitchen for two children. The service here is very fast.

You'll find Mama's on Geary Street at Union Square.

There's another branch, called **Mama's on Washington Square,** at 1701 Stockton St., near Filbert Street (tel. 362-6421), open daily 7am–3pm.

INEXPENSIVE

SALMAGUNDI, 422 Geary St. Tel. 441-0894.
Cuisine: AMERICAN. **Reservations:** None.
$ **Prices:** $2.95–$5.50. AE, MC, V.
Open: Mon–Sat 8am–11pm, Sun 11am–9pm. **Closed:** Thanksgiving, Christmas Day.
Children's Services: Highchairs, boosters.

This soup-and-sandwich establishment is probably the best casual, inexpensive place to take kids before or after an outing—the theater, cable-car rides, walking through Union Square.

They serve 50 different homemade soups, five of them offered daily—our favorites include lentil, country chicken with biscuits, and burgundy beef with noodles. For the price of a bowl you get a refill as well, and, believe me, you'll want one because the soup is delicious. Salads, quiche, and unusual sandwiches round out the bill-of-fare in this buffet-style restaurant; desserts cost extra.

Salmagundi is on Geary Street near Mason Street. On-street parking.

Other branches are at 2 Embarcadero Center (tel. 982-5603) and 39 Grove St. in the Civic Center (tel. 431-7337).

SEARS FINE FOOD, 439 Powell St. Tel. 986-1160.
Cuisine: AMERICAN. **Reservations:** For 6 or more only.
$ **Prices:** $3.95–$6. No credit cards.
Open: Wed–Sun 7am–2:30pm.
Children's Services: Boosters.

There's often a line out the door because the food is scrumptious, but we were assured that it moves quickly and there's usually only a 10-minute wait. World renowned for its sourdough French toast, dollar-sized Swedish pancakes—you get more than a dozen of them per serving—and crisp waffles, this family-oriented restaurant is as popular with locals as it is with tourists. We loved the apple dumpling, and the turkey sandwich is always a big winner with our family.

You'll find Sears at Union Square. On-street parking.

UNION STREET/COW HOLLOW

This is a great area to wander through, with lots of boutiques and little courtyards. You'll find many different places to eat here as well.

MODERATE

DOIDGE'S KITCHEN, 2217 Union St. Tel. 921-2149.
Cuisine: AMERICAN. **Reservations:** Recommended; a must on weekends.
$ **Prices:** Main courses $4.25–$8 or more. MC, V.

Open: Mon–Fri 8am–1:45pm, Sat–Sun 8am–2:45pm.
Children's Services: Boosters.

This little storefront with a little over a dozen tables and a counter area facing an open kitchen is so popular that on the weekends they turn away as many people as they serve. This place really isn't for babies (they don't have highchairs and it's a little cramped), but it's great for slightly older children. The food is excellent, and the service is fast.

For breakfast try the French toast or an omelet stuffed with avocado, ham or bacon, cheese, and tomato, which comes with a choice of potatoes, salad, tomatoes, cottage cheese, even fruit or steamed veggies (extra charge). Lunches include homemade soups, salads, and a wide choice of sandwiches.

MARGARITAVILLE RESTAURANT AND BAR, 1787 Union St. Tel. 441–1183.

Cuisine: MEXICAN. **Reservations:** Accepted.
$ Prices: Main courses $7–$10; combination plates a little more. AE, MC, V.
Open: Daily 11am–2am.
Children's Services: Boosters, highchairs.

Margaritaville usually has a family night when children under 12 dine free. You might call ahead to find out the current night.

This is a lively, fun Mexican restaurant where you can dine in south-of-the-border decor amid hanging plants and servers in tropical-style skirts and shirts. Let the kids enjoy the large aquarium filled with tropical fish. The menu features fajitas, burritos, enchiladas, and tacos, with small plates for light appetites at about $5, and à la carte orders around $2.

PREGO, 2000 Union St. at Buchanan Street. Tel. 563-3305.

Cuisine: NORTHERN ITALIAN. **Reservations:** Accepted for lunch; at dinner for only 6 or more.
$ Prices: Main courses $6.95–$17.50 MC, V.
Open: Daily 11:30am–midnight. **Closed:** Thanksgiving, Christmas Day.
Children's Services: Boosters, highchairs.

The calzone (stuffed pizza) at this restaurant is very good, as is all the food. Pizza ranges from the tame (tomato and cheese) to the exotic (marinated shrimp and salmon). Lots of other items are served as well, including fish, pasta, and poultry dishes.

Prego is located on Union Street at Buchanan Street. There's on-street parking.

INEXPENSIVE

WHAT'S COOKING, 1830 Union St. Tel. 921-4540.

Cuisine: AMERICAN. **Reservations:** Accepted.
$ Prices: Main courses approximately $6. MC, V.
Open: Tues–Thurs 9am–2pm, Fri–Sun 9am–4pm.
Children's Services: Boosters, highchairs.

This homey, informal coffeeshop-type restaurant with under two dozen tables allows for a quick in-and-out meal. Choose from old-fashioned breakfast specialties, such as sausage and eggs (with home fries or two pancakes and sourdough toast) or poached eggs (with sourdough toast and fries) or a large selection of omelets.

What's Cooking cooks at Union Street between Laguna Street and Octavia Street.

MARIN COUNTY: SAUSALITO & TIBURON

CAFFE TRIESTE, 1000 Bridgeway, Sausalito. Tel. 332-7770.
  Cuisine: BISTRO. **Reservations:** None.
$ Prices: $4.95–$9.95; coffee, tea, wine $1–$2.95. MC, V.
  Open: Daily 7am–midnight.
  Children's Services: None.
A little off the beaten tourist path, Caffe Trieste is a good alternative for a quick, fairly reasonably priced bit to eat if the kids don't need highchairs or boosters; in fact, you could keep your child in a stroller in this casual bistro. Frequented by locals, Caffe Trieste serves a changing assortment of sandwiches, pizza, muffins, and delicious specialty coffees, caffè latte, and teas.
  The restaurant is on Bridgeway near the entrance to the town.

FLYNN'S LANDING, 303 Johnson St., Sausalito. Tel. 332-0131.
  Cuisine: AMERICAN. **Reservations:** Recommended.
$ Prices: Lunch $8–$15, dinner $15–$25. MC, V.
  Open: Mon–Thurs 11:30am–10:30pm, Fri–Sat 11:30am–11pm, Sun 11:30am–10pm. **Closed:** Thanksgiving, Christmas Day.
  Children's Services: Boosters, highchairs; service plate.
This restaurant reflects the nautical ambience of Sausalito. Your server will bring the kids crackers and offer paper and crayons when available. The menu features a wide variety of seafood, pasta, soups, salads, and sandwiches—something for everyone. The staff will gladly split orders in the kitchen for children. Our kids have no trouble choosing from the menu, which includes half-pound burgers and club sandwiches.
  Flynn's is on the waterfront just off Bridgeway. There's metered street parking.

GUAYMAS, 5 Main St., Tiburon. Tel. 435-6300.
  Cuisine: MEXICAN. **Reservations:** Recommended.
$ Prices: $7.95–$15.75. AE, MC, V.
  Open: Mon–Fri 11:30am–10pm, Sat 11:30am–11pm, Sun 10:30am–10pm.
  Children's Services: Boosters, highchairs.
This open, airy, traditional Mexican restaurant boasts the best unimpeded view of San Francisco and Angel Island in Tiburon. Guaymas is a colorful place with floor-to-ceiling glass windows, a cement floor, and brightly tinted inside walls of pink, yellow, and turquoise. Even the serving dishes have a Mexican motif.
  Guaymas is a seaport in Mexico, and the staff pride themselves on serving mouth-watering traditional cuisine from that locale. All the food is made from scratch. The open kitchen affords you the opportunity to watch the chefs cook and the local women make fresh tortillas.
  Mexican delicacies are abundant here, and the kitchen has a special flare with them. Have you ever tried chicken with chocolate, chiles, fruit, and spices? You'll also find giant shrimp marinated in lime and cilantro and butterflied baby chicken with tomatillo-jalapeño chile sauce. We find that good choices for the kids include tamales, guacamole and chips, banana-wrapped red snapper, and banderillos de torero (two skewers of beef done over mesquite). The servers will split adult portions at the table for the children and will bring chips and tortillas as soon as you are seated.
  Guaymas is on Main Street, Parking is available.

HOULIHAN'S, 660 Bridgeway, Sausalito. Tel. 332-8512.

Cuisine: AMERICAN. **Reservations:** Recommended.

$ Prices: Lunch $7–$12; dinner $7–$15. AE, DC, MC, V.

Open: Mon–Thurs 11am–10pm, Fri 11am–11pm, Sat 10am–11pm, Sun 10am–10pm.

Children's Services: Boosters, highchairs; children's menu, crayons.

This is another good choice for American food. This smallish restaurant has a glassed-in deck and is quite pleasant. A nice touch is the tray of carrots and celery served before the main course and the cookies after the meal. The children's menu offers burgers, hot dogs, grilled-cheese, peanut butter and jelly sandwiches, chicken fingers, and spaghetti, all of which come with fries or veggies, beverage, and ice cream for dessert. The staff will warm baby bottles and food in the kitchen.

You'll find Houlihan's on Bridgeway on the waterfront.

SAM'S ANCHOR CAFE, 27 Main St., Tiburon. Tel. 435-4527.

Cuisine: AMERICAN. **Reservations:** None.

$ Prices: $5.50–$13; children's portions, $2.75–$4.25. AE, MC, V.

Open: Mon–Thurs 11am–10:30pm, Fri 11am–11pm, Sat 10am–11pm, Sun 9:30am–10:30pm.

Children's Services: Boosters, highchairs; children's menu, crayons.

The service is good and the food is tasty at Sam's. The deck is the place to eat during the day; it offers a spectacular view of San Francisco, the Bay Bridge, Alcatraz, and Angel Island. Although the deck sways, you'll get used to it. The friendly sea gulls are entertaining for the kids, but don't let the kids feed the gulls or the birds will steal the food right off your plate before you can stop them.

If you dine outside, watch your little ones. There are railings all around the deck, which sits over the water, and the servers keep an ever-watchful eye on the kids, but be careful just the same!

This very casual restaurant offers two indoor dining rooms in addition to the outdoor deck. The bar, which is located in front, has a large television; free popcorn is served with the drinks. Sam's is known for its delectable swordfish and salmon, as well as daily seafood specials. Cioppino, steamed clams, and sautéed or deep-fried local oysters are other favorites. Other fare includes sandwiches (the Dungeness crab on a toasted English muffin is yummy), omelets, chicken, steak, and very good burgers.

The children's "color-in" menu—which features a Samburger, spaghetti, fish-and-chips, and a hot dog—comes with crayons.

You'll find Sam's Anchor Café on Main Street.

SCOMA'S, 588 Bridgeway, Sausalito. Tel. 332-9551.

Cuisine: ITALIAN. **Reservations:** None.

$ Prices: $12–$23; children's menu items average $6. AE, MC, V.

Open: Fri–Sat & Mon 11:30am–10:30pm, Sun 11:30am–9:30pm, Tues–Thurs 5:30–10:30pm.

Children's Services: Boosters; children's menu.

For a more formal dining event, we like this attractive bayside restaurant, which has one of the most beautiful views of Sausalito. Overlooking the water, Scoma's has a relaxed atmosphere but a sophisticated seafood menu. Be prepared for a 30-minute wait for a table. You can drop by, leave your name, and continue your seaside stroll for a few minutes.

Scoma's is on the waterfront at Bridgeway. There's on-street parking or validated parking at the City lot.

There are other Scoma's branches at Fisherman's Wharf and in Larkspur.

WINSHIP, 670 Bridgeway, Sausalito. Tel. 332-1454.
   Cuisine: SEAFOOD. **Reservations:** Accepted.
$ **Prices:** Breakfast $7–$10, lunch $8–$14, dinner $11–$24. AE, CB, D, DC, MC, V.
   Open: Daily breakfast and lunch 7:30am–4:30pm, dinner Wed–Sun 5–9:30pm.
   Children's Services: Boosters, highchairs; crayons

This good California-style seafood restaurant has been owned by the same family for more than 25 years. One cute touch is the replica of a tugboat wheelhouse called "Nellie," which you will see when you walk in.

Everything on the menu is made from scratch—including the pastas. Specialties are seafood (don't miss the cioppino if you like the dish) and burgers as well as pasta and veal. At lunch you'll find lots of salads and hot and cold sandwiches. The staff will gladly split adult portions in the kitchen for the children. Be sure to ask for crayons so the kids can draw on the paper tablecloths.

Winship is on Bridgeway, with a view of San Francisco and East Bay.

CHAPTER 8

WHERE KIDS PREFER TO STAY

San Francisco has so many accommodation choices that you won't have any problem finding precisely the kind of hotel or motel that's right for your family. There are even a few bed-and-breakfasts that welcome children. In general, you'll find that hotel prices are comparable to those in most large cities, but you won't find as many budget-priced accommodations as you might in a smaller, less popular town. But expense is relative—what may be expensive to one family isn't to another. In this chapter we've listed our hotel recommendations first by location and then by price. Some price ranges will overlap. An "expensive" hotel might end up being "very expensive" if some of the lower priced rooms are not available. On the other hand, a "very expensive" or "expensive" hotel might become more affordable if you can take advantage of weekend or holiday specials, or family plans. Read each listing carefully to determine which ones meet your needs.

We place a star ✪ on the hotels that are our favorites. Let's face it, it's much nicer to travel with your kids in an environment where they're wholeheartedly welcomed. Hotels get our star usually because of a combination of extraordinary service, amenities, and a helpful attitude toward families. There is a dollar sign ($) preceding an accommodation that is a particularly good value.

Price categories are as follows: "Very Expensive," $200 to $400 per night for a double room; "Expensive," $125 to $200; "Moderate," $100 to $150; "Budget," less than $100.

Note: All rates are subject to change, and *the rates given do not include the hotel tax of 11%.* When you make your reservation, be sure to inquire about family plans, weekend or holiday specials, corporate rates, AAA discounts, senior rates, and any other discounts you might be eligible for.

CAMPING Family camps will take you well out of town. We have included a few camping listings at the end of the excursions chapter. For even more information on camping and other lodging facilities in California, see *Frommer's California with Kids.*

1. EMBARCADERO

VERY EXPENSIVE

HYATT REGENCY SAN FRANCISCO, 5 Embarcadero Center, San Francisco, CA 94111. Tel. 415/788-1234, or toll free 800/233-1234. Fax 415/981-3638. 803 rms. A/C MINIBAR TV TEL

$ Rates: $185–$238 single; $215–$268 double; suites start at $350. Children under 18 free in parents' room. Additional adults $30 per night; cribs free. Specials and weekend rates available; the Family Plan offers two rooms (usually connecting) each at the single-occupancy rate. AE, CB, DC, MC, V.

Parking: Valet parking $18 per day; in-and-out privileges.

Designed by architect John Portman who originated the atrium-court lobby, the 20-story pyramid-like building has seven sides and a 300-foot-long skylight in the roof. The lobby is the center of activity in the hotel (and, we suspect, the neighborhood).

There's no shh, shh, here. Instead there's movement, life, sounds. There are full-size trees, thousands of plants and shrubs, a running stream, and the wonderful Eclipse sculpture fountain. As the water streams down around the fountain's sides, it looks like plastic wrap. You'll see kids stand at the edge of the fountain, carefully running their fingers around the edge to be sure it is water and not plastic wrap. Then there are five glass elevators that are edged with tiny lights, a real treat to children who oooh! and ahhh! as they glide up and down.

Each guest room has a view of either the Bay or the city, and has sliding glass doors. Many of the rooms have balconies with little tables and chairs. There are several one- and two-bedroom suites, as well as the regular rooms that have king- or queen-sized beds with small sitting areas.

Dining/Entertainment: The Market Place Bar and Restaurant has outdoor and indoor eating areas, and offers a nice selection of lighter fare and is open for lunch. Mrs. Candy's is a café in the atrium lobby, serving breakfast, lunch, and dinner as well as light pastries and snacks. The Equinox is the hotel's expensive rooftop restaurant and lounge that makes a 360-degree rotation every 45 minutes; it's open for lunch and dinner daily. Highchairs and boosters available in all the restaurants, and children's plates are half-price. Sunday brunch (with more than 100 different dishes) is served in the atrium lobby from 10am to 2pm. (If you're looking for other restaurants nearby, you might also try Salmagundi or MacArthur Park.)

Services: Airport, RR, and bus transportation, full concierge service (they can arrange baby-sitting), 24-hour room service, doctor and dentist on call, valet parking, same-day dry cleaning and laundry.

Facilities: Shopping arcade, gift shop, barber and beauty salon. Guest privileges available at nearby health club.

CALIFORNIA

Sacramento

San Francisco

Bedford Hotel **1**
Buena Vista Motor Inn **2**
Chelsea Motor Inn **3**
Columbus Motor Inn **4**
Coventry Motor Inn **5**
Cow Hollow Motor Inn
  & Suites **6**
Diva Hotel **7**
Fairmont Hotel & Tower **8**
Four Seasons Clift Hotel **9**
Galleria Park Hotel **10**
Grand Hyatt San Francisco **11**
Handlery Union Square
  Hotel **12**
Holiday Inn-Fisherman's
  Wharf **13**
Hyatt Regency San
  Francisco **14**
Hyde Park Suites **15**
Juliana Hotel **16**
Kensington Park Hotel **17**
Lombard Motor Inn **18**
Marina Inn **19**
Monticello Inn **20**
Petite Auberge **21**
Queen Anne Hotel **22**
Quality Inn **23**
Ramada Hotel at
  Fisherman's Wharf **24**
San Francisco Hilton on
  Hilton Square **25**
San Francisco Marriott
  Fisherman's Wharf **26**
Sheraton at Fisherman's
  Wharf **27**
Travelodge Hotel at
  Fisherman's Wharf **28**
Tuscan Inn at Fisherman's
  Wharf **29**
Vagabond Inn **30**
Villa Florence **31**
Vintage Court Hotel **32**
Westin St. Francis **33**
White Swann Inn **34**

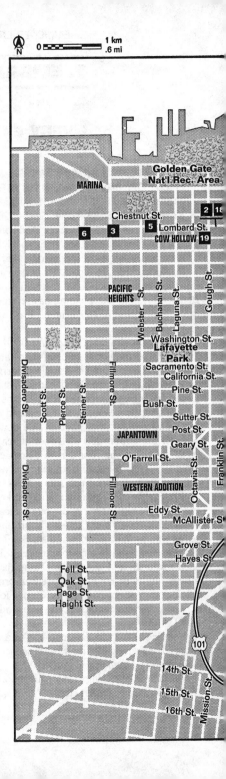

N

0 — 1 km
  — .6 mi

Golden Gate
Nat'l Rec. Area

MARINA

Chestnut St.

Lombard St.

COW HOLLOW **19**

2 1t

6   **3**   **5**

PACIFIC
HEIGHTS

Webster St.
Buchanan St.
Laguna St.
Gough St.

Washington St.

Lafayette
Park

Sacramento St.

California St.

Pine St.

Bush St.

Sutter St.

Post St.

Geary St.

O'Farrell St.

JAPANTOWN

Franklin St.

WESTERN ADDITION

Eddy St.

McAllister S

Grove St.

Hayes St.

Divisadero St.

Scott St.
Pierce St.
Steiner St.
Fillmore St.
Octavia St.

Fell St.
Oak St.
Page St.
Haight St.

101

14th St.

15th St.

16th St.

Mission St.

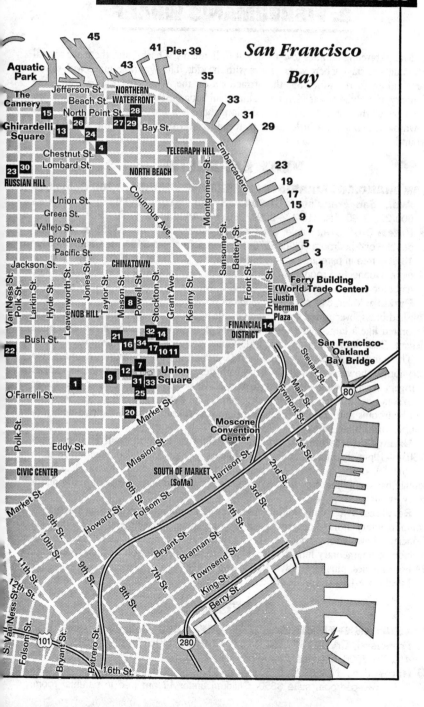

San Francisco Bay

45

41 Pier 39

43

35

Aquatic Park

33

31

29

The Cannery

Jefferson St.

15

Beach St.

NORTHERN WATERFRONT

North Point St.

28

Ghirardelli Square

13

26

24

27 29

Bay St.

4

TELEGRAPH HILL

23

23

30

Chestnut St.

Lombard St.

19

17

15

RUSSIAN HILL

NORTH BEACH

9

7

Union St.

5

Green St.

3

Vallejo St.

1

Broadway

Pacific St.

Jackson St.

CHINATOWN

Ferry Building (World Trade Center)

Columbus Ave.

Montgomery St.

Sansome St.

Battery St.

Front St.

Drumm St.

Justin Herman Plaza

Van Ness St.

Polk St.

Larkin St.

Hyde St.

Leavenworth St.

Jones St.

Taylor St.

Mason St.

Powell St.

Stockton St.

Grant Ave.

Kearny St.

8

NOB HILL

FINANCIAL DISTRICT

14

Bush St.

21

32 14

San Francisco–Oakland Bay Bridge

22

16 34

17 10 11

12 7

9

Union Square

Steuart St.

O'Farrell St.

1

31 33

25

80

Market St.

Main St.

Fremont St.

20

Moscone Convention Center

1st St.

Eddy St.

CIVIC CENTER

SOUTH OF MARKET (SoMa)

Mission St.

Harrison St.

2nd St.

Polk St.

Market St.

8th St.

Howard St.

Folsom St.

6th St.

Folsom St.

Bryant St.

Brannan St.

3rd St.

4th St.

10th St.

9th St.

7th St.

Townsend St.

11th St.

8th St.

King St.

12th St.

Berry St.

S. Van Ness St.

Folsom St.

Bryant St.

101

Potrero St.

280

16th St.

2. FISHERMAN'S WHARF

Many traveling families love to stay at Fisherman's Wharf—and there are several advantages to staying here when you're with the kids. The Wharf abounds with things for children to do—Pier 39, the attractions on the Wharf itself, boat rides, the Cannery, the Hyde Street Pier, and Ghirardelli Square. It's a tourist area, so kids are just part of the general scene. In addition, there is a little more open space than downtown, making it a little easier to meander and stroll and let the children run around.

VERY EXPENSIVE

SAN FRANCISCO MARRIOTT FISHERMAN'S WHARF, 1250 Columbus Ave., San Francisco, CA 94133. Tel. 415/775-7555, or toll free 800/228-9290. Fax 415/474-2099. 256 rms. A/C MINIBAR TV TEL

$ Rates: $164–$192 single; $184–$212 double; junior suites $235 single, $250 double; one-bedroom suites $370; two-bedroom suites $495 up. Children under 18 stay free in parents' room; additional adults $20; cribs free, rollaways $10 per night. Connecting rooms. Weekend packages available; ask about seasonal rates and other special packages. AE, CB, DC, MC, V.

Parking: Valet, $14 per day; in-and-out privileges.

Polished brass, overstuffed chairs, and chandeliers grace the spacious lobby, which is decorated like a large living room with lots of small conversation areas. It is quite elegant. Each floor has an inviting little lobby sitting area off the elevator.

The handsomely decorated rooms have beautiful wood furniture. All have two telephones, shower and bath, and the bathroom amenities we've come to expect. Refrigerators are available upon request for $10 per day. Suites consist of a parlor (with sofa bed), kitchen area (with refrigerator, dining table, and bath), plus the one or two bedrooms that connect. Each bedroom has its own bath, so the two-bedroom suite features three baths.

Dining/Entertainment: Spada—A California Seafood Grill is open from 6:30am–10pm. Breakfasts average $6, lunches average $8, and dinners range from $6–$19.50. It has boosters, highchairs, and a varied children's menu. The lobby lounge has complimentary hors d'oeuvres from 5–7pm and features a piano player every evening.

Services: Twice-daily housekeeping service, complimentary morning newspaper, complimentary hors d'oeuvres 5–7pm, complimentary continental breakfast on Concierge Level, room service (6:30am–11pm), baby-sitting services. Other amenities include complimentary limo service to the Financial District on weekday mornings, 24-hour movies, plus free HBO, ESPN, and CNN.

Facilities: Gift shop. Health club privileges.

EXPENSIVE

HOLIDAY INN–FISHERMAN'S WHARF, 1300 Columbus Ave., San Francisco, CA 94133. Tel. 415/771-9000, or toll free 800/HOLIDAY. Fax 415/771-7006. 580 rms. A/C MINIBAR TV TEL

$ Rates: June–Nov $120–$156 single; $120–$179 double; one-bedroom suite $250; two-bedroom suite $350. Children under 17 are free in parents' room;

additional adults $16 per night; cribs free; rollaways $9 per night. Lower rates rest of year. AE, CB, DC, MC, V.

Parking: Free.

There are a few nice features about this Holiday Inn: the heated outdoor swimming pool, the free parking, and the hotel's location 3 blocks from the Bay and Fisherman's Wharf and 2 blocks from Ghirardelli Square.

The rooms are decorated in soft, muted tones and have bath/shower combinations, table and chairs, and televisions offering free Showtime as well as pay channels. The large one- and two-bedroom suites have a living room with a sofa bed, eating area, kitchen, and large dining table and chairs, with plenty of room for a crib or rollaway.

Dining/Entertainment: Charley's Restaurant and Lounge offers buffets for breakfast, lunch, and dinner. Regular menu items are also available.

Services: Baby-sitting services, bellhops, valet service, room service (6am–10pm).

Facilities: Heated outdoor swimming pool, coin-operated laundry.

RAMADA HOTEL AT FISHERMAN'S WHARF, 590 Bay St., San Francisco, CA 94133. Tel. 415/885-4700, or toll free 800/2-RAMADA. Fax 415/771-8945. 231 rms. A/C MINIBAR TV TEL

$ Rates (May–Oct): $135–$170 single; $150–$185 double; suites with king-sized bed, sofa bed, and wet bar $240–$255; rates lower rest of year. Children under 19 stay free in parents' room if extra bedding is not needed; additional adults $15; cribs free. Connecting rooms available. AE, CB, DC, MC, V.

Parking: $6 in adjacent garage; in-and-out privileges.

The location of this hotel (2 blocks from Fisherman's Wharf) makes it a real find, especially when you consider the limited-fee parking. Another really good feature is the sundeck and jogging track. The gate is locked, so while parents must be there to supervise children, you can feel secure.

The rooms are spacious and bright with either a king-sized bed or two double beds, plus small game tables, and can accommodate even two children, including a baby crib or rollaway. All bathrooms have vanity areas, showers, and tubs. "Superior" rooms with king-sized beds have sofa beds and coffee tables and can sleep four or five people. Master suites are huge, and also sport refrigerators.

Dining/Entertainment: The Conch Pearl Restaurant on premises (open 6:30am–10pm) serves breakfast, lunch, and dinner. The lobby bar is open 4pm–midnight.

Services: Baby-sitting services, room service (6am–10pm), valet service, and pay movies.

Facilities: Sundeck, jogging track, par-course, gift shop.

SHERATON AT FISHERMAN'S WHARF, 2500 Mason St., San Francisco, CA 94133. Tel. 415/362-5500, or toll free 800/325-3535. Fax 415/956-5275. 525 rms. A/C MINIBAR TV TEL

$ Rates: $145–$220, single or double; suites $375 up; many package plans offered. Children under 17 stay free in parents' room if a rollaway is not needed; additional adults $20; cribs free, rollaways $20 per night; connecting rooms available. AE, CB, DC, MC, V.

Parking: $12 per day; in-and-out privileges for registered guests.

★ This isn't a high-rise hotel, but rather one with only four floors that takes up an entire city block 1½ blocks from Fisherman's Wharf, giving the hostelry a resort ambience. It is truly a resort for our kids because it has an outdoor heated swimming pool, quite a treat here in San Francisco.

The attractive, newly decorated rooms are done in muted tones of gray and peach. Each has a TV with free HBO and Sports Channel, and in-room movies are available for $6.75. The large rooms (with two double beds) have enough space for a crib. Bathrooms feature tubs and showers and lots of counter space. All the expected in-room amenities are provided. Refrigerators can be requested for the length of your stay for a flat charge of $20. The rooms open onto large, airy hallways decorated with plants and small trees.

Dining/Entertainment: Mason Beach Grill serves breakfast, lunch, and dinner and features extensive menus for all meals. In the evening there's also an all-you-can-eat seafood buffet at $17.50 for adults and $8.50 for children under 12. A children's menu is available, and there are early-bird specials every night. For a drink, try Chanen's Lounge, an old San Francisco–style saloon.

Services: Baby-sitting services through the concierge, who can also arrange tours and sightseeing; 24-hour room service, twice-daily maid service with nightly turndown; car rental and travel services; express checkout.

Facilities: Outdoor swimming pool with a large shallow area, hair salon, business center, access to health club.

MODERATE

TRAVELODGE HOTEL AT FISHERMAN'S WHARF, 250 Beach St., San Francisco, CA 94133. Tel. 415/392-6700, or toll free 800/255-3050. Fax 415/392-6700, ext. 384. 250 rms. A/C MINIBAR TV TEL

$ **Rates (May–Nov):** $105–$155 single; $115–$170 double; $200–$300 suites; rates lower rest of year. Children under 18 free when sharing parents' room; cribs free, rollaways $10 per night. Connecting rooms available. AE, CB, DC, MC, V.

Parking: Limited free guest parking.

The only Bayfront hotel on Fisherman's Wharf, the Travelodge has a heated outdoor swimming pool set in a landscaped area. Some rooms have balconies with views of either the Bay or the swimming pool.

The rooms are pleasing, but not all the bathrooms have tubs, so request one in advance if it is important to you. Family rooms have two double beds and a sofa bed that opens into a double bed. In theory, you could sleep six people in one of these large rooms.

Dining/Entertainment: Angellina's, a full-service family-priced restaurant, is open 7am–9pm.

Services: Free refrigerators upon request, baby-sitting services, car rental desk, tour services.

Facilities: Heated swimming pool with large three-foot wading area, shopping arcade.

TUSCAN INN AT FISHERMAN'S WHARF, 425 North Point St., San Francisco, CA 94133. Tel. 415/561-1100, or toll free 800/648-4626. Fax 415/561-1199. 199 rms. A/C MINIBAR TV TEL.

$ **Rates:** $140–$160 single or double; one-bedroom suites (nice for family of four)

$175–$215; rates include complimentary continental breakfast. Children under 12 free in parents' room; additional adults $20, cribs free; rollaways $10 per night. Weekend packages. AE, CB, DC, MC, V.
Parking: Valet, $17 per day; in-and-out privileges.

Located one block from the cable car line and only two blocks west of Pier 39 this lovely inn is centrally situated for a good stay in San Francisco. It's obvious that the staff is used to assisting tourists—they're as helpful as they can be. And they are especially pleasant to children, offering a selection of games and videos.

The rooms are extremely attractive, though a bit on the small side. They have TVs with VCR.

Dining/Entertainment: Café Pescatore is open (6:30am–10:30pm) for breakfast, lunch, and dinner everyday. This moderately priced sidewalk café serves Italian food—continental breakfast; pizza, salads, and pastas for lunch and dinner.

Services: Concierge, limited room service, coffee and tea service, complimentary evening wine in lobby, valet and laundry service, tennis and health club privileges. The children's program consists of a printed listing of nearby activities for guests, a dozen kid videos and board games for loan, and crayons and coloring book awaiting the kids in the room when they arrive.

BUDGET

COLUMBUS MOTOR INN, 1075 Columbus Ave., San Francisco, CA 94133. Tel. 415/885-1492, or toll free 800/553-1900. 45 rms. A/C MINIBAR TV TEL

$ Rates: $71 single with king-sized bed; $76 double with king-sized bed or $76 two double beds. Children under 5 stay free in parents' room; $5 for each additional person up to six; cribs free, rollaway $5. AE, CB, DC, MC, V.
Parking: Free on premises.

This is a simple place four blocks from Fisherman's Wharf, with no lobby, just a front desk, but it is pleasant. The rooms are clean and comfortable and feature color televisions and in-room coffee.

Services: Baby-sitting services may be arranged through a bonded service.

3. MARINA DISTRICT/ LOMBARD STREET

BUENA VISTA MOTOR INN, 1599 Lombard St., San Francisco, CA 94123. Tel. 415/923-9600. 50 rms. A/C MINIBAR TV TEL
$ Rates: $71 single, $76 double; additional person $6. AE, CB, DC, MC, V.
Parking: Limited free parking.

Built in early 1989, this hostelry on U.S. 101 on Lombard Street at Gough Street offers lovely guest rooms that are quite spacious. This is a good budget choice.

LOMBARD MOTOR INN, 1475 Lombard St., San Francisco, CA 94123. Tel. 415/441-6000. 48 rms. A/C TV TEL

$ Rates: $71 single; $76 double. Children under 10 stay free in parents' room; additional person $6; cribs free, rollaways $6. Connecting rooms available. AE, CB, DC, MC, V.

Parking: Free indoor parking.

Don't expect anything fancy here, but rates are very reasonable and you'll find it clean and pleasant and conveniently located on U.S. 101 one block off Van Ness Avenue. Standard rooms include a king-sized or extra-long double bed. If you want a bath with a tub/shower, you need to request it. In-room coffee; no charge for local telephone calls.

CHELSEA MOTOR INN, 2095 Lombard St., San Francisco, CA 94123. Tel. 415/563-5600. Fax 415/567-6475. 60 rms. A/C TV TEL

$ Rates: $71 single, $76 double. Children under 5 stay free in parents' room; $5 for additional occupants (four maximum); cribs free, rollaways $5 per night. Connecting rooms available. AE, CB, DC, MC, V.

Parking: Free covered parking.

Located on U.S. 101 at Fillmore Street, this is another attractive budget-priced alternative. Somewhat surprising are the extra touches here: a no-smoking floor, a security elevator that opens only with a room key, king- and queen-sized beds or extra-long double beds. The rooms are large and comfortable and feature showers and cast-iron tubs, plus a vanity area with mirror. Some third-floor rooms have a view. This motor inn is owned by the same folks as the Cow Hollow, the Coventry, and the Chelsea.

COVENTRY MOTOR INN, 1901 Lombard St., San Francisco, CA 94123. Tel. 415/567-1200. 69 rms. A/C TV TEL

$ Rates: $71 single; $76 double; additional persons $5 per night. AE, CB, DC, MC, V.

Parking: Complimentary indoor parking.

This inn is owned by the same folks as the Cow Hollow, and is a pleasant budget accommodation.

COW HOLLOW MOTOR INN & SUITES, 2190 Lombard St., San Francisco, CA 94123. Tel. 415/921-5800. Fax 415/922-8515. 117 rms. A/C MINIBAR TV TEL

$ Rates: $71 single, $76 double for a king- or two queen-sized beds. Children under 5 stay free in parents' room. $5 for each additional occupant up to four; cribs free, rollaways $5 per night. Connecting rooms available. One-bedroom suites with one bath $175, single or double; two-bedroom suites with two baths $225, single or double; each additional person $10; weekly rates available. AE, DC, MC, V.

Parking: Free covered parking.

The spacious rooms at Cow Hollow are tastefully decorated, and some are so large that even with a king-sized bed there's space for a crib, a rollaway, and room to move around in. The rooms are bright and quite lovely. Most have two extra-long double beds. Cow Hollow has recently constructed one- and two-bedroom suites (not budget accommodations) with furnished living room, wood-burning fireplace, fully equipped kitchen, and cable TV. Cow Hollow is on U.S. 101 at Steiner Street.

Dining/Entertainment: The First Watch restaurant on premises serves breakfast and lunch (7am–2:30pm) and offers half-portions for children.

QUALITY INN, 2775 Van Ness Ave., San Francisco, CA 94109. Tel. 415/928-5000, or toll free 800/228-5151. Fax 415/441-3990. 132 rms. A/C TV TEL

$ Rates (Apr–Nov): $78–$108 single; $88–$125 double; lower rates rest of year. AE, D, DC, MC, V.
Parking: Limited free parking.

There are two kinds of rooms here. The first are average-sized rooms with one queen-sized bed, a table and chairs, and a desk, with bathrooms that are small but have shower/tub combinations. These rooms can accommodate a crib or rollaway but may seem cramped. On the other side of the hotel are larger rooms, which have a beautiful view of the Bay and the Golden Gate Bridge. These rooms feature two double beds, a game table and chairs, desk, as well as a good-sized bathroom. On premises Brandi's coffeeshop is open for breakfast (6:30–11am), lunch (11:30am–1pm), and dinner (6–9pm). No lunch on Sat or Sun. The Quality Inn is on U.S. 101 at Lombard Street.

Services: In-room movies, complimentary coffee service, and room service.

VAGABOND INN—MIDTOWN, 2550 Van Ness Ave., San Francisco, CA 94109. Tel. 415/776-7500, or toll free 800/522-1555. Fax 415/776-5689. 132 rms. MINIBAR TV NO A/C TEL

$ Rates: $60–$76 single, $72–$87 double, $125–$150 family units. Children under 19 free in parents' room; additional person $5; cribs free. AE, D, DC, MC, V.
Parking: Limited free covered parking.

The Vagabond is in a great location—on U.S. 101 at Filbert Street. It serves complimentary continental breakfast (7-9am), free coffee and tea, free apples, complimentary weekday newspaper, and has nice-sized pool with a little patio and gazebo. Adjacent is the Midnite Café, which has a full coffeeshop menu and is open 24 hours. The Vagabond Inn is a member of a chain with 42 locations.

HYDE PARK SUITES, 2655 Hyde St., San Francisco, CA 94109. Tel. 415/771-0200, or toll free 800/227-3608. Fax 415/771-2435. 24 suites. A/C MINIBAR TV TEL

$ Rates: $165–$220 single or double; third-floor suites with view of the Bay or with a balcony $190; two-bedroom suites that sleep up to six people $220. Children under 12 stay free in parents' room; additional person $10 per night; cribs $5. AE, CB, DC, MC, V.
Parking: $12 per day; in-and-out privileges.

Located 6 blocks from Fisherman's Wharf at North Point Street, the hotel itself is pretty and only four floors high. The guest suites are built around a contemporary, early-California–style atrium, which gives the hotel an open feeling. The courtyard, with its terra-cotta tiles, wicker furniture, fountain, lots of plants, and small trees that reach up to the skylight, give it an out-of-doors feel.

Suites come with fully equipped kitchens, microwave oven and dishwasher. Although they tend to be on the small side, suites can function like an apartment and have enough space in the living room for a crib and rollaway.

Services: Free limo service to downtown, 24-hour concierge, nightly turndown service, free coffee and tea in your room, complimentary morning newspaper, complimentary continental breakfast every morning in the lobby, a fruit basket filled at all time, grocery delivery service available, limited-menu room service 4pm–midnight.

Facilities: Coin-operated laundry.

4. NOB HILL AREA

VERY EXPENSIVE

THE FAIRMONT HOTEL & TOWER, 950 Mason St., San Francisco, CA 94106. **Tel. 415/772-5000,** or toll free 800/527-4727. Fax 415/772-5086. 597 rms. A/C MINIBAR TV TEL

$ Rates: In the main building: $150–$210 single, $180–$240 double. In the tower: $220–$260 single, $250–$290 double; suites start at $500. Cribs free; additional person, including children, pay $30 per night each. Connecting rooms available. Weekend packages. AE, CB, DC, MC, V.

Parking: $20 per day; in-and-out privileges.

Massive, ornate, enormous, the Fairmont high atop Nob Hill has been the grande dame of hotels in the city for more than 80 years. With almost 600 rooms, it has been called a city within a city. It has all the amenities and services to prove it.

The guest rooms are spacious and well appointed, many with high ceilings and huge picture windows. All have cable television with free HBO.

Dining/Entertainment: The Fairmont has six restaurants: the Bella Voce Ristorante & Bar, open for breakfast, lunch, and dinner; the Fairmont Crown Room, open for lunch, and dinner, and Sunday brunch; Masons, open for dinner; the Squire restaurant, open for dinner; the Tonga Restaurant and Humcan Bar, open for dinner and dancing; and the Sweet Corner, a soda fountain/sweet shop for breakfast, lunch, sandwiches, ice cream and pastries.

Services: There all here—24-hour room service, concierge, baby-sitting services, valet and laundry service.

Facilities: Barber and beauty shops, drugstore, florist, gift shop, bank, exercise room with weights, treadmill, and Nautilus equipment.

5. UNION SQUARE

VERY EXPENSIVE

FOUR SEASONS CLIFT HOTEL, 495 Geary St., San Francisco, CA 94102. **Tel. 415/775-4700,** or toll free 800/332-3442. Fax 415/441-4621. 329 rms and suites. A/C MINIBAR TV TEL

$ Rates: $185–$230 single, $185–$250 double for superior and deluxe rooms;

$265–$285 bedroom/sitting-room combinations; $300 single or double executive suites (French doors separate sitting room from bedroom, 2 baths); $475–$1,000 regular suites. Cribs and rollaways are free. The Family Plan (children 18 and under) offers two rooms (usually connecting), each at the single-occupancy rate. Children stay free in their parents' room; additional adults $25. Rates lower on some weekends. AE, DC, MC, V.

Parking: $18 per day; in-and-out privileges.

One of San Francisco's landmarks, the Four Seasons Clift, 2 blocks west of Union Square, at Taylor Street, is known for its luxurious rooms and superb service. The staff treats you like you're an honored guest; nothing is too much trouble for them. They even take the time to learn your name! The Clift has been catering to traveling families for a while, and they really know how to do it. The hotel staff is gracious and wonderful to children, providing for their every need. Parents will be happy to know that in addition to cribs and refrigerators (available upon request), the hotel can provide bibs, diapers, bottles, strollers, humidifiers, and baby bathtubs. There's even a pediatrician on call 24 hours a day. There are magazines for teenagers, toys for tots, and bedtime snacks of cookies (either Oreos or Mrs. Field's) and milk, and the concierge also offers parents a list of activities and restaurants that cater to children. In fact, parents could conceivably arrive empty-handed and within a short time have the basic necessities to make their stay a pleasant one. In addition, the hotel provides kids with their own plush terrycloth mini-robes, and will send up baseball cards, comic books, and popcorn in a basket with balloons flying. For little Nintendo addicts, you can have a portable Nintendo unit sent to your room. There are even pocket-size electronic games available.

The rooms are elegantly furnished in quiet, understated tones with fine fabrics and Georgian reproduction furniture, some with satin wood inlays. Oversize rooms are standard. A number of rooms feature two bathrooms.

Dining/Entertainment: The Clift's world-famous dining room, the French Room, and its lovely Redwood Room, are treats. The French Room (with its list of over 20,000 bottles of fine wine) serves breakfast, lunch, and dinner and has its share of highchairs. It features a children's menu that includes cheeseburgers, hot dogs, chicken fingers, even macaroni-and-cheese. The Redwood Room is acclaimed as one of San Francisco's cultural and architectural traditions. It is entirely paneled in aged redwood burl polished to a shining luster, and the 20-foot ceiling makes you feel as if you're sitting in the middle of a redwood forest. Designed in classic art deco style, it is an experience not to be missed. *Note:* If you enjoy a classic High Tea (and your children can tolerate the wait—or, better yet, there's another adult to watch them), the Clift is renown for its superb tea service.

Services: 24-hour room service (with special children's menu), twice-daily maid service, complimentary overnight shoeshine service, laundry/dry cleaning, and 24-hour valet, wide array of business services. Additional amenities: toys for children, children's videocassettes, Nintendo.

Facilities: Business services, gift shop, wheelchair accessibility.

GRAND HYATT SAN FRANCISCO (formerly Hyatt on Union Square), 345 Stockton St., San Francisco, CA 94108. Tel. 415/398-1234, or toll free 800/228-9000. Fax 415/392-2536. 693 rms; 33 suites. A/C MINIBAR TV TEL

$ Rates: $195 single, $225 double (with king-size or two double beds); $350–$1,500 suites. Regency Club floors: higher rates. Adjoining rooms available.

Children 18 and under stay free in parents' room; additional adults $15; cribs and rollaways free. Weekend plans. AE, CB, D, DC, MC, V.

Parking: $20 per day; in-and-out privileges.

Perfectly situated in the heart of Union Square at Post Street, and generally thought to cater to businesspeople, the hotel's staff and management go out of their way to encourage families to visit. The emphasis here is on personalized care. Complete with all the usual Hyatt touches, this one has an added benefit if you're taking youngsters: Camp Hyatt (but check ahead of time to be sure of the hours during the time you'll be there).

The lovely lobby is much smaller than you'd expect for such a large hotel, and you can keep track of your children more easily than in the enormous (though breathtaking) sister hotel, the Hyatt Regency San Francisco. Standing in the lobby, it's hard to believe that the hotel has 36 floors (all have views). The hotel has undergone a multimillion-dollar renovation, and everything looks tip-top.

Earth tones and woods predominate in the spacious rooms, which feature televisions with remote control, two phones, and a small game table where the kids can eat or play games. Surprise, surprise, the bathrooms even have tiny televisions.

Dining/Entertainment: The Plaza Restaurant is a great place to take the kids. Its high ceilings, stained-glass dome, and giant picture windows that look out onto Union Square provide an open feeling for dining. The children's menu offers great kid-meals from $1.50 to $3.50, accompanied by coloring book, crayons, and helium balloons. All regular menu items ($3.75–$12.75) are available for children in half-portions at half-price. Open 6:30am–11:30pm daily. Napper's, Too, is another moderately priced restaurant good for families; it's a deli-style room that features homemade soups, salads, and sandwiches.

Services: 24-hour room service (including special Camp Hyatt menu for children), full concierge service, nightly turndown, complimentary fruit at the front desk. Camp Hyatt is a supervised program of children's activities for kids ages 3–15; ask about hours of operation. Games available for loan through the concierge/guest service desk.

Facilities: Tennis privileges at the San Francisco Tennis Club (charge for court fees); free use of Jacuzzi, sauna, steam; exericse room with weights, and Nautilus equipment; aerobics.

SAN FRANCISCO HILTON ON HILTON SQUARE, One Hilton Square, San Francisco, CA 94102. Tel. 415/771-1400, or toll free 800/HILTONS. Fax 415/923-5039. 1,891 rms. A/C MINIBAR TV TEL

$ Rates: $160–$220 single; $185–$225 double; suites start at $250. Luxury tower level, $250 up. Children (any age) sleep free in same room as parents; additional adults $25; cribs free. Weekend packages. AE, CB, DC, MC, V.

Parking: $16 per day; indoor self-parking on the same floor as your room (by reservation).

The $210 million renovation has added some beautiful, unusual touches to this Hilton which was already known for its services and amenities. The lobby is grand indeed, completely done in marble with accents of beige and light-rose hues that accentuate the color of the stone. Two giant crystal chandeliers and enormously high ceilings make for a spectacular entry into the hotel. One very unusual feature of this hotel is the large, heated outdoor swimming pool (open 7am-7pm) on the 16th floor in a garden court, which is protected on all sides to block the wind.

The Hilton on Hilton Square, 3 blocks west of Union Square, offers king-, queen-, and double-bedded rooms, all tastefully decorated, many with views of the city. All rooms have tub/shower combinations, remote-control TVs, and offer SpectraVision, and many have desk and chair.

Dining/Entertainment: Café on the Square is open 6am–midnight, with prices typical of hotel coffeeshops. In addition to regular menu items, the Café offers tempting buffets for breakfast, lunch, and dinner. Kiku restaurant serves authentic Japanese food for lunch and dinner. Phil Lehr's Steakery is a dinner place specializing in steaks and chops. Cityscape, the 46th-floor restaurant with a fabulous 360-degree panoramic view of the city, serves brunch ($31) on Sundays (11am–2:30pm) and dinner nightly. During the holidays, Cityscape has special activities for the kids.

Services: Room service 6:30am–2:30am, car rental, concierge, laundry and dry cleaning, baby-sitting services.

Facilities: Large heated outdoor pool, shopping arcade, barber and beauty shop, business center.

THE WESTIN ST. FRANCIS, 335 Powell St., San Francisco, CA 94102. Tel. 415/397-7000, or toll free 800/228-3000. Fax 415/774-0124. 1,200 rms. A/C MINIBAR TV TEL

$ Rates: Main building: $160 single, $195 double standard rooms; $195 single, $230 double medium-size rooms; $245 single, $280 double deluxe rooms. Tower building: $250 single, $285 double medium-size rooms; $280 single, $315 double for deluxe rooms. Suites $300–$1,800. Children under 18 free in parents' room if additional beds are not needed; cribs free, rollaways $35. Weekend specials; the Family Plan offers two rooms (usually connecting) each at single-occupancy rate. AE, CB, DC, MC, V.

Parking: $20 per day; in-and-out privileges.

The enormous 6,000-square-foot lobby is done in stunning rosewood. With ceilings several stories high, set off with huge crystal chandeliers, it is a stunning picture of old-world opulence. This huge hotel on Powell Street opposite Union Square boasts five outdoor glass elevators (the kids love them), distinctive shops, and one of the busiest lobbies you'll see. You have to keep a close eye on the little ones here—kids can get swept up in the tumult. During Christmas and Easter holidays there are decorations all around, and many schoolchildren come here on class outings.

Ask for rooms in the main building (unless you prefer ultramodern rooms). The hallways of the original building are wide-corridored spaces with beautiful rugs, and the rooms are high-ceilinged and elegant. Some are enormous, with loveseats and plenty of room for cribs and rollaways. The bathrooms feature large sink and counter areas. Suites are two rooms with a connecting door, each with loveseat or couch and loads of space. The tower rooms (all of which have bay windows) are large and have small entry halls.

Dining/Entertainment: There are several restaurants to choose from. The Dutch Kitchen is very pleasant to children and is one of our favorite breakfast places in the city. Open daily 6am–11:30pm, it has a wonderfully complete menu for adults and a special children's menu. There are highchairs and boosters available, and children are given a coloring book and crayons to amuse themselves while they wait. The Compass Rose restaurant is like an English drawing room that opens onto the lobby. Lunch and high tea are served here. Other possible choices are the English Grill and Victor's (you might want to get a baby-sitter and go adult-style for dinner). Victor's also serves a wonderful Sunday brunch.

Services: In-room amenities for all rooms include bathroom scales and deluxe toiletries, SpectraVision; turndown service upon request, 24-hour room service, concierge, airport transportation, laundry and valet, doctor on-call, baby-sitting services.

Facilities: Barber and beauty salons, variety of shops and boutiques, business services, currency exchange.

GALLERIA PARK HOTEL, 191 Sutter St., San Francisco, CA 94104. Tel. 415/781-3060, or toll free 800/792-9636, 800/792-9855 in California. Fax 415/433-4409. 177 rms. A/C MINIBAR TV TEL

$ Rates: $130 single or double; $160–$425 suites. Connecting rooms are available. Children and cribs free; rollaways $15 per night. Family packages; weekend rates. AE, CB, DC, MC, V.

Parking: Garage fee $14 per day; in-and-out privileges.

A creation of developer Bill Kimpton and designer Nan Rosenblatt, the Galleria Park originally opened in 1911 and was completely renovated a few years ago. The atrium lobby is an art nouveau vision, with a gorgeous crystal skylight from 1907. One of the best things about the hotel is the outdoor jogging track (complete with wood benches and trees all around), where you and the kids can retreat when urban life seems too frenetic.

The smartly decorated rooms look less like a commercial hotel than many, and are good sized. Some rooms feature a writing desk, and all are soundproofed. Some bathrooms have showers only, so request a tub if you desire one. The suites are lovely and well-designed, with soothing colors, fireplaces, stereos, and large TVs.

Dining/Entertainment: Brasserie Chambord is located on premises (open Mon–Sat 6:30am–9pm; Sun 6:30am–11pm).

Services: Airport transportation, room service, concierge, valet and laundry service, bellman.

Facilities: Outdoor jogging track, shopping arcade.

HANDLERY UNION SQUARE HOTEL, 351 Geary St., San Francisco, CA 94102. Tel. 415/781-7800, or toll free 800/223-0888. Fax 415/781-0269. 377 rms. Some A/C MINIBAR TV TEL

$ Rates: $99–$130 single, $109–$145 double; suites $130–$280. Connecting rooms available. Handlery Club level: higher rates. Children under 15 free in parents' room; additional adults $20; cribs free; rollaways $10 per night.

Parking: $8.50 per day; in-and-out-privileges.

A beautiful lobby, heated outdoor swimming pool, and a great location make this a really good choice in the Union Square area.

Handsomely decorated rooms have wood furniture, safes, first-run cable movies (for a fee). Each floor has an inviting little lobby sitting area off the elevator.

Dining/Entertainment: New Joe's Restaurant offers breakfast, lunch, and dinner; the cocktail lounge is open from 10am–2am.

Services: Airport transportation, room service (7am–10pm); free coffee in rooms, concierge, bellman, valet and laundry service, baby-sitting service.

Facilities: Heated outdoor swimming pool, poolside service. Barber and beauty shops.

MODERATE

HOTEL BEDFORD, 761 Post St., San Francisco, CA 94109. Tel. 415/ 673-6040, or toll free 800/227-5642, 800/652-1889 in California. Fax 415/563-6739. 144 rms. No A/C MINIBAR TV TEL

$ Rates: $94–$99 single or double; suites start at $155. Children under 12 stay free in their parents' room, additional adults $10; cribs free, rollaways $10 per night. AE, CB, DC, MC, V.

Parking: Valet parking $10.50 per day; in-and-out privileges.

⑤ This newly renovated 1933-vintage hotel is 3½ blocks west of Union Square, near many restaurants and shopping. A charming place, its standard rooms are beautifully decorated, and many of them have panoramic views of the city. Kids are very welcome. They will love the VCRs in every room (you can rent movies in the lobby), and adults love the complimentary wine served every evening in the lovely English-style lobby. Parlor suites consist of a bedroom (with a double- or queen-size bed) and an adjoining parlor that has two overstuffed chairs and a sleeper sofa. The family suites consist of two bedrooms, one with twin beds; there is one small bathroom with bath and shower, but little storage space.

Services: Airport transportation, same-day laundry service, complimentary afternoon wine, morning and evening room service, variety of children's videocassette tapes for in-room VCRs.

HOTEL DIVA, 440 Geary St., San Francisco, CA 94102. Tel. 415/885-0200, or toll free 800/553-1900. Fax 415/346-6613. 108 rms. A/C MINIBAR TV TEL

$ Rates: $109–$134, single or double (depending on size of room); suites $300 up. No charge for cribs or for children under 12 (maximum 2); additional adults and children $10 each in their parents' room, but rollaways cost $10 per night. AE, CB, DC, MC, V.

Parking: 24-hour valet parking, $16 per day.

Architecturally and design wise, the Diva is as far from the traditional European-style hotel as you can get—and a surprise find in San Francisco. Hi-tech, Italian-style, and futuristic, the hotel has its own little gallery of celebrity handprints on the sidewalk in front of the hotel, which is on Union Square between Mason and Taylor streets. As you enter the lobby via the large chrome doors, you'll be struck by the circular chrome reception desk, the floor-to-ceiling mirrors, and the four large video-playing televisions suspended high on the wall behind the front desk.

The rooms are attractive, but vary considerably. Smaller rooms are large enough to include a crib but would be cramped with a rollaway. For families we recommend the bedrooms with a queen-size bed, VCR unit, a little hall (actually part of the vanity area), and a sitting area that is more like a small living room. The sitting room also has a VCR, a closet, and a Sico bed (a Murphy bed) and room for an additional rollaway.

Services: Complimentary continental breakfast (includes croissants, coffee, and tea), videocassette player, VCR library of 300 tapes to rent, free newspapers, overnight shoeshine, and use of IBM personal computers.

VILLA FLORENCE, 255 Powell St., San Francisco, CA 94102. Tel. 415/397-7700, or toll free 800/553-4411, 800/243-5700 in California. 177 rms. A/C MINIBAR TV TEL

$ Rates: $119 single or double; suites start at $139. Children under 17 stay free in their parents' room; cribs free, rollaways $10 per night. Special Christmas packages. AE, CB, DC, MC, V.

Parking: $15 per day, in-and-out privileges (garage about a block away from the hotel).

The lobby at this hotel ½ block off Union Square is 16th-century Italian Renaissance style with a wood-burning fireplace and colonnaded entrance. At first you might not think that this is a place for children. However, the lobby is spacious, the rooms are inviting, and most important, the staff knows how to handle children, and will be glad to do anything they can to help you. Babysitting can be arranged through the front desk.

The rooms are colorfully decorated, and—what a plus—are soundproof. The remote-control televisions feature VCR units. Rooms come with king, queen, or double beds. There are many different types of rooms here, so when you make your reservation, be sure to specify what you want.

Dining/Entertainment: Kuleto's Italian Restaurant (tel. 397-7720) opens into the lobby. Rated by *San Francisco Focus Magazine* as one of the top three Italian restaurants, it is open from 7–10:30am and 11:30am–11pm, serving full breakfasts, lunch, and dinner. Northern Italian specialties. Service plate available for children.

Services: Airport transportation. Room service 6:30–10:30am and 4pm–midnight. In-room refrigerators available. Baby-sitting services.

HOTEL JULIANA, 590 Bush St., San Francisco, CA 94108. Tel. 415/ 392-2540, or toll free 800/382-8800, 800/372-8800 in California. Fax 415/391-8447. 107 rms. A/C MINIBAR TV TEL

$ Rates: $107 regular suite, $135 junior suite, $145 executive suite; rates are per room. Monthly rates available. Cribs free; rollaways $10 per night. AE, CB, DC, MC, V.

Parking: $14 per day; in-and-out privileges.

This lovely little European-style hotel on the Nob Hill side of Union Square at Stockton Street is delightful and may remind you of a pensione in Italy. The lobby is cozy—often there's a blazing fire in the fireplace and classical music in the background. Complimentary tea and coffee are served throughout the day, and complimentary wines are served in the evening.

The guest rooms are comfortable though small, and are done in pastels.

Services: Morning and evening room service; same-day laundry and valet service; on request use of VCR, hairdryer, ironing board, even a lint roller.

HOTEL VINTAGE COURT, 650 Bush St., San Francisco, CA 94108. TEL 415/392-4666, or toll free 800/654-1100, 800/654-7266 in California. Fax 415/392-4666. 106 rms, 53 A/C. MINIBAR TV TEL

$ Rates: $119, single or double. Ask for the larger rooms that have tub/shower combinations; some adjoining rooms available. Children under 12 free in parents' room; additional adults $10 each. Cribs free; rollaways $10 per night. AE, CB, DC, MC, V.

Parking: $14 per day; in-and-out privileges.

This fine boutique hotel between Powell and Stockton streets on the Nob Hill side of Union Square has a wine country theme that is carried throughout. Not only is the decor burgundy, but many guest rooms and suites are named for individual California wineries. In fact, there is even complimentary wine tasting in the evening.

There is no hotel dining room, but adjacent Masa's Restaurant (a nationally acclaimed French restaurant) serves continental breakfast buffet to hotel guests for $6.95 per person. Guest services can arrange babysitting, and can give you lots of information about the Napa Valley area. They'll be delighted to map out a trip to the vineyards for you.

Services: Room service (11am–midnight), complimentary coffee and tea in the lobby during the day and on each floor in the morning; complimentary wine, fruit, and cheese in the lobby every evening. VCRs and first-run movies available at $6 ($1 for a second movie).

Facilities: Arrangements can be made to attend a nearby health club (fee).

KENSINGTON PARK HOTEL, 450 Post St., San Francisco, CA 94102. Tel. 415/788-6400, or toll free 800/553-1900. Fax 415/399-9484. 82 rms. A/C MINIBAR TV TEL

$ Rates: $110 per room, which includes continental breakfast for everyone. Suites $125 up. Monthly rates available. Children under 12 (maximum of two) free in parents' room if additional beds are not needed, cribs free; children 12 and older, extra children and adults $10 per night each. AE, CB, DC, MC, V.

Parking: Valet parking, $14 per day.

The Kensington Park is another small, recently renovated hotel in the Union Square area. It is European style and charming. Complimentary continental breakfast is served daily, consisting of coffee, croissants, and juice.

The rooms are fairly good size and feature a few extra touches such as bathroom amenities and pillow shams. Each floor has three or four connecting rooms available, which are also corner rooms. We recommend these highly.

Services: Airport transportation, room service (6:30–9:30am and 4pm–midnight), complimentary continental breakfast. Concierge will arrange babysitting.

MONTICELLO INN, 127 Ellis St., San Francisco, CA 94102. Tel. 415/ 392-8800, or toll free 800/669-7777. Fax 415/392-8800, ext. 128. 91 rms. A/C MINIBAR TV TEL

$ Rates: $109 single, $119 double; one- and two-bedroom suites $139–$259; all prices include complimentary continental breakfast, tea and coffee throughout the day, and wine in the evening. Children free in parents' room; cribs free, rollaways $15 per night. AE, CB, DC, MC, V.

Parking: Valet, $12 per day; with in-and-out privileges.

This hostelry off Union Square is a delight for anyone who likes Federal-period furniture and history. We recommend it to you if your children are somewhat older. The inviting lobby has a fireplace, Chippendale reproductions, beautiful woods, and an imposing grandfather clock.

The theme is carried out in the guest-room decor as well, with canopied beds and pine furniture. It's like we imagine it must have been in Thomas Jefferson's home.

Services: Complimentary continental breakfast, complimentary tea and coffee, plus wine service in the evening. Concierge, valet and laundry service, VCRs available.

Facilities: There is a health club across the street that guests can use for a fee.

6. OTHER AREAS

MODERATE

QUEEN ANNE HOTEL, 1590 Sutter St., San Francisco, CA 94109. Tel. 415/441-2828, or toll free 800/227-3970. Fax 415/775-5212. 49 rms. No A/C TV TEL

$ Rates: $99–$175 single or double, $175 one-bedroom suite with a queen-sized sofa bed; children under 13 stay free in parents' room; additional person $20. AE, CB, DC, MC, V.

Parking: $10 per day; in-and-out privileges.

This stately Victorian mansion of the 1890s has been elegantly restored to make guests feel as if they are stepping into another era. Dark traditional woods set off the other antique pieces—some of polished brass, others of shining silver.

The lobby has a large parlor area and several conversation groups. There is another small room, called the library, where there is a fireplace, card table and chairs, and upholstered chairs that offer a comfortable place for reading. The atmosphere of the hotel is somewhat quiet, even hushed, without being stuffy, so if your children fit that description, it's a great place to experience the beauty of the city in a lovely setting not far from prestigious Pacific Heights.

The rooms range in size from small to spacious; they all have high ceilings, antique furnishings, telephones, and remote-control TVs. All bathrooms have been completely modernized.

Services/Facilities: Complimentary continental breakfast, tea, coffee, and sherry service in the afternoon; request a small refrigerator, if you need one.

BUDGET

MARINA INN, 3110 Octavia St., at Lombard Street, San Francisco, CA 94123. Tel. 415/928-1000. 40 rms. TV TEL

$ Rates: $55–$85, single or double (depending on size and location of room); includes continental breakfast and afternoon sherry. Children under 5 free in parents' room; additional persons $10 each per night; cribs free. Ask about specials.

Parking:

This little four-story Victorian inn is one of our favorite places, and definitely one of the best buys in San Francisco if you don't mind small space. It is owned by the same people who manage the White Swan and Petite Auberge (see below under "Bed-and-Breakfast" accommodations). This country-style inn (a restored 1928 building) was designed for the family who wants a very intimate setting at a very low price. (You might want to rent two rooms next to each other—no adjoining rooms—since the price is so good.) There is a small common area that houses a microwave, ice machine, and all-day coffee and tea service—this is where the complimentary continental breakfast (juice, muffins, and coffee) is served.

Each room is charming in its own way: some have bay windows with seats; others have pretty pastel-flowered wallpaper. All have queen-sized poster beds and private baths with showers and tubs.

Services: Valet service, bellhops.
Facilities: Barber and beauty shops.

7. BED-AND-BREAKFASTS

PETITE AUBERGE, 863 Bush St., San Francisco, CA 94108. Tel. 415/928-6000. Fax 415/775-5717. 26 rms. no A/C TV TEL

$ Rates (includes full breakfast, full afternoon tea and wine or sherry service): $110–$160 single or double; $195 suite; but the only rooms appropriate for families are the larger ones or the suite. There is a $15-per-day additional charge for children over 4 and additional adults; cribs free. AE, MC, V.

Parking: Valet parking available 7am–11pm for $15 per day; in-and-out privileges.

Just a few doors away from the White Swan on Bush Street, the Petite Auberge is a cozy B&B inn. This lovely little place is probably better for small families with older children. Decorated like a French country inn, it is done in subtle tones of peach and French country blues. This inn also has a small eating area for breakfast—on a smaller scale than the one at the White Swan—and a fireplace in the lobby. Concierge service is available. The staff will arrange baby-sitting services, but they ask you to request it when you reserve your room.

Eighteen of the 26 delightful rooms have fireplaces. Other amenities include a complimentary full breakfast (7–10:30am), English tea in the afternoon (with crudités, breads, and sweets), and wine or sherry service. Room service is available (from an outside source) for light evening meals from 6–11pm. You'll also be given fluffy terry robes.

While cribs are available at no charge, the small rooms and ambience of the inn are more apropos to an older child. If you are bringing young children, let the reservation clerk know when you book and he or she will help with the arrangements.

WHITE SWAN INN, 845 Bush St., Union Square, San Francisco, CA 94108. Tel. 415/775-1755. Fax 415/775-5717. 26 rms. TV TEL

$ Rates (includes full breakfast, full afternoon tea, and wine or sherry service): $145 Queen, $160 King, $250 suite, single or double. Children over 4 and additional adults $15 per day. AE, MC, V.

Parking: Valet parking available 7am–11pm for $15 per day; in-and-out privileges.

The White Swan Inn is an absolutely wonderful place to take the kids! This traditional English-style hotel in the Union Square area has lots of period antique pieces and English accents—hunting prints, black-and-white and green-and-burgundy wallpaper. Beveled glass doors open to the lobby in which many little teddy bears greet you; some sit on the stairs, others are on the floor next to the restored carousel horse. There are fireplaces in three public areas—the upstairs lobby (where you enter from the street), the library, and the lounge—as well as a fireplace in every guest room.

While the White Swan is a bed-and-breakfast style, it is a little easier than a traditional bed-and-breakfast if you're traveling with kids. The 24-hour front-desk staff caters to guests' needs. There is also a concierge.

If you worry that your kids might have problems at mealtime, ask if special arrangements can be made for them; for example, at the White Swan you can take breakfast in your room or to the library. If it's available, the small conference room can be set up so the kids will have more space.

There are two rooms on each floor that have walk-in closets, big enough for a portacrib. And of course a suite is great for people with kids because there are two rooms.

Amenities include terrycloth robes, a wonderful breakfast (croissants, cereal, juices, eggs, potatoes, fruit, and choice of teas or coffee), full afternoon tea (which includes breads, cakes, vegetables and dips, sweets), and wine or sherry service. Breakfast is served in the dining room from 7 to 10:30am—boosters and highchairs are available—or it can be brought to your room. For an extra fee, there is room service (from an outside source) for a light evening meal (6pm–11pm), and the kitchen will heat baby food or bottles or anything else upon request. If you'll require baby-sitting services during your stay, mention this to the reservationist when you reserve your room.

CHAPTER 9

EASY EXCURSIONS

San Francisco is only part of the excitement and beauty in the greater Bay Area. To the north, east, and south, you'll find family activities galore. Berkeley, Angel Island, Tiburon, and Muir Woods are nearby and well worth side trips, especially if you're staying in the area more than just a few days. They make perfect day trips. For overnight excursions you'll never forget, go to Monterey, Pacific Grove, Carmel-by-the-Sea, or Big Sur. These places epitomize California beauty. We have included lodging suggestions for these areas since we believe you might want to stay overnight. There's just too much to see in one day.

1. BERKELEY

The city of Berkeley grew up around the University of California. While the town is an old, established community, it has an intellectual, innovative core that is youthful and forward-looking. In fact, some people say that if everything happens first in California, it gets its start in Berkeley. Even today, a day in Berkeley is like spending time in a small, almost foreign enclave where much of the population is under 30 and vestiges of the counterculture movement of the 1960s are still evident. Street vendors selling candles and jewelry line Telegraph Avenue, musicians play on street corners, and at Lower Sproul Plaza, and political activism is still evident. And while you shouldn't miss the glorious campus, save a little time for some of the other family activities.

GETTING THERE By Car Take the San Francisco–Oakland Bay Bridge to I-80 east. Exit at the University exit and go all the way to Oxford Avenue. Turn right to Bancroft Way, then left on Telegraph Avenue.

By BART Berkeley station is two blocks from the university. The fare from San Francisco is $1.50.

ESSENTIALS Orientation Telegraph Avenue is the main drag for the student populace. It is most colorful between Bancroft Way and Ashby Avenue. Telegraph Avenue deadends at the university's Sproul Plaza and the Student Union.

WHAT TO SEE & DO

UNIVERSITY OF CALIFORNIA AT BERKELEY, east of Oxford Street, between Hearst Street and Bancroft Way. Tel. 510/642-6000.

⭐ Nestled at the foot of the Berkeley hills, this is one of the finest universities in the world. It is also one of the largest. The campus itself is beautiful, filled with distinguished-looking buildings, redwood and oak trees, a delightful creek, and views of the San Francisco Bay.

Before embarking on your explorations, you might want to talk with someone at the **Visitor Information** Center, 101 University Hall, 2200 University Ave. (tel. 510/642-5215). Pick up booklets for self-guided tours or ask about guided tours here.

WALKING TOUR Take a little while to wander along Telegraph Avenue. Some people refer to it as a sideshow at the circus complete with hippie-looking characters, vendors, and "street people." This is where you'll find **Cody's Books** and **Moe's Books** (see Chapter 5, "Their Shopping List," for details).

Just past the entrance to the campus is Sproul Plaza, the most famous area of the campus, home of many demonstrations in years past. To your left (west) is the **Martin Luther King, Jr., Student Union.** The building to your right (east) is **Sproul Hall,** the administration building. This is the place where the Free Speech Movement began in 1964, and today it is still a center for political and social activities. At the foot of Sproul Steps is **Ludwig's Fountain,** where students dangle their feet in the water on hot days. If you look north, you'll see a white stone gate with baroque grillwork. This is **Sather Gate,** a traditional symbol of the university, and still one of the most popular meeting spots on campus.

Just before you get to Sather Gate, there's a path that runs east-west along Sproul Hall. Take that toward the hills (heading east). As you continue, you'll see several interesting buildings. Along the left, redwoods, oaks, and pines grace your walk. You're now at **Strawberry Creek.** There's a trail along the creek if you wish to walk there. The large grassy hill called **Faculty Glade** is a great place for the kids to play. You'll see **Stephens Hall,** a Tudor Gothic building, erected in 1923. The **Faculty Club** is to your east, built by world-famous architect Bernard Maybeck in 1901.

Take the bridge to the north over Strawberry Creek (watch the kids while walking over this bridge—it's a high drop) and keep walking toward **Sather Tower,** better known as the **Campanile.** This is the most famous landmark of the university, built in 1914. For 50¢ you get a great ride to the top, where a heart-stopping view greets you: San Francisco, the Golden Gate Bridge, and Marin County.

Keep walking north to University Drive. Turn right (east). Soon you'll come to the Mining Circle. There is a lily pond and a grassy area. On the north is the **Hearst Mining Building,** built in 1907 in the Italian Renaissance style. Inside are pictures of the California Gold Rush.

Go back to University Drive and walk down to the large white building on your left (south). There are large, sweeping marble stairs to the entrance. This is the **Main Library,** built in 1911. You'll want to walk inside. Take the stairs up to the circulation and reference room. Look up. This has to be the most beautiful room on campus. Three-story windows flank the entire north wall, and four-story arched windows adorn the west and east walls. Leave the library through the same sweeping steps. The street in front of you is **University Drive.** Take it west, over the bridge, and keep walking until you find yourself at West Circle. From here, walk south past the **Life Science Building.** You'll find yourself in the eucalyptus grove as well as the south fork of Strawberry Creek. Kids love this area.

Go over the creek again there will be a fork in the walk area. Veer to your left and you should see the **Alumni House** on your right. Keep walking and you'll be at Lower Sproul Plaza, back where you started.

LAWRENCE HALL OF SCIENCE, Centennial Drive, south of Grizzly Peak Boulevard on the hill above the east side of the campus. Tel. 510/642-5132.

This is a hands-on science center dedicated to educating children (and adults). There is an exhibit that shows how lasers are used. Another popular exhibit features holograms. The earthquake exhibit maps out the earthquake faults and includes a working seismic recorder. Other displays offer colorful computer-activated games on many different scientific topics. A new permanent exhibit is called "Within the Human Brain." It includes a giant-sized brain model and a color brain imager that lets visitors view the biochemical activity of the brain. There is an ongoing schedule of temporary participatory exhibits, including a popular animated life-size dinosaur exhibit that has **Triceratops** babies and a hugh **Tyrannosaurs Rex.**

The Hall presents special events during the summer and on weekends and holidays. There are biology labs where children can touch frogs, chinchillas, rabbits, tarantulas, and other creatures. The Wizard's Lab has physics gadgets and gizmos, so children can learn more about magnetism, electricity, and motion. There are daily planetarium shows during the summer and on weekends and holidays; during the rest of the year there are daily shows at 1, 2:15, and 3:30pm. The Discovery Corner sells science kits, games, and books that are difficult to find elsewhere. The shop also has science-oriented cassette tapes.

Lawrence Hall has complete stroller access. Labs are available on a drop-in basis. Call for information about one-hour workshops and planetarium shows.

Admission: $4 for adults, $3 for seniors and children. Shows $1.50 in addition to admission.

Open: Mon–Fri 10am–4:30pm, Sat–Sun 10am–5pm. Closed New Year's Day, Easter, Labor Day, Thanksgiving, and Dec 25–6.

Directions: From the university, take Centennial Drive south of Grizzly Peak Boulevard.

UNIVERSITY OF CALIFORNIA BOTANICAL GARDEN, Centennial Drive at head of Strawberry Canyon. Tel. 510/642-3343 or 510/642-0849.

This 34-acre complex was started in 1890, and serves as a laboratory as well as a garden. It contains more than 8,000 species, totaling more than 50,000 plants,

Angel Island State Park **4**
Berkeley **7**
Candlestick Park **15**
Charles Lee Tilden
  Regional Park **9**
Children's Fairyland **13**
Fisherman's Wharf
  (Red & White Fleet) **5**
Golden Gate Fields **6**
Jack London Square,
  Oakland **12**
Lake Merritt **13**
Marine World Africa USA **10**
Muir Woods National
  Monument **1**
Natural Science and
  Waterfowl Refuge **13**
Oakland **11**
Redwood Regional Park **14**
Sausalito **3**
Tiburon **2**
University of California
  at Berkeley **8**

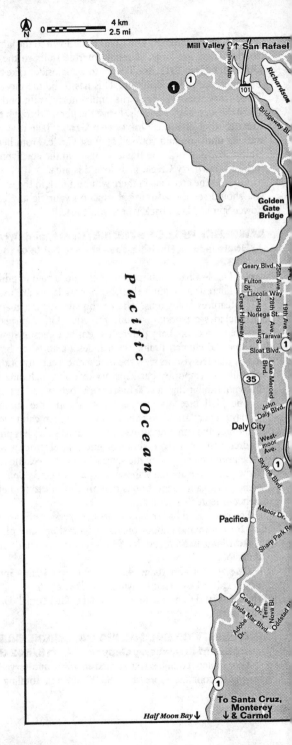

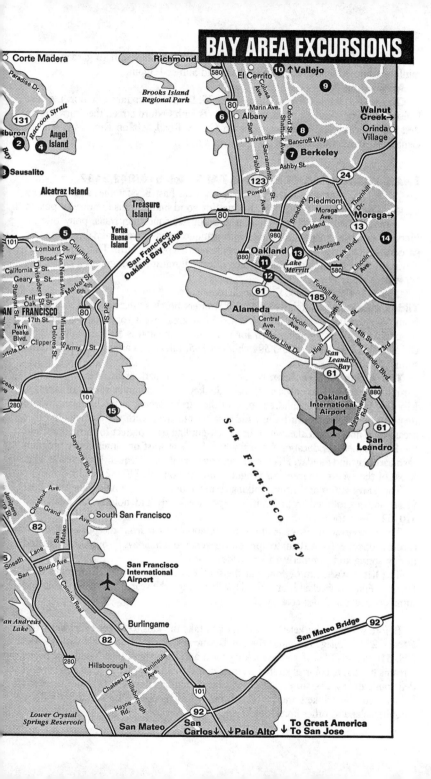

BAY AREA EXCURSIONS

including rare rhododendrons, cacti and succulents, a Chinese herb garden, and a rainforest house. Guided tours offered Sat and Sun at 1:30pm.

Admission: Free.

Open: Daily 9am–4:45pm. Closed Dec. 25. **Directions:** Take I-80 north, exit at University Avenue, go east to where it intersects with Oxford Street, then turn left on Oxford, right on Hearst Street, right on Gayley Road, left on Rim Way, left on Centennial Drive and continue for less than a mile.

CHARLES LEE TILDEN REGIONAL PARK. Tel. 510/843-2137.

This 2,078-acre park is a favorite with local East Bay families and the lucky visitors who know about it. Known for good hiking trails (beware of poison oak, though), lake swimming, a golf course, equestrian trails, pony rides, a Hershell Spillman merry go-round (with antique hand-carved animals), a botanic garden, several playgrounds, and a nature area with a petting farm. Tilden also has an Environmental Education Center, which offers naturalist-led programs.

Admission: Free.

Open: Daily 8am–dusk. Call for directions.

Tilden's Lake Anza (tel. 415/848-3385) offers beach sunbathing and swimming from May through October. There is a shallow area that is roped off for children, which offers great swimming even for toddlers. Admission is $2 for adults, $2 for children 6–17 and seniors, and 50¢ children 2–5. Lifeguards are on duty in summer from 11am to 6pm.

The Tilden Nature Area is one of our favorite park areas. It is where Little Farm is located, with its cows, pigs, goats, donkeys, and a stunning variety of bunnies. Monthly programs have children come in the early morning to the barnyard, where they can milk goats, churn butter, and just get out there with the animals. In other areas you'll find Jewel Lake, which has a self-guiding trail, perfect for little ones, and the Environmental Education Center, which holds at least one interpretive program each Saturday and Sunday. Hikes and wildflower walks are frequently offered as well. Most of the events are free. For program information call 510/525-2233.

The **pony rides** are within walking distance of the Nature Area. The rides cost $1.50 and are offered from 10am to 5pm weekends and holidays all year. Call 510/527-0421 for details.

The **merry-go-ground** is about five minutes by car from the pony rides. The carousel operates from 10am to 5pm on weekends and holidays through the year, and during spring and summer vacation. Rides cost 60¢.

The **little train** can be found at the southern end of the park. It operates from 10am to 6pm on weekends and holidays all through the year, and during spring and summer vacation. Rides cost $1.25.

Before you leave Berkeley, why don't you take the kids to **Sweet Dreams Toy Store,** 2921 College Ave., and **Sweet Dreams Candy Shop,** 2901 College Ave. (Tel. 510/548-TOYS). If you're looking for a good toy store, be advised that Sweet Dreams has large, colorful stuffed animals and the candy shop has rows and rows of delicious candies. The stores don't have a lot of traditional toys; rather, they're a kid's heaven with tiny trinkets and barrels of trendy little goodies. You'll find Betty Boop paraphernalia and other knickknacks.

BERKELEY

Sather Tower 5
South Hall 4
Sproul Plaza 1
Student Union Building 2
University Art Museum 10

Hearst Greek Theatre 12
Lawrence Hall of Science 14
Lowie Museum of Anthropology 9
Paleontology Museum 8
Sather Gate 3

Bancroft Library 6
Botanical Library 13
Charles Lee Tilden Regional Park 16
Cody's Books 15
Earth Sciences Building 7
Faculty Glade 11

You might also want to pay a visit to **Mr. Mopps' Children's Books and Toys** at 1405 Martin Luther King, Jr., Way (tel. 510/525-9633), a wonderful children's bookstore. See Chapter 5, "Their Shopping List," for complete details.

WHERE TO STAY

EXPENSIVE

CLAREMONT RESORT HOTEL AND TENNIS CLUB, 41 Tunnel Rd., Berkeley, CA 94710. Tel. 510/843-3000 (for reservations, write to P.O. Box 23363, Oakland, CA 94623). Fax 510/848-6208. 239 rms. A/C MINIBAR TV TEL

$ Rates: $130–$200 single, $150–$220 double, $235–$535 suites. Children under 18 stay free in parents' room; cribs free, rollaways $10 per night. AE, CB, DC, MC, V.

Parking: Valet, $7 a day.

⭐ This is a classically beautiful Victorian hotel at the foot of the Oakland-Berkeley hills that has hosted the likes of Cornelius Vanderbilt and Eleanor Roosevelt. The imposing structure, with its lavish grounds and facilities, has quite a colorful history, starting in the 1870s when it was known as the Castle. It changed hands several times, endured a major fire, and was finally renovated to its present form just prior to the 1915 Panama-Pacific International Exposition. The hotel has seen several owners—and changes—since that time, and in 1988 complete spa facilities were added.

The rooms are tastefully appointed, and decorated in blues and rich browns. All rooms are spacious and have hill views, and feature televisions with SpectraVision and individual coffeemakers. Suites come equipped with a refrigerator; you can request one for other rooms.

Services: Room service from 1pm–midnight, several snackbars and restaurants with children's selections, nightly turndown service. Baby-sitting services can be arranged through the concierge.

Facilities: 10 tennis courts, a gorgeous outdoor Olympic-size swimming pool with a children's area, a Jacuzzi, exercise par-course, and complete spa facilities.

MODERATE

HOTEL DURANT, 2600 Durant Ave., Berkeley, CA 94704. Tel. 510/845-8981, or toll free 800/238-7268, 800/538-7268 in California. Fax 510/486-8336. 140 rms. No A/C MINIBAR TV TEL

$ Rates (including breakfast): $74–$84 single, $90–$100 double, $125–$200 suites. Children under 12 stay free in parents' room; children 12 and over and additional adults pay $10 each per night; cribs free. AE, DC, MC, V.

Parking: Valet; $3 per day.

The Durant has been hosting visitors for over 60 years. This European-style hotel one block from the university near Bowditch Street has a small, quiet lobby with sofas and loveseats, and is a good place to stay if your children don't need a lot of room to run around.

The rooms are tastefully furnished and all have cable television with free HBO, and AM/FM radio. Many of the rooms have a view of the University of California campus or the Bay, and some can be connected for families.

Dining/Entertainment: Henry's Publick House and Grille serves American cuisine in an English-pub atmosphere. There are Tiffany-style lamps, cluster tables, and lots of polished wood and brass. This is where the free continental breakfast is served. Henry's has highchairs and booster seats, and is best for kids during the breakfast period. As the day wears on, college students frequent the eatery and bar, making it smoky and noisy.

Services: The stately Durant offers complimentary continental breakfast, valet and laundry service, and airport transportation (for an additional fee). They will help you arrange baby-sitting service with students.

BED-AND-BREAKFAST

GRAMMA'S BED AND BREAKFAST INN, 2740 Telegraph Ave., Berkeley, CA 94705. Tel. 510/549-2145. Fax 510/549-1085. 30 rms. TV TEL
$ Rates (including breakfast): $85–$175 single or double, including tax; many rooms $110 with fireplaces—the more expensive rooms accommodate families. Children stay free in parents' room but there is a $10 charge per night for an extra futon. DC, MC, V.
Parking: Free.

⭐ This is a lovely alternative to a regular hotel, and many of the rooms are suitable for families. Gramma's charming restored Tudor houses (a main house, carriage house, garden house, and the Fay house) offer guest rooms decorated with antiques, and loaded with country charm. Each has its own bath or shower and television. Accommodations in the restored carriage house have fireplaces and overlook a garden. There is a huge grassy lawn in the front and a large redwood deck in the back where kids can play.

As the name indicates, breakfast is included in the room price, as is evening wine and cheese or cookies and milk. Sunday brunch, not included in the rates, is also available.

WHERE TO DINE

You won't be surprised to learn that Berkeley is not a small town when it comes to dining. You have your pick of eateries, from traditional to ethnic, from serious eating establishments to simple cafés.

EXPENSIVE

CHEZ PANISSE CAFE AND RESTAURANT, 1517 Shattuck Ave., near Cedar Street. Tel. 510/548-5525.
Cuisine: CALIFORNIAN. **Reservations:** Strongly recommended.
$ Prices: Appetizers $6–$8; main courses $13–$18; fixed-price dinner $55. AE, CB, DC, MC, V.
Open: Dinner seatings Tues–Sat at 6, 6:30, 8:30, and 9:15pm.

Parking: On-street parking.
Children's Services: Boosters.

This is the place where Californian cuisine originated back in 1971. In fact, many famous chefs have worked here with Alice Waters. The award-winning restaurant emphasizes freshness and creativity in its nouvelle cuisine. Naturally, we don't take our kids to the fixed-price dinner, which might consist of caviar; pigeon sausage with cabbage, bacon, and mustard; roasted red onion and garlic soup; grilled rack of veal with green beans and sautéed potatoes; garden salad; and baked figs. Instead, we enjoy the same kitchen (with lighter fare) at the upstairs café, but the menu is simpler and à la carte. We do treat ourselves to an occasional dinner in the downstairs restaurant when we have a babysitter. If you come by BART, the stop is Berkeley; if you drive, take I-80 north, get off at the University exit and turn left on Shattuck Avenue.

CHEZ PANISSE CAFE—upstairs. Tel. 510/548-5049.
   Cuisine: CALIFORNIAN. **Reservations:** Accepted for lunch only.
$ Prices: Lunch average $15–$25, dinner $25–$35. AE, CB, DC, MC, V.
   Open: Lunch Mon–Thurs 11:30am–3pm, Fri–Sat 11:30am–4pm; dinner Mon–Sat 5–11:30pm.
   Children's Services: Boosters, crayons on paper table coverings.

Alice Waters opened the café in 1980 because she wanted a place where her friends, family, and neighbors could eat in a casual setting. The pizza comes from the brick oven, and the pizza-maker will show the kids how he does it, and might even create a pizza using the child's initials. The "tamest" item is the pizza with tomato sauce and sausage, but our kids will share our grilled swordfish and calzone with goat cheese, mozzarella, prosciutto, and garlic. You can also get pasta, salads, and fish. If you went only according to the menu, you'd think your kids would have to have refined taste, but we always tell our server to hold some of the items that seem too "gourmet." To our delight, the food is consistently excellent.

MODERATE

CHRISTOPHER'S CAFE, 1843 Solano Ave. Tel. 510/526-9444.
   Cuisine: AMERICAN. **Reservations:** Recommended.
$ Prices: Lunch $4.75–$7.25, dinner $15–$20. AE, MC, V.
   Open: Lunch Mon–Fri 11:30am–2:15pm; dinner Mon–Thurs 5:30–9:30pm, Fri–Sat 5:30–10:15pm, Sun 5:30–9:15pm.
   Children's Services: Boosters.

This is a lively, noisy place to eat on Solano Avenue, near Calusa Street. Its simple white linens, wood-and-brass wine bar, and mirrors give it a clean look. The service is fast, and bread is put on the table as soon as you're seated.

Good choices for kids are the pastas (they'll serve half-orders), shoestring potatoes, burgers, and steaks (which they'll split in the kitchen). The lunch menu includes a poultry salad of the day, a fresh fish of the day, and a fresh pasta of the day, as well as other selections. Dinner offerings are unusual and diverse. For example, fresh salmon is served with a mango beurre blanc; grilled chicken breast is marinated in chile, cumin, dark beer, cilantro, and orange juice. There is other, more standard fare as well, and Christopher's makes the best Caesar salad in town.

LARRY BLAKE'S R&B CAFE, 2367 Telegraph Ave. Tel. 510/848-0886.

Cuisine: AMERICAN. **Reservations:** Accepted for 6 or more.
$ **Prices:** Lunch $4–$7, dinner main courses $7–$12, weekend brunch $4.50–$6.95. AE, CB, DC, MC, V.
Open: Mon–Sat 11am–2am, Sun 11am–10pm.
Parking: On-street parking is difficult to find.
Children's Services: Boosters, highchairs.

Larry Blake's R&B Café, off Durant Avenue one block south of the campus, has been a tradition in Berkeley since 1940 and has been a student gathering spot for many years. It is a lively place where children fit right in. The menu is primarily traditional American with barbecued and southern fried chicken and ribs, hamburgers made from freshly ground sirloin, salads, pastas, and steaks. The daily dinner specials are exceptional, and they will split orders for children.

There is a downstairs nightclub with live music Monday through Saturday nights, with a jukebox going between sets. Children are allowed if accompanied by an adult. Adults may also wish to visit the second-floor cocktail lounge on nights when they come without children.

INEXPENSIVE

HOMEMADE CAFE, 2454 Dwight Way. Tel. 510/845-1940.
Cuisine: AMERICAN. **Reservations:** Not accepted.
$ **Prices:** $3–$6.75. No credit cards.
Open: Mon–Fri 7am–2pm, Sat–Sun 8am–3pm.
Children's Services: Boosters, highchairs.

If you want to see your kids wolf down a whole order of French toast, this is where it's likely to happen. Homemade Café, on Sacramento Street, corner of Dwight Way, is nothing fancy and is somewhat crowded, but the best breakfasts in town are said to be served here. Since the premises are always packed with locals—and their kids—the restaurant staff knows how to handle youngsters, and the food is served quickly.

Besides the great French toast, you might like to try the homemade corned-beef hash or the lox and eggs scrambled with onions. Creative sandwiches are also a specialty—how about guacamole, cheese, lettuce, and tomato?

FATAPPLES, 1346 Martin Luther King, Jr., Way. Tel. 510/526-2260.
Cuisine: AMERICAN. **Reservations:** Not accepted.
$ **Prices:** $3.75–$6.50. No credit cards.
Open: Mon–Fri 6am–11pm, Sat–Sun 7am–11pm.
Children's Services: Boosters, highchairs.

Simple dishes made from scratch, using quality ingredients, is the way they do things here at Fatapples, the corner of Rose Street and Martin Luther King, Jr., Way. While they're known for their baked goods, the burgers, fries, and soups are also excellent. And the coffee is wonderful too. They'll gladly split portions in the kitchen for children, and the servers will try to bring you whatever you think the kids might like.

CHESTER'S, 1508 B Walnut St. Tel. 510/849-9995.
Cuisine: AMERICAN. **Reservations:** Not accepted.
$ **Prices:** $3.25–$6.75; children's menu. MC, V.
Open: Daily 7:30am–7pm.
Children's Services: Boosters, highchairs.

This casual eatery with wooden benches and chairs offers both indoor and outdoor service. The owners actively promote children coming to the café by presenting a nice children's menu and friendly servers who will actually bring fruit and crackers for little ones. If you prefer to have the children split an adult order, there's no charge if you do it at the table ($1 extra if you request it done in the kitchen). They'll also warm baby bottles and baby food.

Egg specialties, omelets, burgers (seven kinds), crêpes, sandwiches, and salads round out the adult menu. You'll find Chester's in the Walnut Square shopping area.

2. ANGEL ISLAND & TIBURON

GETTING THERE   By Boat   Ferries of the **Red and White Fleet** (tel. 415/546-2896) leave from Pier 43½ (Fisherman's Wharf) and travel to both Tiburon and Angel Island. Boats run on a seasonal schedule; phone for departure information. The round-trip fare is $9.50 to Tiburon, $8 to Angel Island; half price for kids 5 to 11.

Alternatively, you can drive to Tiburon (see below), then board the **Angel Island Ferry** (tel. 415/435-2131 or 415/388-6770) for the short, 15-minute hop to the island. The round-trip costs $5.

By Car   Take U.S. 101 to the Tiburon/Belvedere exit and then follow Tiburon Boulevard all the way into downtown, a 40-minute drive from San Francisco. Catch the ferry from the dock located at Tiburon.

ESSENTIALS   Orientation   Angel Island is only 730 acres big. There are picnic sites with tables, benches, barbecue pits, and rest rooms at Ayala Cove, where you land. Miles of hiking trails lead you around the island and to the peak of Mount Caroline Livermore, 776 feet above the bay.

Tiburon is tiny. The aptly named Main Street is the town's primary thoroughfare. It fronts the water and is a popular bike path. Main intersects with Tiburon Boulevard (known as Paradise Drive). Opposite is a handsome and posh shopping and eating plaza with wood-shingled buildings and brick walkways overlooking its own small body of water. Just across the Beach Road Bridge is Belvedere Island, a pretty little place full of fancy houses.

Information   The rangers at Angel Island State Park (tel. 415/435-1915) will be happy to answer any of your questions.

A federal and state wildlife refuge, Angel Island is the prettiest of the San Francisco Bay's three islets (the others are Alcatraz and Yerba Buena). Most of the people who visit here never leave the large green lawn that fronts the docking area; they bring picnics and enjoy the view of Tiburon across the way. Behind the lawn, inside the ranger station, are displays detailing the history of this largest bay island. Angel Island has been, at various times, a prison, a favorite site for duels, a quarantine station for immigrants, and a Nike missile base. Today, in addition to picnics, it is popular for hiking and biking. More than 12 miles of trails include the Perimeter Road, a partly paved path that circles the island and wends its way past disused troop barracks, former gun emplacements, and other military buildings. Sometimes referred to as the "Ellis Island of the West," Angel Island held Chinese immigrants from 1910 to 1940 while their citizenship papers were being processed. You can still see some faded Chinese scrawlings on the walls of the barracks where the immigrants were held. During warmer months it's possible to camp on the island. There are a limited number of sites, and reservations are required. Call 510/323-2988 for information.

If you want to know why people love living in the Bay Area, grab the kids and go to Tiburon. This tiny village is surrounded by picturesque Richardson Bay. Any way you get there, you'll discover incredible sights. You'll see Mount Tamalpais emerge on the Marin side, all three bridges across the bay (the Golden Gate, the Bay Bridge, and the San Rafael), and spectacular views of San Francisco, Alcatraz, and Angel Island.

WHAT TO SEE & DO

ANGEL ISLAND STATE PARK. Tel. 415/435-1915.

⭐ This park is like a jewel of 750 thickly forested acres sitting in the middle of San Francisco Bay. It offers good hiking trails, bicycle paths, and wonderful picnic spots. On warm summer days the coves are lovely spots to sit with the kids and do some serious work on elaborate sandcastles.

The island has 17 miles of paved trails for easy walking—even if you lug a stroller with you—which may be the best way to go if you have a preschooler who tires easily.

Ayala Cove, which is near where the ferry docks (and the closest beach), and **Quarry Point Beach** both have nice, protected sandy areas. However, there are no lifeguards and there are strong currents, so swimming may not be safe. Throughout the area you'll find lovely picnic sites. Fires are allowed at Ayala Cove and East Garrison.

If you want to venture out of Ayala Cove, **North Garrison** has an old immigration station where tours are given on weekends. At **East Garrison/Fort McDowell** you'll find a large army fort that was in operation from the Spanish-American War through World War II. There are decent tours of the grounds upon request from 11am–4pm on weekends April through October. At **West Garrison/ Camp Reynolds** you'll find a Civil War camp that you can tour. It's a little bit of history for the kids while they're enjoying themselves in the outdoors. Our kids love the cannon firings, which take place at approximately 1pm and 2pm on weekends, April through October.

Walking the island is possible with children. Most kids (even those under 5) can make the easy one-mile walk to the cannon firings at West Garrison without any trouble. Park officials suggest that you bring a wagon or stroller for little tykes. If you decide to take bikes, the terrain is gentle enough that toddler carriers won't present a problem—that is, after you trek up the steep hill to the main road.

The one road around the island is five miles long and is completely suitable for walking or bicycling. The trek up the hill is steep, but, once there, it is a very pleasant, easy walk. This main road is the best for young children, and is where you'll see kids pulling little red wagons or furiously pedaling tricycles.

WANDERING AROUND Tiburon Tiburon was once the hub of the Bay Area, with heavy ferry and railroad traffic; people used it as a main link in their trip to San Francisco. Today the best way to enjoy the quaint village is to walk the main streets and the area called Ark Row. Many of the shops are housed in what used to be summer cottages and old arks (houseboats) built in the 1800s.

Blackie's Pasture Just before you enter town, you'll come across a lovely large green pasture. We often stop here since it's a great place for a picnic. We used to wonder about the name, and then we learned that Blackie was a horse born in Kansas in 1926. He began his career in the rodeo, then worked in Yosemite and at the San Francisco Presidio, and finally arrived in Tiburon in 1938. He grazed in this beloved pasture until his death in 1966 and then was buried here. You can see his grave—it's marked by the white cross. He's a legend in Tiburon.

WALKS AND BIKE PATHS Tiburon is a place to explore on foot or by bike. One of our favorite bike paths runs all along Richardson Bay. (Unfortunately, hordes of bicyclists, joggers, and walkers agree.) Known as the best bike path in Marin County, it passes the Audubon Society's bird reserve and historic Lyford House, which is open Sunday from 1 to 4pm for tours. You'll also ride by beautiful McKegney Green, which faces Sausalito across Richardson Bay and offers wonderful picnicking. You might want to pack that lunch before you hop on the bicycles.

To get to the Tiburon Bike Path, you can take Tiburon Boulevard to Blackie's Pasture. The path leads into town, and is level for about five miles. Once you get into the village, you'll see one of the most spectacular views of San Francisco. Sometimes the city seems so close, you think you could touch it.

A NATURE RESERVE The National Audubon Society's Richardson Bay Audubon Center, 376 Greenwood Beach Rd. (tel. 415/388-2524), is a sanctuary for thousands of waterfowl and is sometimes called a "window on the bay." It has several different habitats that reflect the bay's environment. The center sometimes offers programs for both children and adults. Here you'll find the Book Nest bookstore, one of the largest natural-history emporia in the state. You can visit the center on Wednesday through Saturday from 9am to 5pm. There is no admission fee but a suggested donation of $2 per adult is requested to continue the work here.

OTHER ATTRACTIONS Be sure not to miss taking the family to the **Bay Area Discovery Museum at Fort Baker** (tel. 415/332-9646). For complete details about this family favorite, see Chapter 4, "What Kids Like to See & Do."

WHERE TO DINE

SAM'S ANCHOR CAFE, 27 Main St., Tiburon. Tel. 415/435-4527.
   Cuisine: SEAFOOD. **Reservations:** Not accepted.
$ **Prices:** Main courses $5.50–$13; children's meals $2.75–$4.25. AE, MC, V.
   Open: Mon–Thurs 11am–10:30pm, Fri 11am–11pm, Sat 10am–11pm, Sun 9:30am–10:30pm.
   Children's Services: Boosters, highchairs; children's menu, crayons.
The view at Sam's is special—you can see San Francisco, the Bay Bridge, Alcatraz, and Angel Island from the deck, which is *the* place to eat during the day. Although the deck sways, you do get used to it. There are railings all around the deck, but watch the kids so that they don't fall overboard. The friendly sea gulls are entertaining, but don't let the kids feed the birds or they'll swoop down and steal the food off your plate before you can eat it.

The café offers savory food and the service is good. The delectable swordfish and salmon dishes are the stars, but the daily seafood specials are popular as well. Other treats include cioppino, steamed clams, and sautéed or deep-fried local oysters. Even the burgers here are very good. Delicious sourdough bread and butter comes with all main courses. The children's "color-in" menu (which features a Samburger, spaghetti, fish-and-chips, and a hot dog) comes with crayons.

GUAYMAS RESTAURANTE, 5 Main St., Tiburon. Tel. 415/435-6300.
   Cuisine: MEXICAN. **Reservations:** Recommended.
$ **Prices:** Main courses $7.95–$15.75. AE, CB, DC, MC, V.
   Open: Mon–Fri 11:30am–10pm, Sat 11:30am–11pm, Sun 10:30am–10pm.
   Parking: Available.
   Children's Services: Boosters, highchairs.

This open, airy, authentic Mexican restaurant boasts the best unimpeded view of San Francisco and Angel Island in Tiburon. Guaymas is a colorful restaurant with floor-to-ceiling glass windows, a cement floor, and brightly tinted walls of pink, yellow, and turquoise hung with colorful Mexican masks. Even the serving dishes have a Mexican motif.

Guaymas is named after a fishing village on Mexico's Sea of Cortez, and the staff pride themselves on serving mouth-watering traditional cuisine from that locale. All the food is made from scratch. Kids love watching the chefs cook and the local women making fresh tortillas through the open kitchen area.

The kitchen has a special flare with the Mexican delicacies served here. Have you ever tried chicken with chocolate, chiles, fruit, and spices, for instance? The restaurant is famous for their giant shrimp (camarones) marinated in lime and cilantro. Another favorite is butterflied baby chicken with tomatillo-jalapeño chile sauce. We find that good choices for the kids include tamales, guacamole and chips, and banana-wrapped red snapper, or banderillos de torero (two skewers of beef done over mesquite). At Guaymas they'll split adult portions at the table for your kids, and the servers will bring chips and tortillas to the table as soon as you are seated.

3. MUIR WOODS NATIONAL MONUMENT

GETTING THERE   By Car   To get to **Muir Woods,** drive across the Golden Gate Bridge and take the exit for Calif. 1/Mount Tamalpais. Follow the shoreline highway about 2½ miles and turn onto the Panoramic Highway. After about a mile, take the signed turnoff and follow successive signs.

WHAT TO SEE & DO

MUIR WOODS NATIONAL MONUMENT, Mill Valley, CA 94941. Tel. 415/388-2595.

Less than 20 miles northwest of San Francisco, Muir Woods feels like a million miles from civilization. It is such a popular place, you might want to go on a weekday or late in the day; the woods are open daily from 8am to sunset. To get to the woods, you drive on winding two-lane roads through the coastal hills that take you through groves of eucalyptus. You feel as if you've gone a long way.

There's something about the huge grove of giant coast redwoods (*Sequoia sempervirens*)—this monument to nature—that is at once exhilarating and calming. The towering redwoods that have stood for hundreds of years, the fern thickets, and the moss that covers the barks of some of the trees are simply beautiful. Our kids love to run along the paved pathway, but they, too, seem to revere these natural giants.

The tallest trees here are in Bohemian Grove. Some stand 250 feet tall. The widest is 13½ feet across. Most of the main trails are level and paved, easy for strollers and young children.

A wonderful Muir Woods offering is the Junior Ranger program. It is designed to heighten children's enjoyment and skills of observation. Kids are encouraged to stop by the Visitor Center to pick up a Junior Ranger Pack, which comes equipped with cards that correspond to a map and activities to be done in certain areas of the park. Included also are bug boxes, a dip net, a magnifying lens, a clipboard, and a trash bag. The cards present many different activities for the kids to participate in. It's a wonderfully involving way for children to be introduced to nature.

Muir Woods has a snack counter, a gift shop, a bookstore, and a Visitor Center. No picnicking or camping is allowed in the forest. Bring warm clothing, as the forest is cool.

Admission: Free.
Open: Daily 8am–sunset.

4. MARINE WORLD AFRICA USA

GETTING THERE   By Ferry   The **Red-and-White Fleet** (tel. 415/546-2896 in San Francisco, or toll free 800/445-8880 in California) operates a high-speed catamaran service from Pier 41 at Fisherman's Wharf. The pretty cruise, passing Alcatraz and the Golden Gate Bridge, takes 55 minutes, including a brief bus ride. The round-trip, including park admission, is $37 for adults, $30 for seniors 55 and over and students aged 13 to 18, and $20 for kids 4 to 12. Service is limited; call for departure times.

By Car   From San Francisco, take I-80 north to Calif. 37 and follow the signs to the park; it's less than an hour's drive.

MARINE WORLD AFRICA USA, 1000 Fairgrounds Dr., in Vallejo. Tel. 707/643-ORCA for a recorded message.

A must-see for families who love animal and marine life, a day at this state-of-the-art oceanarium and wildlife park promises to be an adventure to remember. The 160-acre park features hundreds of animals—land, sea, and air, exotic and common—with the goal of offering families wonderful entertainment and learning experiences. The trainers have such close relationships with their animals that park visitors are able to experience the animals close up. Visitors learn while they're having fun.

We usually try to arrive at opening time. Then we get a show schedule at the Clock Tower and choose those we intend to see (shows run 20 to 30 minutes each). Next, we hightail it over to the storage lockers (to the left of the admission gate) to stow extra sweaters, baby food, and everything we don't want to carry around. We always lather sunscreen on the kids at this time, just in case we can't grab a wiggly, excited child later on. We choose a meeting place in case someone gets lost, load our cameras, and get ready. We also remind the kids not to feed the animals. Then we're off.

Everyone loves the scheduled shows, including the Killer Whale and Dolphin Show, the Sea Lion Show, the Waterski and Boat Show, the Jungle Theater (with tigers, lions, elephants and chimps), and the Bird Show. Our family favorite, though, is the **Killer Whale and Dolphin Show,** where the 9,000- and 6,000-pound killer whales swim and leap effortlessly through the water. One word of caution, though. At the marine shows, there is a "wet zone." If you sit in this area in any of the shows, be prepared to be splashed with salt water, which can burn the eyes; during the whale show you'll simply be drenched. Unknowingly, we sat there once and were soaked.

The **Elephant Encounter** is a very exciting show where people can enjoy these endangered animals. There's even a tug-of-war and other safe encounters. The **Gentle Jungle** is a great area where toddlers can hang out with llamas, goats, prairie dogs, and bunnies. Pony rides (75¢) are available for children 65 pounds and under. The **Whale of a Time World Playground** is an innovative active play area for children under 90 pounds. The ball crawls, rope crawls, and net climbs are a treat for preschoolers to preteens. This playground is very well supervised by park attendants, and is a favorite place for kids to spend an hour.

The small but respectable **Aquarium** is set up to give a view of the Tropics, the Caribbean, and the California coast, and is arranged so comparisons can be made between the different habitats. There are tidepools where kids can touch and pick up their favorite creatures—anemones, hermit crabs, sea stars, and the like. The Discovery Room inside the Aquarium is staffed by assistants who will answer questions and show you how animals adapt to specific environments.

To everyone's delight, animals and their trainers abound throughout the park. Chimps, snow leopards, and monkeys wander with their human companions, giving us a chance to watch them close up. Our kids loved the elephant rides, and were entranced at **Tiger Cove,** where trainers and cats are always together.

If you know ahead of time when you'll be at the park, you might be able to participate in one of the family evening programs (usually 7–9pm; $11 additional fee). There are also sunrise and moonlight tours (coinciding with the full moon) that give people a chance to see animals at different times of day. Children's workshops, such as the Afterschool Seafari (for school-age children), help children learn what animals eat, what their tracks look like, and what their habitats consist of. Most of these programs are offered in the spring and fall. For more information, call 707/644-4000, ext. 433.

A wide variety of fast food is available at the restaurant plaza—everything from burgers and pizza to nachos and chicken. Prices are moderate, averaging about $6 to $7 for a light bite. A sit-down restaurant completes the food choices. Or you can bring your own picnic—there are barbecue facilities on the grounds.

Finally—and we hope you won't need it—the first-aid station is located at the main gift shop.

Admission: $19.95 for adults, $16.95 for seniors, $14.95 for children 4 to 12 and seniors over 60, free for children under 4. Stroller and camera rentals available. AE, MC, V accepted.

Open: Open daily Memorial Day through Labor Day 9:30am–6:30pm; the rest of the year Wed–Sun 9:30am–5:30pm, with special winter holiday schedule.

5. GREAT AMERICA

GETTING THERE   By Car   Take Calif. 101 south to Santa Clara and exit at the Great America Parkway.

ESSENTIALS   Information   For advance information, contact the Santa Clara Visitor Information Center, 1515 El Camino Real, Santa Clara, CA 95050 (tel. 408/296-7111). Or write Great America, P.O. Box 1776, Santa Clara, CA 95052.

GREAT AMERICA, Great America Parkway, Santa Clara. Tel. 408/988-1800 for recorded message.

Great America, best known for its classic wooden roller coaster, the Grizzly, is a 100-acre theme park that caters to children of all ages. Teens and preteens who love wild rides, thrilling roller coasters, and action are going to love this park. So will the junior set. Designed around the general theme of North America's past, there are six theme areas, each with rides, shows, shops, and restaurants—**Carousel Plaza, Hometown Square, County Fair, Yukon Territory, Yankee Harbor,** and **Orleans Place.** The park has a total of 33 rides. It can be crowded, yet the atmosphere is not frenzied. People are friendly and helpful.

According to a spokesperson for the park, they try to be particularly sensitive to the needs of small children and offer many attractions and services geared to kids under 12. In fact, she reports that a primary goal of Great America is to help parents enjoy their day at the park as well. The double-decker **Hanna-Barbera Carousel,** denoting Carousel Plaza, is the entrance to **"Fort Fun,"** the action area for little ones. In addition to the carousel are rides such as **L'il Dodge 'Em, Yakki Doodle's Lady Bugs,** and **Handy Biplanes.** Favorite Hanna-Barbera cartoon characters roam the area. Our kids went wild over Scooby Doo.

A hit with the little ones is **Smurf Woods.** The **Blue Streak,** located in Smurf Woods, is a mini roller coaster—a "training" roller coaster for the kids (and the adults who need it) with speeds of only 25 mph. Comparing the Blue Streak to the Grizzly is like comparing a skier's bunny hill to a mogul field! Surprise! Our baby as well as the older tots loved Smurf Woods.

The Grizzly and the Revolution may be the favorite rides of teens who go to the park. The **Grizzly,** a classic wooden roller coaster—the largest ever built in Northern California—speeds up to 50 mph for almost three minutes. Another attraction, the **Revolution,** is a 360-degree swinging ship that works like a pendulum. As it goes higher, passengers are suspended upside down—two complete loops before the ride is over. The **Demon** and **Tidal Wave** roller coasters, and the free-fall ride, **The Edge,** will keep you and your teens shook up for hours. **Skyhawk** is a flight ride where riders use a control stick to regulate the angle of flight and rotate the cabin. These, along with **Yankee Clipper, Logger's Run,** and **Whizzer,** are the most popular rides in the park and are busiest between noon and 5pm. The newest addition—**Whitewater Falls**—is a great family ride.

When you tire of the thrill rides, or just want to experience something different, there are a number of shows—musical productions, puppet shows, and the like—that you'll enjoy. Don't miss the **Pictorium Theatre,** which, using the IMAX projection process, gives spectators the feeling they are in the action. While this is fabulous for older kids (our 8- and 10-year-olds wanted to see it three times), inquire about the specific show and seating arrangements if you're taking in little ones. It can seem very loud and overwhelming to them.

Another place jammed with young teens is the **Recording Studio,** where you can record your voice singing over the soundtrack of a favorite song (an extra fee required).

Stroller rentals are available inside the front gate ($2 plus deposit). In Fort Fun is a **Pampers Infant Care Center** for changing and nursing (carpeted, roomy, with two rocking chairs, and free diapers, tissues, and baby lotion; there's even an attendant on duty). The **Lost Children's Center** is a large, carpeted place filled with toys and supervised by a caring attendant who watches the kids until lost parents arrive.

We also suggest you bring lots of liquids for the little ones (unless you want your toddler drinking soft drinks all day)—it can get hot, and only a few places sell milk. Plan to spend lots on drinks and snacks in the park. Bring sun hats, sunscreen, and cool clothing if you're there during the summer; otherwise your crew may get sunburned.

Admission: $18.95 adults, $9.45 children 3–6, $11.95 seniors, children under 2 free.

Open: Daily during Easter Week, Memorial Day weekend, and early June–Sept from 10am; closing times vary; weekends Mar–May and Sept–mid-Oct. **Closed:** mid-Oct–spring.

6. SAN JOSE

GETTING THERE By Car From San Francisco, take U.S. 101, I-280, or I-880 south to San Jose.

ESSENTIALS Orientation A close 50 miles south of San Francisco, San Jose is like another world. It is located at the southern end of San Francisco Bay and is considered the capital of the Silicon Valley. It is the third-largest city in California, has more than 50 wineries, 70 parks, and the largest children's museum on the west coast.

Information For information contact **San Jose Convention & Visitors Bureau,** 333 W. San Carlos St., Suite 1000, San Jose, CA 95110 (tel. 408/295-9600, or toll free 800/726-5673, 800/295-2265 for recorded announcement). Or you can stop by the **San Jose Visitor Center** located in the lobby of the San Jose Convention Center (tel. 408/295-9600, ext. 141).

WHAT TO SEE & DO

WINCHESTER MYSTERY HOUSE, 525 S. Winchester Blvd., at I-280 and Calif. 17. Tel. 408/247-2101 for recorded message.

This is the strangest house you'll ever see. It has 160 rooms, 47 fireplaces, 13 bathrooms, 10,000 windows, and countless spiritual symbols throughout the mansion. The story goes that Sarah L. Winchester, heiress to the Winchester rifle estate, was convinced by a spiritualist that the untimely deaths of her husband and baby daughter were caused by the spirits of people killed with Winchester rifles. She was told that she would be killed too, unless she built a home for the spirits. As long as construction continued, she believed she would not die.

Sarah (even today, the tour guides refer to her as if she is still their employer) kept a crew of carpenters working 24 hours a day from 1884 until her death in 1922, ultimately spending over $5 million on the bizarre mansion.

Winchester House is at once strange and splendid—strange because Sarah's dread and fascination with the spirits motivated her to construct ways to foil ghosts who might come to kill her, and splendid because it's filled with fabulous articles of Victorian culture and art (furniture, accessory pieces, etc.). There are several staircases that lead nowhere, a switchback stairway that has seven turns and 44 steps but rises only nine feet, and several doors that open to blank walls. There's one room without a doorway. Sarah was obsessed with the occult, and the number 13 comes up again and again—she even had 13 sections to her last will and testament and signed it 13 times!

The **Winchester Historical Museum** is located here too, and features a huge collection of rifles and antique firearms. And don't miss the **Victorian Gardens** either.

Admission: $10.95 adults, $5.95 children 6–12, $8.95 seniors; free for children under 5. You can rent cameras and backpacks (to carry babies).

Open: Daily mid-June–Labor Day 9:30am–5:30pm; Oct and Mar–May 9:30am–4pm (weekends and holidays till 4:30pm); Nov–Feb 9:30am–4pm; June 1–15 and Sept 9:30am–4pm (weekends and holidays till 5pm).

CHILDREN'S DISCOVERY MUSEUM OF SAN JOSE, 180 Woz Way at Auzerais Street. Tel. 408/298-5437.

This is a new museum in the San Jose area, and the largest children's museum in the West. Designed for children between 3 and 13, the interactive exhibits teach science and technology and the arts and humanities in a creative way that encourages exploration. Your kids will have a great time here.

Guadalupe Park surrounds the museum and has picnic facilities.

Admission: $6 adults, $3 for children 4–18 and senior citizens.

Open: Tues–Sat 10am–5pm, Sun noon–5pm.

KELLEY PARK, On Senter Road between Story Avenue and Phelan Avenue. Tel. 408/292-8188 or 408/277-4192.

This 176-acre family-oriented park complex has large grassy areas, picnic tables, barbecues, games, and activities geared to kids 10 and under. It's easy to spend more than a few hours here with such attractions as the *Happy Hollow Park and Zoo, Japanese Friendship Garden, and San Jose Historical Museum*. We take the **Kelley Park Express** miniature train around the area.

The Happy Hollow Park and Zoo at 1300 Senter Rd. (tel. 408/292-8188 and 408/295-8383), a tiny theme park and petting zoo, is a favorite of youngsters. The park and rides—Danny the Dragon, Mini-Putt-Putt Car Ride, and King Neptune's Carousel—are perfect for younger children and parents alike. Kids can run around here and just play with a minimum of supervision. The zoo is small but interesting, and makes viewing the animals easy for the very young, very short, or handicapped. There are some interactive informational displays that add a nice touch. A combina-

SAN JOSE

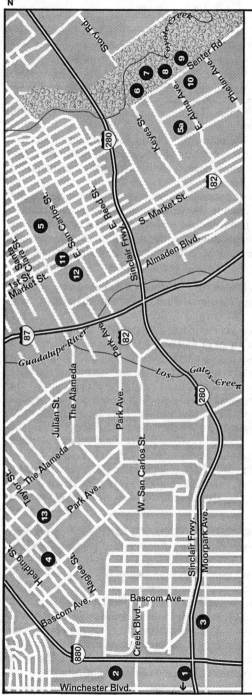

Civic Auditorium 11

Happy Hollow Children's Park 7

Japanese Friendship Garden 8

Kelley Park 6

Municipal Rose Garden 4

Performing Arts Center 12

Rosicrucian Museum & Planetarium 13

San Jose City College 3

San Jose Historical Museum 9

San Jose Municipal Baseball Stadium 10

San Jose State University 5

Valley Fair Shopping Center 5a

Winchester Mystery House 2
 1

CALIFORNIA

SAN JOSE

tion ticket for the playground and zoo costs $2.25 for adults, $1.75 for children 2–14 and seniors 65–79; children under 2 free. Rides cost 50¢ each. Parking is $2 per car on weekends and in summer. Happy Hollow is open May–Oct Mon–Sat 10am–5pm, Sun 11am–6pm; the rest of the year Mon–Sat 10am–5pm.

The **Japanese Friendship Garden and Teahouse** at 1300 Senter Rd. (tel. 408/292-8188 or 408/295-8383), is a lovely traditional Japanese stroll garden patterned after Korakuen Park in Okayama, Japan. Children will enjoy feeding the koi fish with food purchased in the garden. There is no admission charge. The stroll garden is open daily from 10am to dusk.

The **San Jose Historical Museum,** 635 Phelan Ave. at Senter Road (tel. 408/287-2290), is a collection of restored turn-of-the-century Victorian buildings. There's an original post office, firehouse, doctor's and dentist's offices, bank, stables, print shop, candy shop, hotel, and homes.

There's lots of space surrounding the museum, just perfect for picnic lunches and playing on the grass. It's an easy place to take strollers, and diaper changing can be done on the tables outside in the park. Special events abound here. Call ahead to see if there's something going on. Admission costs $2 for adults, $1 for children 6–17, $1.50 for seniors. The museum is open Mon–Fri 10am–4:30pm, Sat–Sun and hols noon–4:30pm. It's closed on New Year's Day, Thanksgiving, and Christmas Day.

RAGING WATERS, 2333 S. White Rd., off Capitol Expressway at Tully Road in Lake Cunningham Regional Park. Tel. 408/238-9900 and 408/270-8000.

This 14-acre water-theme park has more than 30 waterslides and other aquatic activities. For little dippers, there's a small slide area and two wading pools with a large sandy area and picnic areas. For kids a little older, but not quite ready for the speed slides (you have to be 42 inches tall for those), the three serpentine slides are good. These are five stories tall with curves and turns but are slower than slides for the older kids. **Slide Creek** is another good attraction—it's an inner-tube ride. For older kids (10 and up), there are the speed slides, which are 400 feet long and go about 25 miles an hour. There's also **Shotgun Falls**—a slide about 50 feet long that gets you going fast enough to fly off a six-foot drop into ten feet of water. As with all water parks, we advise parents to tell their kids to be extremely careful.

Admission is $12.95 for adults; $10.50 for children under 42 inches, $6.50 for senior citizens, children under 2 free, and includes all-day use of rides. Raging Waters is open daily June 11–Labor Day 10am–7pm, Sat–Sun Sept 4–30, weather permitting.

ROSICRUCIAN EGYPTIAN MUSEUM AND PLANETARIUM, Rosicrucian Park, Park Avenue between Randolph Avenue and Naglee Avenue. Tel. 408/287-2807.

This unusual attraction deserves mention. It's the kind of place that will delight some children and bore others. Only you know your kids. Housing the West Coast's largest collection of Egyptian, Assyrian, and Babylonian artifacts, there are mummies, ornate coffins, jewelry, sculpture, and the Rosetta Stone. Admission $4 for adults, $2 for children 7–15, $3.50 for seniors and students; under 7 free. The museum is open Tues–Sun 9am–5pm; it's closed New Year's Day, Thanksgiving, and Christmas Day.

The Science Museum Planetarium next door will delight children. Check for planetarium show times, as they change. Children under 5 are not admitted to the shows. Admission is $3 for adults, $2.50 for seniors and students, $1.50 for children ages 7–15; children 5–6 free. The planetarium is open Tues–Sun 9am–4:15pm; closed New Year's Day, Thanksgiving, and Christmas Day.

WHERE TO DINE

MARIE CALLENDER'S RESTAURANT, 620 Blossom Hill Rd. Tel. 408/ 578-0643.

Cuisine: AMERICAN. **Reservations:** Not accepted.

$ Prices: Lunch $3.95–$6.95, dinner $3.95–$11. AE, MC, V.

Open: Mon–Thurs 10am–10pm, Fri–Sat 10am–11pm, Sun 10am–10pm (brunch 10am–2pm).

    Parking: Ample nearby.

    Children's Services: Boosters, highchairs; children's menu, crayons.

For a quick bite of lunch if you don't want to picnic, try Marie Callender's. A cut above the standard coffeeshop fare, this restaurant chain's members are always a good bet. The kids will enjoy the puzzles and the drawings to color on the children's menu. This family-style restaurant not only offers great deep-dish meat and poultry pies, burgers, and pasta, but also has some of the best fruit pies around.

7. SANTA CRUZ

GETTING THERE By Car From San Francisco, take Calif. 1 straight down the coast to Santa Cruz. It will take you at least one hour to drive, perhaps more if traffic is heavy.

ESSENTIALS Orientation Santa Cruz is a picture-perfect seaside town of 41,000 hugging the shoreline of Monterey Bay. With good swimming beaches, an old-fashioned boardwalk, and the historical Roaring Camp Steam Railroad, Santa Cruz is a favorite family fun spot.

Information For information about the area, contact the **Santa Cruz County Conference & Visitors Council,** 701 Front St., Box 8525, Santa Cruz, CA 93061 (tel. 408/425-1234, or toll free 800/833-3494).

WHAT TO SEE & DO

THE SANTA CRUZ BEACH BOARDWALK, off Calif. 1. Tel. 408/423-5590 or 408/426-7433.

    Dating back to the early 1900s, the Santa Cruz Beach Boardwalk is everything a boardwalk should be. At either end are rides for small kids, and in the middle is a wonderful merry-go-round (a treat for all ages). There's an enormous game-filled arcade with an assortment of video games, skee-ball, pinball, and "oldies" that date back to the 1920s.

    With rides galore (more than 20), there's a lot to choose from. Teenagers pass the tame rides by and line up for the Pirates Revenge and the Giant Dipper roller coaster, or stroll self-consciously in swimsuits and shorts, trying to see and be seen. The fee for rides range from $1.20 to $2 each, or $14.50 for unlimited use.

While there is lots of boardwalk-style food, it's hard to find juice and milk, so you might want to bring those or any other healthy snacks you desire. Bring sunscreen, as sunburn is a major problem here. Rest rooms are huge (located in the middle of the boardwalk) but have no changing counter. Although you can make room for yourself, you'll have to improvise.

Along the boardwalk are benches for crowd-watching and resting. Infants and toddlers can sometimes be overwhelmed by the crowds here, so it's a good idea to bring your stroller.

The sandy beach is popular with swimmers, surfers, and sunbathers. Located just off the boardwalk, it has rest rooms, parking, and a lifeguard.

SANTA CRUZ CITY MUSEUM OF NATURAL HISTORY, 1305 E. Cliff Dr. Tel. 408/429-3773.

You'll recognize this museum by the full-size statue of a whale in front (and probably five little kids climbing on it). This little museum has a superb Ohlone Native American exhibit and a few wonderful hands-on exhibits, including a tidepool where kids can touch sea creatures. If you haven't been to the Monterey Bay Aquarium, this will be a real treat.

While the beach across the street is inviting, it can be a bit windy for picnicking. We use the picnic tables and lawns behind the museum instead.

Admission: $1.50 adults, 50¢ seniors; children free.

Open: Tues–Sat 10am–5pm, Sun noon–5pm. **Closed:** Holidays.

ROARING CAMP & BIG TREES NARROW-GAUGE RAILROAD, 6 miles north of Santa Cruz on Graham Hill Road in Felton. Tel. 408/335-4484.

This is billed as a way to relieve the excitement of the 1880 pioneer days. Located on land covered with remarkable redwoods, the authentic steam logging train recalls a time when locomotives took giant logs from the forest to be made into lumber. This is one of our kids' favorite places. It's the site of an original steam-gauge railroad, and the site of Bret Harte's short story, "The Pride of Roaring Camp." It has been wonderfully restored.

The camp also has good bathroom facilities, plus a stationary set of train cars that kids adore playing on. There are picnic tables, barbecue pits, and lots of grassy areas where you can plunk down a blanket and enjoy your lunch while lazing in the sun. Sometimes country-and-western musicians perform, and during the summer there are a few volleyball nets set up.

The glorious 6-mile ride up the mountain in the open cars takes about 75 minutes. The train goes in and out of sun and cool forest (don't forget hats and light sweaters—sunscreen, too). You might want to bring along a snack and juice, and be sure your kids use the bathroom before you board, as there are no facilities on the train or at the top of the mountain where the train stops among the elegant grove of redwoods. Everyone gets a chance to stretch. When we have gone with only older kids, we've actually disembarked and hiked down. Check with the conductor and the ticket seller before you do that (or be prepared to hike down), since you can only be let back on a train if there are seats available, and during the summer months trains tend to be crowded.

Admission: $10.75 adults, $7.75 children 3–15; under 3 free.

Open: Daily departures June–Sept at 11am, 12:15, 1:30, 2:45, and 4pm; call for schedule rest of year.

There is also a vintage train that runs from the Roaring Camp to the beach boardwalk at Santa Cruz (round trip takes 2½ hours), called the **Santa Cruz, Big Trees & Pacific Railway** (tel. 408/335-4400). There are daily departures from June 9 through Labor Day. Round-trip passage costs $12.95 for adults, $7.95 for children ages 3–15; under 3 free.

Another option is the **Moonlight Steam Train Parties** (June through October on Saturday night at 7pm). Call for reservations (tel. 408/335-4400)—a must—and fares. Also from May through October on Saturday and Sunday from noon to 3pm, there is a chuckwagon barbecue.

You might be lucky enough to be at Roaring Camp on a special-event day. If you do, be prepared to witness a train robbery or participate in an egg hunt or autumn harvest fair. If you're in Santa Cruz on Memorial Day weekend, you'll enjoy the Roaring Camp Annual Civil War Memorial. This reenactment of Civil War battles and camp life is played out by hundreds of soldiers in Union and Confederate uniforms.

WHERE TO DINE

TAMPICO'S KITCHEN, 822 Pacific Ave. Tel. 408/423-2240.
　Cuisine: MEXICAN. **Reservations:** Accepted for 6 or more.
$ **Prices:** Lunch $5.95–$13.95, dinner $5.95–$13.95. AE, MC, V.
　Open: Daily 11am–10pm.
　Parking: Available.
　Children's Services: Boosters, highchairs, children's menu.
This family-style Mexican restaurant has a little mariachi band that will play requests or simply serenade you at your table. Dine on tacos, burgers, and beef or chicken fajitas.

ZACHARY'S, 819 Pacific Ave. Tel. 408/427-0646.
　Cuisine: AMERICAN. **Reservations:** Not accepted.
$ **Prices:** Breakfast $2.75–$5. DC, MC, V.
　Open: Daily 7am–2:30pm.
　Parking: Ample parking nearby.
　Children's Services: Boosters, highchairs.
A fine place to begin the day with a great brunch or breakfast (they're open for lunch too but serve the same foods). We love their homemade breads, but for a special treat, be sure not to miss the jalapeño cornbread. This casual restaurant is bright—full of natural light—and the servers are great with kids. They'll split adult portions for two kids.

8. MONTEREY & PACIFIC GROVE

GETTING THERE **By Car** From San Francisco, take Calif. 1 south. Monterey is situated at the southern end of crescent-shaped Monterey Bay, 120 miles south of San Francisco.

ESSENTIALS **Orientation** Many people think of the Monterey Bay area as romantic—leisurely strolls near Lover's Point overlooking Monterey Bay, a cozy room warmed by a fireplace, or gallery-hopping in the quaint village of Carmel. But the Monterey Peninsula has much to offer families, too. Rich in historical significance, Monterey is a charming seaside town that feels very much like a working fishing village. Until recently, the canneries were a major part of city life, and even today the wharf bustles with fishing activity.

The main areas of town are located along the waterfront (Cannery Row, Fisherman's Wharf, the Monterey Bay Aquarium) and near downtown (Alvarado Street).

Information A stop at the **Monterey Visitors and Convention Bureau,** 380 Alvarado St. (tel. 408/649-2211 or 408/649-1770), will be very helpful in getting you started. Pick up the walking tour brochure called "Historical Monterey: Path of History Walking Tour."

WHAT TO SEE & DO

MONTEREY

MONTEREY BAY AQUARIUM, 886 Cannery Row (West end). Tel. 408/ 648-4888.

Go ahead, "ooooh" and "ahhhh" as you enter the tremendous, cavernous building designed to reflect the atmosphere of the huge cannery which used to be here. This is the largest aquarium in the country and one of the largest in the world, with more than 6,500 creatures and 100 exhibits, many of them interactive. In fact, if you have time for only one activity, this is where you should spend the time. Don't expect marine life in simple fish tanks, though. What makes this aquarium unique is that it gives you an "undersea tour" of Monterey Bay and the rich marine life that inhabits the region. Children may not grasp the superb nature of this place at first. It will help you if you inform them beforehand that it is not like Sea World or Marine World. This is marine life in its natural habitat, not a collection of performing animals.

It's a place you'll return to again and again, to re-experience favorite exhibits and try new ones as the kids get older and their interests expand. You will want to allow different amounts of time for kids of different ages. Little ones may find the experience too educational to be exciting (except the seal feedings), but children 5 and over will love certain exhibits—especially the touch **Tide Pool,** where they can handle sea stars, anemones, and sea cucumbers under the guidance of patient volunteer instructors who show them what to do. Kids also love the bat-ray pool,

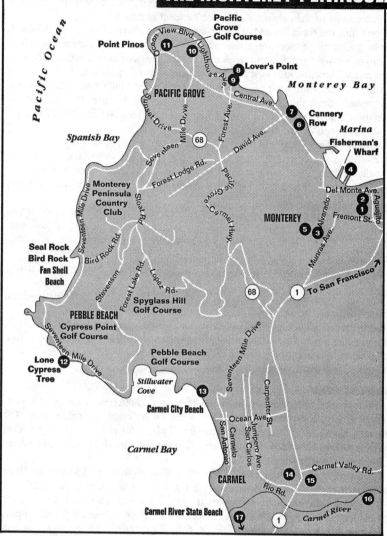

THE MONTEREY PENINSULA

0 1 mi
1.6 km

Pacific Ocean

Point Pinos

Ocean View Blvd

11

10

Pacific Grove Golf Course

Lighthouse Ave.

8
9

Lover's Point

PACIFIC GROVE

Central Ave.

Monterey Bay

Sunset Drive

Mile Drive

Forest Ave.

68

David Ave.

7

6

Cannery Row

Marina

Fisherman's Wharf

Spanish Bay

Seventeen

Forest Lodge Rd.

Pacific Grove

4

Del Monte Ave.

Monterey Peninsula Country Club

Sloat Rd.

Carmel Hwy.

2
1

Aguajito

MONTEREY

5 3

Alvarado

Fremont St.

**Seal Rock
Bird Rock
Fan Shell Beach**

Bird Rock Rd.

Lopez Rd.

Munras Ave.

1 **To San Francisco**

Stevenson

Forest Lake Rd.

Spyglass Hill Golf Course

68

PEBBLE BEACH

Cypress Point Golf Course

Seventeen Mile Drive

Pebble Beach Golf Course

Seventeen Mile Drive

Carpenter St.

Lone Cypress Tree

12

Stillwater Cove

13

Carmel City Beach

Ocean Ave.

San Antonio

Carmelo

Junipero Ave.

San Carlos

Carmel Bay

CARMEL

Carmel Valley Rd.

14

15

Rio Rd.

16

Carmel River State Beach

17

1

Carmel River

where they can watch—and pet—the fish. Plan to spend lots of time there. Teens will appreciate most of the exhibits if they don't expect gimmicks.

Don't miss the **Kelp Forest,** a diver's-eye view of a towering forest of California's giant kelp. One of the most impressive exhibits of the aquarium, it is three stories high and can be viewed from different levels. Amazingly, the giant plant can grow up to ten inches a day! Show the kids how the light changes depending on how far it is filtered from the surface. And don't miss the **sea otters.** California's 1,600 sea otters are found mainly along the central coast. This two-story exhibit gives kids a chance to watch these animals at play, in and out of the water. And feeding time for the otters is an event you won't want to miss.

Monterey Bay Habitats is a spectacular 90-foot-long hourglass-shaped exhibit that re-creates the environment of the bay. It's what you would see if you went scuba-diving in the area, in the order in which you would see it—that is, you see the habitat from the deepest part of the bay to the shallowest, from the reef and the sandy sea floor to the wood pilings of the wharf.

The Sandy Shore is an open-air bird sanctuary that re-creates the shoreline. As the waves come in, you can watch the fish that swim just below the surface. You enter this aviary via a revolving door (which helps to confine the birds). Be aware that strollers are not allowed through the revolving door. There is a new exhibit featuring live video broadcasts from a research submarine deep in the Monterey submarine canyon.

You might want to stop for a snack or lunch at the Portola Café, open 10am–5pm. We were surprised at the pleasantness of the café and the varied menu.

Admission: $9 adults, $6.50 students and seniors over 65, $4 children 3–12; children under 3 free. To avoid standing in line you can buy tickets at Ticketron before you arrive in Monterey, or purchase them at your hotel.

Open: Daily 10am–6pm.

CANNERY ROW

Children love to wander through the renovated canneries—parents too—but you'll have to ask about stroller access in some of the buildings. Don't miss **700 Cannery Row,** which houses several delightful places for children of all ages. Our favorite was **Old Fashioned Fudge and Candy Co.** (tel. 408/373-6451), where we were in "sugar heaven."

The same building houses **Steinbeck's The Spirit of Monterey Wax Museum** (tel. 408/375-3770), which tells the story of old Monterey. Admission costs $4.95 for adults, $2.95 for children ages 7–13; $3.95 for students, military personnel, and seniors, children under 7 free. The museum is open daily 9am–10pm.

Up one block from Cannery Row at 640 Wave Street, the attraction at the Edgewater Packing Company (tel. 408/649-1899) is the antique carousel built in 1905. It has 34 hand-carved horses, two zebras, and two chariots, as well as 940 lights! Open daily at 11am.

When you're finished with your activities at Cannery Row for the day, stroll to Fisherman's Wharf. It's an easy walk along the waterway that takes about 25 minutes. It is fine for strollers.

FISHERMAN'S WHARF

Monterey's Fisherman's Wharf is lined with gift shops, restaurants, and fresh seafood stands in an authentic wharf atmosphere. The wharf is a great place to watch the sea lions. It is still a working pier (although the commercial fishing fleet is now at the Municipal Pier, Wharf 2—which you can also walk to). It was once a pier for trading schooners to unload their wares when Monterey was the major port on the Pacific. Today, however, the wharf is where you'll find boats for sport fishing, sightseeing, and whale watching. **Randy's Fishing Trips,** 66 Fisherman's Wharf (tel. 408/372-7440; open 5am–5pm daily), rents poles, tackle, and anything else you or the kids will need to fish (kids don't need fishing licenses—adults do). They also offer group-charter boats, sightseeing trips to Big Sur and, during the season, bird- and whale-watching excursions. **Princess Monterey Cruises** (tel. 408/372-2628) offers 35- to 45-minute sightseeing cruises during the summer to Carmel Bay, where you can see Carmel from the air—a wonderfully different perspective. Cruises depart daily on the hour from 9am to 3pm and cost $12 for adults, $6 for children under 12. They also offer bay cruises at a cost of $6 for adults, $3 for children under 12. Whale-watching cruises are available December through March; a 1½- to 2-hour trip costs $15 for adults, $8 for children under 12.

EL ESTERO LAKE. Tel. 408/375-1484.

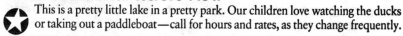
This is a pretty little lake in a pretty park. Our children love watching the ducks or taking out a paddleboat—call for hours and rates, as they change frequently.

DENNIS THE MENACE PLAYGROUND, in the park at Camino El Estero. Tel. 408/646-3866.

This park was designed by cartoonist Hank Ketcham, creator of "Dennis the Menace." We've spent many hours here, the kids playing on the steam locomotive, the roller slide, and the spaceship-like structure, while we simply took advantage of the fresh air and beauty of nearby El Estero Lake.

Open: Daily 10am–dusk.
Admission: Free.

MONTEREY STATE HISTORIC PARK, 525 Polk St. at Custom House Plaza. Tel. 408/649-7118.

This is a group of historically important adobes and other buildings located in Monterey. The buildings, which are owned by the state, are open to the public for viewing, and many have guided tours of the "Path of History." You can pick up a brochure detailing the 45 historic landmarks on the Path at the Visitors Center or at the park's offices and you may begin your tour at any location. If you plan to visit several of the sites in the state park, you can purchase an all-day pass.

Admission: All-day pass: $4 for adults, $2 for children ages 6–17. Single-building admissions: $2 for adults, 50¢ for children.

Open: Daily 10am–5pm in summer; 10am–4pm in winter. **Closed:** New Year's Day, Thanksgiving, Christmas Day.

ALLEN KNIGHT MARITIME MUSEUM, 550 Calle Principal, between Madison and Jefferson streets. Tel. 408/375-2553.

If your children are sea lovers, they may enjoy the Allen Knight Maritime Museum, which has a large collection of maritime artifacts, pictures, and models. Kids love the huge 1880 Fresnel Light from Point Sur Lighthouse, which is on display. Another favorite is the old captain's cabin.

Admission: No charge, but donations are welcome.

Open: June–Sept Tues–Fri 10am–4pm and Sat–Sun 2pm–4pm; rest of year Tues–Fri 1–4pm. **Closed:** Mondays, holidays.

PACIFIC GROVE

PACIFIC GROVE MUSEUM OF NATURAL HISTORY, 165 Forest Ave. at Central Avenue. Tel. 408/648-3116.

This little museum is where you can learn about the natural history of Monterey County and the Monarch butterflies' annual winter return to Pacific Grove. There's also an extensive collection of shore and aquatic birds.

Admission: Free.

Open: Tues–Sun and holidays 10am–5pm. **Closed:** New Year's Day.

LOVER'S POINT, near Ocean View Boulevard.

⭐ Lover's Point offers a spectacular view of the bay, and is not to be missed. There are stairs down to the beach, but swimming is not suggested.

POINT PINOS LIGHTHOUSE, Lighthouse Avenue at Asilomar Boulevard. Tel. 408/648-3116.

This is the oldest working lighthouse on the West Coast—it's been in operation since 1855. The grownups in our group were more excited about it than the kids (whose great pleasure was counting the number of steps up to the top). If your group has never seen a lighthouse before, take them to this one—the kids will enjoy it in their own way, and you don't need to spend much time there. There is a small museum downstairs.

Admission: Free.

Open: Sat–Sun (except holidays) 1–4pm.

SEVENTEEN-MILE DRIVE

The Seventeen-Mile Drive meanders through exquisite coastal scenery from Pacific Grove to Carmel. Many people love this route. Others with kids who are poor car travelers aren't so sure. If your kids will cooperate, you'll find it a highlight of your visit to the coastal region. Begin your drive at the Calif. 1 Gate—take Munras Avenue to Calif. 1. Although there are three gates that will take you to the drive, this one is the most convenient.

Family Activities

BICYCLING Bicycling in the area is wonderful. You have a choice of scenery and terrain. You can either stay on designated bike paths or ride in lovely residential areas. One of the most scenic paths is the **Shoreline Bike Path** from Lover's Point (Pacific Grove) to Fisherman's Wharf (Monterey). This path is also good heading south, where you ride along the shore of the Seventeen-Mile Drive (an easy six-mile ride). **Adventures by the Sea,** 299 Cannery Row, Monterey (tel. 408/372-1807), is a full-service bicycle-rental company that has free pickup and delivery (in Carmel, Carmel Valley, Monterey, and Pacific Grove), as well as package rates and preplanned tours. They have mountain bikes, beach cruisers, and tandem bikes, plus helmets and locks. They also have children's bikes, bicycles with training wheels and toddler carrier seats. **Bay Bikes,** 640 Wave St., Monterey (tel. 408/646-9090), is a bike rental shop located on the Shoreline Bike Path at Cannery Row, one block from the

Aquarium. They also rent quadricycle/surreys that will hold three adults sitting next to each other, with a basket in front that holds two children up to age 6. Helmets are included in price of bike.

FISHING Pier Fishing If fishing is an activity enjoyed by your family, you might want to try your luck at Monterey Municipal Wharf #2 (tel. 408/646-3950). Or for deep-sea fishing, contact **Randy's Fishing Trips,** 66 Fisherman's Wharf (tel. 408/372-7440), or **Chris's Fishing Trips,** 48 Fisherman's Wharf (tel. 408/375-5951). Trips (7:30am–2:30pm weekdays and 6:30am–2:30pm weekends) cost $23 on weekdays and $26 on weekends. The children's rate (under 10) is $12 on weekdays and $15 on weekends. There's no minimum age as long as you're willing to keep track of your own kids.

HORSEBACK RIDING The **Pebble Beach Equestrian Center,** Portola Road and Alva Lane, Pebble Beach (tel. 408/624-2756), offers one-hour escorted trail rides through Del Monte Forest. The route takes you on sand dunes and around some of the beautiful golf courses.

Admission: $30 per hour. By reservation only (no more than six in a group). Children must be at least ten years old.

Open: One-hour escorted trail ride twice daily except Monday, 10am and 2pm.

TIDEPOOLING Look for good tidepools along the rocky areas between Point Pinos and Asilomar Beach in Pacific Grove during low tide. **Caution!** Remember that the ocean waves can be unpredictable and may surprise you. Always be careful. Remember, too, that the area is slippery.

Here are some tips for tidepooling (courtesy of the Monterey County Visitors and Convention Bureau):

1. Remain with your group—do not go off alone.
2. Don't fool around on the rocks.
3. Walk slowly and carefully, since the rocks are very slippery.
4. Wear tennis shoes.
5. Don't get trapped by the rising tide.
6. Waves can knock you down, so always watch for them.
7. Don't bring glass containers in the tidepool areas.
8. Don't pry animals from the rocks.
9. Return animals to the same area from which you removed them.
10. Return each rock to the exact spot you took it from.
11. Sea animals do not like being stepped on or having fingers poked at them.
12. Leave empty shells on the beach—they may be some animal's future home.
13. Remember that all tidepool life is protected by law.

WHERE TO STAY

MONTEREY

Expensive

SHERATON MONTEREY, 350 Calle Principal at Del Monte Boulevard, Monterey, CA 93940. Tel. 408/649-4234, or toll free 800/325-3535. Fax 408/372-2968. 344 rms. A/C MINIBAR TV TEL

$ Rates: $185–$225 double (depending on the floor, the view, and the room setup), suites $225–$850. Children under 18 free in parents' room if no additional bed is needed; cribs free. Additional adults or rollaways $20 per night. Connecting rooms available. AE, CB, DC, MC, V.

Parking: Valet; $5 per day.

★ This 10-story hostelry offers panoramic views of Monterey Bay from many of the rooms. The two-story atrium lobby absorbs much of the tumult and noise while serving as a comfortable and popular gathering spot. We saw dozens of young'uns, many of whom were rambunctious, and the style of the lobby accommodated them well.

What makes the Sheraton exceptional is the service. The staff are warm and attentive, and have a sense of humor, which is great when you're traveling with children. From the valets who park your car to the bellmen and staff in the coffeeshop, everyone is friendly. They treat the whole family with respect, and they're only too pleased to talk to you about their own children and their likes and dislikes.

The rooms have refrigerators, game tables and chairs, and dressing rooms with vanity areas. They're spacious and airy, and there is plenty of room for kids to play with blocks and puzzles on the floor. You can request a room with two double beds or one with a king-sized bed. Many rooms have a couch or loveseat as well.

Dining/Entertainment: Continental breakfast is served in the lobby (for an additional charge). The Three Flags Café, a family-style restaurant, is open (6:30am–1am) for breakfast, lunch, and dinner, and has a full menu. Highchairs and booster seats are available here. Ferrante's, located on the tenth floor, is an Italian restaurant and bar with a spectacular view. Even if you don't eat here with the kids, take them for a look-see at sunset. There's a cocktail lounge with live jazz entertainment nightly—the Monterey Bay Club (open 4pm–2am).

Services: Full concierge staff, limousine service, baby-sitting arrangements, daily morning newspapers, 24-hour room service, and, if you give housekeeping a call, nightly turndown service.

Facilities: Outdoor swimming pool and Jacuzzi that are sheltered from the wind on three sides. Health club with exercise equipment, weights, and bicycles (you must be 18 to use it), barber and beauty shop, gift shop.

MONTEREY PLAZA, 400 Cannery Row, Monterey, CA 93940. Tel. 408/646-1700, or toll free 800/631-1399, 800/334-3999 in Calif. Fax 408/646-0285 or 646-5397. 290 rms. A/C MINIBAR TV TEL

$ Rates: $150–$280, single or double; suites $300–$675. Children under 12 stay free in parents' room; cribs free; additional adults and rollaways $20 per night. AE, CB, MC, V.

Parking: Valet; $9 per night.

This "grand hotel on the Bay" has beautiful rooms with breathtaking views. Many of the deluxe rooms are built over the bay (watch the windows if you have young children since they open wide), affording an unparalleled view of Monterey and the curving coastline of the bay. This is indeed elegance. The lobby is quiet, but there is a large outdoor plaza area where kids can wander.

Rooms are beautifully decorated and come with luxurious amenities, including sewing kits.

Services: Room service available 6:30am–midnight. Baby-sitting services may be arranged through the concierge. Tennis, golf privileges.

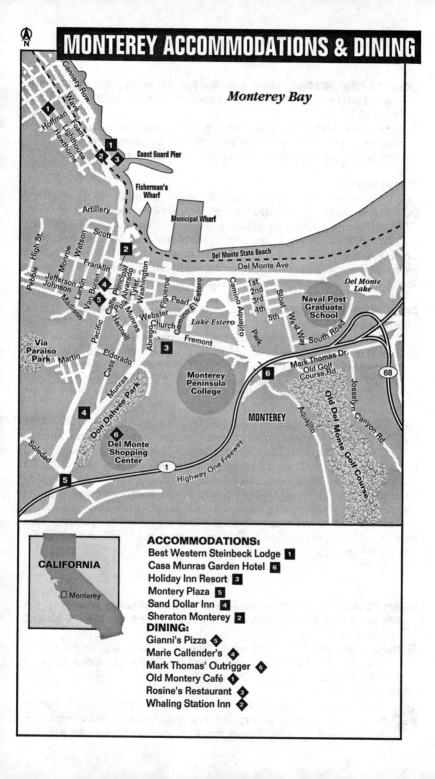

MONTEREY ACCOMMODATIONS & DINING

Monterey Bay

Cannery Row
Wave
Foam
Lighthouse
Hawthorne
Hoffman

Coast Guard Pier

Fisherman's Wharf

Municipal Wharf

Artillery

Scott
Watson
Monroe

High St.
Pebble
Jefferson
Johnson
Larkin
Madison

Franklin
Van Buren
Calle Principal
Polk Alvarado
Tyler
Munras
Washington
Figueroa
Pearl
Webster
Church
Abrego
Camino El Estero
Camino Aguajito

Hartnell
Pacific

Del Monte State Beach
Del Monte Ave.

1st
2nd
3rd
4th
5th
Sloat
West Way
South Road
Park

Del Monte Lake

Naval Post Graduate School

Via Paraiso Park

Martin
Eldorado
Cass
Munras

Fremont
Lake Estero

Don Dahvee Park

Monterey Peninsula College

Mark Thomas Dr.
Old Golf Course Rd.

68

Soledad

Del Monte Shopping Center

MONTEREY

Aguajito
Josselyn Canyon Rd.
Old Del Monte Golf Course

1
Highway One Freeway

ACCOMMODATIONS:
Best Western Steinbeck Lodge 1
Casa Munras Garden Hotel 6
Holiday Inn Resort 3
Montery Plaza 5
Sand Dollar Inn 4
Sheraton Monterey 2

DINING:
Gianni's Pizza 5
Marie Callender's 4
Mark Thomas' Outrigger 6
Old Montery Café 1
Rosine's Restaurant 3
Whaling Station Inn 2

CALIFORNIA

Monterey

Moderate

HOLIDAY INN RESORT, 1000 Aguajito Rd., Monterey, CA 93940. Tel. 408/373-6141, or toll free 800/HOLIDAY. Fax 408/655-8608. 204 rms. A/C MINIBAR TV TEL

$ Rates: $69–$195 single, $84–$195 double, depending on season. (Ask for a room facing the pool or garden.) Children under 16 free in parents' room; cribs free, rollaways and additional adults $15 per night. AAA special rates. AE, D, DC, MC, V.

Parking: Free.

⑤   This modest resort one mile north off Calif. 1 at Golf Course Road offers a heated swimming pool (that Andrew and Elizabeth didn't want to leave), shuffleboard, a putting green, Jacuzzi, and sauna, and a location that is perfect if you're planning activities in Carmel and Big Sur as well as in Monterey and Pacific Grove. Room service is available for breakfast, lunch, and dinner, with hamburgers and fried chicken prominent on the menu. Babysitting can be arranged. The Monterey Rose Restaurant is open 6:30am–10pm, and has boosters and highchairs.

CASA MUNRAS GARDEN HOTEL, 700 Munras Ave. (P.O. Box 1351), Monterey, CA 93940. Tel. 408/375-2411, or toll free 800/222-2558, 800/222-2446 in Calif. Fax 408/375-1365. 150 rms. No A/C MINIBAR TV TEL

$ Rates: $69–$119, single or double, for room with king-sized bed, sleeper-sofa, and fireplace; suites $149. Children under 12 free in parents' room if no additional bed is needed; cribs free, rollaways or additional adults $12 per night. Some connecting rooms available. AE, CB, DC, MC, V.

Parking: Free.

⑤   Of the motels in Monterey, this is one of our favorites. Originally built in 1824 as the official residence of the last Spanish ambassador to the state of California, Casa Munras is set on 3½ acres of landscaped, flowering gardens, and it is just 5 blocks from the wharf. There is a heated outdoor pool with a large shallow area for children. The rooms are good sized, with plenty of space for a crib and toys for kids. Extra care is shown in the decor—for example, brass beds and comforters are part of the standard room. Baby-sitting may be arranged through a referral service.

Although there is no room service, the Casa Café is on the premises (open Sun–Thurs 7am–9pm and Fri–Sat till 10pm); boosters and highchairs are available. The bar is open daily 4:30pm–1am; entertainment Thurs–Sun.

Budget

SAND DOLLAR INN, 755 Abrego St. at Fremont Avenue, Monterey, CA 93940. Tel. 408/372-7551, or toll free 800/982-1986. Fax 408/372-0916. 63 rms. No A/C TV TEL

$ Rates: $59–$69 (smallest room) to $89–$109, depending on the season. Children 12 and under free in parents' room; cribs free; additional people or rollaways $10 per night. AE, D, DC, MC, V.

Parking: Free.

⑤   There is a heated swimming pool and Jacuzzi here. Other notable features include a coin-operated laundry, free in-room perked coffee, and complimentary continental breakfast. Rooms vary from queen-bedded rooms with fireplaces to double-queen suites. Some have only showers, others have shower/bath combinations, plus some have honor bars and private balconies.

BEST WESTERN STEINBECK LODGE, 1300 Munras Ave., ¾ mile south of Calif 1 exit, Monterey, CA 93940. Tel. 408/373-3203. Fax 408/372-3505. 32 rms. No A/C TV TEL

$ Rates (including continental breakfast): $55–$85 single, $55–$95 double, depending on the season and kind of room. Cribs $6 per night; rollaways $8. AE, CB, D, DC, MC, V.

Parking: Free.

This modest little motel boasts a good location and clean rooms; even a heated pool. Room rates include a continental breakfast of danish, pastry, and coffee for each guest.

PACIFIC GROVE

Budget

PACIFIC GARDENS INN, 701 Asilomar Blvd., Pacific Grove, CA 93950. Tel. 408/646-9414, or toll free 800/262-1566. 28 rms. No A/C MINIBAR TV TEL

$ Rates: $70–$98 one or two queen-sized beds or one king-sized bed, $99–$145 one- and two-bedroom suites. Rates include complimentary continental breakfast, and wine and cheese in the evening. Children under 12 stay free in parents' room if additional beds are not needed; children over 12 and adults pay $5 each per night. AE, MC, V.

Parking: Free.

Nestled in the trees and lovely gardens across from the beach, this is a cozy, rustic motel. Most of the units have fireplaces. There are two hot tubs on the property. Kitchen units and adjoining rooms are available upon request. All rooms have refrigerators, plus a popcorn maker and popcorn.

BEACHCOMBER INN, 1996 Sunset Dr. at Asilomar State Beach, Pacific Grove, CA 93950. Tel. 408/373-4769, or toll free 800/445-7745, 800/237-5885 in Calif. 26 rms. MINIBAR TV TEL

$ Rates: Winter rates $55 (queen- or king-size bed)–$100; summer rates $65–$150. Refrigerator in every room. AE, DC, MC, V.

Parking: Free.

This is a small inn—basic but very clean. It's the last property before the beach. If you have very little ones, you'll love the free bikes with child carriers. They have a few kids' bikes to lend as well. The rooms are small, but adjoining rooms can be rented. The outdoor swimming pool is heated year round and has a large slide that delights kids. The Fishwife Restaurant is on the premises (see the dining recommendations which follow, for details).

Bed-and-Breakfast Inns

GREEN GABLES INN, 104 Fifth St. at Oceanview Boulevard, Pacific Grove, CA 93950. Tel. 408/375-2095. 11 rms, 7 with bath, 4 share bath. No A/C

$ Rates (includes full breakfast and afternoon tea): $155, single or double. Children over 5 pay $15 per night; cribs free. AE, MC, V.

Parking: On-street parking.

★ This is a Queen Anne–style mansion and you'll be amazed as you first step into the high-ceilinged living room. It is elegantly decorated with antiques and faces the sea. The view through the large bay windows is spectacular. Complimentary afternoon tea, sherry, and wine are served with hors d'oeuvres in the parlor, and a full breakfast is served in the English-style dining room. Across the street is a trail for jogging or strolling, and a lovely public beach.

The guest accommodations in the main house are furnished with antiques and have common bathrooms, so they are not advisable for kids. Instead, the Carriage House has five separate accommodations with queen-sized beds, fireplaces, sitting rooms, private baths, and color television. These are the rooms to request for families.

GOSBY HOUSE INN, 643 Lighthouse Ave., Pacific Grove, CA 93950. Tel. 408/375-1287. 22 rms. No A/C

$ Rates: $85–$130, single or double; children over 5 and additional adults are charged $15 per night (for food). *Note:* There is a no-smoking policy at the inn. AE, MC, V.

Parking: On-street parking.

★ With older children, you might consider the Gosby House Inn, owned by the same people who run Green Gables. Inspired by European country inns, this bed-and-breakfast has been in operation since 1887, and was placed in the National Register of Historic Places in 1980. It is considered an excellent example of authentic Queen Anne architecture, with bay windows and a rounded corner tower reminiscent of a turret. This charming inn is a two-story wooden building painted yellow with white trim. Formal and traditional, this is a wonderful place for children who are quiet and restrained. Girls (and adults, too) will delight in the antique doll collection located in the parlor. And the small garden is a perfect place for reading and breakfast.

Some 20 of the 22 rooms have baths, so reserve ahead if you insist on one with a tub. (If you're an antique buff, ask for a room with a clawfoot tub.)

Services: Concierge service, nightly turndown, and breakfast in bed (on request). The staff will fix a picnic basket of fruit and cheese—and wine if you desire (at an extra charge). Breakfast and afternoon tea, sherry, and hors d'oeuvres are included in the room price.

WHERE TO DINE

MONTEREY

Expensive

WHALING STATION INN, 763 Wave St., Cannery Row, Monterey. Tel. 408/373-3778.

Cuisine: AMERICAN. **Reservations:** Recommended.

$ Prices: $15.95–$35. AE, DC, MC, V.

Open: Sun–Thurs 5–9:30pm, Fri–Sat 5–10pm.

Parking: Valet parking.

Children's Services: Boosters, highchairs.

⭐ We couldn't believe it when we were told that the famous Whaling Station Inn catered to families. This gem of a restaurant is the perfect place to spend a relaxed evening with or without children. Don't let the candles and elaborate dessert table fool you. While the ambience of this legendary restaurant is quiet and elegant, the service is gracious and helpful to children and their parents. Manager Bert Simpson, the servers, and the bus persons have an appreciation for a dining experience with children, and, even more important, all have a sense of humor and camaraderie with the parents. "It happens all the time" is the response to a spilled Shirley Temple. They believe you can have a fine dining experience even when you take your children along. Fussy infants are greeted with little goldfish crackers and warm bread. Older children are greeted with a "hello" and a big smile.

Our server was chatty and efficient, making suggestions about the menu, but never being pushy. There's a children's menu but if you order from the regular menu your server will gladly bring you a half-portion of the pasta dishes, or split a fish or a steak dinner between two children. It's hard to imagine anything the staff won't try to do to accommodate your family—three cherries in the Shirley Temple if your child asks, telling you all about their own children, and making suggestions for places you'll enjoy in the area with your family.

Complete dinners include artichoke for two, soup, fresh vegetables, and warm homemade bread. Fresh abalone, lobster, and seafood are specialties here.

Moderate

MARK THOMAS' OUTRIGGER, 700 Cannery Row, Monterey. Tel. 408/ 372-8543.
   Cuisine: AMERICAN/SEAFOOD. **Reservations:** For 6 or more.
$ **Prices:** Dinner $6–$30. AE, MC, V.
   Open: Daily 11:30am–10pm.
   Parking: Available for fee in nearby lots.
   Children's Services: Boosters, highchairs; children's menu.

This is a moderately priced seafood and steak restaurant overlooking the water of Monterey Bay. It is a fine spot in which to enjoy a leisurely meal while watching the seals and pelicans. Ask for a window seat and your children will likely spend their time observing the activity on the water—by day the wealth of boats and fishing vessels; near sunset, the small fields of floating kelp and the ever-changing colors on the distant shoreline of Seaside and Santa Cruz.

Or you might want to request seating in the back dining room, which is bright and spacious, for obtrusive highchairs and wandering children. If you have to wait for a table, there's a little beach area next to the restaurant that keeps the kids occupied. (Be careful of the rocks, though.)

The children's menu caters to a variety of sophisticated palates and includes a kid's shrimp Louis, deep-fried calamari, and fish-and-chips. Their drink list includes nonalcoholic daiquiris (banana, coconut, strawberry, etc.) and piña coladas, along with the more traditional Shirley Temples and Roy Rogerses.

OLD MONTEREY CAFÉ, 489 Alvarado St., Monterey. Tel. 408/646- 1021.
   Cuisine: AMERICAN. **Reservations:** Not accepted.

$ Prices: $2.95–$8.95. No credit cards.
Open: Breakfast and lunch daily 7:30am–2pm.
Parking: On-street parking.
Children's Services: Boosters, highchairs.

This is where locals go for breakfast and lunch. Centrally located, it's a good place to try during a walk downtown (if you're doing part of the Path of History Tour) or after a jaunt in Dennis the Menace Park. The food is fabulous, and the menu is varied and unusual. The old-fashioned hash browns are well worth the trip, as are the homemade muffins. For omelet lovers, choose from such exotic combinations as avocado, bacon, and onions, or artichoke hearts, bacon, and Jack cheese—they're all made with four eggs. You can even invent your own omelet filling. Lunch offers the same kind of variety in sandwiches, half-pound burgers, salads, and homemade soups. There is no children's menu, but they'll gladly serve a child's half-portion for you, and will warm baby bottles and baby food.

Inexpensive

GIANNI'S PIZZA, 725 Lighthouse Ave., at Prescott Avenue. Monterey. Tel. 408/649-1500.
  Cuisine: ITALIAN. **Reservations:** None.
$ Prices: $4–$11. No credit cards.
  Open: Mon–Thurs 4–11pm, Fri–Sat 11:30am–midnight, Sun 11:30am–10pm.
  Parking: On-street parking.
  Children's Services: Boosters, highchairs.

Gianni's is an inexpensive family-owned restaurant that has wonderful Italian food to eat in or take out as well as a cocktail bar, dessert bar, and coffee bar. While the artichoke frittata and fresh breadsticks are a find, Gianni's specializes in traditional Italian pizzas. This is a great place to come after a walk through the aquarium or a few hours at Cannery Row. While there is no children's menu, pizza and pasta are made for sharing, and the servers gladly warm baby bottles and baby food in the kitchen. Pizzas take about 20 minutes to prepare, and at peak hours on Friday, Saturday, and Sunday (from 5:30 to 9pm) you may have to wait 10 minutes to get a table.

ROSINE'S RESTAURANT, 434 Alvarado St., Monterey. Tel. 408/375-1400.
  Cuisine: AMERICAN. **Reservations:** Not accepted.
$ Prices: Sandwiches average $3.50, dinner $6.25–$14.95. DC, MC, V.
  Open: Mon 7:30am–4:30pm, Tues–Wed 7:30am–9pm, Thurs 7:30am–9:30pm, Fri–Sat 7:30am–10pm, Sun 8am–10pm.
  Children's Services: Boosters, highchairs.

When you step into this restaurant it's like you're entering an early-California outdoor plaza. If there's such a thing as "faux outdoor early California," this is it. The walls are painted to look as if you're sitting in an outdoor plaza, complete with blue shutters on the walls that "open" into the restaurant. There is no children's menu and there's a charge for splitting food; however, at dinner one pasta dish for children is offered. Some of the menu items—such as a half sandwich with soup or salad, or a bagel with cream cheese and soup or salad—are fine for small appetites. Breakfast is served all day.

For more grown-up tastes, there are Reuben, Philly, and calamari sandwiches, as well as full dinners served after 5pm.

MARIE CALLENDER'S, 1200 Del Monte Shopping Center, Monterey. Tel. 408/375-9500.

Cuisine: AMERICAN. **Reservations:** Not accepted.

$ Prices: Dinner $5.95–$8.95; children's menu $1.75–$2.75. AE, MC, V.

Open: Mon–Sat 8am–10pm, Sun 8am–9pm.

Parking: Available in the shopping center lot.

Children's Services: Boosters, highchairs; children's menu.

For anyone not familiar with Marie Callender's restaurants, these are generally good family places to eat. While each one is slightly different (some have children's menus; others don't), you can feel secure that your meal—breakfast, lunch, or dinner—will be a step above coffeeshop fare. Known for their excellent fruit pies (20 to 30 kinds daily) and heartland pot pies (Charlie Chan chicken pot pie, chicken divan pot pie, and Mexican beef pot pie, as well as the more ordinary chicken, turkey, and tamale pot pies), they also serve very good soup and chili, and a surprising variety of entrées. This location also has good lasagna, spaghetti marinara, and quiche. Cornbread is another of their specialties.

Marie Callender's restaurants tend to be very popular, so you may have to wait for a table at prime time. It's a good idea to go early for dinner or lunch. If you have to wait, the Del Monte Shopping Center has several stores of interest for you and the children to browse through while passing the time.

PACIFIC GROVE

Moderate

FISH WIFE, 1996½ Sunset Dr. at Asilomar State Beach, Pacific Grove. Tel. 408/375-7107.

Cuisine: CALIFORNIAN/CARIBBEAN. **Reservations:** Recommended.

$ Prices: Breakfast $2.75–$6.50, children's breakfasts $1.95–$3.50; lunch $5–$9; dinner $10–$16; Sunday brunch $4.95–$6.95.

Open: Daily except Tues 11am–10pm. **Closed:** Thanksgiving, Christmas Day.

Parking: Nearby.

Children's Services: Boosters, highchairs; crayons, children's menu.

This moderately inexpensive restaurant offers consistently good Californian cuisine and is off the beaten track so you don't have to compete with all the other tourists. However, the food is so good the locals flock to this place. If you go for Sunday brunch, lunch, or an early dinner, you'll have the beauty of Asilomar to enjoy.

The owners really care about food being healthy and nutritious, and offer special dishes to accommodate weight watchers as well as low-sugar and low-salt dieters. The kids will love the crayons and paper on the table. Adult dinners include fresh vegetables, French bread, and potatoes. You can choose from prawns Belize and calamari abalone style to New York steak with cracked peppercorns (as well as many of the salad and pasta selections also available for lunch). The children's dinner includes potatoes and fresh vegetables (plus chicken or fish entrees) and costs $3.95 to $4.50. Your server will warm baby bottles and baby food, or will split adult entrees for kids.

Inexpensive

THE FIRST WATCH, 125 Ocean View Blvd., near Monterey Bay Aquarium, Pacific Grove. Tel 408/372-1125.
   Cuisine: AMERICAN. **Reservations:** Not accepted.
$ **Prices:** Breakfast $2.75–$5.95, lunch $3.75–$5.25. MC, V.
   Open: Daily 7am–2:30pm. Coffee service is provided if you have to wait.
   Children's Services: Boosters, highchairs.

This is our favorite restaurant for breakfast or lunch. The great atmosphere, large portions of good food, and low prices make this a perfect place before or after your visit to the Monterey Bay Aquarium, a short two-block walk. The restaurant is housed in the old American Tin Cannery building, and the rough cement-and-brick walls and huge two-story windows draw you back into the time when sardine canning was the big industry in Monterey.

The homey atmosphere (thermos of coffee and pitcher of water at the table) even comes across in the menu, from which children can order gourmet pancakes or luscious French toast by the amount they think they can eat. Unique breakfast items include raisin-walnut pancakes (made from scratch) and fresh vegetable frittata. Their fresh orange juice may be the best around. Salads and sandwiches are available too. Try a Hawaiian sandwich—pineapple and sliced ham on English muffin—or maybe a classic Reuben.

TOASTIES CAFE, 702 Lighthouse Ave., Pacific Grove. Tel. 408/373-7543.
   Cuisine: AMERICAN. **Reservations:** For 6 or more.
$ **Prices:** Breakfast $3–$6, lunch $4–$6, dinner $5–$8; children's menu $1.95–$3.95. MC, V.
   Open: Mon–Sat 6am–3pm, Sun 7am–2pm, Tues–Sat 5pm–9pm.
   Parking: On-street parking.
   Children's Services: Boosters, highchairs; children's menu, coloring books and crayons, plus 20 hand-held water toys to borrow.

This is a wonderful homestyle American café. "When it comes to kids, we basically do anything you want," says owner Robert Yee. That includes creating items for young palates, an extensive children's menu, having toys for kids, warming baby food, and splitting adult portions for children. This homey café boasts great country specialties made from scratch. The corned-beef hash and Philly steak are favorites, as are the pancakes, waffles, and French toast. Try San Francisco Joe's Omelette (ground beef, onions, spinach, and cheese with country potatoes, toast or pancakes). We had French toast and blueberries (delicious) and Baby Cakes (dollar-size pancakes). They'll even make omelets without egg yolks for people who are watching their cholesterol intake.

9. CARMEL, CARMEL VALLEY & BIG SUR

GETTING THERE   By Car From San Francisco, take scenic Calif. 1 straight to Carmel. Big Sur is 26 miles south of Carmel on Calif. 1.

ESSENTIALS Orientation Nestled among the Monterey cypress and other pines, with grand vistas of washed-white beaches and sapphire-colored ocean, the village of Carmel is a place you'll long remember. It is truly a town for romantic getaways, fabulous shopping, and gallery-hopping. There are places for kids to go, things for kids to do, but don't plan extended days in town. We spend a day in Carmel and another in Big Sur.

Information For information in advance, including a brochure called *Carmel-by-the-Sea* with art gallery listings, contact the **Carmel-by-the-Sea Business Association,** P.O. Box 4444, Carmel, CA 93921 (tel. 408/624-2522). Or stop by when you're in town—it's on the second floor of Vandervoort Court, on San Carlos between Ocean Avenue and 7th Street. The **Monterey Visitors and Convention Bureau,** 380 Alvarado St., Monterey, CA 93940 (tel. 408/649-2211), will also send you material.

WHAT TO SEE & DO

CARMEL & CARMEL VALLEY

Beautiful stores and boutiques line Ocean Avenue and the surrounding streets in the **downtown** area. While you may be more interested in art galleries and gift stores, your youngsters will enjoy **Thinker Toys,** on the lower level of Carmel Plaza, on Mission Street off Ocean Avenue (tel. 408/624-0441). Kids are welcome to play in the store while parents browse through the array of European-made Brio toys, mobiles, model trains, radio-controlled cars, and the like. Open Mon–Sat 9:30am–9pm, Sun 9:30am–5:30pm.

CARMEL MISSION (Mission San Carlos Borromeo del Rio Carmelo), 3080 Rio Road off Calif. 1. Tel. 408/624-3600.

This was the second mission founded by Fray Junípero Serra in 1770. Set on lovely grounds, its Moorish-style tower and sandstone exterior made it one of the prettiest missions in the state. This was Fray Serra's headquarters as he continued to found missions throughout California, and it is the place he chose to be buried. You can walk through and see the spartan rooms in which Fray Serra lived and the cemetery where he's buried. There is also a museum and library with displays of interesting relics of the California mission period.

Admission: By donation, $1 suggested.

Open: Mon–Sat 9:30am–4:30pm, Sun and holidays 10:30am–4:30pm. **Closed:** Easter, Thanksgiving, Christmas.

CARMEL CITY BEACH (at the end of Ocean Avenue)

Exotic gnarled Cypress and Torrey pines grace the stretches of white sand. Although it can be chilly (and downright cold at times), we've spent hours building sand castles and flying kites at these beaches.

CARMEL RIVER STATE BEACH

This 106-acre area also has a lagoon for frolicking and a marshy area that is a bird sanctuary. There are picnic tables and rest rooms available. To get there, go south (if you're coming from Monterey) on Calif. 1. Take a right on Rio Road and a left after the Carmel Mission, and continue taking left turns until you're there.

THE BARNYARD SHOPPING COMPLEX, at the entrance to Carmel Valley on Calif. 1, off Carmel Valley Road. Tel. 408/624-8886.

This shopping complex has over 55 shops and 7 restaurants. What is most appealing, however, is its setting—flowers, trees, walkways, and terraces create a ranchlike atmosphere. The Barnyard was born years ago with the **Thunderbird Bookshop** (see the "Where to Dine" section for details). When the owners decided to expand, they left the natural feeling of a ranch and built authentic-looking barn structures to house the new shops. You won't want to miss taking the kids to the Thunderbird Bookshop. If you have time, your kids will also enjoy the **Thunderbird for Kids** bookstore. We enjoy eating at **From Scratch** (tel. 408/625-2448), a casual breakfast-and-lunch place that specializes in fritattas, egg dishes, quiche, soups and salads (open daily 7am–3pm).

POINT LOBOS STATE RESERVE, 4 miles south of Carmel on Calif. 1. Tel. 408/624-4909.

Point Lobos is referred to as the "Crown Jewel" of the California State Park System. Plan to spend at least 2 hours here. It's a spectacular living museum where flocks of pelicans, gulls, and cormorants (as well as 250 other animal species and over 300 plant types) can be seen on the fantastic granite rock formations in the little coves and in the rolling meadows. The ocean is wonderfully wild here, and if you look closely, you'll notice sea otters floating offshore.

Two-thirds of the Reserve is an underwater refuge (diving restrictions apply), protecting the rich and varied sea life. You can visit six different areas—the sea lion area, the cypress grove, the pine wood, Bird Island, North Shore Trail, and Whaler's Cove. This is a simply wonderful spot for children over 6, who will love everything about it—from the vividly colored wild mushrooms to the thick, lush ferns.

We always love taking the Cypress Grove Trail (a 30-minute walk starting at Sea Lion Point parking area), which wanders through the stand of Monterey Cypress. The ocean views along here are spectacular. Another favorite of the kids is Sea Lion Point (a 30-minute walk, same starting point), an easy trail that takes you to the barking sea lions and past Headland Cove, where you can see sea otters. Bring binoculars, so you can get a better look at the sea lions. There are wooden steps that lead to an overlook of Devil's Cauldron and Sea Lion Point, and if you're lucky enough to be there during the whale migration, you might see the enormous blow sprays and the huge flapping tails of a grey whale.

Warning! Poison Oak is abundant in the Reserve. Have your children stay on the trails to avoid contact with it. Show them what it looks like before you start out, so they don't touch some accidentally. Also, the wild surf and dangerous cliffs make the Reserve a place where you want to hold the hands of any young child.

During the summer there are guided nature walks twice a day. The rest of the year, check with the ranger at the entrance, as guided walks are less frequent. On weekends, when weather is clear, you can see cars lined up waiting for admittance. Go early if you want to get in. When the reserve is full, visitors are asked to wait in line and are permitted in one at a time as others leave.

Admission: $5 per vehicle, but you can also park outside the Reserve and walk in.

Open: Daily spring-fall 9am–7pm, rest of year 9am–5pm.

Picnic Supplies

MEDITERRANEAN MARKET, at the corner of Ocean and Mission streets. Tel. 408/624-2022.

Before we're off for the day, we always get a picnic basket full of goodies from the Mediterranean Market. You'll find yummy treats here—and such nice people to help with selections. The market is open daily 9am–6pm, closing an hour later in summer. They take MC and V credit cards here.

BIG SUR

Without doubt, Big Sur has to be 90 miles of nature's most incredible coastline. To the west, the crashing sea meets steep cliffs that jut out of the sand. Small coves of vibrant aquamarine- and sapphire-colored water greet you on many turns. Huge jagged black rocks that have tumbled into the sea are hosts to gulls and otters. To the east are pine forests and redwoods which create a veil for the wanderer in the woods and provide astonishing backdrops for hiking and camping.

Calif. 1 on the Big Sur coast (also known as Cabrillo Highway and the Coast Highway) can be some of the most treacherous driving in California. While the road is well maintained, a healthy respect for Calif. 1 is good, and caution is necessary, especially if you're not used to winding roads. Drive defensively, and—although this might sound preachy—never drive it if you have had anything to drink, or if you are fighting sleep. Also check weather conditions, as dense fog or heavy rains can make the highway difficult—if not impossible—to drive.

The drive from Monterey to Big Sur Village takes from 45 to 60 minutes. As you head south past Point Lobos, the coastline gets increasingly rugged. There are plenty of turnouts where you will undoubtedly want to stop and take pictures.

Warning! Because of the makeup of the terrain, it's easy to lose your footing. Little ones must be held by the hand. Exquisite as the vistas are, it is important to wait until you get to a big turnout or vista point where you can park.

Although the beaches are breathtakingly beautiful, don't be fooled. There are few approachable beaches, and swimming is *not* safe along the coast because of riptides and treacherous currents.

Probably the one Big Sur landmark that most people recognize is **Bixby Bridge.** This often-photographed bridge, with its huge arch, was built in 1932 and was considered a spectacular engineering feat. The bridge spans Bixby Canyon, where little Bixby Creek runs. There is a turnout on the north end of the bridge.

Although there's no hiking to recommend for families here, you can drive the South Coast Road, a dirt road that winds through Bixby Canyon across the Little Sur, and comes out at Andrew Molera State Park. You travel through redwoods and high meadows, and the drive affords sensational views of the ocean.

ANDREW MOLERA STATE PARK, about 21 miles south of Carmel. Tel. 408/667-2315.

This is a lovely beach and walk-in campground. Enter the park via a short driveway off Calif. 1 that leads you to the parking lot. You'll have to walk to the park (¼ mile—and it's flat). From the camp to the beach is about ½ mile. There is a river, equestrian trails, firepits, pit toilets, but no drinking water.

If you like to hike, this is a great place. The Bluffs Trail is an easy two-mile trail that goes along the ocean to the bluff. The Headlands Trail is about a one-mile hike that takes you to the headlands above the mouth of Big Sur River as it flows into the ocean. You get a beautiful view of the river, the ocean, and the canyon. The Bobcat Trail is about two miles that takes you through the redwoods along the Big Sur River.

Admission: $5 day-use fee.

The **Nason Ranch/Molera Trail Rides Big Sur** (tel. 408/625-8664) is located here. All rides are four hours long and go to the beach. Open daily March to November, rides are offered at 9am, 1:30pm, and 4 hours before sunset. These half-day trips cost $50 per rider. Minimum age is 7. There are horses for advanced, intermediate, and beginner riders. Reservations are recommended.

As you travel south from Andrew Molera State Park, you enter **Big Sur Village**, the place many consider the heart of Big Sur. This is where you can get something to eat, find a place to stay overnight, and gas up the car.

PFEIFFER–BIG SUR STATE PARK, about 26 miles south of Carmel. Tel. 408/667-2315.

Even if you're not camping, you'll enjoy a day of fabulous hiking and picnicking among the redwoods and dense forests. There's no beach access in this 820-acre forest, but the Big Sur River runs through the park. As you enter the park on the east side of the highway, the rangers in the Information Booth (which operates like a visitor center) will give you detailed maps and let you know if there are any restrictions on hiking, picnicking, or camping. A Nature Center is located near the Pfeiffer Falls trailhead. The center has displays of natural history of the area. Ask about the ranger-guided walks.

The most popular hike for families with young kids is the easy ½-mile trek that goes up to Pfeiffer Falls. Another one is the Oak Grove Trail (1¼ miles long) that takes off from the Pfeiffer Falls trailhead. The Valley View Trail begins at the falls and goes up from there; the climb is 400 feet in a distance of ½ mile). The quarter-mile trail takes you to a high point that gives you a view of the entire Big Sur Valley and Point Sur. Kids can also fish in the river, and if you time it right the fish may really bite.

Admission: $5 day-use fee.
Open: Daily 7am–10pm.

JULIA PFEIFFER BURNS STATE PARK, south of Pfeiffer Big Sur State Park. Tel. 408/667-2315.

Further south from Pfeiffer Big Sur State Park is a 1,800-acre wooded day-use park (there is no camping). In addition to telephones, rest rooms, and a picnic area with fire grills, there are several trails, some suitable for novice hikers. One easy trail (a third mile long) runs from the parking lot to McWay Cove, where you'll get a wonderful view of McWay Falls as it drops 50 feet into the ocean.

Admission: $5 day-use fee.

Near Julia Pfeiffer Burns State Park is **Coast Gallery** (tel. (408/667-2301), a gift store and art gallery with a large selection of puppets as well as fine art, wood items, and ceramics pieces. There is a permanent exhibit of watercolors done by author Henry Miller, who once lived in Big Sur. The grounds on which the gallery sits has all sorts of succulents and flowering plants. There is also a good place to buy original gift items. It is open daily from 9am to 5pm in winter, till 6pm in summer.

WHERE TO STAY

CARMEL

Expensive

LA PLAYA HOTEL, Camino Real at 8th Avenue (P.O. Box 900), Carmel, CA 93921, Tel. 408/624-6476, or toll free 800/582-8900 in Calif. Fax 408/624-7966. 75 rms. MINIBAR TV TEL

$ Rates: $95 to $175, single or double; suites $275–$375; cottages $175–$500. Children under 12 stay free their parents' room; cribs free; children over 12 and additional adults pay $10 per night each. AE, DC, MC, V.
Parking: Free.

La Playa Hotel is an elegant old Mediterranean-style villa that was built in 1904 and converted into the only full-service hotel in Carmel. Each room has a view either of the ocean, garden, residential Carmel, or the red-tiled patio area. There is a beautiful outdoor swimming pool, exquisite formal gardens, and lawn areas where kids can play. The rooms carry out the Mediterranean motif. Decorated in light, airy colors, they have hand-carved furniture, plus refrigerators and hairdryers.

Dining/Entertainment: The Spyglass Restaurant (tel. 408/624-4010) serves breakfast, lunch, dinner, and Sunday brunch. There is the Spyglass Terrace and the wood-paneled Spyglass Lounge for cocktails. These folks are friendly and will do anything they can to help you and the kids enjoy your stay. Breakfast averages $5–$12, lunch $6–$15, and dinner $14–$45. Sunday brunch costs $19.50 per adult; $10.50 for children under 12.

Services: Nightly turndown, concierge desk, valet services, same-day laundry (Mon–Fri), and room service (7am–11pm) with tasty items available for kids including burgers and sandwiches; you can ask for peanut butter and jelly or other goodies.

Facilities: Golf and tennis.

Moderate

CARMEL MISSION INN-BEST WESTERN, 3665 Rio Rd., Carmel, CA 93923. Tel. 408/624-1841, or toll free 800/348-9090). 165 rms. A/C MINIBAR TV TEL

$ Rates: $79 to $139, single or double; suites start at $195. Children under 12 free in parents' room if additional beds are not needed; cribs free. Connecting rooms available. Ask for seasonal and holiday special rates. AE, CB, D, DC, MC, V.
Parking: Free.

Enjoy the warmer weather and beauty of the Carmel Valley. Surrounded by sculptured gardens and winding walkways, this inn has a heated outdoor pool and Jacuzzi. Because it's located near the Barnyard Shopping area, we found it convenient to wander over there when the kids wanted something to do but wanted to stay close to the hotel.

The recently remodeled rooms are spacious and well maintained, and open onto hallways, not parking areas. Refrigerators are available on request and there are free in-room movies.

Dining/Entertainment: Sassy's Bar and Grill (tel. 408/624-1841) is open for breakfast, lunch, and dinner and serves American and continental cuisine. For breakfast, try the yummy waffles, pancakes, omelets, even the eggs Benedict. For lunch, you can choose from salads, hot and cold sandwiches, and a buffet that includes prime rib and seafood; items cost $3.75 to $7.50. For dinner there's fresh fish, fresh pasta, Kansas City baby back ribs, and sinful desserts.

Services: Baby-sitting services can be arranged; room service is available, offering such children's favorites as waffles, grilled cheese, pizza, and peanut butter sandwiches; poolside food service is available.

MISSION RANCH, 26270 Dolores St., 1 mile south of downtown, Carmel, CA 93923. Tel. 408/624-6436. 26 rms. MINIBAR TV TEL
$ Rates: Cottages $95–$125, motel units $50–$75. Cribs free; rollaways $10 per night. MC, V.
Parking: Free on-premises parking.

Mission Ranch is a real "find" if you like ranch-style living. Originally a working dairy farm, the grounds are spacious and dotted with 100-year-old Monterey cypress trees and even older redwoods. The ranch looks out onto a meadow, Point Lobos, and the Pacific Ocean.

Wonderful for children, it has 20 acres (with 8 tennis courts), dotted with grazing sheep and huge eucalyptus trees. In fact, the ambience is such that many families come back year after year. Located between the mission and a school, the owners are accustomed to having kids move through the property all the time. On weekends and during the summer, children can use the playground equipment at the school next door. If you need a babysitter, the office staff will give you a few names, and then you can make the arrangements yourself.

Several kinds of accommodations are available here. Meadow- and ocean-view cottages include kitchens/kitchenettes and televisions, but only showers—no baths—and some have living rooms and multiple bedrooms, perfect for families. Finally, there are rooms in the farmhouse, but these are set up for couples. Children under 16 are discouraged from staying in this area. Included in the room price is a continental breakfast of cereal, croissants, fruit, juice, and beverage.

Dining/Entertainment: Mission Ranch Restaurant (tel. 408/624-3824) began serving meals in 1937. It is a funky old ranchhouse featuring a sing-along piano bar. Most of the tables look out onto the sheep pastures. A casual, comfortable place where the locals go to eat, it is surrounded by the grassy play area that is the ranch. The restaurant, which is open daily for dinner, serves American cuisine and specializes in prime rib, but they also offer lamb, back ribs, chicken, and fish. Prices for full dinners, which include relishes, bread, soup or salad, vegetables, and potato, are $10.75–$22.95. The children's dinner costs $7 and includes soup, fries or rice, choice of entrée, vegetable, dessert, and milk.

Budget

COLONIAL TERRACE INN, San Antonio Street at 13th Avenue (P.O. Box 1375), Carmel, CA 93921. Tel. 408/624-2741, or toll free 800/345-1818 in Calif. 25 rms. No A/C TV TEL
$ Rates (includes continental breakfast): One queen bed $60, two double beds $75,

one queen and one hideabed $130, two queens $130, one queen and one double bed (with two baths) $160; cribs free. Weekends: 2-day minimum stay. AE, MC, V.
Parking: Free on-site parking.

Tucked away in a quiet residential area one block from the beach, the Colonial Terrace Inn doesn't even look like a hotel. All rooms look out on manicured gardens or quiet courtyards, and there are grassy play areas for energetic kids. Each room is uniquely furnished. Some have fireplaces, some have refrigerators, others have sitting rooms. Connecting rooms are available and may be your best buy.

Because each room is different, rates vary widely. Tell the reservationist what you need when you call and she'll help you. All rates include a complimentary continental breakfast, which is served in the lobby.

Bed-and-Breakfast

COBBLESTONE INN, Junipero Avenue between 7th and 8th streets (P.O. Box 3185), Carmel, CA 93921. Tel. 408/625-5222. Fax 408/625-0478. 24 rms. MINIBAR TV TEL

$ Rates (includes continental breakfast and hors d'oeuvres and tea/sherry service): $95–$110 queen-sized bed and shower; $130–$145 king-sized bed, shower, and wet bar; $155 two-room suite with queen-sized bed, shower, and sitting room; $170 two-room suite with king-sized bed, tub/shower combination; all rates same single or double occupancy. Cribs free; children over 4 and additional adults $15 each per night. AE, MC, V.
Parking: 4 parking spaces plus 24-hour street parking.

If you're looking for a bed-and-breakfast experience in Carmel, you'll love the Cobblestone Inn. Each of the 24 guest rooms has its own entrance, and is decorated with fresh flowers, antiques, a fireplace, telephone, color television, and private bath with shower or tub. Fresh fruit and a refrigerator are provided in every accommodation, as are bathrobes and complimentary toiletries.

Many rooms open onto a U-shaped courtyard. But remember that this, like other older inns, doesn't have the level of soundproofing that newer hotels might have.

Cross the courtyard to the communal living room with a fireplace, where complimentary sherry, wine, tea, and hors d'oeuvres are served every evening. Breakfast is served here too. Guests can dine inside or at tables outside for breakfast in the summer. This is great for kids because they are able to get up from the table and run around.

Other amenities offered, not often thought of as part of a bed-and-breakfast inn, are concierge service, nightly turndown, complimentary shoeshine and morning newspaper.

BIG SUR

Budget

BIG SUR LODGE, on Calif. 1 in Pfeiffer–Big Sur State Park (P.O. Box 190), Big Sur, CA 93920. Tel. 408/667-2171. 61 rms.

$ Rates: June–Labor Day $85–$95 single or double; rest of year $65–$95. Units with fireplace $15 additional; with kitchen $20 extra. Extra person $10–$20 per night. MC, V.
Parking: Free for lodge guests.

If you're lucky enough to get a room, this is a wonderful place to experience the redwood forest while having some of the comforts of home. Located within the Pfeiffer–Big Sur State Park, it is only a short distance from the park entrance, which means that you and your family can enjoy the evening activities (or take sunset hikes) without having to drive anywhere afterwards. Open year round, the lodge has a grocery store, gift shop, and restaurant. For those who are just looking around, the lodge has one of the few public rest rooms in Big Sur.

Tucked in among the pines and redwood, the guest cottages are on a hill surrounded by the mountains and the Big Sur countryside. Surprisingly, there's a heated outdoor swimming pool, but even when it's too cool to swim, the large grassy areas bid children to play Frisbee and tag. Other amenities include a sauna, laundromat, and a recreation room. Some rooms have kitchenettes (without cooking equipment), and refrigerators are available upon request. (Note that there is no television.) Some units can accommodate up to 6 people, but no cribs are available.

Camping

ANDREW MOLERA STATE PARK, 21 miles south of Carmel. Tel. 408/667-2315.

This is a walk-in campground with 50 sites that charges a fee of 50¢ per person per night.

PFEIFFER–BIG SUR STATE PARK, 26 miles south of Carmel, Big Sur, CA 93920. Tel. 408/667-2315.

There is wonderful camping along the Big Sur River with terrain that varies from redwoods to oak groves. The 218 developed sites (with table and campfire ring) run through the canyon, but no campsite is more than 300 yards away from the river. Flush toilets and showers are nearby. The sites can accommodate trailers up to 27 feet and motorhomes up to 31 feet.

During the summer, there are interpretive ranger programs that include guided walks and campfire programs. The fees are $10 per campsite and $3 per extra vehicle. You can reserve through MISTIX, toll free 800/444-7275 in Calif. and 619/452-1950 outside Calif.).

VENTANA CAMPGROUND, Calif. 1, Big Sur, CA 93920. Tel. 408/667-2331.

Privately owned and located on Calif. 1 just 1½ miles south of Pfeiffer–Big Sur, Ventana has 65 campsites set in among the redwoods. Each site has a fireplace and table, and there are bathrooms with hot showers nearby. No facilities for RVs or campers. Call in advance for reservations. The fees are $15 per night per campsite.

WHERE TO DINE

CARMEL

Expensive

CLAM BOX RESTAURANT, Mission Street and Fifth Avenue. Tel. 408/624-8597.

Cuisine: CONTINENTAL/SEAFOOD. **Reservations:** Not accepted.
$ Prices: $10–$25; children's plates $6.50. No credit cards.
Open: Tues–Sun 4:30–9:00pm. **Closed:** Mon, Thanksgiving, Christmas week.

Parking: On-street parking.
Children's Services: Boosters, highchairs; children's menu, crayons.

⭐ We love the Clam Box Restaurant, a lively, fast-moving place that serves excellent seafood and caters to families. The atmosphere is casual and the tables are close together, but it all adds to the geniality of the place. The service is fast—soup and bread and butter are delivered immediately—and the servers are very agreeable. There are not only highchairs and boosters, but our kids were given crayons and coloring books to while away the time. We've heard talk that storybooks and toys often make their apperance as well.

There is a huge selection of seafood, and dinners start with both homemade soup (get the clam chowder if you like chowder) and salad. Dine on tender abalone, broiled filet of salmon, and whole Pacific lobster, and enjoy. For the under-8 set, there's a choice of filet of sole, old-fashioned ham, or hamburger with fries, plus soup or salad.

With all of this going for it, you'd expect a line—and that's what you'll get if you come after 6pm (waits can be up to an hour long). If you get there before 6pm, we've been assured that it is easy to get a table. If you do have to wait, take a leisurely stroll along the nearby streets, and don't miss the park, where your kids can run off any excess energy before they sit down.

HOG'S BREATH INN, San Carlos Street between 5th and 6th avenues. Tel. 408/625-1044.

Cuisine: AMERICAN. **Reservations:** Not accepted.
$ Prices: Lunch $5–$6, dinner $18–$23. AE, CB, D, DC, MC, V.
Children's Services: Boosters.
Open: Daily lunch 11:30am–3pm, dinner 5–10pm. Bar open until 2am.
Parking: On-street parking.

Most people go to Hog's Breath Inn (yes, that's the name of the restaurant) because Clint Eastwood owns it and is often seen there. Eastwood and his friend Walter Becker opened this unusual place many years ago. Most impressive is its outdoor patio, where you can lunch surrounded by trees, five fireplaces (and warming heaters), wood burl tables, and sculptures of hogs—an experience, indeed. The Dirty Harry burger is a favorite (includes soup), or there's the Eiger sandwich (roast beef), and Sudden Impact (Polish sausage with jalapeño peppers on a French roll). The dinner menu offers Coogan's Bluff (a 12-ounce steak), a 16-ounce steak, and High Plains Rancher (prime rib). There are daily specials as well. Anything on the menu is available in a child's portion at a lower price.

Moderate

THUNDERBIRD BOOKSHOP CAFE, 3600 Barnyard. Tel. 408/624-9414.

Cuisine: AMERICAN. **Reservations:** Accepted.
$ Prices: Lunch $4–$8, dinner $9–$14. AE, CB, DC, MC, V.
Open: Lunch daily 11am–3:30pm, dinner Tues–Sun 5:30–8:30pm, Fri–Sat 5:30–9pm.
Parking: In the Barnyard parking lot.
Children's Services: Boosters, highchairs.

⭐ A Carmel landmark, the Thunderbird Bookshop Café is unique. Take your meal surrounded by 40,000 books. You can dine year round in the Solarium Patio that has a retractable glass room and opens to the whole life center. Wooden tables and a blazing fire in the fire pit make this casual, rustic-style place a real find. Lunch consists of soups, sandwiches, and salads. Dinner includes pasta and prawns, three different steak and chicken dinners, as well as angel-hair pasta and linguine Alfredo. They'll warm baby bottles but not baby food in the kitchen.

KATY'S PLACE, Mission Street between 5th and 6th avenues. Tel. 408/624-0199.

   Cuisine: AMERICAN. **Reservations:** Not accepted.

$ Prices: $3.95–$9. No credit cards.

   Open: Daily 7am–2pm.

   Children's Services: Boosters, Sassy Seats.

We love this one. Country charm and excellent food are what you're likely to find at Katy's Place. Famous for their eggs Benedict (they have seven different kinds, including crab, salmon, and vegetarian), we luxuriate in the eggs while our kids order dollar-size pancakes, all while sitting at the counter and watching the chefs.

You're given juice and coffee as soon as you sit down, and the service is generally very fast. The outside patio is lovely and is a wonderful place to sit on sunny days. While there is no children's menu, a regular-size breakfast easily feeds two or three children, and the side orders (bacon, cereal, fruit, waffles) will satisfy any picky eater. Portions are enormous. If you like home fries, go off your diet for the home-fried red potatoes here.

BIG SUR

BIG SUR LODGE RESTAURANT, next to Big Sur Lodge, Big Sur. Tel. 408/667-2171.

   Cuisine: AMERICAN. **Reservations:** Not accepted.

$ Prices: Breakfast $3–$8, lunch $6–$8, dinner $7–$15. MC, V.

   Open: Breakfast 8am–11:30am, lunch noon–2pm (no lunch during off season), dinner 5–9pm.

   Children's Services: Boosters, highchairs; children's menu.

Big Sur Lodge Restaurant serves its fare in a lovely glassed-in dining room that makes you think you're eating among the pines. With a children's dinner menu that features everything from hamburger with fries to squid rings, eggplant parmesan, and black bean tostada, your kids will find something appealing, and you'll be delighted with the place, too.

NEPENTHE, on Calif. 1, 3 miles south of Big Sur State Park. Tel. 408/667-2345.

   Cuisine: AMERICAN. **Reservations:** Accepted for 5 or more.

$ Prices: Lunch $8.50–$10, dinner $8.50–$22.50.

   Open: Daily lunch 11:30am–4:30pm, dinner 5pm–midnight.

   Children's Services: Boosters, highchairs.

Perched high over the pounding sea, looking out over redwoods and oaks is Nepenthe. Magic surrounds the place. Movies have been filmed here, and it remains a favorite spot of some of the celebrities who live in the area. The walk to the restaurant takes you up steps that follow a little fern-lined stream. It's as if you're walking deeper into the forest. You're met at the top with a breathtaking view of Big Sur (if it's not foggy).

If you dine on the terrace at night amid the candlelight and the blazing fire pit, you'll agree that it's one of the most romantic places on earth. But during the day it's a fabulous place to while away time having a coffee or good lunch with your family.

The patio area is especially inviting for wandering children. Large tables make family seating easy, and the wide-open spaces are great for accommodating families with young children. Because the place is so famous, the owners are used to children trekking in and out. Crackers are brought to the table right away, or you can walk up to the bar and grab a handful yourself. Ask and they'll bring your hungry kids carrots to munch on. If the wait is long, you'll enjoy exploring the area around the restaurant or you can visit the famous Phoenix gift shop downstairs. (You'll see it as you drive up.)

For dinner or lunch, try the famous Ambrosiaburger, a delicious ground-steak sandwich on a French roll, or sample the wonderful French Dip. Also available are soup and salad, steak sandwiches, and Holly's (crustless) Quiche. There is no children's menu, but they will gladly split adult orders into halves or thirds.

RIVER INN, Pheneger Creek, south of Big Sur Village. Tel. 408/625-5255.

Grab a cup of coffee, here. Be sure to wander out back by the river where people sit with their chairs in the water, letting it run over their feet. A truly peak Big Sur experience.

10. THE NAPA VALLEY

GETTING THERE   By Car   From San Francisco, cross the Golden Gate Bridge and continue north on U.S. 101. Turn east on Calif. 37, then north on Calif. 29. This road is the main thoroughfare through the Wine Country.

ESSENTIALS   Orientation   California Highway 29 runs the length of Napa Valley, which is just 35 miles long. You really can't get lost—there's just one north-south road, on which most of the wineries, hotels, shops, and restaurants are located. Towns are small and easy to negotiate. Any local can give you directions.

Information   For a detailed description of the area and many of the wineries, pick up the free guide *California Is Wine Country* from the Wine Institute at 425 Market Street, Suite 1000, San Francisco, CA 94105 (tel. 415/512-0151). Once in the Napa Valley, make your first stop the **Napa Chamber of Commerce,** 1556 First Street, in downtown Napa (tel. 707/226-7455). They have information on the local vineyards, as well as listings of antiques dealers and walking tours. All over Napa and Sonoma, you can pick up a very informative—and free—weekly publication called *Wine Country Review.* It will give you the most up-to-date information on wineries and related area events.

Tucked among the California coastal mountains about an hour northeast of San Francisco, the tranquil Napa Valley awaits, ready to unfold all her gardenlike splendor to families. Each season brings its own delights. Known simply as "The Wine Country," the 30-mile-long Napa Valley includes the towns of Napa, Yountville, Oakville, St. Helena, Rutherford, and Calistoga. Be prepared for it to be pricey, though, since this is a place that attracts wine lovers. Realistically, to truly enjoy the area, the older your children the better.

While visiting wineries and wine-tasting have become a tradition, there are other, more family-oriented ways to spend time together. On clear mornings, brilliantly colored hot-air balloons grace the sky. Soaring and gliding are other air adventure possibilities. There is golf and tennis, and an exquisite place to picnic. Or maybe you'd like to go horseback riding. Near Calistoga, you can see one of the world's three geysers and visit a petrified forest.

The Napa region is an interesting blend of traditions. The Gold Rush was the initial impetus for building the area. In the mid-1880s, Napa (among others) was host to the Great Silver Rush. The most famous mine was the Silverado, made immortal by Robert Louis Stevenson's *The Silverado Squatters*. In 1865 a railroad line was completed, linking Napa city with Vallejo to the south, and stagecoaches were already making their regular trips as far north as Calistoga. To this mining area mix, add a dash of early California mission influence. The Spanish settlers brought with them vine cuttings from the nearby missions, where wine was made for sacramental uses. Because of Napa's perfect wine-growing climate, these took hold and the Napa Valley is now known throughout the world for its excellent California wines.

Before your trip you might want to do a little research. Maps are available from the **Napa Chamber of Commerce,** 1556 First St., Napa (tel. 707/226-7455), and you can get more information about the entire wine-growing region from the **Redwood Empire Association,** 785 Market St., 15th floor, San Francisco 94103 (tel. 415/543-8334).

WHAT TO SEE & DO

Although half a dozen little towns dot the Napa Valley, it's so small we will talk about it as a region. Here's a brief rundown of the time it takes from one place to another: from Napa to Yountville is 9 miles (about 15 minutes); to St. Helena is 18 miles (about 30 minutes); to Calistoga is 28 miles (about 40 minutes.)

The combination of exquisite scenery and interesting sights (especially the wineries) is the main reason people come to the Napa Valley. Let's start with . . .

THE WINERIES

It's likely your kids will appreciate the wineries in an educational light, much as they would if you took them on any other industrial tour. Approach it that way. Winery tours show the wine-making process from grape picking to crushing, fermenting, storing, and bottling. You see different aspects of the process at different times of the year.

Adults will find the history and architecture of the buildings themselves fascinating. Children will enjoy the wine-making process—huge oak barrels, stainless-steel vats, crushers, and bottles with their labels.

But first you have to decide which wineries to stop at. Here are a few we think are the most interesting for children. A word of caution: Don't try to visit too many. People who've tried it say that two wineries is the limit for most children. We've done a few more with older kids, but with several activity breaks in between.

You might want to start at the south end and work north.

ROBERT MONDAVI WINERY, 7801 St. Helena Hwy. (Calif. 29) Oakville, CA 94562. Tel. 707/963-9611.

THE NAPA VALLEY

The tour at the Robert Mondavi Winery gives a complete overview of the wine-making process in a modern state-of-the-art facility. The guide will take you through all phases of production—from grape to bottle—in a 60-minute tour, which ends with a wine tasting. There is a large lawn with stylized sculptures outside the tasting room where kids can wander while Mom and Dad sample the vintages. In July the winery holds an outdoor jazz festival, and at Christmas there are other musical performances.

Open: Daily April–Oct 9am–5pm, Nov–March 10am–4pm. Reservations are necessary for the guided tour.

V. SATTUI WINERY, White Lane at Highway 29, 1½ miles south of St. Helena, CA 94574. Tel. 707/963-7774.

This may be the best winery to take the kids. We love to time it so we "do lunch" in the beautiful tree-shaded picnic area, complete with tables. Don't worry about buying lunch beforehand; they have a large gourmet cheese shop and deli on premises.

Open: Daily 9am–6pm in summer, 9am–5pm in winter. Tours by appointment only.

BERINGER VINEYARDS, 2000 Main St. (Calif. 29), St. Helena, CA 94574. Tel. 707/963-4812 or 963-7115.

This winery is unique. Built in 1883, the Beringer family home, called the Rhine House, is an example of old German architecture and is a California National Landmark. You will be able to view the house as well as take a walking tour of the aging cellars, during which you will learn some California history. These hand-dug tunnels were carved out of the mountainside by Chinese laborers, and are currently used to store the barrels of wine for aging.

Open: Daily 9am–5pm.

CHRISTIAN BROTHERS GREYSTONE WINERY HOSPITALITY BUILD-ING, 2555 Main St. (P.O. Box 391), St. Helena, CA 94574. Tel. 707/963-0763.

This is another good choice. Located just north of St. Helena (near the Beringer Vineyards), the magnificent four-story building (which the kids call "the castle") is one of the largest stone buildings in the world. Our kids love Brother Timothy's corkscrew collection. There are over 3,000 corkscrew, some of them unusual animals and figurines. During the wine-tasting session, you might want to have one adult take the kids to the gift shop or to play in the grassy area in front of the mansion.

Open: Daily 10am–4:30pm. The free guided tours last about 35 minutes.

STERLING VINEYARDS, 1111 Dunaweal Lane, Calistoga, CA 94515. Tel. 707/942-5151.

Farther north than Beringer and Christian Brothers, located 2 miles south of Calistoga, Sterling Vineyards is a good family place. Board the four-seater aerial tram for a fun ride up the mountains to the hilltop winery. You'll get a sweeping view of the surrounding mountaintops, valley, and vineyards (the steep climb can be scary for those afraid of heights). The stark-white monastic-style building is also an unusual visual treat. Once there, the tour is guided by signs, not people, allowing you and the kids to move at your own pace. Be prepared to carry your infants and toddlers, however, because there is no stroller access. There is a large gift shop and lots of open places for children to wander.

Open: Sales hours and tasting times are 10:30am–4:30pm daily. There's a $5-per-person visitor fee for those over 16.

OTHER RECREATIONAL ACTIVITIES

There are many other family activities to pursue in the Napa Valley also. Here's just a sampling of our favorites.

Natural Wonders

OLD FAITHFUL GEYSER OF CALIFORNIA, 1299 Tubbs Lane, Calistoga, CA 94515. Tel. 707/942-6463.

This is one of the three Old Faithful Geysers in the world (the other two are in Yellowstone National Park and in New Zealand). The geyser is approximately 60 feet high and it erupts about every 40 minutes—great fun for kids. There is a picnic area, snackbar, and a gift shop. Strollers can navigate the area. Old Faithful is about 45 minutes from Napa City via Calif. 29 or Calif. 428.

Admission: $2.50 Adults, $1 children 6–12; under 6 free.

Open: Daily 9am–5pm in winter, 9am–6pm in summer.

THE PETRIFIED FOREST, 8 miles west of Calistoga at 4100 Petrified Forest Rd., Calistoga, CA 94515. Tel. 707/942-6667.

Giant redwoods, covered with volcanic ash from an eruption years earlier by Mt. St. Helena, have been turned into stone, permanently preserving them. Kids enjoy touching the stone-like redwoods, and will marvel at all the petrified specimens. The museum describes the process of fossilization and petrification, of interest to young and old alike. You can picnic here, and strollers are fine on the trail. The Petrified Forest is about a 50-minute drive from Napa City.

Admission: Adults $3, children 4–11 $1, under 4 free.

Open: Daily 9am–6pm in summer, 10am–5pm the rest of the year.

BOTHE-NAPA VALLEY STATE PARK, 3801 St. Helena Hwy. North, Calistoga, CA 94515. Tel. 707/942-4575, or toll free 800/444-7275.

This beautiful state park 4 miles from St. Helena is a great place for picnicking, horseback riding, swimming, hiking, and even camping. There is a public swimming pool open from mid-June through Labor Day. There are 50 developed campsites. Make reservations in advance for the busy summer months if you want a campsite. You can reserve through MISTIX at 619/452-1950, or toll free 800/444-7275 in California.

Admission: Adults $2, children under 17 $1; day-use fee $3 per vehicle, $1 per day, $10 per campsite.

Open: Daily.

Picnic Spots

In Napa itself, **Skyline Park** at Fourth and Imola (tel. 707/252-0481), with more than 900 acres of wilderness grounds, is a lovely place to hike or picnic. Admission is $4 per vehicle, $2 for walk-ins and bicycles. No dogs are allowed in the park. Two other pretty picnic spots in Napa are **Fuller Park** at Jefferson and Laurel (this one has a playground, too) and **J. G. Kennedy Park,** 2291 Streblow Dr., which has boating, fishing, barbecue pits, and a playground. No admission fee for either park. **Conn Dam-Lake Hennessey** is 15 miles north of Napa off the Silverado Trail. This park offers fishing and picnicking, and has no admission fee. Another good place to picnic is **Crane Park** on Grayson Avenue off Calif. 29 in St. Helena, which has a playground, tables and barbecue pits, but no admission fee.

Bicycle Riding

Although this is a very popular way to experience the lushness and beauty of the vineyards, parents who take their children bicycling need to be wary of the cars—and the drivers who have been wine tasting. That said, the relatively flat, historic **Silverado Trail** is considered by many to be one of the best routes. There's no doubt that the trail affords lovely views of the green Mayacamas Mountains and lush vineyards. It has wide 8-foot shoulders, but drivers hit speeds of 45–65 mph, so your kids better be experienced bicyclists. Another less scenic but much safer road that we prefer is the **Solano Bicycle Path** (locals just call it the Frontage Road), which runs from the Clarion Hotel in the south (that's at Trancas Road and Redwood Road) to Yountville in the north. It follows the Wine Train and Calif. 29, but it is separated from the highway and tends to be used by residents driving to and from their normal activities at speeds of approximately 35 mph.

You can rent bikes at **Bryan's Napa Valley Cyclery,** 4080 Byway East, Napa (tel. 707/255-3377). Bryan's doesn't rent ordinary bicycle seats for toddlers but rather little trailers that go behind the bicycle and will carry children up to 125 pounds. Rates are $4 for the first hour, $2 for each additional hour to a maximum of $12 for a business day. Overnight, or 24 hours, costs $20. The shop is open Mon–Sat 9am–6pm, Sun 10am–5pm; in winter they close at 4pm.

Horseback Riding

This is another adventure we love and **Wild Horse Valley Ranch,** Wild Horse Valley Road in Napa (tel. 707/224-0727), is the place to go. Guided trail trips cost $25 for a two-hour ride through 3,000 acres of gorgeous countryside. Children must be 8 years old to ride. Each March, July, and October there are equestrian events—horse trails, including cross-country and stadium jumping—that spectators can watch for free.

Hot-Air Ballooning

The balloons take off in the early morning when the air is cool and the winds are gentle. The flight over exquisite countryside is an expensive adventure. Some kids do quite well in the balloons and love floating up high. Others find it very frightening to have nothing but the balloon between them and the ground hundreds of feet below. This is one activity in which it's difficult to ask the operator to stop and let the kids out.

Adventures Aloft, at the Vintage 1870 complex in Yountville (mailing address: P.O. Box 2500, Yountville, CA 94599; tel. 707/255-8688), is the oldest outfit in the Valley. Be prepared to spend three to four hours for the preflight breakfast, the flight itself, and then the postflight champagne brunch. The cost is $175 per person.

Other choices are **Napa Valley Balloons,** P.O. Box 2860, Yountville, CA 94599 (tel. 707/253-2224). **Balloon Aviation of Napa Valley,** 2299 3rd St., Napa, CA 94558 (tel. 707/252-7067), and **Once In a Lifetime,** P.O. Box 795, Calistoga, CA 94515 (tel. 707/942-6541, or toll free 800/722-6665).

A Special Museum

The Silverado Museum, 1490 Liberty Lane, St. Helena, CA 94574 (tel. 707/963-3757), is devoted to memorabilia of Robert Louis Stevenson. You'll find first and variant editions of the author's work, original letters, and manuscripts, plus paintings, sculptures, and photographs. Admission is free and the museum is open Tues–Sun noon–4pm, closed Monday and holidays.

WHERE TO DINE

JONESY'S FAMOUS STEAK HOUSE, 2044 Airport Rd., Napa. Tel. 707/255-2003.

Cuisine: AMERICAN. **Reservations:** Not accepted.

$ Prices: $4.75–$12.75. MC, V.

Open: Tues–Sun 11:30am–9pm in summer; Tues–Fri 4:30am–8pm, Sat–Sun 11:30am–9pm in winter.

Parking: Available nearby with plenty of room for RVs, too.

Children's Services: Boosters, highchairs; children's menu.

Don't let the bland decor fool you. Kids love to watch the small planes take off out front and we love the good hearty fare they offer here. The servers are friendly and especially fast—no wait for food here. The kitchen is quite an operation to watch—food is prepared on an open grill—and the owner is only too happy to walk through the place making sure that diners are satisfied.

The children's menu features steak, an ample portion for two small children; also chicken and hamburger. The children's dinner comes with a cup of soup or tossed salad plus french fries; the real favorite is the block of Jello-O on the kiddie's plates. The food and the entertainment make this is a great place for lunch or an early dinner. Be sure to request a window seat.

RIVER CITY, 505 Lincoln St., Napa. Tel. 707/253-1111.

Cuisine: AMERICAN. **Reservations:** Recommended.

$ Prices: Lunch $5.75–$7.95, dinner $9.75–$13.75. MC, V.

Open: Daily lunch 11am–5pm, dinner 5–10pm.

Children's Services: Boosters, highchairs.

This is a good, casual place for hamburgers, sandwiches, lamb, steaks, pasta, and chicken. One of the amenities of this restaurant is the outdoor deck and the big fish pond that the children just love.

PICNIC FIXINGS & LIGHT BITES

The **Oakville Grocery,** 7856 St. Helena Hwy., Oakville (tel. 707/944-8802), has everything you'd expect in a gourmet grocery—and some items you wouldn't. In fact, you can even pick up cellophane-wrapped packages of picnic place settings. And don't miss the Napa bread, or the fresh fruit and vegetables, cheese and meats, and other gourmet items you might want to take home for your special cooking.

WHERE TO STAY

THE CLARION INN NAPA VALLEY, 3425 Solano Ave., Napa, CA 94558. Tel. 707/253-7433, or toll free 800/CLARION. Fax 707/252-6791. 191 rms. A/C MINIBAR TV TEL

$ Rates: Apr–Nov $70–$105 single or double, higher rates Fri–Sat nights; lower rates rest of year. Suites $200–$300. Children under 17 free in parents' room; cribs and rollaways free. A few connecting rooms available. AE, MC, V.
Parking: Free.

This is a great moderate-priced hotel in the heart of Napa Valley. The lobby feels warm and welcoming and has the charm of a country inn. The fireplace and inviting chairs and sofas make the lobby a cozy, relaxing place to be. The hotel staff is extremely helpful and congenial. They'll recommend restaurants, shops, bike trails, and will help solve general problems.

The oversized rooms continue the country theme. Decorated with oak furniture and brass headboards, they all have a shower massage and remote-control TV, equipped with HBO and in-room movies. Many of the rooms face the grassy courtyard and pool. If you want a refrigerator, request it in advance—there will be a charge of $10 per night.

Dining/Entertainment: The country-style Signature Restaurant, an open, spacious dining area just off the lobby, is open daily (7am–2pm; 5–11pm) and has a special children's menu.

Services: Baby-sitting service requires 24 hours advance notice; room service is available 5:30am–10:30pm; valet service.

Facilities: Heated pool, Jacuzzi, lighted tennis.

THE INN AT NAPA VALLEY, 1075 California Blvd., Napa, CA 94559. Tel. 707/253-9540, or toll free 800/EMBASSY. Fax 707/253-9202. 205 rms. A/C MINIBAR TV TEL

$ Rates (includes full breakfast and evening cocktails): Winter $89 single, $129 double; spring, fall, and summer $109 single, $149 double. Children under 12 stay free in parents' rooms; those over 12 and additional adults $15 per night each; cribs free; rollaways are not available. AE, DC, MC, V.
Parking: Free.

This Spanish-style hotel has a spacious lobby. There is a large mill pond outside with a working paddlewheel, all manner of ducks and swans, and the courtyard has tables and chairs, inviting guests to sit and relax. The indoor and outdoor swimming pool and Jacuzzi are relaxing retreats year round. Bicycles are available for use.

All accommodations are two-room suites, though they are a bit on the small side. All come with a full kitchen that features a microwave, wetbar, and coffee maker. For longer stays you can request a full range of utensils and cookware. The front desk will provide you with the names of baby-sitting agencies upon request.

INDEX

GENERAL INFORMATION

SIGHTS & ATTRACTIONS

SAN FRANCISCO

NOTE: An asterisk indicates an Author's Favorite

EXCURSION AREAS

ACCOMMODATIONS

SAN FRANCISCO

KEY TO ABBREVIATIONS: *B* = Budget; *B&B* = Bed-and-Breakfast; *Cg* = Camping; *E* = Expensive;
M = Moderately priced; *VE* = Very Expensive; *$* = Special Savings; * = an Author's Favorite

EXCURSION AREAS

RESTAURANTS

SAN FRANCISCO & ENVIRONS

BY CUISINE

KEY TO ABBREVIATIONS: *B* = Budget; *E* = Expensive; *I* = Inexpensive; *M* = Moderately priced; *VE* = Very Expensive; *$* = Special Savings; *** = an Author's Favorite

BY AREA

EXCURSION AREAS

NOW, SAVE MONEY ON ALL YOUR TRAVELS!
Join Frommer's™ Dollarwise® Travel Club

Saving money while traveling is never easy, which is why the **Dollarwise Travel Club** was formed 32 years ago to provide cost-cutting travel strategies, up-to-date travel information, and a sense of community for value-conscious travelers from all over the world.

In keeping with the money-saving concept, the annual membership fee is low—$20 for U.S. residents and $25 for residents of Canada, Mexico, and other countries—and is immediately exceeded by the value of your benefits, which include:

1. Any TWO books listed on the following pages;
2. Plus any ONE Frommer's City Guide;
3. A subscription to our quarterly newspaper, *The Dollarwise Traveler;*
4. A membership card that entitles you to purchase through the Club all Frommer's publications for 33% to 40% off their retail price.

The eight-page *Dollarwise Traveler* tells you about the latest developments in good-value travel worldwide and includes the following columns: **Hospitality Exchange** (for those offering and seeking hospitality in cities all over the world); and **Share-a-Trip** (for those looking for travel companions to share costs).

Aside from the various Frommer's Guides, the Gault Millau Guides, and the Real Guides you can also choose from our Special Editions, which include such titles as *Caribbean Hideaways* (the 100 most romantic places to stay in the Islands); and *Marilyn Wood's Wonderful Weekends* (a selection of the best mini-vacations within a 200-mile radius of New York City).

To join this Club, send the appropriate membership fee with your name and address to: Frommer's Dollarwise Travel Club, 15 Columbus Circle, New York, NY 10023. Remember to specify which single city guide and which two other guides you wish to receive in your initial package of member's benefits. Or tear out the pages, check off your choices, and send them to us with your membership fee.

FROMMER BOOKS
PRENTICE HALL TRAVEL   **Date**_____
15 COLUMBUS CIRCLE
NEW YORK, NY 10023

Friends: Please send me the books checked below.

FROMMER'S™ COMPREHENSIVE GUIDES
(Guides listing facilities from budget to deluxe, with emphasis on the medium-priced)

☐ Alaska	$14.95	☐ Italy	$19.00
☐ Australia	$14.95	☐ Japan & Hong Kong	$17.00
☐ Austria & Hungary	$14.95	☐ Morocco	$18.00
☐ Belgium, Holland & Luxembourg	$14.95	☐ Nepal	$18.00
☐ Bermuda & The Bahamas	$17.00	☐ New England	$17.00
☐ Brazil	$14.95	☐ New Mexico	$13.95
☐ California	$18.00	☐ New York State	$19.00
☐ Canada	$16.00	☐ Northwest	$16.95
☐ Caribbean	$17.00	☐ Puerta Vallarta (avail. Feb. '92)	$14.00
☐ Carolinas & Georgia	$17.00	☐ Portugal, Madeira & the Azores	$14.95
☐ Colorado (avail. Jan '92)	$14.00	☐ Scandinavia	$18.95
☐ Cruises (incl. Alaska, Carib, Mex, Hawaii, Panama, Canada & US)	$16.00	☐ Scotland (avail. Feb. '92)	$17.00
		☐ South Pacific	$20.00
☐ Delaware, Maryland, Pennsylvania & the New Jersey Shore (avail. Jan. '92)	$19.00	☐ Southeast Asia	$14.95
		☐ Switzerland & Liechtenstein	$19.00
☐ Egypt	$14.95	☐ Thailand	$20.00
☐ England	$17.00	☐ Virginia (avail. Feb. '92)	$14.00
☐ Florida	$17.00	☐ Virgin Islands	$13.00
☐ France	$15.95	☐ USA	$16.95
☐ Germany	$18.00		

0891492

FROMMER'S CITY GUIDES

(Pocket-size guides to sightseeing and tourist accommodations and facilities in all price ranges)

☐ Amsterdam/Holland	$8.95	☐ Minneapolis/St. Paul	$8.95
☐ Athens	$8.95	☐ Montréal/Québec City	$8.95
☐ Atlanta	$8.95	☐ New Orleans	$8.95
☐ Atlantic City/Cape May	$8.95	☐ New York	$12.00
☐ Bangkok	$12.00	☐ Orlando	$12.00
☐ Barcelona	$12.00	☐ Paris	$8.95
☐ Belgium	$7.95	☐ Philadelphia	$11.00
☐ Berlin	$10.00	☐ Rio	$8.95
☐ Boston	$8.95	☐ Rome	$8.95
☐ Cancún/Cozumel/Yucatán	$8.95	☐ Salt Lake City	$8.95
☐ Chicago	$9.95	☐ San Diego	$8.95
☐ Denver/Boulder/Colorado Springs	$8.95	☐ San Francisco	$12.00
☐ Dublin/Ireland	$10.00	☐ Santa Fe/Taos/Albuquerque	$10.95
☐ Hawaii	$12.00	☐ Seattle/Portland	$12.00
☐ Hong Kong	$7.95	☐ St. Louis/Kansas City	$9.95
☐ Las Vegas	$8.95	☐ Sydney	$8.95
☐ Lisbon/Madrid/Costa del Sol	$8.95	☐ Tampa/St. Petersburg	$8.95
☐ London	$12.00	☐ Tokyo	$8.95
☐ Los Angeles	$8.95	☐ Toronto	$8.95
☐ Mexico City/Acapulco	$8.95	☐ Vancouver/Victoria	$7.95
☐ Miami	$8.95	☐ Washington, D.C.	$12.00

FROMMER'S $-A-DAY® GUIDES

(Guides to low-cost tourist accommodations and facilities)

☐ Australia on $40 a Day	$13.95	☐ Israel on $40 a Day	$13.95
☐ Costa Rica, Guatemala & Belize on $35 a Day	$15.95	☐ Mexico on $45 a Day	$18.00
		☐ New York on $65 a Day	$15.00
☐ Eastern Europe on $25 a Day	$16.95	☐ New Zealand on $45 a Day	$16.00
☐ England on $50 a Day	$17.00	☐ Scotland & Wales on $40 a Day	$18.00
☐ Europe on $45 a Day	$19.00	☐ South America on $40 a Day	$15.95
☐ Greece on $35 a Day	$14.95	☐ Spain on $50 a Day	$15.95
☐ Hawaii on $70 a Day	$18.00	☐ Turkey on $40 a Day	$22.00
☐ India on $40 a Day	$20.00	☐ Washington, D.C., on $45 a Day	$17.00
☐ Ireland on $40 a Day	$17.00		

FROMMER'S CITY $-A-DAY GUIDES

☐ Berlin on $40 a Day	$12.00	☐ Madrid on $50 a Day (avail. Jan '92)	$13.00
☐ Copenhagen on $50 a Day	$12.00	☐ Paris on $45 a Day	$12.00
☐ London on $45 a Day	$12.00	☐ Stockholm on $50 a Day (avail. Dec. '91)	$13.00

FROMMER'S FAMILY GUIDES

☐ California with Kids	$16.95	☐ San Francisco with Kids	$17.00
☐ Los Angeles with Kids	$17.00	☐ Washington, D.C., with Kids (avail. Jan '92)	$17.00
☐ New York City with Kids (avail. Jan '92)	$18.00		

SPECIAL EDITIONS

☐ Beat the High Cost of Travel	$6.95	☐ Marilyn Wood's Wonderful Weekends (CT, DE, MA, NH, NJ, NY, PA, RI, VT)	$11.95
☐ Bed & Breakfast—N. America	$14.95		
☐ Caribbean Hideaways	$16.00	☐ Motorist's Phrase Book (Fr/Ger/Sp)	$4.95
☐ Honeymoon Destinations (US, Mex & Carib)	$14.95	☐ The New World of Travel (annual by Arthur Frommer for savvy travelers)	$16.95

(TURN PAGE FOR ADDITONAL BOOKS AND ORDER FORM)

0891492

☐ Paris Rendez-Vous $10.95	☐ Travel Diary and Record Book........$5.95
☐ Swap and Go (Home Exchanging).....$10.95	☐ Where to Stay USA (from $3 to $30 a
	night).......................$13.95

FROMMER'S TOURING GUIDES

(Color illustrated guides that include walking tours, cultural and historic sites, and practical information)

☐ Amsterdam....................$10.95	☐ New York $10.95
☐ Australia $12.95	☐ Paris $8.95
☐ Brazil........................$10.95	☐ Rome.........................$10.95
☐ Egypt........................$8.95	☐ Scotland......................$9.95
☐ Florence......................$8.95	☐ Thailand......................$12.95
☐ Hong Kong....................$10.95	☐ Turkey $10.95
☐ London $12.95	☐ Venice $8.95

GAULT MILLAU

(The only guides that distinguish the truly superlative from the merely overrated)

☐ The Best of Chicago $15.95	☐ The Best of Los Angeles $16.95
☐ The Best of Florida..............$17.00	☐ The Best of New England $15.95
☐ The Best of France $16.95	☐ The Best of New Orleans..........$16.95
☐ The Best of Germany $18.00	☐ The Best of New York $16.95
☐ The Best of Hawaii...............$16.95	☐ The Best of Paris $16.95
☐ The Best of Hong Kong...........$16.95	☐ The Best of San Francisco $16.95
☐ The Best of Italy................$16.95	☐ The Best of Thailand.............$17.95
☐ The Best of London $16.95	☐ The Best of Toronto $17.00

☐ The Best of Washington, D.C. $16.95

THE REAL GUIDES

(Opinionated, politically aware guides for youthful budget-minded travelers)

☐ Amsterdam $9.95	☐ Mexico......................$11.95
☐ Berlin........................$11.95	☐ Morocco.....................$12.95
☐ Brazil........................$13.95	☐ New York $9.95
☐ California & the West Coast $11.95	☐ Paris $9.95
☐ Czechoslovakia.................$13.95	☐ Peru........................$12.95
☐ France $12.95	☐ Poland $13.95
☐ Germany $13.95	☐ Portugal.....................$10.95
☐ Greece.......................$13.95	☐ San Francisco $11.95
☐ Guatemala $13.95	☐ Scandinavia $14.95
☐ Hong Kong....................$11.95	☐ Spain........................$12.95
☐ Hungary......................$12.95	☐ Turkey $12.95
☐ Ireland.......................$12.95	☐ Venice $11.95
☐ Italy.........................$13.95	☐ Women Travel $12.95
☐ Kenya........................$12.95	☐ Yugoslavia $12.95

ORDER NOW!

In U.S. include $2 shipping UPS for 1st book; $1 ea. add'l book. Outside U.S. $3 and $1, respectively.

Allow four to six weeks for delivery in U.S., longer outside U.S. We discourage rush order service, but orders arriving with shipping fees plus a $15 surcharge will be handled as rush orders.

Enclosed is my check or money order for $_____

NAME_____

ADDRESS_____

CITY_____ STATE_____ ZIP_____

0891492